The publisher and author wish to thank Alfred A. Knopf, Inc. for permission to use the quotes from THE DEATH AND LIFE OF GERMANY by Eugene Davidson and LIFE Magazine for the permission to use the quotes from their issue dated May 10, 1954.

Library of Congress Catalog #64–15762

Printed and bound in the United States of America
by American Book–Stratford Press.

THIS GERMANY

The Story Since the Third Reic

RUDOLF WALTER LEONHARDT

TRANSLATED AND ADAPTED
FOR THE AMERICAN EDITION BY
CATHERINE HUTTER

NEW YORK GRAPHIC SOCIETY PUBLISHERS, LTD.

GREENWICH, CONNECTICUT

If you know aught that might be preferable
to these maxims, let me hear it; if not,
I beg of you, make use of these.

Horace, THE EPISTLES

CONTENTS

FOREWORD:

"WHY DON'T YOU
WRITE THE BOOK?"

"Do you like being a German?" asked Yvonne.

She was what Rilke might have called a "dainty little French girl." Her name was unmistakably French—Lefranc. She was twenty-nine, not pretty, but very attractive.

We were sitting in the Kloten airport, near Zürich, a rather international group: Dick O'Connor, an American publisher; Ralph Stevens, an English journalist; Professor Pierre Spälti, a Swiss university professor; and Andreas von Hattesdorf, an Austrian. All these people exist. Their names have been changed, but everything they say and ask on the pages that follow, they said and asked. Anyway, Yvonne asked me if I liked being a German. I'm sure of that because it wasn't easy to answer.

My foreign friends sometimes came up with quite a few unpleasant items: what they consider to be the truth, for instance, and the truth is not always pleasant. They were not anti-German. Frankly, I find it a too simple explanation to sense anti-Germanism behind every honest observation or opinion of Germany. Of course some people like the Germans more, some less. In that the Germans find themselves in the same position as the French, the English, cats, or tobacco. To be hated for the right reasons is not always pleasant, but to be loved for the wrong ones can be downright embarrassing. Germanophiles, by the way, are quite often dull individuals.

Only very few people are forthright or simple enough to make a sound appraisal of the individual from an antipathy of the group. Many Germans, for instance, undoubtedly went along with the anti-Semitism that became a national doctrine before World War II, but insisted on exempting three or four Jews—usually the three or four they knew personally—just as most Americans and English people didn't hesitate to speak about "the Huns," and "my German friend," in one and the same breath during World War I. And a French girl like Yvonne would say "*mon ami allemand*," which wouldn't prevent her from speaking of the Germans collectively as "*les boches.*"

"You mean, do I like to be a *boche?*" I asked.

"*Boche?*" Yvonne's charm took the edge off her scorn. "You mean *chleugh.*"

We made progress, if I may call it that, when instead of the *boche*-pig of World War I, the name of a despised Arab tribe was used in World War II to express collective unfriendliness toward the Germans. We come across the same thing in Anglo-Saxon countries. There, in the end, they called us "Krauts," or "Fritz." The latter also became a nickname for the German in France. In World War II there was scarcely any mention of the Hun of World War I.

"You know," said Ralph Stevens, the Englishman in our group, "it's strange that you should think *we* saddled you with the name 'Hun,' just to be nasty, when it was your Kaiser who did it." And he was right. It really was Kaiser Wilhelm II who, fourteen years before the First World War spoke the memorable words, "There shall be no pardon. We shall take no prisoners. As the Huns of a thousand years ago made a name for themselves under King Etzel, which has given them a tradition of might in legend and fairy tale, the name 'German' must be reaffirmed in a way that will make it impossible for anyone to look down on a German again!"

Yet they do. . . .

The list of German sins is long. Here is a summary:

1. *The Germans are ruthless toward the weak.*

A hangover of resentment from the last war? Not at all. Eliza Marianne Butler, once Professor of Germanics at Cambridge University in England, now deceased, writes in her autobiography, *Paper Boats* (Collins, 1959), of the time she spent as a student in Bonn before the First World War. What she found most distasteful in that pretty little town on the Rhine was the "devil take the hindmost attitude," as she calls it, the pushers and shovers who didn't care who got left behind.

2. *The Germans can feel very sorry for themselves, but much less so for others. Love of their fellow men—let's call it humaneness—is foreign to them.*

After the last two wars, this reproach seems quite natural, so I am going to call in Miss Butler again, since the roots of her grudges go back to the beginning of our century. In the same autobiography she writes: "In the total indifference to the sufferings of others (as Belsen and Buchenwald were to prove) it was lovelessness toward humanity as a whole. It was—I always come back to it—the lack of '*Humanität.*' We are all subject to it of course; but in Germany it was chronic, endemic, and acute."

3. *When given the chance, the Germans are arrogant; when they can't be arrogant, they are craven.*

American President Franklin D. Roosevelt stated repeatedly that, beside the provincialism of the Germans, their arrogance bothered him more than anything else. As for their cravenness—you have only to read the reports of the occupation forces to find out about that. It doesn't make pleasant reading, but there's nothing new about it. In 1795, when the French took Düsseldorf without a fight, the inhabitants of that town, according to Heinrich Heine, "put on new faces . . . and their Sunday clothes . . . and looked at each other in French, and said '*bon jour.*' "

4. *The Germans glorify war.*

In May, 1959, in the editorial of a special issue of *Life* magazine dedicated to Germany, you could read: "Germany's neighbors have fought Germans not only twice in the last 40 years but five times in the last ninety and 17 times in the last 200," for what seemed to them "good reasons." And to prove the incorrigibility of this *furor teutonicus*, people like to quote Tacitus: "The Germans hate peace." In a handbook of the English occupation forces (called simply *Germany*) you could read on page 24: "There are signs that the German leaders are already making plans for a Third World War. That must be prevented at all costs."

5. *The Germans go in for extremes: cock-eyed idealism or crass materialism, uninformed apathy or hybrid intellectual detachment.*

"German history lacks balance and continuity," writes the French historian, Pierre Gaxotte, in his book, *Naissance de l'Allemagne*. "It expresses itself in contrasts and extremes. Germany is a country of miraculous progress and apocalyptic catastrophes." I. F. Stone reports in the German *Frankfurter Hefte* (July, 1959), that: "The basic mood in West Germany is satiation, self-satisfaction, and crass materialism," and in the issue of *Life* just mentioned—for which Chancellor Adenauer wrote a foreword—we find: "Down through all the centuries the German intellectual remained too aloof from his country's political life. This tradition of political irresponsibility . . . shared by the German middle class, eventually helped bring on the 20th century's cataclysmic wars—the last bitter illustrations of Germany's strange dualism of cultural progress and political retrogression."

6. *The Germans don't know and don't want to know the meaning of freedom.*

Instead of calling in a lot of witnesses on this, I shall let a famous sentence suffice. It was written by Madame de Staël, whose book, *Of Germany* (1810) is still considered a classic: "*L'amour de la liberté n'est point developpé chez les Allemands.*" (Love of liberty has not been developed at all among the Germans.) The words are all the more significant because they were written during the Napoleonic Wars, which we Germans like to call, "Wars of Liberty," and Madame de Staël's sympathies were with the Germans at the time.

7. *The Germans will never be democrats, but will always remain subjects.*

The Swiss historian, Gonzague de Reynold, writes in his book, *D'où vient l'Allemagne?* (1939): "The Germans are not cut out for democracy and parliamentary rule, and they never will be." The Swiss poet, Max Frisch, in a speech on the Swiss national holiday in 1957, expressed his fear of a Germany that "would turn out to be the opposite of a democracy just as soon as enough German helmets, boots, and atomic missiles have been produced." These reactions are typical, and historic. "There are no revolutions in Germany because the police would not permit it."—Alexis de Tocqueville.

"And what have you to say about it?"
If I were to say, "It is all true," it would be simple, but sad. If I were to say, "It is all untrue," it would be simple too, and consoling. But the reproaches included in this roster of sins—which exist quite apart from the fact that similar lists could be constructed for other nations—have one embarrassing quality: they are half-truths.

"My dear friends from America, England, France, Austria, and Switzerland, to all these accusations I have nothing to say. We will just have to let them be what they are—talk. But I have a suggestion. Come with me. Let us take a closer look at this Germany."

My suggestion was accepted. Technical difficulties were overcome by mutual good will. But again it is impossible to express the results of the whole undertaking in a few sentences. One would have to write a book about it.

"So why don't you write the book?"
Dick O'Connor asked the question as we sat in the immaculate Bayerische Hof, in the pretty little island town of Lindau, looking down at the pretty little harbor, where an imposing (but pretty) lion on a high column at the end of the mole testified to the fact that Lindau was Bavarian. Two weeks had gone by since the six of us had sat together at the airport in Kloten. In the meantime we had traveled crisscross through Germany. Dick was the only one still with me, and he was on his way to Zürich, where a super-Constellation was waiting to take him back to the land of so many German dreams—the United States.

"Why don't you write the book?"
Why? A selection of recent literature on "the New Berlin" includes 138 titles, comprising in all 35,385 pages. Anyone wanting to study Berlin alone, and able to read a printed page in two minutes, would therefore have to read four months, ten hours daily. If he wanted to buy the books, the price would be 1,633.50 German marks.

"Why don't you write the book?"

One of my illustrious predecessors, author of the best book on Germany to date, was threatened with a law suit because he didn't quote the circulation figures of an illustrated magazine correctly. . . . A journalist reporting on German hotels drew the following comment from the president of the German Hotel and Restaurant Owners' Association: "I find the man's criticisms superficial. Everybody is going to wonder why such conclusions have been drawn from the experiences of one man." A young chemist with the highest academic qualifications described to the readers of a leading German newspaper, "How Chemistry Is Studied In Germany," to which the president of the Association of German Chemists had this to say, "Apart from a few references that might be worth discussing, the series of articles is full of the most grotesque distortions, malicious untruths, and unacademic—I would go so far as to say—partially offensive recriminations."

"Why don't you write the book?"

Now I was thinking of my potential readers. A lot of them would be Germans who know better than I do what they think right and important. And what they don't know, they won't think is right and important. . . .

"The Americans still don't know very much about Germany," said Dick.

"That may be. But why bring that up?"

"Because I want to publish the book in the United States."

"For heaven's sake!" And I told Dick about the poet Heinrich Heine, whose greatest offense, which has been held against him for over a hundred years, was that he published some things that were not very friendly toward Germany in France. . . . That could only have happened a long time ago? . . . I told Dick about Kay Lorenz, whose Düsseldorf Little Comedy Theater is one of the best political cabarets in West Germany, and no one gives a damn when they air their satirical material, aimed at the leading lights of state and society, in front of a (fortunately) limited audience of approximately two hundred people, which is all the place will hold. But when Kay wanted to take his little troupe to the United States, what a clamor! How could he think of fouling his own nest in the country of such an important ally?

"To foul one's own nest"—that is the *terminus technicus* of these peculiar nest-hygienists who are so proud of their national sentiments and would be dismayed if someone were to say to them, "I presume we may gather from your indignation that if any nests are to be fouled, they should be other people's?"

"A book about Germany for America, Dick? You've got to let an American write that. He can't offend anyone."

On the harbor boulevard of Lindau, a laughing crowd was passing by, young girls provocatively taking their ballerina skirts for a walk. The park band was playing *"Einmal am Rhein . . ."* That's right, we were on the Rhine, only it was hiding in Lake Constance. The sun was setting over Switzerland, casting its last rays on Austria, to which this little town of Lindau had belonged at the beginning of the last century.

It was nearly time for us to say good-by. Dick was impatient. "Well, are you going to write the book or not? We have enough books about Germany written by Americans; a few of them are even quite good. But I don't have to tell you that a foreigner may see some things very clearly, then again he sees just as many falsely, and some things he doesn't see at all. I want a book about Germany by a German."

"But why me?"

"Because you're so typically German. 'Why me?' Your country's almost gone to the dogs several times because of that question. Of what concern of mine is the Kaiser? Hitler? Adenauer? What business of mine is this nation? Why me? In the States a man like you would say, 'I've got to do it because if I don't, maybe no one else will either. If you Germans would only learn that!'"

That did it. I promised Dick I would write the book.

MIDDLE GERMANY: RED SPARTA

1. LADIES AND GENTLEMEN, OUR NATIONAL ANTHEM

Deutschland, Deutschland über alles,	Germany, Germany, above all things,
Über alles in der Welt,	Above all things in the world,
Wenn es stets zu Schutz und Trutze	If in defense and in offense,
Brüderlich zusammenhält!	We like brothers together hold.
Von der Maas bis an die Memel,	From the rivers Meuse and Niemen,
Von der Etsch bis an den Belt:	From the Adige to the Belt,
Deustchland, Deutschland über alles,	Germany, Germany, above all things,
Über alles in der Welt!	Above all things in the world.
Deutsche Frauen, deutsche Treue,	German women, German fealty,
Deutscher Wein und deutscher Sang	German wine and German song,
Sollen in der Welt behalten	Must through the entire world
Ihren alten schönen Klang;	Keep their old and lovely sound;
Uns zu edler Tat begeistern	Inspiring us to actions noble
Unser ganzes Leben lang:	Our entire existence long;
Deutsche Frauen, deutsche Treue,	German women, German fealty,
Deutscher Wein und deutscher Sang!	German wine and German song!
Einigkeit und Recht und Freiheit	Unity and right and freedom
Für das deutsche Vaterland!	For the German fatherland!
Danach lasst uns alle streben	And for this let us all strive
Brüderlich mit Herz und Hand!	Like two brothers hand in hand.
Einigkeit und Recht und Freiheit	Unity and right and freedom
Sind des Glückes Unterpfand;	Are good luck's security;
Blüh' im Glanze dieses Glückes,	Thrive in the glow of this good fortune,
Blühe, deutsches Vaterland.	Thrive, oh German fatherland!

In a survey made by the Allensbach Institute for Research and Statistics, thousands of West Germans were asked the following questions:

"Can you show us the River Meuse on the map? The Niemen? The Adige? And where is the Belt?"

Barely half of those asked succeeded in finding the Meuse and Niemen, but not two out of ten knew where to look for the Adige and Belt. Yvonne couldn't get over this. She had recently acquired a little faith in statistics, which was now seriously shaken. And the rest of our small group didn't know either whether they should believe the results of the survey.

"I always thought *Deutschland, Deutschland, über alles* was Germany's favorite song," said Dick.

"And the Germans are much too conscientious to sing anything if they don't know what it's all about," said our English friend, Ralph.

"Well, it's been the German anthem since time began, and still is," said our Swiss friend. Our Austrian friend was wise enough to keep silent.

"But I've often read and heard," Yvonne assured us, "that Germany's urge for aggrandizement was clearly demonstrated in *Deutschland, Deutschland über alles*, because the rivers in it aren't even in Germany. Everybody knows that!"

"But eight out of ten Germans don't," I said, "and unfortunately you haven't got it right either." Nothing to be done about it but correct her. Not only Yvonne. Inserted in quite a few French travel brochures, you'll find a little booklet about Germany, *L'Allemagne*, by Joseph Rovan. It is benevolently written and often quite clever. But it also says: "For over a hundred years, the German national anthem has extolled the dimensions of a fatherland bounded by the Maas (Meuse), the Memel (Niemen), the Etsch (Adige), and the Belt, *i.e.*, three rivers which don't even touch Germany and a strait that doesn't either."

Most foreigners are aware of this, but how many Germans are?

In the year 1841, August Heinrich Hoffmann, age forty-three, German professor in Breslau, Silesia, better known as Hoffmann von Fallersleben after his birthplace, Fallersleben, near Braunschweig, was staying on the island of Helgoland, which was English at the time. Could it possibly have annoyed him that only in excursion-boat-trip's distance down the Elbe from Hamburg, England abruptly began? Be that as it may, the fact that Germany consisted of too many different states had been annoying him for a long time. In 1841, after Napoleon had done a fairly good job of eliminating a lot of the smaller German states, there still existed—beside Prussia and Austria—the Duchy of Holstein, the Grand Duchy of Mecklenburg-Schwerin, the Grand Duchy of Oldenburg, the Kingdom of Hannover, the Duchy of Braunschweig, the Duchy of Anhalt, the Electorate of Hesse, the Grand Duchy of Hesse, the States of Thuringia, the Kingdom of Saxony, the Duchy of Nassau, the Palatinate, the Grand Duchy of Baden, the Kingdom of Württemberg, the Kingdom of Bavaria, to say nothing of such small-fry principalities as Mecklenburg-Strelitz and Schaumburg-Lippe.

As a protest against this conglomerate Reich, the professor from

Breslau, who until then had never composed anything more serious than a few pleasant children's ditties and love songs, wrote the three verses just quoted, along the lines of a song made famous by the celebrated German medieval lyric poet, Walther von der Vogelweide, a good six hundred years before. The latter's verses however had concerned themselves mainly with women:

> From the Elbe to the Rhine
> And to Hungarian ground,
> That's where you will find the best
> On this earth to be found. . . .

The professor saw no reason for adhering to the narrow limitations of his predecessor. In his verses he expressed himself more specifically and was definitely more demanding. He courageously called his poem *The Song of the Germans*, and for forty-four years, from 1870 to 1914, it was just that. Before 1870, it was not in the public domain; after 1914, political-party overtones could be heard above the melody. If the Allensbach Institute survey had included questions about the text of the song, I would venture that less than two out of ten would have known all three verses.

At the time the song was composed, the three rivers mentioned in it constituted a perhaps not very modest, but certainly defensible choice of German boundary rivers. The Meuse, coming from France, flowed 50 kilometers through North Limburg, which is today a part of Holland, but in Fallersleben's day, Limburg had joined the German Bund two years before. The Niemen formed the border between East Prussia and Lithuania; the last 100 kilometers of the river were in German territory. (Today it is under Soviet rule.) The Adige ran through South Tirol and was its most important river; South Tirol was then a part of Austria and belonged to the German Bund until 1866. During Fallersleben's time of writing, therefore, it was well "in." And the Belt was the northernmost sea frontier with the Duchy of Schleswig, which, granted, still belonged to Denmark at the time.

That these waterways came to lie farther and farther outside Germany's borders while the Germans were preoccupied with their notorious struggle for more "living space," is one of the paradoxes of German history. And it certainly cannot be denied that the controversial "Germany above all things" was no more hurrah patriotically interpreted between 1870 and 1914, than the national anthems of many other countries. The composer let himself be fêted accordingly. The Prussian authorities, however, did not hear in the song a lust for world conquest, but rather a threat to the German Duchies, and relieved the professor of his duties in Breslau!

The song, with its fine Haydn melody, did not become the official anthem until 1922, and then at the instigation of the first President of the Weimar Republic, Social Democrat Friedrich Ebert, a man to whom all thirst for domination and "above-all" in the sense of "superior-to-all" feelings were absolutely foreign. The same applies to his successor, Theodore Heuss, who on May 6, 1952—after a substitute anthem by Rudolf Alexander Schröder had achieved little popularity—reinstated verse three as the national anthem. During Hitler's era, only the first verse was sung as a sort of overture to the "Horst Wessel Song," which still leaves us the especially endearing second verse should the need ever arise.

Professor Hoffmann von Fallersleben defined the boundaries of Germany, and was dismissed. That was over a century ago. Today he wouldn't fare much better, not because of the prevailing political conditions, but because the boundaries themselves helped to create these conditions. Germany is a country without obvious boundaries. Nearly everyone knows that, and you can read it in every book on Germany. But that doesn't help. It has to be experienced.

"Take a look at this lake," I said. We were still on the south shore of Lake Constance. "Three countries border on it, yet you'll find the same people in every one of them. All of them speak German, and in much the same way. Would you say that they were really different countries?"

"I certainly would," Professor Spälti said briskly. "Since 1684."

"In our case," said von Hattesdorf, "it's not so simple. After all, we were lumped together with the Germans for two thousand years . . . the first thousand to 1866, and then Hitler's thousand—from 1933 to 1945."

Where nature defines no borders, languages don't either. West Germany has more neighbors than any other country in Europe, and the German language doesn't stop at its borders. Try traveling from Cologne via Coblenz to Trier; from there to Völklingen, Saarbrücken, Forbach, Metz. Take time to talk to the people. On this attractive journey through three river valleys—the Rhine, the Mosel, the Saar—you will hear every conceivable mixture of German and French: German with a smattering of French in Cologne; French with a smattering of German in Metz; but in Lorraine, the natives have had more borderline experience and trouble than anywhere else. The following story of a friend of mine from that province is not only indicative, it also happens to be true.

When I met Jean first, he was French without, however, being a citizen of France. True, Metz, where he lived, became French in 1918; but in 1905, when he had been born there, it had been German. Since he was one of those innumerable Lorrainers who insist on sympathizing with the nation to which they don't happen to belong, he couldn't see why he should pay a few thousand francs for a French passport. He lived peacefully, minded his own business, drank his aperitif and a little more when it suited him, photographed bridal couples and naked babies on bearskins because that was his profession, and was carefree.

Came 1939, and the war. The French interned Jean after declaring him "stateless." The internment camp was not pleasant, and the only way of getting out was to become a French soldier. Jean became a

French soldier and as such was taken prisoner by the Germans. This nearly turned out very badly for him because, as far as the Germans were concerned, he was German—a German, and a French soldier! The only way out of this miserable situation was to become a German soldier as speedily as possible. The war with France seemed as good as over— by now it was 1942—and Metz was "German again" anyway, so Jean became a German soldier.

But the war was not over. Suddenly there was a French army again, which entered Metz in 1944, and took the German soldier, Jean, prisoner. And now Jean, a Lorrainer who had put on and taken off his uniform in accordance with every threatening power, but who certainly had never done anybody any harm because he just wasn't that kind of fellow—now Jean was something terribly dangerous—he was a *collaborateur!* Fortunately for him, but not for a lot of others in the first excitement, he was not shot. All they did was deport him, not from France, but from Lorraine. Somewhere in the south he had to report to the police every day. Then I lost track of him.

"That makes you think," said our American publisher, Dick O'Connor.

The borders of the West German republic are 4,279 kilometers long. Anyone who cared to walk along them at an easy tempo of 5 kilometers an hour, would have plenty of time to think day and night for five months and might come to the conclusion that it is astonishing that anything like the Federal Republic of (West) Germany can exist at all! There isn't another country in the world more arbitrarily bounded—unless it be the (East) German Democratic Republic. And there isn't another country in the world which, by its nature and through history, is so *open* to the world as the West German Republic, unless it is the East German Republic. Let's say for short therefore that this *resumé* of conditions applies to *all* of Germany.

2. WHO IS TO BLAME FOR THE PARTITION OF GERMANY?

I don't see why I should interpret the word "Germany" differently now from the way I did when a child. I can still remember Saxony, Anhalt, Thuringia, Mecklenburg, and Brandenburg, even if it is quite a long time—longer than suits me—since I visited these parts. In fact, I remember them very well. Unfortunately many young Germans do not. They experience Germany as a whole more in festive speeches than in the realities of everyday life. A generation is growing up for whom the Masurian lakes blend in with the Russian steppe. You already find more people in West Germany who have been in Capri than in the Elbe Sandstone Mountains of Central Germany. Well-meaning friends advised me to write only about the Federal Republic, but I don't feel like writing about half of Germany as if it were the whole. Besides, it seems only fair to examine the territories of West Germany and East Germany together, for the governments of both states have frequently stressed their togetherness, and the majority of those governed—although shrinking—seem to want it, too. And it seems just as fair to *not* include the former German territories now under Polish and Soviet jurisdiction, because the government of East Germany ceded these territories to Poland in a treaty on June 6, 1950; and the government of West Germany, in repeated and solemn declarations, has renounced any idea of reclaiming them by force.

"Who is to blame for the partition of Germany?"

Who was asking? Our American, Dick O'Connor? Our Englishman, Ralph Stevens? The others wanted to know the answer, too.

All of us are to blame: the occupation forces whose goal was the dismemberment of Germany; the Germans, among whom there wasn't one who wanted to and scarcely a man who would have had the physical strength to bother about the borders of a future Germany, which no one believed in anyway. Would there have been a time to avoid it later? And when was it really too late? This is a controversial issue in the West German parliament. There are a lot of people in West German Munich and in East German Dresden who know the answers; unfortunately their views are diametrically opposed. . . .

It is a fact that at Teheran (February, 1945) Churchill declared that England, America and Russia, were agreed on the necessity for a partition of Germany. It is a fact that the Soviet Union was the first of the victorious powers to change its mind and suddenly stand up for German unity. It is a fact that the French, who at first did not participate in the conference of the victorious powers, urged the partition of Germany more doggedly than any of the other allied nations. It is a fact that it was a four-power decision, on June 30, 1946, that closed the border between the Soviet Zone and the Western Zone, thereby officially recognizing the Iron Curtain. And it is a fact that this measure permitted the western half of what was left of Germany to blossom overnight while the east had to be written off, for the time being at any rate. Although the financial reforms in West Germany on June 20, 1948, were followed by similar steps in East Germany on June 23; although the West German Basic Law of May 1949, was followed by a similar document in East Germany at the end of that month; although the proclamation of the West German Federal Republic on August 14, 1949, was followed on October 7 by a proclamation of the East German Democratic Republic, or DDR, the picture formed by this series of related events is deceiving. The development of the two areas did not run parallel at all.

When the Federal Republic was formed, no one could really foresee the shape of things to come. The question of which party would form the government was wide open and was decided in the end by a very slight majority. But when the DDR was formed, the Unity Party or SED, created for this purpose by a coalition of Social Democrats and Communists as far back as April 21, 1946, had already filled all key positions. Soon scarcely a soul honestly believed that the Christian Liberal Party—which strangely enough still pretends to exist in the

DDR today—had anything but a purely decorative function. And the economic demands of Marxist-Leninism had been fulfilled long before the proclamation of the DDR. All estates of over 100 hectares had been expropriated; all large industries nationalized, all private business establishments driven to the wall, to be finished off one by one in the ensuing years.

Richard Thilenius, whose book *Die Teilung Deutschlands* (The Partition of Germany) is the best book on the partition of Germany to date, writes: "Thus, in west and east, two German states were formed on German soil according to the ideas of the momentarily responsible victorious powers, and were absorbed into their spheres of power: two German states, as completely divorced from each other as fire and water. Although each only a part, both demanded from their momentary protectors the right to speak exclusively for all of Germany, with the result that they avoided each other like the plague."

"Do you believe in the reunification of Germany?" asked Yvonne.

I don't like the word "reunification." It has become an all-too-flimsy alibi for people who can't even assemble an all-German football team. It removes the main emphasis of the problem into purely political spheres, and I think it is out of the question that the DDR and the Federal Republic could possibly have common borders or a common government in our time. This type of German unity only lasted for seventy-four years anyway—from the founding of the Reich by Bismarck, January 18, 1871, to the capitulation of the Donitz government on May 9, 1945. But there is another Germany which is no less real because it isn't so easily defined. This Germany has existed for at least twelve hundred years, and I consider it premature to bury it and then go running around desperately asking, "Do you believe in its resurrection?"

"When you say 'another Germany,' do you mean the land of Schiller, Goethe, and Bach?" asked Dick.

Among other things. But here we come to a point where we must be cautious. Schiller of Jena from Marbach, Goethe of Weimar from Frankfurt, Bach of Leipzig from Eisenach—according to the stupid geographical aspect of things, all three happen to belong (yes, *happen to* belong!) to East Germany, in spite of which they naturally belong to all-Germany. That their names are mentioned so often is further proof of the dilemma we face when we try to define this Germany, which is not dependent on boundaries or governments.

3. ON SEEING RED

I spent my first years as a journalist in England. In 1955, I returned to Germany, and six months later was on the verge of giving up my profession because I was sick to death of being accused daily of corruption, incompetence, and ignorance on every imaginable subject, and of being considered an inferior character, capable of the most serious moral crimes. Then an older colleague enlightened me. Since he was a Rhine-lander, he put it this way: People have a *Dollpunkt,* a point at which they see red.

Where so much has been destroyed, as is the case in Germany, which has after all been in the thick of all great conflicts for centuries, much has also been wounded. Superficially most of the wounds have healed, but deep down they are still highly sensitive. Touch them, and you get an emotional reaction. Say "Hitler's war was a crime," and the little Nazi who isn't meant at all sees red. "Yes, he was a party member, but he always behaved decently," and the refugee whose family was murdered suspects neo-Nazism. "Where Tachism begins, the art of painting ends," and the young painter who has sacrificed his all for abstract art feels his livelihood threatened. "In the end, the young people are always right," and whoever is eighty at heart although his birth certificate may read forty, protests at being discounted in such an infamous fashion. "If drivers would drink less, we would have fewer accidents," brings a clamor from the liquor salesmen. "Some people can drive much more steadily with half a bottle of whisky in their blood than you milk drinkers,"—outcries of horror from those who already see themselves as victims of a head-on crash.

Whoever begins to grasp the principle of the *Dollpunkt,* or the point at which a man sees red, must soon notice that the numbers of his friends and relatives whom he would like to clear of this frailty, dwindles away. Germans are not the only race afflicted, but there is perhaps not another country in the world with so many vulnerable cases. Because there isn't another country which, in two generations, has lost as many wars and experienced two revaluations of its currency and two complete revolutions of its basic social and moral ideas. In Germany seeing red is an institution you can count on. That is why, for the Germans more than for any other people, it is organizable. Germany suffers—and will suffer for a long time to come—from organized *Dollpunkts.*

Some people are afraid for Germany, others are afraid in Germany, and these fears and anxieties are often determined by a see-red or boiling point. We are not dealing here with philosophical differentiations but with something remarkable from a sociological point of view. What are we most afraid of in Germany? The complacent man fears war; the successful man, the loss of what he has gained; the Jew, anti-Semitism; the European, nationalism; the cold-war monger, East-West contacts; the East-West German, the cold war; the agnostic, the "bigotry of the Catholic Church"; the religious Catholic, a revival of atheistic materialism; the dedicated man, neutralistic tendencies; the liberal democrat, an anti-Communist dictatorship; many East Germans, West German militarism; most West Germans, the Communist plan of world domination, with such fine differentiations as: we have grown accustomed to Russian communism; we find the Polish version of the same thing tolerable; but we detest German communism in the DDR more than anything else in the world.

4. IN FLIGHT FROM GERMANY TO GERMANY

After all we have experienced, no one likes to revive the subject of blood ties, yet the so-often-abused term, "our brothers and sisters in the east," also has a meaning void of all pathos, and may be interpreted literally and simply as indicating that there is kinship between all of us who call ourselves German. To talk about a history in common isn't easy either. The borders and governments of this nation in the heart of Europe, which has felt pressure constantly from one side or another, or from more than one side at a time, have changed so often that it is almost impossible for any outsider to imagine it. And among a hundred Germans, only one was able to tell me how it could happen that a native of Coburg, for instance, should be supposed to feel he is a defender of Western civilization, while his fellow German from Gotha, forty miles away, his former brother during the days of the old Duchy of Coburg-Gotha, whose aristocracy once ruled over half the world and still rules the society of Coburg, should be expected to participate in the Socialist revolution. The declaration that there are personality differences, that their *natures* are different, cannot be traced back to any sensible opinion, only to a boiling point. To be sure, some people from Gotha are model Socialists today, class strugglers, more Soviet than the Soviets; and a few Coburgers are quite exceptionally North Atlantic Treaty minded, more American than the Americans, but does this prove personality differences? I would say, on the contrary! But we do still speak the same language, interspersed with a lot of Anglo-Americanisms on the one side, and with a lot of Party-Chinese on the other.

This Germany is partitioned in many ways. The three most important divisions are: 1. The River Main between north and south Germany. Its importance is historic rather than topical. 2. Topical and historic at the same time, but easier to recognize than to describe: the Oder-Neisse Line, the present eastern boundary of Germany. What was East Germany before 1945 lies beyond it; what is called East Germany today lies west of it. 3. Still without historic tradition and therefore topically all the more sensitive—the western boundary of the Soviet Zone as defined at Yalta. Today, twenty years later, it is still the eastern border of the Federal Republic. Since no river was handy to name it after, a formulation of the greatest orator of our time, Winston Churchill, was used and it was called the Iron Curtain.

Since 1945, the Germans have been able to choose between the two states on either side of this barrier. From 1945 to 1949, they were not called states but zones, to be precise—Occupation Zones. There are quite a few West Germans who feel that for the DDR, this still applies; they therefore never use or even tolerate the expression DDR for the *Deutsche Demokratische Republik* or German Democratic Republic, unless in quotes or preceded by a snide "so-called." Yet it is hard to deny that even this part of Germany can no longer be described correctly as an Occupation Zone. The use of "East Zone" for "Soviet Zone,"

and—more vaguely—"East Germany," came in and went out again fast
(in Germany) when the news got around that East Germany lay farther east, beyond the Oder. The latest results of the all-out effort to
irritate no one—the use of "Middle Germany" for "East Germany,"—
turned out to be out of the frying pan into the fire, since it seemed to
stress the fact that Germany should one day extend farther east, an idea
the Poles (and many Germans) don't like at all.

Call the country ruled by a government in Berlin (East) what you
will, you can't avoid trouble. A state-conscious citizen of the Federal
Republic is probably safest when he calls the German Democratic
Republic "East Zone," or in spite of the objections just mentioned,
"East Germany." In the same way, a state-conscious citizen of the
German Democratic Republic—according to the popular Germany
sport of tit-for-tat—is probably safest when he calls the Federal Republic the "West Zone," or "West Germany." Non-Germans, who apparently also like to be on the safe side, seem to prefer "West Germany" (as they call it in the east), and "East Germany" (as they call
it in the west).

If such a thing as public opinion had existed in the years 1945 to
1947, and the institutions to study it, then without doubt the results
would have been as follows: by far the most popular zone was the
British Zone; next came the American Zone; then for quite a while no
zone at all, followed by the French and Russian zones in that order.
That, in spite of this, the British Zone did not become overpopulated,
containing as it did 31 of Germany's 53 major cities, and the Soviet
Zone did not become completely depopulated, proves that either the
Brandenburgers and Saxons living in the east had leanings toward communism, or that the freedom of choice, as at first maintained, was handicapped from the start by quite a few limitations.

Everyone knows that by no means all Germans may decide freely
where they wish to live. But it is customary to shroud this simple fact
in a fog of misleading propaganda, and to decide in a clear-cut fashion: there are good Germans (democratic citizens of a free Western
World), who live in—let's say again—the West German town of Coburg; and there are bad Germans (agitators, functionaries, rowdies,
Communist fellow travelers) who live forty miles north in today's
East German Gotha. On the other hand, and depending entirely on
where you are, there are good Germans (democratic citizens of a peace-
loving Socialist world) who live in East German Gotha, and there are
bad Germans (agitators, functionaries, rowdies, fellow travelers of
capitalist imperialism) who live forty miles south, in West German
Coburg. This may have to be because of our mania for logical cate-
gorizations which probably gave the world a third, perhaps even a
half of its most famous philosophers. The sad part of it is that among
the inhabitants of this Germany, where you will find good and bad as
everywhere else in the world, there are more people who fanatically
believe this nonsense than there are anywhere else.

"But does anybody *seriously* think that the Germans in one part of

Germany are 'worse' than those in the other part?" Andreas von Hattesdorf had had enough of such oversimplifications.

No, nobody thinks so seriously; they come to this conclusion
thoughtlessly. The young man who, in order to be able to study, joins
the Communist Youth Organization, the FDJ, as so many of us joined
the Hitler Youth Movement, is despised in West Germany as a "functionary"; the harmless little skier from the Thuringian Forest, whose
government prescribes the insignia he has to wear on his jacket, is not
allowed to wear it at our West German sports meets because it stamps
him as a "secessionist." When a soldier of the Soviet-German People's
Army is pictured in a representative West German newspaper with the
subtitle, "One of Ulbricht's henchmen," it evidently doesn't bother
those who, as German soldiers of World War II indignantly (and
justly) refused to be called "Hitler's henchmen." And how often we
hear the phrase, "Well, he doesn't have to stay over there!"

Do we really want the entire population of the DDR to move west,
to "vote with their feet" as it has been called in Soviet political propaganda since Lenin? Nobody likes to think this through to the end.

Efforts to classify our refugees are as necessary as they are hopeless.
There are few groups but many individual destinies, all of which would
be deeply moving if they did not have to be banished from the realm
of living experience into the maw of statistics because there are millions
of them. In the beginning only he who had had to move from his domicile under a threat of life or death was rated a refugee, especially if he
was living even farther east, beyond the borders of the DDR. Whoever
had been dismissed from a prison camp of one of the Western allies, and
whose domicile (which very often existed only on paper) was in the
Soviet Zone, was not permitted to stay in one of the three west zones.
Even today, a man deciding against the Communist way of life in the
DDR of his own free will, and acting accordingly by moving to West
Germany, is entered in the statistics but not automatically recognized
as a refugee, which is greatly to his disadvantage, because to be recognized as a political refugee means very decisive state help in one's efforts
to start a new life. And all this had to be taken into consideration when
it came to answering Andreas' "simple" question, "But does anybody
seriously think that the Germans in one part of Germany are 'worse'
than those in the other part?"

"I have read something by Eugene Davidson," said Dick, "to the
effect that most of the refugees who left East Germany did so because
they hoped to earn more in the West, and thought they would be able
to do more with the money they earned. Many were disappointed.
And for every three refugees from east to west, you could count two
from west to east. How do you feel about that?"

Eugene Davidson, who did say as much in his book, *The Death and
Life of Germany*, was a member of the board of governors of the Yale
University Press at the time and would be very surprised if the govern-
ment in Bonn were to accuse him of spreading Communist propaganda.
Whatever the motives for flight may be, they are not to be grasped sta-

tistically, and the number of refugees is not so easily come by either. Of 15,000, 10,000 went west and 5,000 went east, say the statisticians of the DDR; 13,500 to the west, 1,500 to the east, say the statisticians of the Federal Republic. No one is in a position to check these figures in which anywhere from 5 per cent to 15 per cent must be counted as professional border crossers who swing back and forth from east to west, from west to east, to fish in the troubled waters of both areas. At times the fairly steady stream of refugees was overwhelmed by a tidal wave of fear. This was especially evident before the Berlin rebellion of June 17, 1953, and before the erection of the Berlin wall on August 13, 1961. Such waves differed in two essential ways from the steady flow of refugees to which we had grown accustomed in the fifteen years before 1961: they moved exclusively from east to west, and the reasons were clear. Before the wall, which for many Germans and for all Berliners, is a date equivalent to "before the war," or even to "before Christ," it was the fear that one day all access to the West would be closed that drove more Germans westward, in addition to the "normal" stream, for whom no general and irrefutable interpretation of motives is possible. And the fear turned out to be only too justified. Since the Iron Curtain has been rung down in Berlin, only very few have succeeded in finding a loophole.

We visited a doctor—let's call him Dr. Muller—living in a suburb of the West German spa of Baden-Baden. Many streets in Baden-Baden are named after cities in the East, indicating that a colony of refugees has been created there. There are innumerable such colonies in West Germany; as far as I know, none exist in East Germany.

Dr. Muller lives in a five-room apartment which he shares with his wife, his two children, his wife's parents, his father and brother. His office is in town. He gets there in a quite decent-looking car, which makes him appear wealthier than he could possibly be, judging by his living quarters.

"Do you think there is a stream of refugees from west to east," asked Dick, "which is not as great as from east to west, but still constitutes a quarter of that number, or a third?" (We have to keep in mind that this conversation took place in 1960.)

Dr. Muller belongs to the generation of the Hitler Youth Movement, and they have no more illusions. "As I see people," he said, "nothing is impossible. But I do believe that most of the west-to-east refugees come back very fast. If they can."

"Would you tell us why you came west?"

"Of course. Because I had had enough. At first I thought: They're playing crazy; one day they'll come to their senses. As far as medical care is concerned, they do a lot; you can't take that from them. So that's not the reason. How shall I explain it? I don't know if a man has a soul—in such matters I'm not always sure of myself—but every doctor knows there are illnesses that are easier to diagnose if we accept the fact that a man has a soul, or if you prefer it, a subconscious mind.

And in the DDR I sometimes had nightmares. I was surrounded by incurably ill people."

"And that's why you fled?"

"I know it sounds stupid, but if you want to put it in a nutshell—yes, that's why. Because the science of healing can't heal when it can be applied only externally. And because I couldn't bear it any more when the doorbell rang in the morning . . . not being sure what it might mean."

"Were arbitrary arrests a daily occurrence?"

"No. I wouldn't say that. I had many friends and many patients, but I heard of it happening only twice. But you"—and he turned to address me—"you experienced the Third Reich. You know that of the average men in an average town, hardly anyone was sent to a concentration camp, still all of us had it in our subconscious: "Watch your step. . . . Don't say too much. . . . It's better not to get mail from abroad. The German look. A chronic tenseness. So, sometimes, when the bell rings, it startles you."

"Would you say economic considerations play a part?"

"We refugees—if you will permit the expression, even if I have been living in this house for six years and feel quite at home here—we refugees don't like to hear that. It is said much too often. Of course everyone in our little town in the DDR talked incessantly about "the Golden West." Of course there are young people who have come here for that reason. But we who are not so young don't pull up our roots so easily. Take my family. I don't make any more than I did in East Germany, and at the beginning it was considerably less. My wife and children came here of course because I did. Before they left, my wife's parents were living under great pressure. They owned the last private book store in town, and their daughter had "defected to the republic," as it is called over there. There was a constant stream of callers—from the Party, from the city authorities. Deliveries from the state publishing houses were late; sometimes they didn't deliver at all. When a few good old customers stayed away because they were afraid to patronize the shop, my mother-in-law made up her mind. I know how hard it was for her to give up the business her grandfather had founded, and be dependent on me. Money played a part only in my father's case. He was a teacher. Like all the teachers in our town, he had been a member of the Nazi party, but he didn't want to join the SED, the new Communist party in the DDR. Finally he got a job as a janitor in the school of which he had once been the principal. At first I sent him money. But that got to be more and more difficult, and risky. Here, as a '131-er,' he at least gets a pension."

A 131-er is a man who, under paragraph 131 of the laws of the military occupation, lost his job because the occupation forces considered him undesirable. When a similar position became vacant later, he was given preferential treatment if proved not guilty, for the rights of a German civil servant may be taken from him only by a court of law, and then only for criminal reasons.

And so they move, some from west to east, many from east to west. One family member makes a start, makes a go of it, sends for the rest of his family. In the land they have forsaken, they are considered criminals, and a few questionable characters may undoubtedly be found among them, but the great majority of those who decide to give up so much and start all over again are people filled with great determination and energy. Sociological investigations have revealed that the IQ of refugees is far above the average, and that refugee families hold together very well.

The wanderers from west to east could take any route they pleased, since "defection" from the Federal Republic is not a punishable offense, but until August, 1961, the stream of refugees from east to west coursed mainly through Berlin. It is hard to believe that it will ever again be possible for hundreds of thousands to flee the DDR; it isn't even such an easy thing to wish for, since it would mean for us to be prepared and to ask the world to put up with another German war. In 1945, Dr. Muller was still able to walk across "the green border," but since then more and more iron has been added to the Curtain. From the Baltic Sea east of Lübeck to the Czech border in Hof, runs a barbed-wire fence, 1,381 kilometers long, interrupted in only a few places, for instance where a river—the Elbe, the Werra—can take its place, or at the 13 open crossings: 8 railroad beds and 5 highways. 36 railroad lines and about 100 main roads, as well as thousands of secondary roads, end at the barbed wire, and perhaps no more than a hundred yards beyond it look as if they were not the same road. East of the wire lies a 10-meter strip of scorched earth, officially "the control strip," in the language of those living in the border areas, "the death strip," because so many refugees have died on it under the fire of border guards.

This frontier, devised at Yalta, probably took quite a few historic facts into consideration. It was the borderline between different German Länder and provinces, but some of these states were still quite young, and, as far as historical tradition was concerned, scarcely established. That is why this frontier now cuts straight through cohesive native groups, folk and economic entities, landscapes. And yet, if a borderline had to be drawn down the middle of a country, this one seems almost sensible when compared with the present East German eastern border, the notorious Oder-Neisse Line.

5. THE ODER-NEISSE TABOO

On July 6, 1950, the DDR came to an agreement with Poland whereby it recognized the line formed by the Oder and the western section of the River Neisse as an "inviolable peace and friendship line between Germany and Poland."

"And because you refuse to recognize this boundary, you can't recognize the DDR and have to behave as if a state which exists—

whether you refer to it as a 'Zone' or 'the so-called DDR'—were not there."

Ralph could work himself into a great state of excitement over this topic, which was quite unlike him. All in all, this "peace and friendship" boundary put the peace and friendship of our little group to a hard test. And how could it be otherwise, since there isn't another German boundary which has created so much discontent and enmity in so short a time? The Polish government in exile that asked for the boundary was never permitted to return home; George Dertinger, Foreign Minister of the DDR, who drew up the agreement with Poland, was arrested three years later as a traitor and spy and condemned to fifteen years penal servitude. Whenever a statesman of the Western powers has to mention the eastern boundary of Germany, he has to choose his words very carefully if he doesn't want to jeopardize his relationship with the Federal Government. Whenever during the last decade, overtones of hysterical German nationalism have shattered the democratic harmony, in fifty out of a hundred cases it was directly or indirectly because of this border.

"Well now, tell me—am I right?" Ralph Stevens again.

"No, Ralph, in spite of everything, you are not even half right. You know that I don't 'recognize' the DDR—to do so fortunately lies beyond my jurisdiction; I do accept the fact that it exists. But that has nothing to do with the Oder-Neisse Line. Just as you have no right to give my garden to anyone else, neither does the government of the DDR, nor of the Federal Republic, have any right to renounce a fourth of Germany which does not belong to them. On the other hand, we appreciate Poland's difficulties and want to live in peace with her. And at present there is no better way out of this dilemma than to stick to the two formulas already established. The three-power Potsdam agreement of August 2, 1945, states that the Oder-Neisse Line is to remain in force until the final establishment of Poland's western frontiers, which was to be left to a universal peace conference. And in his statement of October 20, 1953, Chancellor Adenauer said, "The problem of the Oder-Neisse Line is not to be solved by force but by peaceful means only."

"But isn't that just empty talk?" This time our French Yvonne was dissatisfied. "What does it mean anyhow? What do they have in mind?"

Generally speaking, I don't think much of taboos. There are few difficulties in this world that would not be simplified by discussing them openly, but the Oder-Neisse Line is one of these few. It can't do any harm, though, to recall how it was created.

After World War I, in the Treaty of Riga (1921) the Soviet Union, weakened by war and revolution, was forced to cede its western provinces to Poland. This was contrary to the council of an independent committee under the chairmanship of British Foreign Minister Lord Curzon, who defined these areas as belonging ethnographically to Russia. After that it was a Russian rather than a Soviet ambition to create a "just border," the Curzon line.

In the pact between Hitler and Stalin, August 24, 1939, the Soviet Union succeeded in this respect, and later, when it allied itself with the West against Germany, it kept the Polish territories it had been granted by Hitler. At Yalta, the Allies were agreed that not the Poles but the Germans should bear the brunt of this Soviet territorial expansion; Poland was therefore to receive substantial territories in the northwest. If Poland had been satisfied with an Oder Line at the time, the result might have been a final and lasting agreement, but the Polish demand for Middle and Lower Silesia as well, changed the Oder Line into an Oder-Neisse Line, something the Allies could not say yes to.

Neither the Oder nor its extension southward through the River Neisse have ever been boundaries in an historic sense. After all, they slice straight through six large cities, although these cities, unlike Berlin, are already divided by rivers. But in the case of the largest and most important one, the old Hanseatic city of Stettin, the Oder-Neisse Line, which would have left the more prosperous and beautiful part of Stettin in Germany, was bent so that all of Stettin is now Szczecin, a Polish city. The proud old government buildings on the Hakenterasse still tower over it, but it is no longer the teeming city it used to be when it was a major Baltic seaport.

About 150 kilometers up the Oder, at the mouth of the River Warthe, lies the old Prussian fortress town of Cüstrin, where Crown Prince Frederick, later called "Frederick the Great", was imprisoned by a stern father; and where his friend Katte was executed before his eyes. The town, a sad ruin, lies for the most part on the eastern bank of the Oder and is called Kostrzyn. The suburb of Kietz has remained German. Next we come to Frankfurt on the Oder, a city truly divided; the suburb across the river is called Slubice. Witnesses testify to the fact that "peace and friendship" are not the first emotions experienced on this once so busy but now sparsely traveled Oder bridge. Frankfurt, the largest city on this arbitrary border, is famous for its town hall, Marienchurch, and old university, the three most impressive buildings in the partially restored medieval heart of the town. Whoever wishes to travel from Berlin to Posen, Warsaw, Moscow, must pass now as then through Frankfurt on the Oder; but there apparently aren't many people nowadays wishing to travel from Berlin to Posen, Warsaw, Moscow. . . .

Still farther south, the Oder curves to the east. Now the border runs straight across Brandenburg, cuts off the western tip of Silesia, and continues along the River Neisse to Guben, a typical provincial town with mixed memories for various types of people. Mention of Guben always reminds me of the fact that in August, 1939, gigantic troop concentrations took place there, in preparation for the invasion of Poland. Citizens of the other, "more eastern" Germany are probably reminded of the fact that on January 3, 1876, Wilhelm Pieck, the first President of the DDR was born in Guben. The now Polish city may continue to call itself "Gubin," and the 'i' is justified, since Gubin is basically a Slavic town; but the newer section, prosperous because of its industry, was to be renamed Wilhelm-Pieck-City in Pieck's honor after his death in 1960, just as the Saxon industrial city of Chemnitz was renamed Karl-Marx-Stadt, though no one was ever able to ascertain what Karl Marx had to do with Chemnitz. But the town fathers of industrial German-Guben protested with all sorts of economic arguments and therefore with some success. "Our hats," they declared (Guben being a hat-producing town) "are sold all over the world as "Guben hats." Who in God's name is going to buy Wilhelm-Pieck-Stadt hats?" Guben is therefore now called Wilhelm-Pieck-Stadt Gubin.

But the partitition bureaucracy reached its ultimate absurdity when it let the River Neisse divide the Silesian city of Görlitz into a Saxon Görlitz and a Polish Zgorzelec.

This city can teach us a lot. The young people who have been reared in West Germany see no difference between the two halves of Görlitz, since they hardly know where the town lies. Is it "over there," in Poland? Or "in the Zone"? Or "Communist"? And the young people raised in East Germany are not allowed to see any difference. After all, don't both halves of Görlitz belong to that "great block of freedom loving Socialist peoples which eradicates all national differences," making East Germany and East Poland one, at least theoretically?

Görlitz contradicts both hypotheses. In 1945, when the Oder-Neisse Line had to be taken seriously, chance would have it that apparently all the inhabitants of Görlitz were "domiciled" in the western part of the city. Thus German Görlitz soon became an overpopulated and once more prosperous town, while Polish Zgorzelec stood empty for years, nothing was rebuilt, and the town fell apart. Finally industrial workers from East Poland were moved to Zgorzelec.

When partition ceased to be a rhetorical hypothesis and became a practical reality, events proved that Görlitzers did not want to become Zgorzelecers, although the Polish variation of communism is the most liberal, whereas German thoroughness and organizational zeal have made communism in Germany into something unbearable. Reality is often very different from what is described in text books and proclaimed in ideologies—that is the lesson of Görlitz. And that is what the Peace and Friendship Border looks like. The Polish government in exile persuaded the British it would serve as a "security line," but this could not prevent it from breeding instead insecurity, dissatisfaction, and enmity.

Beyond this line lies one-fourth of Germany: Pomerania, West and East Prussia, and the old Hanseatic City of Danzig. There lie the big estates which used to provide almost half the German population with meat and fats, with bread and potatoes. There, in Upper Silesia, lies the Ruhr of the East, the second largest German industrial area, cut up in World War I, separated from Germany by World War II. Almost 10 million Germans lived there, of which 8 million have been driven away, dragged away, or killed in flight. In this territory there were cities that could be counted among the most beautiful in Germany, not only Danzig, but Königsberg, Stettin, and many smaller ones: Allenstein and Marienburg in East Prussia, Waldenburg and Hirschberg in Silesia.

"And now would you like to balance the record? The loss of those eastern provinces and the driving out of their people against the horrors of the Second World War, the concentration camps, the destruction of six million Jews?"

This is a question that is asked over and over again. Apparently there are many Germans who have restored their spiritual equilibrium and "overcome the past" through such an accounting.

"No, Ralph. I would consider such accounting insane. You cannot counter guilt with guilt. Who is to tell us where to subtract and where to add? To put it simply: what does it profit a Polish Jew who was gassed in Auschwitz that two years later an East Prussian peasant is beaten to death?"

"Well then for heaven's sake write off those eastern provinces and we'll have peace! All you do is embarrass your friends in the West by keeping the subject alive. And actually you have written them off. . . ."

"I don't know, Ralph. Are you talking to me personally, or are you addressing the German people? None of the existing German governments has the right to write off territories that never belonged to them. As for me . . . no one I know has any idea of winning back the eastern territories by force, not even the official representatives of the refugee groups with their sometimes quite rash and foolish speeches."

But should I—can I—forget the summer evenings on the Masurian lakes? What of the feelings evoked when I see pictures of the Langgasse in Danzig, and the Krantor, rebuilt just as they were? It took us twenty-five minutes to get to the beach in Oliva. . . . Zoppot was the most internationally famous Baltic Sea resort; for me there was always something exotic about it. I don't grieve for that megalomaniac piece of sculpture, the Tannenberg Monument; but the Marienburg. . . .

Others have other memories: of Pomerania, East Prussia, Silesia. Should such memories be kept alive artificially, or stifled? Both things happen. In a surprising show of unity, school children in both West and East Germany learn very little about Silesia, unless they happen to have a geography teacher who is a refugee. But two generations are still alive for whom East and West Prussia, Danzig, Pomerania, and Silesia belong to Germany, regardless of where the border runs, which they can't change, and don't want to change by force. As long as we live, the world that was our world remains a part of us.

6. DRESDEN, THE CITY THAT WAS MURDERED

In West Germany we find 53 big cities; in the DDR, 5; in the eastern territories lost to Germany, 5. If Berlin were not divided it would be the twelfth largest city in the world, after Tokyo, New York, London, Shanghai, Paris, Moscow, Buenos Aires, Calcutta, Peking, Bombay,

Chicago. West Berlin alone would be twenty-second, and the largest West German cities would be thirty-fifth (Hamburg), and seventy-ninth (Munich).

Which German city do those Germans who still remember all of Germany consider the most beautiful? I asked at least a hundred people and the twelve cities that came out on top were: 1. Rothenburg on the Tauber. 2. Dresden. 3. Heidelberg. 4. Hamburg. 5. Freiburg in Breisgau. 6. Munich. 7. Würzburg. 8. Lübeck. 9. Nürnberg. 10. Meersburg. 11. Passau. 12. Bamberg. Also-rans were: Dinkelsbühl, Goslau, Marburg, Danzig, Trier, Regensburg, Lüneburg, Hannoversch Münden, Königsberg, Wesserburg/Inn, Schwerin, Hirschberg, Linz/Rhein, Bernkastel, Naumburg, Neisse.

Since I happen to be a big-city man—and for me the most beautiful city has to be a living city—Hamburg and Munich would rank high on my list. But at the top would stand Dresden, with which my memory is playing me a trick, because Dresden is dead. It was murdered.

The city was overflowing with treks of refugees trying to escape the Red Army which had reached the Oder. For the first time, the women and children felt a certain precarious safety from the heavy attacks of the Soviet soldiers. Nobody took seriously the air-raid alarm on the evening of February 13. Hadn't the city, which contained few military targets, been spared so far? Didn't everybody know that the war couldn't last much longer? Could there be any sense in bombarding Dresden now, a famous art center in which the oldest and most gracious part was called "the English quarter," next to which lay an "American quarter," and an English, an American, a Scotch and a Russian church?

But the seemingly senseless thing happened. In three attacks, well over 2,000 English and American planes dropped first incendiary, then high explosive bombs; 135,000 human beings died, a greater number than in any single military action in the history of mankind. They burned to death in the streets, sought in vain to save their lives by jumping into the icy waters of the Elbe, were buried in the ruins of the city, which since then has remained dead.

"If you have forgotten how to cry, you will learn it again in the destruction of Dresden," wrote the eighty-three-year-old poet and dramatist, Gerhart Hauptmann, who witnessed the saturation raid. "I stand at the exit portals of my life and envy my dead friends who were spared this experience. I weep."

There wasn't a major German city, except Heidelberg, that was easy to recognize for anyone who saw them again in 1945, after a lapse of years. None were spared. But some took clever and energetic advantage of the opportunity to begin again and—to the man unprejudiced by memory—seem more beautiful today than they were before. Hannover, for instance. Others—Hamburg and Munich, to name two—have been astonishingly successful in literally saving their faces. Cities like Cologne, Frankfurt-am-Main, Nürnberg, Cassel, or Leipzig, are certainly not what they were before, but their citizens show no evidence of letting sentimental memories dim what they have achieved in rebuilding their cities. Berlin, for quite different reasons, and the German cities beyond the Oder and Neisse, could be compared with Dresden in that the city that once bore the name no longer exists.

This is not because Dresden was destroyed with exceptional brutality. Hamburg suffered almost as much; Cologne more. And it is not only because reconstruction in East Germany proceeded at a much slower pace than in West Germany. It is because of the irreconcilable difference between the hedonistic baroque princes who made Dresden the city it was once, and the Communist puritans who rule there today.

Dresden was basically a gay city; now even admirers of the East German Communist regime would hardly find its gayety something to stress. The gravity, sometimes called "moral," sometimes "brutal," of a people who, in the course of their history have often had every reason to be unable to laugh, celebrates a macabre triumph in East Germany. But as an admirer of the old, festive, and resplendent Dresden you find yourself in good company. "A wonderfully agreeable situation . . . the town is the neatest I have ever seen in Germany," was how Lady M. Wortley Montagu, put it in the eighteenth century. The German poet, Herder, called the city "the German Florence," and another poet, Heinrich von Kleist, describes a trip down the Elbe as follows: "Suddenly the river abandons it right bank and makes a quick turn toward Dresden, as if fleetingly kissing a beloved. What a grandiose, festive location the city has, wreathed by the Elbe hills which seem encamped around it, keeping their distance as if too awestruck to come closer."

Finally, a writer of our day, a Dresdener who "emigrated" to Munich when his native city was taken over by a government that threatened to burn his books—books which had already been burned once by Hitler's professors: "Dresden was a wonderful city . . . in it past and present lived together in harmony . . . and with the landscape, the Elbe, its bridges and hillsides. . . . If it may be said that I know not only what is bad and ugly, but also what is beautiful, I have Dresden to thank for it, the city where I grew up." This was written by Erich Kästner.

Visualize Dresden as a circle, its circumference indicated lightly by hills. In the circle, envision a large Y, and with that you have the ground plan. The foot of the Y points southwest and runs up from the circumference straight through Old Dresden, more or less along the Schlosstrasse. At its end, in the center of the circle, you come to a bridge which today is named after the Bulgarian, Dmitrov. When Dresden was still Dresden, it was the Augustus Bridge.

The two arms of the Y are formed by the River Elbe, which describes a wide arc in the center of the city, flowing from east to northwest. North of the river, clasped in the arms of the Y, lies Dresden Neustadt (or New City), which isn't a day newer than the Altstadt (or Old City) and the New City was called Old Dresden until the city burned to the ground in 1685. By 1732, it had been rebuilt. However, the Altmarkt, or Old Market, did not lie in Old Dresden but in the Old City; and that's where you'll also find the New Market, which is not in the New City—all of which used to be complicated enough. But since the König Johannstrasse, the street which helped to connect the two, has been renamed the Ernst Thälmannstrasse (after the German Communist leader), nobody knows how to get around.

Dresden is not a very old city in the European sense. It was not really important until the Princes Ernst and Albert, of the ruling house of Wettin, quarreled, and Albert made Dresden the residence of the Alberts, or *Albertiner*, in 1485. In the sixteenth century, the Renaissance was in flower, without, however, making much impression on the city. The real Dresden, the celebrated and unforgettable Dresden, never grew to be much older than two hundred. It was created in the eighteenth century by two hedonistic, art-loving men of the world who had a slight tendency toward megalomania. As Electors of Saxony, their names were Friedrich August I and Friedrich August II; as Kings of Poland, which they also happened to be, they were August II and August III. August II became very popular as August the Strong, a title referring mainly to his phenomenal progenitive faculty. His offspring, however, were for the most part illegitimate. As the residence of this King of Poland, Dresden became a world-famous metropolis.

In Matthew Daniel Pöppelmann, August the Strong found a congenial architect. When the old Georgian building that served him as a palace did not turn out to his liking, he and Pöppelmann planned a super-colossal, ostentatiously gorgeous construction. It took twelve years, (1711–1722) to build the courtyard alone, famous since then as the Dresden Zwinger, so famous that the new rulers in Dresden have gone to a great deal of trouble to rebuild it as it was, stone for stone. "*Fehlt leider nur das geistige Band* . . . naught missing but the spiritual link." (Faust.)

The Catholic Hofkirche (built 1737–1756, according to the plans of Italian architect Chiaveri) has also been restored with exemplary devotion. Its slender tower was as much part of the city's silhouette as the majestic dome of the Frauenkirche, built by another genial master of Dresden baroque art, George Bahr (1726–1738). But that is gone.

To complete the list of Dresden architects, we have Gottfried Semper, the Hamburg art professor, who also designed the Vienna Burg Theater. His classicism, derived more from the Italian Renaissance than Greece, complemented the city's baroque buildings—his opera house, for instance, which has been rebuilt in part, but above all, his art gallery. Even today it can hold its own with the galleries in Florence and the Louvre in Paris. The palaces of the aristocracy and the baroque façades of patrician houses, which often equaled them in splendor, stood side by side with royal residences and churches. But prayer is not a desirable element now in Dresden's churches which for reasons of prestige have been rebuilt, and confessions are taken care of by Party functionaries and come under the heading of "self-criticism."

Not even the desire to revive some of the Old City's past glory could persuade the new Dresden city fathers to restore a middle-class baroque atmosphere. Of the central German cities, Dresden is still the most beautiful. Whoever has traveled in East Germany for a few days enjoys a sense of release there. The stage is set, but no gay performance is being held.

7. AN ALL-GERMAN DISCUSSION

People used to converse in Germany; today they have discussions, preferably "real" discussions. These differ from those that are unreal in that they deal with "real" concerns. An example of a real concern is the fraternal strife within Germany. When a journalist from Chemnitz (alias Karl-Marx-Stadt), a professor and his wife from Leipzig, a deputy from Borna—all living in East Germany—and a West German journalist from Hamburg, like myself, talk about Dresden, then about the DDR, and finally about art, literature, and science, they do what we did one dreary November evening in Borna—they broaden the scope of the "real" discussion and turn it into an "all-German" discussion.

Toward such all-German discussions we find three basic all-German attitudes: 1. They are senseless. 2. They are desirable. 3. They are dangerous. These three basic attitudes depend on the intellectual stand of those taking part in the discussion, on its location geographically, on its point of departure, on the prevailing political situation, and on many imponderables. Whoever lets himself in for such a discussion should be fully aware that he is engaged in something at once senseless, desirable, and dangerous. And whoever decides to report on Germany must learn to bear with composure: reproaches (because he is doing something senseless), praise (because he is doing something desirable), and suspicion (because he is doing something dangerous). The names of those participating in the following conversation are therefore disguised. A few other aspects of the talk are also camouflaged for political reasons.

My foreign friends were duly interested in the Federal Republic of (West) Germany, especially whenever prejudices could be aired, explained away, confirmed or corrected, but they were incomparably more interested in the DDR. We did our best to get into the DDR as a group; unfortunately we did not succeed. Six Americans might have been able to do it, or six French citizens, in the last analysis perhaps even six Germans. But to procure visa and visitor's permit for an American, an Englishman, a French girl, a Swiss, an Austrian, and a German, so that all six might travel together, turned out to be more than the East German bureaucracy could cope with. The talk here described therefore took place without them. For the fact that it took place in Borna, twenty-eight miles southeast of Leipzig, there is an autobiographical explanation: long, long ago, when Germany was still a whole, democratic nation where Communists and Nazis brawled, I went to school in Borna.

My old teachers are ruined or dead. Not one of them survived the two changes of regime—Weimar to Hitler, Hitler to Ulbricht—without being broken. My old schoolmates can be divided easily into three groups of almost equal number: those who were killed in the war, those who fled to West Germany, those who occupy key positions in Borna and its surroundings. It would be interesting if one could divide these approximately hundred persons into the three just-mentioned groups according to some recognizable characteristic—as for instance: the best were killed, the second best fled, and the scum stayed and did well in East Germany. Reality isn't so simple. The smart, the strivers, the staunchly narrow-minded, the average citizen, the tough, and the unsavory customers—you can spread them fairly evenly across all three groups. Our valedictorian, who won every sport event for us, the sort of boy every father wants for a son, became a doctor and fled to West Germany. The president of our class got himself a not-very-significant job in a completely insignificant bank in Borna, which he probably still has today unless he is dead. His brother—considered a genius in my day, a musical prodigy—died in the war. The most repulsive fellow was first an important Hitler Youth leader, then he became a leading deputy in East Berlin. The four smartest—according to the *consensus omnium* of their schoolmates rather than their report cards—may be accounted for as follows: one died in action, the second emigrated to the United States as an engineer, the third is Karl Thal, the Chemnitz journalist, mentioned previously, and the fourth is the Leipzig professor, George Schmidt, with both of whom I spent the evening just mentioned. Also with us—or I should say, we were with him, since he was the only one of us still living in Borna—was a minor deputy, a friend of Karl Thal, who described him to me privately as "no shining light, loyal to the Party line, but loyal in other ways too."

Karl had read an article by me about Dresden. As a journalist in a confidential position, he could—unlike his fellow citizens—take cognizance of things printed in West Germany. "You're right in a way," he said. "Still what you write isn't entirely correct. The people living in Dresden today have made an all-out effort to rebuild their city, with more emotional involvement than you people in Hamburg are in a position to imagine."

"Oh, the true citizens of Hamburg are really very proud of their city, to which I would like to add: justly so."

But Karl was dogged. "Did they help to rebuild it with their own hands, as so many thousands did in Dresden?"

"I should say so. Thousands. Above all, the construction workers. Forgive me, I didn't mean to be cynical, but we believe the work of building should be left to those who know how to do it and who make good money at it."

"I'd say that the contractors do most of the earning. What are you paying for your apartment in Hamburg?"

"Four hundred marks a month."

Triumph on every face around me, and in unison, everyone's variation of the basic melody: *That's* what we thought capitalism looked like! Then Karl again. "I know Dresden very well, and I was very fond of the old Dresden. But I like the new city, too. My sister just got an apartment there, for thirty-eight marks a month. You see? Not even a tenth of what you pay."

All right. In West Germany the construction business is operating at an all-time high, and many people looking for a place to settle are attracted to Hamburg. Still, this Dresden rental couldn't possibly be the true market value.

"She had to wait quite a few years for the apartment," Karl admitted. "And, of course, there isn't much choice. And she had to become a member of the AWG, for the time being at any rate."

"Of the what?"

"I'm sorry. We have an initial craze here. Of the *Arbeiter-Wohnungs-baugenossenschaft*, the Workers' Apartment Building Union. That meant a down payment of three hundred marks, and a certain number of hours work clearing debris, excavating. . . ."

"What does your sister do, Karl?"

"She's an X-ray technician."

"Wouldn't you say that was a rather foolish way to utilize her capabilities?"

"On the contrary," said Karl, "Inge thought it was wonderful to be a laborer for a change, to create material things with her own hands."

"Excavating?"

"Excavating."

I long ago gave up taking Marxist terms such as "worker," "farmer," and the old hue and cry of their relationship to "the means of production" seriously. But what are the facts?

In fact, the "worker" Inge, née Thal (whom I later visited in her three-room 38-DM-a-month apartment with plush furniture and cheap carpeting) is a middle-class woman, lower middle class. She worries about her children, works in a hospital, thinks the powers that be know what they are doing. She plays badminton (tennis is still rather expensive and therefore considered quite fashionable in all of Germany) and hopes to win in the lottery. Officially she enjoys equality with her husband; in private life she is devoted and submissive to him. She dotes on a figurine with the head of a hedgehog, which was created and named by a big illustrated paper in—strangely enough—*West* Germany. Like her opposite number in West Germany, she calls this queer animal Mecki. She hopes, fears, and does exactly what thousands of lower-middle-class women in West Germany hope, fear, and do.

"To get back to Dresden," said Karl, "I don't say I approve of everything. Those little towers on the apartment houses on the Altmarkt are terrible, and I'm allowed to say so. There was a lot of bickering when it came to rebuilding Dresden, but the fact remains: they did try to preserve the central part of the city. Around it, instead of narrow, unsanitary houses with dark rooms, you have roomy workers' apartments, and in the Altmarkt, shops and restaurants. They're not stylish, but they're modern."

Stylish. Modern. Words, words, words. And whoever put the words into an ideological system can't be contradicted by words any more. Just try to tell a native of Dresden, convinced that his socialism is a blessing, that there is no festiveness within the city's walls, and he probably won't even know what you're talking about. Instead, he'll refer you to a "complex territorial seven-year plan" which demands that "socialist life be effectively expressed by festivals and demonstrations" on that very turreted Altmarkt Karl was complaining about. These abysmal slogans!

"Yes, they are dreadful," Professor Schmidt admitted, "but the people need them. As for us, we don't pay any attention to them any more. But you'll have to admit that, compared with Borna, Dresden is still a beautiful city."

The laughter that followed was a little too bitter to come as a relief.

Borna, on the Whyra, is one of the thousand small towns in which one-third of the Germans of the DDR live. In this region, names often end in 'a': Riesa, Rötha, Hartha, Grimma, Pirna, a sign that the founders were Slavs. The most important street in such towns usually runs from the market square, which today is usually called Karl Marx Platz, to the station which is still called *Bahnhof*, or station. In the good old days, the street was called simply and solidly, Bahnhofstrasse.

In Borna, this simple Bahnhofstrasse was renamed Friedrich-Ebert-strasse under the Weimar Republic; Adolf-Hitlerstrasse in the Third Reich; and Wilhelm-Pieckstrasse in the Workers' and Farmers' State, in the course of which the street didn't get any prettier. I'm afraid I'll have to admit that the whole town hasn't grown any prettier. It always did take a lot of love for my home town to see anything at all in it, in spite of the fact that, although it didn't have a castle, it did have old town gates; no miracles of Romanesque or Gothic architecture, but churches that bore staunch witness to the sacrifice and simple taste of pious people. There were never any *salons* or grand *soirées* in Borna, only cozy taverns and sport clubs. Words such as "impressive" and "glamorous" would never have been evoked by Borna even at the best of times, but pleasant, idyllic, *gemütlich* . . . a little something for the heart. The garrison of a royal Saxon cavalry regiment—later a tank unit—and the state high school (more nearly the equivalent of an American junior college) were the focal points, socially, of this small town of 7,000 inhabitants who lived by modest manufacture and a little agriculture. Borna had a fine reputation for its onions and was therefore known by those at home as *Zwibbelborne*, dialect of that region for Onion-Borna. In the 1880's improved drying methods for briquetting peat made Borna, lying as it did in a rich brown coal area, the center of a new industrial region. Its inhabitants grew to 12,000. Brown holes gaped in the landscape, factory chimneys belched thick clouds of smoke into a sky that was never quite so blue again. Houses, streets, and fields were veiled by a light layer of soot. The town had already elected a Social Democrat deputy during the last years of the Kaiser's rule. After World War I, the Workers' Party split into SPD (Socialists) and KPD (Communists).

Then came 1933. The National Socialist Party came to Borna, as it did to all of "Red Saxony." The *Ortsgruppenleiter*, or Local Troop Leader, was more important than the mayor. A reliable Pg. (*Parteigenosse* or Party Member) replaced the old superintendent of the high school without any of his teachers protesting; soon Borna was a garrison town again. . . .

Its industrial importance increased when chemists of the Third Reich succeeded in considerably broadening the usefulness of brown coal. Benzine, synthetic rubber, and textiles were now produced between Borna and Leipzig. Then came 1945. Borna had to open its gates to refugees from the east. They swelled the population to a count of 20,000, who were soon absorbed by the brown-coal industry, which was still operating. Today it works in three shifts and determines the life rhythm of the region. Coal is East Germany's most important export. In the DDR exports to West Germany, brown coal takes first place; second is motor fuel. The Communist Party took over this heritage from the National Socialists. Again all streets were renamed, again the superintendent of schools was changed, and the *Gymnasium* or high school is now an *Oberschule*, or Upper School.

All schools are Upper Schools in East Germany, just as every waiter is a *Herr Oberkellner*, or Mr. Upper-waiter. Usually the "waiter" is omitted, making of him simply a Mr. Upper, to say nothing of all the other little Mr. Uppers: *Oberpostschaffner* for the mailman; *Oberwachtmeister* for the policeman; *Oberregierungsrat* for a (not top ranking) civil servant, which only goes to show that a German Communist state remains basically German.

Yes, compared with Borna, Dresden is a beautiful city. "Don't be offended, but Borna has more in common with Dresden than with any small town in West Germany," I said.

"Of course," said the deputy, "because both places are no longer seats of bourgeois capitalism but workers' cities."

"Do you mean to tell me you believe that nonsense?"

"You don't have to be so aggressive about it," said the deputy. "But we understand, of course. It all ties in with the position of the bourgeoisie. Seen socially as a whole, they have to be ideologically on the defensive."

Helplessly I turned to George Schmidt, the professor. "What's the man talking about?"

"If you want a lesson in Marxist-Leninism——"

"No, just tell me in plain German what the gentleman—I beg your pardon—what our comrade just said, and what it has to do with Borna and Dresden."

I have never been able to find out to what extent my schoolmates—the Leipzig professor George Schmidt, and the journalist from Karl-Marx-Stadt, Karl Thal—have been able to adopt the new ideology that has been rammed down their throats the last fifteen years. I don't think they're too sure about it themselves. One thing did come clear though in the course of our conversation: within the framework of the Marxist-

Leninist thought system, intelligent and clever speakers are on their own terms uncontradictable: that a man's position on this earth depends upon his relationship to the means of production; that world history nurtures the secret ideal, revealed only to a favored few, of an evolution toward Marxist-Leninist socialism; that the individual owes everything to the collective, the collective nothing to the individual. The Marxist-Leninist reality has the brilliantly conceived characteristic of taking place for the most part on paper (hence the popularity of "plans") and remaining uninfluenced by facts, observed or experienced.

8. PROFESSOR IN LEIPZIG

Of the German universities that have remained German, Leipzig is the second oldest, dating back to the year 1409. Only Heidelberg (1386) and Cologne (1388, closed in 1798, reopened in 1919) are older. Of those which have not remained German universities, Prague (1348) is today in Czechoslovakia; Vienna (1365) is Austrian.

On the surface, the founding of Leipzig University sounds impressive: four hundred German scholars and masters left the Prague University in protest again Czech domination, and supported by the Pope and the Wettin electors, founded their own university in Leipzig. However, at the time nationalism and the Reformation were ushering in a new era, and the new teachings were being propagated in Prague by the pioneer Czech, Jan Hus. It was therefore the anti-Reformers, the restorers and conservatives, the "reactionaries," who withdrew to Leipzig. Actually, while the humanities were flourishing in Erfurt (1392, closed in 1816) scholasticism, and the obscurantism of the Middle Ages still reigned supreme in Leipzig.

"Compared with the scholastic regime," said Professor George Schmidt, "the pressures of socialism are light. Of course we must take into account that, as a scientist, I am in a favorable position. That's why I can afford to have middle-class parents and even a few bourgeois-capitalist contacts."

"As a scientist? Why?"

"Because Marx and Lenin had the good sense to realize that scientific findings can't be class-bound."

A professor of the humanities, on the other hand, *is* affected by the Marxist-Leninist teachings, which are as obligatory today on the other side of the Harz Mountains as the dogma of scholasticism ever was. But the scientist gets into trouble only when his research has undesirable results, as for instance—and this really happened—the official discovery that the despised, privately owned farms of approximately thirty hectars, which have been abolished, were more profitable than the collectives prescribed by Marxist-Leninist ideology. The theologian, philosopher, historian, philologist, must always be "sociological" too; he can't afford objective knowledge. He busies himself, according to dialectical Marxism with the "superstructure," a rather airy edifice as the name implies, erected on the solid foundation of "production ratio" and therefore dependent on it. When the production ratio changes, philosophy has to change with it, for the faculty members have to represent the class viewpoint; anything else would be heresy or, as they say in Leipzig: objectivism.

"But all that doesn't concern me," George assured me. "I have Karl Marx to thank for the fact that my computer doesn't have to take social systems into consideration."

"And you see no difference between Leipzig and Heidelberg?"

"Oh, Heidelberg is a much prettier town." George grinned.

Of course Leipzig never was an obviously beautiful city. Since Goethe's day, you could hear people call it a "Paris in miniature," and claim for it an aura of culture. But this Saxon Paris lacks not only the Louvre and the Tuileries—the River Pleisse just can't replace the Seine, and I even prefer the Eiffel Tower, the esthetic merits of which are controversial, to the bombastic mass of stone, the Völkerschlachtdenkmal, which commemorates the Battle of Leipzig (1815). But Leipzig was a pleasant city, lacking any prominent triumphs of architecture, yet with a certain attractive uniformity, thanks to the preferential use of Rochlitz porphyry as building material. It was a flourishing city. Tobacco, textiles, and leather were traded, and three times a year there was a fair. Few books were written in Leipzig, but many were published there; and since the establishment of commission sales, they have been sold there, too. Leipzig is the home of such famous publishing houses as Anton Kippenberg's *Insel* books, Teubner, Brockhaus, Reclam, and the Bibliographic Institute. Ernst Rowohlt learned bookmaking in Leipzig, and in the first volume he published on his own, he listed "Leipzig & Paris" as places of publication. The many people who came to Leipzig on business wanted to be entertained. The Old and New Theaters did what they could, without ever exerting much influence on the German theater as a whole. Thomasschule and Gewandhaus catered successfully to the connoisseur of music.

"What I really wanted to know," I asked my friend, "is whether you notice any difference between educational methods practiced at the university here and those in West Germany? Or as they used to be before Germany was divided?"

"In research methods you'll find very little change, but where staff and students are concerned, practically everything is different. Students, study plans, political education—nothing's the same."

"What political education?"

"Well, I'm expected to take part in a so-called Marxist conference every two or three weeks."

"And who expects you to?"

"The SED. They arrange the whole thing. Sometimes it's quite funny. Do you know, for instance, what your world viewpoint is, as a citizen of West Germany?"

"I can hardly wait!"

George was quite evidently having a wonderful time explaining my world viewpoint to me. "I found out a few evenings ago, at one of these conferences. Your state philosophy in West Germany is neo-Thomism."

Well, well, well! I had never taken time off to see my philosophy as eclectically dependent on Thomas Aquinas.

For George Schmidt, professor of chemistry, these conferences—from which he may occasionally stay away—are the only direct encroachment by the Party on his private life. Occasionally it is suggested that he join the Party, but only suggested; nothing more than that. He is, however, required to know the generally propagated theories of Marxist-Leninism, and now and then he must solemnly reaffirm his faith in "Peace and Progress."

"But I shall have to join the Party soon," said George.

"Why?"

"If my oldest boy wants to attend the university—and he does—he has to be either a worker's or a farmer's son, which he is not; or he must move to West Germany, which we don't want him to do; or he must have a father who is a member of the SED. In that case this father—even as a member of the 'old intellectuals'—may be found worthy of having helped to produce, for once purely biologically, a 'new intellectual.' "

"Worker's and farmer's" children is an *idee fixe* in East Germany. The quite correct observation, in countries such as West Germany, that not all children have yet reached the point where it can be said they enjoy the same start in life, appears in East Germany as an "ideological" glorification of the worker's and farmer's child. What this child is supposed to be will grow increasingly difficult to define as the remnants of the old bourgeoisie, who even in East Germany still contribute to everyday life, are used up. This anachronistic residue can be sure of at least one thing: they do not enter the picture as procreators of worker's and farmer's children. But in due course it will have to be decided whether the child of a professor (who was once a worker's or farmer's child) is automatically demoted to the underprivileged ranks of a non-worker's or farmer's child. . . .

This glorification of worker's and farmer's children is not an innovation of communism, or of East Germany. It had its beginnings in the French Revolution. "With the founding of the Republic," said Fabre d'Eglantine, addressing the National Convention, "the time has come at last to demonstrate to all nations that in France, the worker—in industry or in the fields—is worth more than all the crowned heads in the world put together." In 1794, D'Eglantine went to the guillotine.

Be that as it may, out of 100 students, 60 have to be "workers' and farmers' children." That is what the directives of the Ministry of Education, established in East Germany in 1951, prescribe, and that's the way it has to be.

A former Leipzig student, returning to Leipzig today, is more likely to recognize the city than the university. Both were crushed by Allied bombings in December, 1943—but the city recovered. The Leipzig Fair has again become a major attraction; the railway station is once more the focal point of a sociable community with its arms wide open to tourists. The professors live today where professors always lived, in the quiet residential sections of Marienbrunn and Markleeberg. But the university . . .

Now, they call it the Karl Marx University, although it could count such men as Gottsched and Gellert, Wilhelm Wundt, the psychologist, and Wilhelm Ostwald, in chemistry, as its professors; although Ulrich von Hutten, Leibniz, Klopstock, Lessing, Goethe, Jean Paul, and Robert Schumann studied there—*not* Karl Marx of Mosel-Rhine-English origin, who never had anything even remotely to do with the University of Leipzig. They could have called it the Thomas Münzer University. Münzer, the militant disciple of Luther, who in the sixteenth century managed somehow to distill a rather noble communism from the text of the Bible, had a farmer's state in mind even then (workers did not yet exist) and what's more, he was a Leipzig student. But if they didn't want to latch on to Leipzig's Christian traditions—which is understandable—then the only century in which the University of Leipzig really played a leading role in Germany's intellectual life—the eighteenth "Century of Enlightenment"—could have provided quite a few illustrious names, any one of which would have served well as patron of a university that until then had been proud of the fact that it had no patron. But no, it had to be Karl Marx.

"I don't know why either," said George. "The Nazis named everything they could after Hitler; we name everything we can after Marx. Frankly, I prefer Marx."

The desire to do honor to Karl Marx seems stronger than another tendency, also noticeable in East Germany, which is, wherever possible not to disturb any old all-German traditions popular with the small-German citizenry, small in the sense of local, regional. Wherever the name of a square has been changed from Adolf-Hitler Platz to Karl-Marx or Marx-Engels Platz, the name is spelled out in the script of yesteryear—black Gothic lettering on a white background. In East Berlin, cars have the same old Berlin license number, IA, and the taxis are striped black and white as in the Führer's day. The broadcasting station, *Deutschlandsender*, in Königswusterhausen, hasn't changed its name, and the Prussian Academy is now the German Academy. The German Reich was destroyed, but the railways of East Germany are still called *Deutsche Reichsbahn*, and though the West German army, after a considerable display of hamstrung imagination, came up with new uniforms (which were discarded when it was found that they pleased no one), the antimilitaristic, anti-Fascist People's Army of East Germany took over the uniforms of the former German Wehrmacht without a trace of embarrassment or any visible alterations.

"Yes," said George, "we're a strange homogenization of Greater Germany *petits bourgeois* and small-German secessionists, but you can say what you like—we're not doing so badly."

From the limited perspective of a university professor who, as a scientist, is spared all ideological pressures, such an interpretation of conditions is understandable. Only some 300 members of a faculty of 1,600 have left the University of Leipzig since it became Communist— Theodore Litt, renowned pedagogue, now deceased; the jurists, Weber and Nikisch; philosopher and first postwar dean, Gadamer; at five minutes to twelve, one day in August, 1961, when the last all-German hole was barricaded by a wall in Berlin, philosopher of Marxism, Ernst Bloch, and the master of coal chemistry, Wilhelm Treibs; most recently, the literary historian, Hans Mayer. Physicist and Nobel prize winner, Gustave Hertz, stayed at Leipzig; so did Germanics professor Theodore Frings; Romanist Werner Krauss; professor of pediatrics, Albrecht Peiper; agrarian Otto Rosenkranz.

All these men have been honored by the government of the People's Republic. They love to hand out medals in East Germany. During the first decade of the SED state, 3.8 hundredweights of metal were used to cast all the honors distributed for special services. During the same period, there were more than a million festive acts of recognition for some form of valor or other which did not require confirmation in metal. Such national honors also have a financial aspect which should not be overlooked. They pay 25,000 DM. (Class III), 50,000 DM. (Class II), and up to 100,000 DM. (Class I).

9. RED SPARTA

"You will never understand our state," said George, "if you see in it anything but the final and therefore most valid expression of man's ancient desire to give his life meaning."

"But, George, I don't have a thing to say against any such effort. Only look here, out the window, the results are terrible!"

Outside a uniformly gray mass of workers and employees was streaming out of dozens of railway cars and buses, seeping into streets and alleyways, in a steady flow as they changed shifts. The sight was indescribably depressing.

"Tell me one thing—if you were called to a West German university today, would you go?"

"I don't know what I'd have answered to that three years ago. Such an offer would have been very unlikely anyway. Today I know the answer—no."

"Why?"

"I can even tell you that," said George. "For two reasons. One—things are looking up here. You can work decently here now, as long as you respect a few taboos. You can eat decently and live with a semblance of comfort. Social security and vacation benefits in the various holiday homes of the Free German Unions Association do a great deal for ____"

"But for heaven's sake, George, was that what we were aiming at when we were sent forth from school into what is commonly known as life? 'A new day beckons us to splendid shores . . .'"

"That brings me to the second reason," said George. "The only rivals—if you'll permit me to call them that—to our form of socialism would be Catholicism, or other metaphysical explanations of life which I find even stranger; or a consistent liberal humanism, but you don't have either of them anymore, even in your part of Germany."

"But we have thousands of faithful Catholics!"

"They have them in Poland, too."

"As for 'liberal humanism,' what do you mean by that? I can say and write what I think."

"Would you be allowed to write, 'Walter Ulbricht does more for peace than Adenauer'?"

"Why should I? I don't think he does."

"Would you be allowed to think so and write it?"

"I'd make myself unpopular."

"Exactly."

"But if I did think and write that I preferred Ulbricht to Adenaeur, and East Germany to West Germany—I don't think I'd go to jail for it. What about you?"

George was smart enough to parry the question. He said instead, "They'd probably suggest, as they did to Martin Niemöller, that you emigrate to the DDR."

"If I could believe all you tell me, I could wish for nothing better."

This was followed by a conversation about the boundary running down the middle of Germany, which becomes no less of a boundary because out of ten West Germans, seven don't want it, and three would be ready to remove it at great personal sacrifice; whereas of ten East Germans . . . But that's such a controversial statistic. All that can be truthfully said is that among the average citizens of East Germany, the wish for reunification is stronger than among the same average type in the West, which is in part a matter of historical heritage: the east of Germany has always felt more strongly drawn to the west than vice versa. It is also true that the government of neither state is in a position to make such far-reaching concessions as would be necessary for a voluntary political reunification.

How much longer will East Germany look like an artificial state, created by power politics and geographic caprice? How long will the memory of Saxony, Thuringia, Saxony-Anhalt, Brandenburg, and Mecklenburg remain alive?

I put Saxony first on purpose, although of all the middle Länder, it has the smallest territory. (Brandenburg, Saxony-Anhalt, and Mecklenburg are larger.) But Saxony does have the largest population, more than five million, whereas Saxony-Anhalt has four, Brandenburg three, Mecklenburg more than, and Thuringia less than, two. But Saxony is above all a Land with borders that have remained more or less the same since the sixteenth century. Of all the German Länder, only Bavaria can boast an equally old and uninterrupted history.

The three most important cities of the DDR lie in Saxony: Dresden, Leipzig, and the industrial city of Chemnitz, now Karl-Marx-Stadt, not beautiful but very active. Saxons and Swabians are generally believed to have produced more famous men than any other Germanic race. Since "famous men" and "race" are terms with which one can juggle, this theory can't be proved or contradicted. Just the same, almost half of German philosophy seems to be rooted in Saxony, from Leibniz through Fichte to Nietzsche. Music is represented by Robert Schumann and Richard Wagner. In an anthology of Saxon poets and writers, you will find Paul Gerhardt, Gellert, Lessing, Theodore Körner, Joachim Ringelnatz, Kurt Kluge, Erich Kästner, Ernst Schnabel, Peter Bamm; and I would like to include a Saxon author of best sellers, our only writer of the Wild West (the American Wild West), the German answer to Zane Grey, and Hitler's favorite author—Karl May. Even artists, who are supposed to prefer the warmer and more church-oriented southern climes, are well represented in Saxony; in the last century alone by Heinrich Zille, Paula Modersohn-Becker, Erich Heckel, Max Beckmann, T. T. Heine, Karl Schmidt-Rottluff. One of the first German professors to lecture in German, the great reformer Thomasius, as well as the historian Heinrich von Treitschke and the sociologist Friedrich Naumann, were Saxons.

This list of Saxon "greats" could be impressively augmented if we included in it Thuringians and natives of the former province of Saxony, which would be characteristically perfectly fair. Then we could include Martin Luther from Eisleben, the poet Klopstock from Quedlinburg, and Novalis from Halle. The musicians would include Johann Sebastian Bach, born in Eisenach, achieved fame and died in Leipzig, and Händel, a Halle-man before he became an Englishman. Oswald Spengler from Blankenburg and Max Weber from Erfurt would also belong and, sunning themselves in Goethe's fame, Christiane Vulpius (Weimar), and Charlotte von Stein, who moved to Weimar from Eisenach when she was fifteen. Goethe, the Hessian, and Schiller, the Swabian, made Thuringia Germany's cultural center. Weimar has preserved a trace of this glory. But apart from the Protestant Church, only two all-German institutions still function to some extent in Saxony today—the Bach Society in Leipzig, and the considerably more active Goethe Society, founded in Weimar in 1885. Its members convene there every two years.

Whoever cares to wander in Goethe's footsteps will find Weimar almost unchanged. The Goethe House on the Frauenplan has been lovingly restored; close by on the Esplanade stands the less elegant Schiller House; and the path to Goethe's summer house still runs through a beautifully tended park and from there to Schloss Belvedere. All-German memories. Another place belongs among them, only a half hour away, west of Weimar—Buchenwald.

In day trips from Weimar, one can enjoy scenery that can't be equaled between mountains and sea anywhere—Thuringia, "the green heart of Germany." In the north, the valley of the River Unstrut runs into Thuringia's main waterway, the Saale, past the Kyffhäuser Mountains where Holy Roman Emperor Friedrich I, called Barbarossa, is supposed still to be sitting with his long red beard grown through the wooden table in front of him, waiting for his people to summon him. In the east lies Jena, Goethe's "dear, foolish nest," a university town since 1558, where Karl Marx got his degree, where Schiller and Schelling, Schlegel and Hegel taught, and where Carl Zeiss erected his world-famous factories for optical instruments. In the west, a broad highway leads to Eisenach and to the Wartburg, the "castle invulnerable" for almost a thousand years, and actually never taken. Such very dissimilar figures as Martin Luther, Tannhäuser, and Wolfram von Eschenbach contributed to its fame. This highway runs through two cities—Gotha, since 1640 the seat of a line of constantly changing Thuringian princes; and Erfurt, where the monk Martin Luther was made a priest, studied, and got his degree. The latter presents the visitor with a successful mixture of Renaissance and baroque styles. Once such churches stood cheek by jowl in Erfurt, and to this day the cathedral on one side of the city and the three slender green spires of St. Severi on the other are architectural focal points. Sixty kilometers by car to the south of Weimar lies Neuhaus am Rennsteig. From here to Eisenach, one travels through the most beautiful part of the province, the Thuringian Forest. The Rennsteig runs along the summit of a chain of hills, a footpath more than 100 kilometers long as the crow flies. It takes ten days to traverse it. They were ten unforgettable days in the life of this hiker who didn't tire easily at a time when one could still enjoy the trail alone, with another person, or in a small group, on foot or on skis, and could find a friendly inn to stay at every night without being dependent on the "welfare" of any union, or any other mass organization.

The East German law, that was intended to obliterate Thuringia and all the other German Länder, was enacted on July 23, 1952. It stands opposed to the constitution which this Soviet state wrote for itself, of which Article I reads, "Germany is an indivisible democratic republic consisting of German Länder." Here, as so often, the German People's Republic turns out to be an unconstitutional state.

In any country where a strong authoritarian government wants to govern centrally, the Länder, with their historically developed self-will, must seem an irritating anachronism. If they are to be only administrative districts, why not create uniform administrative areas with fixed and ideal size; in other words—the most sensible borders possible, with no awkward corners, edges, enclaves, and exclaves? So that's what was done. Where formerly there were Saxony-Anhalt, Brandenburg, Mecklenburg (with West Pomerania), Saxony (with a tip of Silesia) and Thuringia, fourteen new administrative areas were created: Dresden, Leipzig, Karl-Marx-Stadt, Gera, Erfurt, Suhl, Halle, Magdeburg, Potsdam, Frankfurt on the Oder, Cottbus, Neubrandenburg, Rostock, Schwerin. But it wasn't until December, 1958, that the Zweite Kammer or Second Chamber of the administration, seated in East Berlin and consisting of representatives from Länder that had ceased to exist, was finally dissolved.

For Saxony-Anhalt, the change was minimal. This formerly Prussian province of Saxony had been artificially created as far back as 1816 out of leftovers of Old Prussia, the Electorate of Saxony, and Mainz, to which the old Duchy of Anhalt was added in 1945. In the west lie the Harz Mountains, with the Brocken, a region unparalleled in all Germany for its wild romanticism, evident in such names as Hexentanzplatz (Witches' Dancing Ground), Teufelsbrück (Devil's Bridge), Teufelskanzel (Devil's Pulpit), Hexenaltar (Witches' Altar), Hexenwaschbecken (Witches' Washbowl). And whoever loves the Lower Rhine will be equally moved by stretches of the Elbe between Wittenberg and Wittenberge. All of which is as it should be, and yet . . . "Saxony-Anhalt" doesn't have much meaning.

As for the Land of Brandenburg, its independence lies in the distant past, yet it can't really be regarded as a Land. If Saxony-Anhalt can be considered a stillborn child, Brandenburg is a mother who died in childbirth. The child's name is Prussia, and the birth dates back to the year 1618. The greater and more powerful Prussia became, the more Brandenburg seemed to lose in individuality and importance. In the end it wasn't much more than a landscape characterized by such descriptive passages as *"märkische Heide, märkischen Sand* . . . the moors of the Mark and their sands . . ."* It did have a part to play though, the importance of which wasn't really brought home to most people until 1945, when it was all over. In the midst of this landscape lies Berlin. The vicinity of Berlin—*that* was Mark Brandenburg, from Eberswalde to Treuenbrietzen, from Perleberg and Pritzwalk to Spremberg and Guben.

Mecklenburg has been a Land in its own right for eight hundred years, since Henry the Lion, Duke of Saxony, whose great fortress *mikilin borg* gave it its name. It had no natural boundaries except the Baltic Sea and therefore changed its shape from time to time, splitting once into two duchies—Mecklenburg-Schwerin and Mecklenburg-Güstrow, later called Mecklenburg-Strelitz, which were united again in 1934. After the Second World War, when new borders were to be drawn for Brandenburg, it was comparatively simple to tack on a fifth of a province very like it—Pomerania.

The cultural center of Mecklenburg is the old Hanseatic university town of Rostock. The harbor was reason enough for industry to develop there, particularly shipbuilding. The ports of other Mecklenburg coastal towns—Wismar, Warnemünde—do the same thing for them. The sandy Baltic seacost, very suitable for summer vacationists, resulted in such seashore resorts as Kühlungsborn, Heiligendamm, Warnemünde, Graal, Müritz, Wustrow. The annexation of parts of Pomerania brought in the university town of Greifswald, and another vacation spot for those who love the sea, the largest German island—Rügen.

But two university towns, harbors, ship industry, and the constantly rising tide of holiday traffic are things that touch the Mecklenburgers literally only on their periphery. The rest of this fruitful land lives by its farming, and its tragedy lies in the fact that these farmers have never been permitted to live undisturbed.

Let's begin with the Thirty Years War, with which all German misery officially starts. The times before that seem to be happy and peaceful only because we are prone to romanticize the Middle Ages and see history as a chronicle of ruling houses before anything else.

After the Thirty Years War there began in Mecklenburg the famous *Bauernlegen*, or dispossession of the peasants. The noble landowners—very often coarse fellows like the most famous of them all, Prince Blücher—enriched themselves quite uninhibitedly at the expense of the peasants dependent on them, many of whom remained slaves until well into the nineteeth century. In the year 1820, electric magnetic fields were discovered and calculated; in 1820, Friedrich Engels was born; and in 1820, slavery was finally abolished in Mecklenburg! After that the little man in the fields of Mecklenburg enjoyed peace and quiet for 140 years, if you want to call a period quiet and peaceful that includes four wars, one inflation, two military occupations, and change-overs from duchy to kingdom to republic to Hitler to the new gentlemen in the entourage of the Soviets.

In 1960, the second dispossession of the peasants took place, as it was described in the Western press. The fact is that in January, 1960, about one half of East Germany's agricultural industry was still privately owned, but by the summer of that year, not a single farmer still owned the land he was working. The average monthly quota of 10,000 east-to-west refugees, increased by several thousands, and these thousands were farmers. But now we must let Professor George Schmidt have his say.

"I'm glad to see you disassociate yourself from the expression *Bauernlegen*. It doesn't bother me because it's an insult, but because I find it stupid to use the same expression for two fundamentally different events. In the seventeenth century, it was a question—let's put it genteelly—of transferring the property of the peasant to the great landowners. Today it is a question of taking seriously the Marxist-Leninist demands for the abolition of private ownership. That the farmer isn't always able to see the difference doesn't justify the intelligent observer in coming to forced and confusing conclusions."

"Look here, George, what you've just said fits in very well with an impression I get here every now and then, and it's getting stronger all the time. In fact, it's becoming a sort of intellectual common denominator which I'd like to boil the whole DDR down to: unlike the Poles, for instance, you people take all the demands of Marxist-Leninism so terribly seriously."

"That may be," said George. "What else did you notice?"

"How very seriously the young fellow at the border checked my papers, instead of saying to himself, 'If this man wants to come here, why not? We're both Germans, aren't we?' I notice the fanaticism with which some of your younger officials apparently really believe that we have two worlds clearly separate from each other: the freedom-loving East and the warmongering West; the way your vacations are organized from A to Z, and how deadly serious you are about even the most harmless private fun. Then there's your rigorous puritanism that's ready to attack anything it suspects of being Western decadence, and the relentless hierarchy that rules over this allegedly classless society _____ "

"If you're referring to our deputies, they'd be risking their lives if they ever mistook the privileges of their position for any personal license to indulge in luxury."

But I wasn't going to be interrupted until I'd had my say. "If things go on like this, the East Germans are going to be the Chinese of Europe."

"Well, I think quite a few things still differentiate us from the Chinese," said George, "though not all of them are to our advantage. But if you've got to have a comparison, then with all due respect to your humanistic tendencies, I can see the West Germans and East Germans facing each other as the Greeks did once, Athenians and Spartans."

"We're the Athenians?"

"Yes. And we're the Spartans. After all, isn't Spartacus one of our saints?"

HISTORICAL FLASHBACK: In the fifth century before Christ, Athens and Sparta faced each other, at first not inimically; they were just different. The Athenians were prosperous, cultured, and democratic in a highly liberal sense; the Spartans were poor, especially the helots who cultivated the land and had to give up half of what they earned. Sparta's culture consisted of strictly ceremonious festivities. The individual didn't count; all that mattered was the collective. The people's decisions were made by a *gremium* consisting of twenty-eight men; all the people had to do was agree with them. For this state form, when carried over to other states, the word *tyrannis* (of Asiatic origin) was used for the first time.

As long as these two half-states held together, they were able to keep in check even the Asiatic power of Persia. But as time went by, they ceased to hold together. When the Athenians called an all-Greek meeting to end the split between them, Sparta refused to attend. Then came the downfall of Athens. And it began with the Athenians giving up their political forms so as to be better able to cope with the more austerely organized Spartans. Liberalism and democracy were no longer valid. The governing body became all powerful; individual freedoms were sacrificed to the cause of anti-Spartanism. This Athenian effort to be more Spartan than the Spartans was doomed to fail. In the war of Greek against Greek, which history calls the Pelopenesian War (431–404 B.C.), the Spartans were victorious.

But it was a sad victory. To be sure, Athens was crushed, but Sparta, too, was laid low. The only one who profited was the Asiatic power, Persia. Through a dictated peace treaty (387 B.C.) a reunification of the two Greek states was to be prevented "for all time." Well, the Greeks didn't have to wait forever, but it did take almost two thousand years. There was no Greece again until January 1, 1822.

2

CRAZY-QUILT GERMANY

1. PRUSSIAN SCRAPS MAKE GERMAN LÄNDER

In 1945, everyone seemed happily agreed on one thing: If Germany was ever to rise again, then it should be as a federal state. But it was a deceptive unity, born of the mutual desire—please God, no more disagreements now, no fresh complications!

Actually the Americans, Russians, English, French, and the first postwar German statesmen were agreed on one point: that no Greater Germany, strictly organized and centrally governed, should be permitted again to become a world power. Guided by a conception of history which lets past developments mold the world of tomorrow, they were also agreed on the best means toward that end: Prussia had to be destroyed. This was achieved by a reorganization of Germany. Skeptical observers like to say it was the only thing achieved.

"Are you a skeptical observer?" my foreign friends asked me. They never let me get away with the aloof use of the third person plural.

"Yes, I am skeptical, but not without hope."

He who has eyes to see and ears to hear can't fail to observe that in the part of Germany called the Federal Republic, a name that in the English language has deteriorated altogether too casually into an oversimplified "West Germany," forces are shaking the two basic pillars of the state; the federalist structure, and the constitution, or Basic Law. The men behind this are not monarchists, nor do they belong to any specific political group. The whole thing is more a vague but general tendency which I call the new German anti-ideology. It consists paradoxically of preferring to do exactly what is being done in the other part of Germany which calls itself the German Democratic Republic. Since the federalist structure has been done away with in

East Germany, why shouldn't it be done away with in West Germany, too? And since freedom is curtailed in East Germany, why not do the same thing in West Germany? And the reasons for this? Only then shall we West Germans be strong enough for a conflict which we do not desire (that's what the West Germans say, and nine out of ten mean it), but which we fear, and on this fear *all* Germans are agreed.

This was too much for Ralph. "But you sound as if in past conflicts only centralized and autocratically governed states were victorious. And I'm not even thinking of armed conflicts. Future disputes—if we are spared a nuclear catastrophe, against which an autocratically ruled state will be just as helpless as a federated one—future disputes are going to be concerned with markets and souls, if you'll excuse my lumping them together like that. And nothing gives us the right to believe that dictatorships—or since no state will admit to being a dictatorship, let's say states that restrict the freedom of their subjects more than is absolutely necessary to preserve order—are superior in such disputes to any others."

The discussion became lively. And we hadn't set out to discuss dictatorships, but to talk about my country with its so-called federalist structure, in which the power of the state is divided among numerous Länder and co-ordinated in a representative federal government, an arrangement that would make it very difficult for a dictatorship ever to be established in West Germany. In East Germany a dictatorship became possible only when the Länder were done away with.

This is how the Germany of the future was envisioned in 1945: The Americans had their own federated nation in mind as a model. The French were evidently agreeable to anything that would help to prevent a unified Germany—which was by this time just what the Russians wanted after a political about-face that had astonished and dismayed the rest of the world. The English Labor Party, which after the war had formed a government and taken over the responsibility for what was to become of Germany, must certainly have felt that a unified Germany would form a suitable basis for a socialist economy, yet to enforce it they were not prepared to go so far as to side with the Russians against the French and Americans.

The German diplomats, after their experience with Hitler's centralized Reich, tried desperately to find a new form for the future German state. The conservatives were already thinking along federalist lines, and the Social Democrats were ready to moderate their demands for centralization. Today, because all the political power the Social Democrats have been able to exert since the founding of the Federal Republic comes from the Länder they administrate, they have developed a certain affection for federalism; no cautious young lady though would find it a sufficient basis for marriage.

But the strongest influence toward a federalization of Germany in 1945–46 were the four territories or zones which, although they were called Occupation Zones, did tend to form a federated state of sorts, even if it had an only very inadequate government in the Allied Control Council.

Justified resentment against Hitler's Reich, an anti-Prussian complex, the reality of the four zones of occupation, and, soon to follow, east-west tensions—these were the four most prominent midwives at the birth of the German Federal Republic. Under such conditions it was hardly surprising that this child could not develop into a model of health and proportion.

Instead of one federated state, two separate states developed, a fact which those who feel it is politically expedient to deny the DDR will one day have to admit. Of these two separate states, one abolished its Länder; in the other you can hear the complaints growing louder daily because the constitution makes it so difficult to abolish theirs. All pressures in West Germany tend toward a centralization which is supposed to be so un-German. Those opposing it find themselves in strange company. Here you will find politicians who are happy to play, on the level of the Länder, parts they couldn't find in a centralized national government because there wouldn't be enough roles to go around: functionaries of the Länder administrations who don't like to see their existence threatened; local VIP's who are fortunate in that the territories they help to govern are no broader than their intellectual horizons. But a North-Rhine Westphalian or Rhine-Palatinate or Baden-Württemberg Länder consciousness exists only in the publications of these Länder administrations.

Prussia, however, was smashed. Of the fifteen present German Länder, only four were created without the addition of any part of Prussia, and they are the four sturdiest: Bavaria, Bremen, Hamburg, and Saxony. All the others got pieces of Prussia: Baden-Württemberg got Hohenzollern Sigmaringen; Hesse consists more than 50 per cent of the former Prussian province of Hesse-Nassau; Mecklenburg-Pomerania was presented with the part of Prussia that was called Pomerania; Rhineland-Palatinate received the Rhenish part of Prussia; Thuringia, a number of small Prussian enclaves. A few West German Länder didn't receive scraps of Prussia, but were put together solely out of such scraps, augmented by some non-Prussian elements: Lower Saxony plus the Grand Duchy of Oldenburg and the Duchy of Braunschweig; North-Rhine Westphalia plus the principality of Lippe; Saxony-Anhalt plus the Duchy of Anhalt; Schleswig-Holstein plus a piece of Oldenburg and Lauenburg. Brandenburg and the Saar consist entirely of Prussian provinces.

When you take into consideration as well that all of Germany east of the Oder-Neisse Line was Prussian, it becomes clear that the war objective on which everyone was agreed—that Prussia be destroyed—was fully realized, and of what other war aim can that be said?

There remains the question whether it was really a "consummation devoutly to be wish'd." If the German Reich of 1871 didn't always find favor in the eyes of its neighbors, was this because of Prussian leadership or because it was a unified German Reich?

"Of course we would have preferred a Germany under Austrian leadership," said Ralph.

"But the First World War started in Austria," Andreas von Hattesdorf volunteered helpfully, "and one could probably say that National Socialism did, too, certainly with more validity than that it started in Prussia."

"But the Bavarians are much more sympathetic than the Prussians," said Dick.

"They have prettier churches," said Professor Spälti. "But then, of course, Bavaria also includes Munich, the Capital City of National Socialism, and Nürnberg, the City of the Party Rallies."

"But the bad thing was Prussian militarism," said Yvonne.

"Don't forget," I told her, "that Ralph is one of those people who like to think that our Federal Republic and its Defense Department have military aspirations, whatever he means by that. So we seem to appear militant even without Prussia!"

"But your ministers and generals—aren't they all Prussian?"

"Our Defense Minister [at the time he was the Bavarian Franz-Joseph Strauss] wouldn't like it at all to be called a Prussian, not if I know him. As for 'my' generals—that they are all Prussian isn't true; it is true that the best of them were very often Prussian."

"How do you feel about the fact that Hitler's generals are influential again?" asked Ralph.

I prefer to answer this question in another context. Right now we are concerned with Prussia, a land which no longer exists; a land that succeeded in making itself unpopular throughout the world thanks to characteristics considered virtues everywhere else: obedience, a strong sense of duty, incorruptibility, righteousness, and frugality. In Teheran, Churchill advocated severity for Prussia but leniency for Bavaria, Württemberg, Baden, the Palatinate, and Saxony. And at Yalta, Stalin declared that the North Germans had to be treated more severely than the South Germans.

Here we have a very characteristic categorization which also has its supporters in Germany: the North Germans are Prussians; the non-Prussians live in South Germany. If you take a look at the map as it was at the beginning of the century, it does not appear to contradict this distribution. Only a few seemingly minor discrepancies ricochet against the massif of the Prussian provinces north of the River Main. But are they really so minor? Oldenburg, Hamburg, Mecklenburg, Braunschweig, Lippe, and the Grand Duchy of Hesse, were never Prussian. And the Swiss historian, Gonzague de Reynold, states that, "actually Prussia was founded by a dynasty: the Hohenzollerns." And the Hohenzollerns came from South Germany, no doubt about that. . . .

In dividing Prussia into Bundesländer, the borders of the individual Prussian provinces were left intact wherever possible. But the Prussian provinces were administrative areas. Thus an anti-Prussian complex forced a Prussian administrative structure on one-half of the Federal

Republic, while in the non-Prussian Lands, historic developments and dynastic relationships were allowed to play a part.

The Federal Republic consists therefore of Länder with uninterrupted traditions of their own (Bavaria, Hamburg, Bremen); split provinces (Schleswig-Holstein); conglomerates with their own traditions (Baden-Württemberg, Hesse); Länder with their own traditional core (Lower Saxony) with primarily economic reasons for being (North-Rhine Westphalia, Saarland); and a Land that is explicable only in terms of occupation-force policy: the Rhineland-Palatinate. To these must be added West Berlin, which occupies a unique position.

When the first postwar German statesmen were supposed to take over this heterogeneous mixture from the occupation forces that had created it, they were understandably not very happy about it. That was why they wrote Article 29 into the West German constitution: "The federal territory is to be reorganized by federal law with due regard to regional ties, historical and cultural connections, economic expediency and social structure. The new reorganization should create Länder which by their size and potentiality are able to fulfill efficiently the functions incumbent upon them."

Since this Article, except for a few minor corrections, has been invoked only once—to consolidate three southwestern Länder into one southwest Land: Baden-Württemberg, we may presume that all the nice things covered by Article 29 haven't been fulfilled yet. In spite of which we can't really hope for any new arrangement of the Republic's federated states. And if we may not in the near future count on Länder that even remotely fulfill what the statute promises, there are reasons for it.

Those who have the power to influence the structure of the Federal Republic may be divided into three groups: One, which is growing stronger all the time, for whom the provinces are nothing but a nuisance, hindering an organization and administration that could otherwise run smoothly. Another group, still quite large, is interested in a specific Land and ready to use its influence on its behalf—its own Land, of course. And then there is a small group which thinks it would be worth the trouble to form a unified federal state out of the Federal Republic. This last group is handicapped not only by the opposition of the other two, but also by the wording of Article 29, which comes very close to having your cake and eating it. "With due regard to regional ties, historical borders, and cultural connections . . . economic expediency and social structure." King Solomon with all his wisdom couldn't have got all that under one hat!

2. THE LÄNDER AND THEIR CULTURE

When in March, 1961, the Federal Constitutional Court decided that the Federal government had no right to a television program of its own because that interfered with the Cultural Autonomy of the Länder, it was interpreting the literal meaning of the statute absolutely correctly. But in the aforementioned Article 29, the same statute envisions the Länder to which it extends this cultural autonomy as something quite different from what they actually are.

No German city has an older cultural history than Cologne, which lies in North-Rhine Westphalia. A Cologne culture may quite possibly be said to exist; there certainly is such a thing as a Rhineland civilization, but a North-Rhine-Westphalian culture is nonexistent. Mainz and Trier can hold their own with Cologne and Aix as a meeting ground for Celtic, Roman, and Franconian cultures. They lie in Rhineland-Palatinate, but there is no such thing as a Rhineland-Palatinate culture. Munich, on the other hand, is historically further removed from Nürnberg than the white-blue flag they share indicates. Still there is such a thing as a Bavarian culture. But what is fair for Bavaria should be fair for Rhineland-Palatinate, and for North-Rhine Westphalia, too, because a federal republic must treat its Länder with absolute equality.

That the Länder should have their own individual culture is as it should be. You may read it *expressis verbis* in the statute, and none of the provinces have given an inch on this point. Other things were included in the statute, less *expressis verbis*, and it was possible to talk the Länder out of them, or to simply take them away, with the result that a rather grotesque definition came pretty close to the truth: a Land is a territory which is supposed to have its own culture; what it definitely has is its own police force!

The problem is how to get hold of a culture which you can't buy with German marks. This problem has been resolved bureaucratically. Every Land has a radio station assigned to it, and the Land's cultural independence rests with the radio station's *Hauptabteilungsleiter Kulturelles Wort*, a mouthful meaning Head-Departmental-Chief of the Cultural Word! If he is in Hamburg, it is up to him to produce Hamburg, Schleswig-Holstein, and Lower Saxony culture. But since there happens to be such a thing as *Plattdeutsch* literature, indigent to that part of Germany, the fellow in Hamburg is to be downright envied when compared with his colleague in Saarbrücken, who is supposed to supply the Länder administration week by week with a justification for the Saar in the shape of Saarland culture!

That Berlin was once a cultural center for all Germany is a myth. As the largest city in Germany, it naturally attracted the arts that have to go where the money is. It could afford better orchestras and more theaters than other cities, and it had the newspapers to see to it that art didn't go unnoticed. But Berlin was never the focal point toward which Germany's total culture was drawn; it was less and more than that. A cultural center with a rank all its own, a Berlin—or, if you like, a Prussian—cultural center under Hohenzollern patronage was created by the coming together of Prussians, Silesians, French (Huguenots), and Jews.

When I speak of culture in this sense, I mean a profusion of the arts and sciences; and a cultural center is created whenever anyone—be he prince, city administration, or producer—has the power, over a long period of time, to effect this profusion in three specific ways: as patron, as promoter, and, consciously or unconsciously, by leaving the impress of his style on it. There is no reason why it should not be possible to keep cultural centers alive today or even create new ones. Wherever this fails to happen, there are two reasons for it: the profusion is lacking, there is a paucity of cultural material; or protection, promotion, and impressive style are lacking.

Do the German Länder have the power to protect, promote, and leave a lasting impression on the arts and sciences over a long period of time? The power that would really put them in a position to practice "cultural autonomy" cannot be drawn simply from the fact that to practice it is their statutory right. Wherever this power is lacking, one finds—not cultural centers—but provincial culture.

Do the borders of today's German Länder coincide with ethnological borders, or to phrase it as our constitution does: Do they take regional ties into consideration? Which brings us to those mysterious elements known as the German *Stämme*, or tribes.

All the folk nonsense about the Germans that was being propounded when we were going to school can't change the fact that philology needs the German tribes and can prove they existed. Today's Germany was the territory of the West Teutons. In his *History of the German Language*, Adolf Bach writes: "The West Teutons, from whom the Germans issued after the Great Migration of Peoples, may be divided into two major groups that can be called Danube-Alpine and Lower Rhine–North Sea groups, according to their territories." After the Great Migration of Peoples, therefore, philologists find a border separating Germany *horizontally*, north from south.

All this was and is partially true as long as you don't start theorizing and schematicizing in an all-too-thorough German way. Whoever does would evoke a protest from historian Golo Mann. In referring to the Napoleonic era, he writes: "For some time now, the German states had taken very little interest in their legendary tribal characteristics with the result that they disappeared completely: dialects, landscape, religious and historic traditions mingled with the new state forms which could demand only the fulfillment of an abstract state principle."

You might say that this protest goes too far. Cultural life certainly was concerned with tribal characteristics and still is, but in a way that is difficult to analyze and not simple to organize. An ideal West German Federal State, taking into equal consideration tribal, native, historic, economic, social, and cultural developments, couldn't even be designed on paper, and not, in the last analysis, because the West German Republic was forced into a structure where such factors can only be considered very inadequately. Let us go back to the language groups of philology: one in the north, one in the south of Germany. That was in the seventh century. But six hundred years further back, we find another border in Germany, again dividing north from south: the Iron

Curtain of the Romans, the *limes*, begun in the first century A.D. under the Emperor Domitian and secured by hundreds of watchtowers which stretched from the Middle Rhine across the Taunus Mountains straight through Hesse. Then it followed the Main for a while, as far as Wörth, where it curved off to the Neckar and carried on from there to the Danube. And now a leap forward into the sixteenth century when reformation and counter-reformation resulted in a Germany divided between Protestant and Catholic. As long as the prince prescribed the religion of his land, its borders—even if constantly changing—were at least defined. And this Protestant-Catholic border ran straight through Germany, separating north from south.

These three demarcation lines ushered in a fourth. In 1866, when Prussia was faced with the question of how far it could extend the power of the North-German Bund southward, an obvious border presented itself, running from west to east, dividing Germany into . . . north and south.

Teutons, Protestants (Swedes) and Prussians, were the powers in the north; Roman Catholics (Habsburgers) and Austrians, were the powers in the south. Between them lay a great area of tension, drawing its own borderline across Germany, and whenever Germany was torn, it usually tore between the two, just about in the middle, sometimes a little more to the south along the Roman *limes germanicus*, sometimes farther north, along the language barrier, approximately along the Main.

In the twentieth century something happened that resembles the effect on a crystal when you turn its magnetic plane 90 degrees: the old formulas no longer apply. There it lay, that Germany, with its poles north-south. Suddenly it was flung into a magnetic field running east-west, where it didn't belong at all.

For Germany to be divided horizontally was nothing new. The differences between North and South Germany are self-evident; they can't be ignored. But that Germany could be divided vertically, straight through the heart of Prussia, straight through the Harz Mountains, through the hyphen of the Dukedom of Coburg-Gotha—that is something we have known only for a few years, and there are some who still don't know it or want to believe it.

Are Germany East and Germany West capable of surviving on their own? That is the great question. And a more minor one: Can the western part settle down and accept the federalist structure that east-west tensions, tradition, arbitrariness, and the geography of occupation bestowed upon it?

3. BONN

There still exists a Germany which does not have to rise from the dead because it has never been buried, which has to be kept together rather than reunified, a land whose people are related in a perfectly ordinary, family sense; a land nourished by a common heritage in its

schools, universities, museums, concert halls, libraries, theaters; a land
that speaks a common language, in which twelve centuries could not be
erased by fifteen years, even if these fifteen years resulted in the two
separate states that now form this land, two states that can be boiled
down to the formulas: Pankow and Bonn.

Once upon a time there was a cosy little university town and its
name was Bonn.

Zu Bonn am Rhein
Da möcht' ich sein . . .

"In Bonn, on the Rhine, that's where I'd like to be," the students sang
when they still set the style in that city. The first changes in this
idyl took place before November 3, 1949, when the German parliament,
in a secret ballot, chose Bonn as the capital of the new German Federal
Republic by a vote of 200 to 176. Student songs became less gay and
harmonious in 1933, when Hitler came to power, and many old student traditions were forbidden. In 1944 there were no more students in
Bonn; those who survived 1945 returned to their *alma mater Bonnensis*
in uniforms painstakingly made over into civilian clothes, and found
little cause for singing and less alcohol to induce it. For them the Court
Garden was the center of town. On one side lay the ruins of the
University Palace, where only a few rooms were left intact and considered safe or fit for seminars and lectures. On the other side, undamaged, stood the Academic Museum of Art where most lectures were
being held.

In the Court Garden you may read everything that happened to
Bonn. During the war, potatoes were planted there. In 1945, this heart
of the university served as a camp for war prisoners. In 1946, when they
were freed, the wildly overgrown grass was ours—half-starved men
lounging in the sunshine after lectures. On two plates of sweetened soup
daily, we found it advisable to conserve our strength. Today the University Palace is in tiptop shape again; the Art Museum has been renovated, the grass is once more lawn and walking on it is forbidden.

On November 3, 1949, Bonn moved into the limelight of world politics and ceased to be a little university town. Nobody really knows why
or how. What persuaded a majority of serious and, on the whole, well-
meaning men to forego making Frankfurt-am-Main the capital, a city
obviously both geographically and historically better suited for the
purpose, would be worth investigating.

At the time there were seven arguments in favor of Bonn, of which
two were weak, three were malicious imputations, and two turned out
to be false.

1. The Parliamentary Council had already convened in Bonn and felt
at home in the Pedagogic Academy, which is the Bundeshaus today.

But political decisions don't succumb so easily to the laws of inertia.

2. The capital should not be in the same place as the Allied Administrative Offices.

Why not? The relationship was a good one. Anyway, distance between the German government and the Americans, English, and French, was not sought or found in Bonn.

3. Konrad Adenauer, deputy of the CDU for Bonn, wanted "his" parliament as close to home as possible.

In 1955 his wish might have been reason enough. But in 1949?

4. Bonn lies on the left, the "safer" bank of the Rhine.

Whatever one may care to say of the men who formed the parliament of 1949, the urge for safety did not play a prominent part in their outlook. Not yet. And what is safe anyway?

5. Frankfurt lies in predominantly Protestant-Social-Democratic Hesse; Bonn is in the predominantly Catholic-Christian-Democratic Rhineland.

Even granting the supposition that party politics influenced a decision that would have been best kept out of party politics—of the 402 members of Parliament, the majority of whom chose Bonn as a capital, only 139 were members of the CDU, or Christian Democratic Union.

6. Bonn would be economical.

Operations actually began with a budget of three million marks, but it turned out to be feasible only on paper. To date, at least a hundred times that amount has been spent; possibly more.

7. Frankfurt, as a capital, might demand that status forever; Bonn would not.

Tempora mutantur. This argument, which was probably the strongest at the time, and certainly persuaded all delegates from Berlin to vote for Bonn, is heard less and less as time goes by. Bonn is the capital of the Federal Republic of West Germany, and for half the people on this globe, it is the capital of Germany. It is difficult to imagine that this will change in our time.

It is much easier to get to Bonn than to get through it. Our little party approached the city on the left bank of the Rhine from Cologne. We stayed at the Hotel Königshof, a pretentious alien body in the town picture, marking the beginning of the government quarter.

Bonn is a long tube, bounded on the one side by the Rhine, on the other by hills. Two large traffic arteries cut through it: the railway, and the highway from Cologne to Coblenz. On paper, Rhine, highway, railroad, and hills look like four parallel lines running north-south. They connect Cologne and Coblenz, but they also separate Bonn-east from Bonn-west. Since the Rhine can be crossed in Bonn by only one bridge, one must use time-consuming ferries or make detours that are no quicker. The heights of the Kreuzberg and Venusberg are traffic deterrents that are becoming more and more a part of the town. And then there are the railroad tracks. . . .

Approximately one hundred and fifty trains pass through the streets of Bonn daily, and from beginning to end of the city there are only three grade crossings. A little ministerial clerk from Bonn, whose efficiency was being criticized, excused himself with the desperate words, "You can't get anything done here. Either it's raining, or the climate's worn you out, or the gates are down!"

Sociological borders separate the residential sections of the native Bonners in the north from the university town in the center; and the latter is kept strictly apart from the capital of (immigrant) Bonners which stretches farther and farther southward, is all of a sudden called Bad Godesberg and, finally, Mehlem, without anyone being able to notice where Bonn suddenly ends. But you can't fool the telephone company. Anyone placing a call from Bonn to Godesberg—though separated from the person he is talking to by perhaps not more than two hundred feet—is making a toll call.

The House of Parliament, the seat of the Chancellor in Schaumburg Palace, and of the President in the Villa Hammerschmidt; the Foreign Ministry with its "house of eleven hundred windows," make the Coblenzstrasse the center point of Bonn. Its triple image as a medium-size Rhenish city, university town, and capital, is much clearer sociologically than could ever be demonstrated on a map. A parliamentary delegate, for instance, will not really feel at home in Bonn; a student at the university wouldn't stay at the Königshof in the quarter reserved for the capital's illustrious guests. Journalists from Munich know the members of Parliament better than do the citizens of Bonn.

Everything is neatly separated. You can't find out anything about the town from the guests at the Königshof; not much from the students about what's going on in Parliament; as good as nothing at all from the delegates about the university. My foreign friends were astounded. They called this provincial. Hm . . . !

A little town awakened out of its sleep by political events? You hear this often, but it isn't quite true. German provincial towns don't have so much time to sleep. Bonn, founded by the Romans and even mentioned by Tacitus, was for centuries the seat of the Archbishops and Electors of Cologne. "O thou unique and fortunate Bonn," according to a hymn of the Middle Ages. "Famed city, illustrious land, flowering in thy martyrdom, God-hallowed ground . . . ever a happy haven for the persecuted; the alien finds a home within thy walls. . . ."

Fortunate Bonn? The heart of the city has been destroyed twice: in the war of the Palatinate succession in 1689, and in 1944 by Allied air attack. For thirteen years, Bonn belonged to Napoleon's France. After the downfall of Napoleon, it was added to Prussia and has this decision of world politics to thank for the fact that it is a university town. Prussia's King Friedrich Wilhelm III hoped in this way to win over the recalcitrant Rhinelanders. A historian, called to the new university, was relieved of his post two years later because he had dared to write derogatively not only of Napoleon but also of the new rulers. His name was Ernst Moritz Arndt, and his monument looks down from the Alte Zoll, bastion of the Rhine, onto the Siebengebirge. An era that was more easily enthusiastic than ours described this view as the world's eighth wonder.

At the university in Bonn, classic philology and Romanistics had their beginnings; the first Institute for Advanced Chemistry was set up there; works of world literature were written in Bonn and burned there; Thomas Mann was given an honorary degree, and it was taken from him—all in Bonn. That's what the "idyll of the German provinces" looks like in Bonn, and elsewhere.

Actually Bonn isn't a provincial town any more. People only go on saying it is and making Bonn-mots about the place, calling it a Bundeshaupt*dorf* (village) instead of a Bundeshaupt*stadt* (city) where people live in Ver*bonn*ung rather than Ver*bann*ung (exile), and they excuse the absence of night life in Bonn with the explanation that "the lady just left for Cologne." As a matter of fact, Bonn has seventeen night clubs which are allowed to stay open until 4:00 or 5:00 A.M., to say nothing of Germany's largest gambling casino in Bad Neuenahr, only a half hour's drive away. Before 1949, nothing of that sort could be found in Bonn.

At the beginning of the century, Bonn had a population of 50,000 of which 1,200 were students and 120 professors, figures which make the faculty of today green with envy. At Gronau on the banks of the Rhine south of Bonn, where today houses stand one beside the other, there were wide meadows. Here the students, even in 1948, still swam in the Rhine. It was the thing to do. Today bathing in the polluted waters is inadvisable.

In 1948, the city's population was 100,000; today it is more than 150,000, but that is only Klein-Bonn, the small heart of the city. Greater Bonn extends from Wesseling, south of Cologne, to Mehlem on the border of Rhineland-Palatinate, and 350,000 people live there; soon it should be 500,000.

Bonn is one of the most traffic-jammed, richly populated and debt-encumbered of all the larger German cities. How can it be called provincial when the atmosphere of a provincial town usually includes such pleasant aspects as repose and contemplativeness? Of course Bonn has also been accused of having an atmosphere of "hectic boredom . . ."

On the other hand, in the Beethoven Hall, Bonn has Germany's most beautifully situated concert hall, and the one richest in tradition. The new State Theater which has been built next to it on the banks of the Rhine, boasts the most up-to-date technical equipment. And there is nothing provincial about the wide view from the palace (today's university) across the fountains of the Kaiserplatz and the Poppelsdorfer Allee, with its chestnut trees, to the Poppelsdorf Little Palais of Elector Clemens August, which now houses the Mineralogical Institute. On the contrary, it could be said that Bonn exhibits a largesse in keeping with its modest circumstances; a grandeur in good taste that knows its place. If, in spite of all this, almost every visitor feels he must complain about the "sleepy provincialism of this town of retired people," there are reasons for it.

Greater Bonn exists only in the minds of rational thinkers; actually, each of the little villages and towns that make up Greater Bonn is fighting for its own town hall. Bonn still behaves as if it seriously looked upon itself as a provisory capital, and so-called "improvisations" are consuming millions. The more the money is spent without plan, the more an aura of improvisation is preserved, all of which is supposed to appease the die-hards. And finally, as previously demonstrated, even the core itself, Klein-Bonn, is not a city but a conglomerate of original Bonn natives, Federal Republic Bonners, and university people. And each of these three towns within a town withdraws jealously within its own borders. Consequently, the President of the Republic lives in an industrial-type villa which is neither suitable nor in very good taste, while the highly representative baroque castle in Poppelsdorf houses a collection of academic stones.

Bonn is what it always has been—a beautiful city, a center for learning, and, for a small nation, a not unsuitable metropolis. Perhaps there are too many people there, people who take themselves a little too seriously; perhaps the climate is excessively humid; but realistically, it is hard to understand why some Germans look upon Bonn as the source of all evil.

We had a chance to speak to a few such people in Berlin. Some were dedicated Communists, others were fellow travelers, but all of them behaved as if the world would be more beautiful if Bonn did not exist. Of course they didn't mean the town. For them the word "Bonn" was a formula, a symbol. The emotions it arouses can be understood most clearly by a citizen of West Germany if we let him say one word: "Pankow."

4. BERLIN: A BROKEN CAPITAL

Where does Pankow lie? The question has never been asked in German surveys, so I had to do a little amateur research of my own. Of several people asked, only one gave the right answer which is, "It's part of the City of Berlin." The others declared that it was in the DDR, in the so-called DDR, in the East Zone, in the Soviet Zone, "over there," near Berlin (the most frequent wrong answer); also: on the Zone border, in Saxony, in Poland—but these last, including the answer, "I don't know," were exceptions.

As far as I know, the formula "Pankow" was invented by West German journalists and eventually incorporated in the treasure of German bureaucratic idiom. When an East German says, "Pankow," it implies conscious opposition to the Communist regime there. When somebody in West Germany—where such opposition may be considered natural—uses the expression in any other than a thoughtless way, he is expressing his scorn for a state guided by Pankow on the River Panke, and his disapproval of those at the helm. Whoever in West Germany avoids using the formula is automatically under suspicion that he doesn't disapprove enough.

But there are better explanations for such reticence. One is that the formula doesn't fit because the ministries of the DDR are not situated in Pankow at all; most of them lie in the government quarter of prewar Germany, in or not far from the Wilhelmstrasse, where Bismarck once lived. The second is that the word "Pankow" conceals the fact that the founders of the DDR made Berlin their capital in flagrant violation of the Four Power Agreement. According to this agreement, East Berlin is as much or as little a part of East Germany as West Berlin is of West Germany. According to international law, there may be no changes in the status of West Berlin which would not be automatically applicable to East Berlin.

From the roof garden of the Hilton Hotel on the Budapesterstrasse—still in the west, but close to the border—you can see far across the old capital of the Reich. Dick felt at home at the Hilton. "It all sounds very convincing," he said, "but it can't be that simple."

And it isn't that simple. Juristic opinions on Berlin's position according to international law have succeeded, in the course of many volumes, in complicating the situation to such an extent that no one can find his way through it. According to the West German constitution—which is full of nice things about man's basic rights—Berlin belongs to West Germany. But the West German constitution isn't valid in Berlin. According to the East German constitution—which is full of nice things about man's basic rights—Berlin belongs to East Germany. But the East German constitution isn't valid in Berlin. It isn't valid in East Germany either, for that matter. . . .

Wherever the facts are allowed to speak for themselves, they prove quite clearly that the city is divided, but with this difference: whenever the West German government chooses to ratify an act of state in West Berlin, it is bombarded with East German protests; whereas the Federal Republic of (West) Germany had apparently resigned itself to the fact that the (East) German Democratic Republic was being governed from Berlin by simply declaring that, in this case, Berlin wasn't Berlin, but "Pankow"; until that bleak thirteenth of August, 1961, when the East German government chose to separate its seat of administration from the west by drawing its own state border and lo—suddenly there was no Pankow; the border ran straight through the heart of Berlin!

Half a century ago, Pankow really was a small village in the district of Niederbarnim, under the jurisdiction of Potsdam, famous for its mental institutions and flowers. To the north lay the village of Niederschönhausen. Here there used to be a castle where the Prussian King Frederick II deposited his unloved wife, Elizabeth Christine. On October 11, 1949, in true workers' and farmers' style, Communist leader Wilhelm Pieck moved into this castle, the first President of a government that had been given power by Soviet Russia, a government that likes to call the territory over which it rules (territory identical by the way with the former Soviet Occupation Zone) a Workers' and Farmers' State and a German Democratic Republic. It was the trick of the week on the part of the SED or Socialist Unity Party, supported by the Soviet Occupation Administration, when they declared Berlin to be their capital, thereby creating a constantly smoldering source of crisis which political tacticians could let flicker to the proportions of a fire whenever they so pleased; which could, however, also erupt into a conflagration of world-wide proportions at any time without anyone having so pleased. Since the Thirty Years War, the German lands proved fairly easy to divide again and again, but the *cities* were always considered distinct entities. They were young, therefore they matured, grew old, surrounded themselves with satellites; some died. In short, they were something akin to an organism. It is hard to join two cities. Efforts made toward this end since 1929 prove this, for instance, the attempt to make Elberfeld and Barmen, and a few smaller towns into one city called Wuppertal. For years no one will be able to tell what the results of the DDR's efforts to halve it are going to be for the life of Berlin.

Berlin lies on the rivers Spree and Havel, which are too small or lie too far outside the city proper to be part of it as the Rhine is of Cologne or the Elbe of Dresden. Berlin looks like a broken city. A sketch of the center of town, which we drew so that my traveling companions would have something to start from, looked like a dumb-bell: two centers of gravity—Charlottenburg with the Kurfurstendamm and what used to be the Knee (now called Ernst-Reuter Platz) on the one side; the old center of the city with its Lustgarten or Pleasure Park, now known not so pleasantly as Marx-Engels-Platz, and the Alexanderplatz on the other. They are connected by the bar of the East-West axis. The names of the streets along this axis provide a capsule history of Berlin: the Seventeenth of June Street, Brandenburger Tor, Pariserplatz, Unter den Linden, Liebknechtstrasse. But at the Brandenburger Tor, the bar has a crack. For more than ten years it has been broken here by one of the main East-West conflicts, and since the wall was put up, the area across which both sides glare at each other has assumed the character of a spectral battlefield. Tourists go there to learn how to shudder. Those directly affected—the Berliners and all those sympathizing with them—have been shuddering for a long time.

Two cities that have nothing in common—still the same city: you may hear both opinions, even from experts. Each is a half-truth, which seems analogous not only for Berlin but for all Germany. But only analogous. Berlin grew from two fishing villages on the Spree—Berlin and Kölln—into the entity that has been divided today.

Heine was joking when he wrote: "A lot of bears live in the city . . . some go so far as to say that 'Berlin' has the bears to thank for its foundation, and is really called 'Bearlin.' " But historical research can add little to his etymology. Actually Berlin may not have bears but *a* bear to thank for its origin: Albrecht the Bear, who became Margrave of Brandenburg in 1150 after the conquest and death of the Wend Prince Pribizlav. As for the name "Berlin," its derivation from the word *Bär* or "bear," rather than from a Slavic root, satisfies those who are of the opinion that the role of the Slavic Wends in the creation of Berlin should not be overevaluated, especially not today with the Slavs breathing down our necks! Hans Scholz is one of these men, a West Berlin writer who is considered the leading chronicler of the broken German capital by all the enthusiastic readers of his novel, *Am Grünen Strand Der Spree* (*Through the Night,* Crowell, 1959). Anyway, the Berliners accepted themselves as "Bärliners," like the "Bärners" of Bern, Switzerland, who chose a bear for their crest. But Berlin did not become an important city until the Hohenzollern Swabian-Franks made it an elector's, later a king's, and finally a kaiser's residence. Its development may be read in the count of its population: in 1654, for Berlin and Kölln (they wern't really united until 1709 under Frederick I) 10,000; in 1707—55,000; in 1800—172,000; in 1840—322,000; in 1871—825,000; in 1892—1,624,000; in 1939—4,340,000.

The old and true Berlin, the Berlin of the Hohenzollerns, but also of Bismarck and Stresemann, of the painter Zille and the writer Döblin, lies in "the East," or, speaking nonpolitically, in the northeast: Schlossplatz, Wilhelmstrasse, Unter den Linden, Alexanderplatz, German Theater and State Opera, Cathedral and University. West Berlin may be found on earlier maps of Berlin, let's say those of 1900, in the lower left-hand corner, and there's not much of it: Moabit, Tiergarten, Zoologischer Garten, Schöneberg, which is the present seat of the West Berlin city government.

A French visitor, Bernard Dort, writing in a German magazine, says, "In Berlin, church spires and glass cages no longer face each other, but two worlds, two epochs. The false riches of the one are repulsive to us; the other is excoriated, still filled with dust and rubble, still dreaming of the future. Because of its modern architecture, Berlin looks on one side like a gigantic airfield, a city where you can buy everything; on the other, still blackened by the smoke of war, stifling in the hysterical fascination of an all too enticing tomorrow. Red-hot, overheated capitalism, and charred socialism. . . ."

Yes and no.

Quite apart from the rather unusual division of color—red for the west and black for the east—the elegant Kurfürstendamm ("Kudamm" in the vernacular) and the residential section of Dahlem, in fact the entire quite fashionable Westend of Berlin, were never popular with the Socialist reformers even when Berlin was one city; and the Alexanderplatz area, or a part of the city like the Prenzlauer Berg, could have been called "excoriated" even then. What I am trying to say is that the elegant section of Berlin was elegant long before 1945 or 1949. But the metaphor of West Berlin as an airfield is good. Generous in its use of space; in spite of all restrictions, less restricted than most West German cities; actually a city reached most safely by air; glass and concrete predominate in the experiment-crazy reconstruction of a city which is a true anthology of modern architecture.

"The hysterical fascination of an all-too-enticing tomorrow," is also true, in a way, of East Berlin. But apart from the architects of East Germany—I use the word "architect" in its broadest sense—I don't think so many are fascinated. And where this fascination has tried to create a style of its own, things look sad, because some of the buildings of this, oh-so-enticing tomorrow smack of yesterday. The colossal baroque houses of the Stalinallee which were to be showplaces, belong—like Khrushchev's predecessor—to a despised past. The gigantic statue of Stalin was dismantled on the night of November 13, 1961; the eastern section of the Allee is again called Frankfurter Allee, as it was in the days of One Berlin; for the western stretch, Karl Marx—whom no one could accuse of Stalinism—served as name giver.

Berlin is a broken city. Can a wall that is hated on both sides be strong enough to make two cities of it? On the demands of an ideology, a terrible experiment is being imposed on four million people, and you may ask in vain who will profit by it. Oh, yes, Berlin was a leak in the hermetical sealing of East to West, a highly embarrassing leak for those who felt threatened by a free exchange of men and ideas. But it was at the same time a point of contact between the two enemy camps, a last thing they had in common, with advantages for both sides, or at any rate for those on both sides who saw the coexistence of two worlds as the only alternative to constantly threatening destruction. Are their voices, the voices of common sense, going to be drowned out again?

3

A LITTLE...WELL, NOT SUCH
A LITTLE SOCIOLOGY

1. A SHORT ECONOMIC HISTORY

The year 1945 was entered as Point Zero for Germany. Most of the stories dating back to that year open with the assurance, "There really was nothing." Although the all-night bombings had knocked out only one-tenth of Germany's industries, and the German economic potential was still the largest in Europe, nobody seemed to feel like doing anything with it. Whoever happened to have any strength left beyond that needed to stay alive, was attracted to enterprises not always legal, but certainly more lucrative than working eight hours a day at a lathe. Whoever was capable of running a factory had probably done so before 1945 and was in no hurry to stick his neck out again. Actually there was very little for everyone: 1,000 calories for the stupid ones who had no "Vitamin B," which was what good connections were called; 6 marks for a cigarette, 300 for a pound of butter; there wasn't enough money in the world to buy a bicycle.

Economic experts measure a country's prosperity by its steel production. In 1934, Germany had produced 11.9 million tons annually and been in second place, behind the United States, 26 million. In 1945, when Germany's steel quota was to be determined and with it Germany's future industrial potential and standard of living, the Allies still pretty much shared the viewpoint of American Secretary of the Treasury Morgenthau, who recommended making "a pasture" of Germany. The English were ready to grant Germany 9 million tons, the French 7, the Russians 4.5, Morgenthau's compatriots only 3.5. When General Clay accepted a steel quota for Germany of 5.8 million tons, he was reprimanded by the State Department. But gradually the Morgenthau influence waned, to be replaced by the view which had persuaded H. G. Wells to write in his *Washington and the Hope for Peace* (Collins. London, 1922): "It is impossible to destroy such a people [as the Germans]; it is impossible to wipe them off the map, but it is possible to ruin them economically and socially. And if Germany is ruined, most of Europe is ruined."

A year later, the State Department had to agree to a steel quota for Germany of 7.5 million tons yearly, as established in the so-called first industrial plan of March 26, 1946. It was the aim of this plan to keep German production at half its 1938 level. To the more generous composer of the second industrial plan (August 28, 1947), the year 1936 provided a more reasonable comparative production rate. Steel production in Germany was to be allowed to reach 10.7 million tons. Two years later this was upped to 11.1. Then came the Korean War, after which the sky was the limit. Today, West German steel production stands at 30 million tons annually; only the United States (85 million) and the new steel colossus, the Soviet Union (60 million), produce more.

German business conditions may be measured against steel production, at first with the brakes on, then benefiting by the five most important and certainly most spectacular events of the last fifteen years: the dismantling of factories, the currency reform, the Marshall Plan, the Common Market, and the encouragement of the Free Social Market Economy.

The story of the dismantlings has a double twist. Its purpose was to ruin German industry, but tearing down, loading, transporting, and reassembling equipment elsewhere usually cost more than it was worth, and the dismantlers found themselves out of pocket. The procedure was terminated in 1950, after the outbreak of the Korean War, when it suddenly seemed desirable to help German industry back on its feet. And what turned out to be astonishingly helpful were the dismantlings! Wherever a factory had been torn down or bombs had dug holes, new machinery had to be set up, and while you were at it, you put in what was best and most modern. An international upsurge of business found West German industry in an enterprising mood, like a freshly shod horse that has been standing in the stall too long.

June 20, 1948, was a big day, which no one who had received his quota of 40 brand-new D-marks is likely to forget. What was he going to do when they were gone? Suddenly the mark had become worth 6.5 pfennige, but as soon as you found out you could actually buy something with it, a roll of bread for instance, white bread, then 6.5 pfennige suddenly seemed like quite a lot of money. Confidence in the new currency was fuel for the motor of a German industry that had remained more or less intact.

On June 5, 1947, American Secretary of State Marshall delivered his famous speech at Harvard University in which he recommended a program that would expand the long-term economic aid granted to

Greece and Turkey to include other European nations as well. The Soviets refused to accept any such aid for the parts of Germany occupied by them. For the three West Zones, however, the Marshall Plan money arrived at an exceptionally favorable moment psychologically, coinciding as it did with the currency reform.

There is no better proof for the old adage: a stitch in time, saves nine. The right moment is often far more important than the amount of aid. Up to 1954, West Germany had received $29 per capita of Marshall Plan money, Italy $33, France $72, England $77, and Austria $104. But this relatively small amount of aid—which certainly doesn't justify the Soviet reproach that the Americans "bought" West Germany—meant at the time the difference between having to manage economically or trying to work on a shoestring; and to manage economically—that's something Germans know how to do!

Does a comment like this already sound surprising? An English lady who preferred to remain anonymous, wrote a very revealing commentary on Germany published by Longmans, Green & Co., London, in 1884, under the title *German Home Life*. In it she pokes fun at the "frugality which never deserts the true German from his uprising to his downlying, at home and abroad, traveling and stationary."

The last two points to be dealt with are more the concern of the businessman and the politician: the Common Market, and a market economy sometimes called "free," sometimes "social."

On February 10, 1953, the directors of the Coal and Steel Union declared a joint market for coal, scrap metal, and iron ore, in the six countries of the European Common Market. My colleague Jacques Stohler has told me over and over again what a blessing this was, especially in view of its political consequences. And it all did sound very plausible at the time. Actually the little man in Germany hasn't noticed very much difference in his life to date because of the European Common Market. If in the meantime duty and tariffs have been abrogated, then the news hasn't got around to the customs officials who still turn your automobile inside out in the hope of finding a can of Nescafé.

The Market Economy, "a multi-colored, glittering soap bubble," as Professor Kogon once called it, is just as controversial, but however much it may glitter, no one can doubt its blessings any longer. Chancellor Ludwig Erhard, who may not have been its inventor, but who certainly was its most enthusiastic and adamant champion, became the most popular Economics Minister of all time in Germany because of it: Father of the German Economic Miracle and the second greatest Father-Image in West Germany.

How the terms "free" and "social" came to be allotted to this economic system remains a disputed question. The former American ambassador, James B. Conant, an expert on Germany, says of it: "The socially conscious free market economy, as we have observed it, has perhaps not been altogether free nor especially outstanding for its social consciousness. Its chief characteristic, one might say, is the scope and incentive it has given to individual initiative . . . by rapidly lifting total income . . . it eventually raised everybody's income."

Professor Röpke, to whom the theory of the Market Economy owes a lot, must have felt he had to sound a warning when he wrote in his book, *The Science of Economics,* that the businessman was being left only his losses, while his profits were being taxed out of sight. Later, Professor Erhard, to whom the practice of the Market Economy owes a lot, had to point out that "free" and "social" should not be permitted to mean "free profits" and "social losses."

The strongest powers in West Germany are economic powers; in this respect West Germany is no different from the rest of the world. It is only clearer for everyone to see: the Bank Deutscher Länder, the German mark, and the renowned German big industrialists were there long before the Federal Republic. And many smaller entrepreneurs had their big moment in the years 1945–1949, when Germany was non-existent and regulations, such as they were, allowed for a good deal of latitude and maneuvering. The important thing was to have been there when it all began, not with one's legal 40 marks but with property, houses, machinery, stockpiles (or "hoarded material" as the ugly phrase had it), with credit and connections, with willing hands, plans, energy, and the will to succeed. In those days, a "white shirt" (as opposed to the former "brown") and a petition granted were worth millions. Often the only capital needed was 5,000 marks (equal to 800 cigarettes) and sometimes that was borrowed from a friend. All that mattered, was *to be there.*

Axel Springer, heir to a respectable but not spectacular printing press in Hamburg-Altona, which the bombs had not spared, was there with an idea for a radio magazine and with the means to start it: contact with radio people and a man who knew how to edit (he is still editor-in-chief today). Springer's first efforts were small issues, just the programs. When he finally got his permit from the occupation forces, the corner-stone had already been laid for the biggest newspaper publishing house in Germany, one of the fifth largest in the world today. The currency reform came at a time when the number of German radio owners could be counted in the millions, all of them glad to spend 30 pfennige for *Hör Zu* (*Listen*).

And then we have Max Grundig, who got his experience in the radio business when he was selling radios. During the war, he learned how transformers and coils were made, and at the same time made the right contacts. Somehow he managed to assemble the necessary machinery for a small workshop. He transported the stuff in a wheelbarrow from the village where it was stored to a laundry in some courtyard or other in Fürth, which happened to be his home town. Fürth welcomed the development of any kind of industry because, since all Jewish business had been driven out, it hadn't been able to hold its own too well with its neighbor, Nürnberg. "Industry" is really a rather big word for the eight men who put together the first Grundig radios in the laundry in Fürth. But everything was ready for them; all that was needed was the spark.

Grundig called his product *Heinzelmann*, or *Elf*. It was a construction kit with which even those with no technical aptitude whatsoever could construct a radio for themselves. Old radios confiscated by the occupation forces were scarce; new ones were rationed. The Heinzelmann filled the gap between them and found an almost limitless market. Today Max Grundig owns the largest television factory in Germany, the largest radio factory in Europe, and the largest sound-track factory in the world!

In the same years, between Reich and Republic, two other men stepped up to the starting line and waited for the currency reform to give them the signal, "Go." They were also the entrepreneur types to whom the German economy owes so much. To be sure, Heinz Nordhoff had already been made director at the Opel Works in Rüsselheim during the war. In the autumn of 1947, an English colonel persuaded him to take over the Wolfsburger Volkswagen factory. Today he is president of the largest automobile factory outside the United States. Berthold Beitz, though, was unknown before an English major gave him the chance to make good as an insurance agent, and—more important—as an organizer in the business. When the starting shot was fired, Beitz, at thirty-five, was on his way to becoming the president of Iduna Germania, the biggest German insurance company. Thanks to the intervention of a sculptor who had done some work for Iduna Germania and for the Essen steel magnates, Beitz met Alfried Krupp, and in 1953 had a decisive talk with him. Result: Beitz became managing director of the most powerful corporation in German heavy industry.

That is how the fates of men changed in Germany, and who would like to stick out his neck and say that these are examples of the unpredictability of the German character? Alfried Krupp, accused and condemned for war crimes in Nürnberg, freed after a few years in jail, soon after that again a power in German economy. His case got a lot of publicity, but he didn't stand alone. Probably none of the leaders of industry wanted Hitler's war, but without them it would have been impossible. In 1946, this was still considered a crime. In the autumn of 1950, many people—Americans most of all—thought differently about it. The 300 top men of Germany's heavy industry, the owners and chief stockholders of the famous old German firms, returned and demanded their former rights. One hears the old names again: Krupp and Thyssen, Haniel and Flick, Klöckner and Röchling, and many more. In the less heavy industries: Henkel, Bosch, Oetker, Reemtsma, and hundreds of others I would have to mention to make the list complete.

Among the fifteen biggest industries in the world (according to 1959 figures) there are four German firms whose names were well known before the Federal Republic. In seventh place, Siemens; in eighth, the Volkswagen Works; in ninth, Krupp; in fifteenth, Mannesmann.

The Krupp-Beitz connection is typical: often it was the younger generation (today of course they are in their fifties), men of the world with open minds, frequently trained in the United States, who gave the old firms a fresh glow. To get to the top demanded toughness, toughness by the way also toward oneself. Where there was no trace of order, these people could hardly have succeeded without superdimensional self-confidence. But to get to the top is not enough; you have to know how to stay there. And for that other, more admirable qualities are needed: cleverness, perhaps even wisdom, and a sense of responsibility.

Many whose names should be mentioned here had a great deal more than the prerequisite toughness and self-confidence; it is not their fault that they gave a false picture to those who could emulate only these two attributes, with the result that toughness became ruthlessness; self-confidence, arrogance. To succeed as Springer or Nordhoff did these qualities did not suffice, but to rake in a lot of money—for that they were adequate. The money-rakers are still among us. . . .

It is our misfortune that those outside Germany often form a picture of it today from this type of uninhibited, narrow-minded *nouveaux riches* who can't see beyond the fenders of their Mercedes 400. And even worse than the fathers—who at least proved themselves by working hard—are their sons, howling sports-car *jeunesse talmiée*, loud-mouthed and arrogant because they are unsure of themselves. You can't see them sprawled on bar stools in St. Anton or Lech without feeling shame, an emotion as foreign to them as the Germany we love is an unknown factor in their lives.

2. THE PYRAMIDS OF GERMAN SOCIETY

"I was very much interested in what you wrote in your book on England about the upper classes," said Ralph Stevens. " 'The elite,' the 'happy few,' or 'upper ten'—call them what you like. But I would be much more interested to know who belongs to this 'happy few' in Germany."

A foreigner's questions may be unpleasant, even when you think you know the answer, but in this case I had to admit, "I don't know."

"Well, first and foremost—the professors," said Yvonne helpfully.

There is nothing like a group of curious foreigners who won't give up, for helping one to clarify one's own ideas about one's country. "Could be."

"Probably all academic people," said Dick.

Wasn't he going too far? "Could be."

"Certainly the leaders of industry," said Professor Spälti, coming a little closer to reality.

"Hm! Yes."

"The aristocracy still plays an important part in Germany," said Andreas, who in his homeland called himself simply "Hattesdorf," which didn't prevent people from calling him *"Herr Baron."* But when he came to Germany on behalf of his publishing house, he found it advantageous to have his cards printed with his title and the "von" that went with it.

"Could be."

By this time my "could be" was getting on my nerves more than on those of my friends. To move the discussion onto the more solid ground of economic fact, I stuck out my neck and said, "I suppose the man who drives a six-cylinder Mercedes or a luxury sports car has to be considered a member of the upper class. The man who can spend five thousand marks or more on himself every month. The man who lives in at least six rooms in a decent neighborhood; has not only a tux or tails in his clothes closet, but both. A man who can spend his free time hunting or playing golf, and his vacations on the Riviera or at an expensive spa; in short, the man who shows he can afford it."

My definition was a great success, with the result that I was embarrassed. It sounded convincing enough, but on second thought, I had my doubts. To be sure, that's the way the little man sees the big wide world, and the big wide world of Germany has plenty of little men whose conspicuous consumption helps build their prestige with headwaiters, doormen, bartenders, and also among business associates, government officials, and ladies of society. You may put this to an irrefutable test: try making the same trip three times—once by train in a cheap suit; then in an average tailor-made suit and a medium-size car; and finally in a suit made by a first-class tailor and in a flashy car. Only if you have a very strong character will you manage to *not* feel like a different person every time. And yet . . . Generalizations are always dangerous, but when applied to the German social structure, they become absolutely senseless. Is there a "society" in Germany? And does it have any sort of structure? It is easy and has become customary to say no to both questions. But that, too, is only a half-truth.

Things are simplest in this respect in East Germany. As the social order decreed by bureaucracy and ideology becomes more and more secure, social levels come clear which, in this classless society, may with impunity be called classes: the official leaders, the intelligentsia (especially the scientific intelligentsia), the middle and minor functionaries, the workers and farmers, the employees who did not succeed in becoming functionaries, and finally—fallen angels, criminals, and the undesirable elements of bourgeois society. All this is not as simple as it sounds, but it is roughly accurate.

Such a picture is not available for West Germany, and of all possible viewpoints, the Marxist one that would distinguish between "exploiters" and "exploited," according to the individual's share of the means of production, is the least useful. West German society is far from being a class society in the orthodox sense. The term "worker" may scarcely be used any more as a professional title; the title "citizen" denotes either a good example or a bogeyman. But popular groupings reveal a great deal. Here we have "manager-employers," "directors," "contractors and entrepreneurs," but they describe functions in the economic life of the nation, not social position.

Still, there is a hierarchic order, often experienced, yet hard to describe. Every German has a social position, a prestige co-efficient or whatever the sociologists want to call it, which is complicated in three ways: it consists of varying factors; it is not constant; it is not generally binding.

In a small town like Gusselbach, for instance, there can be no doubt about who belongs to the upper class. The *Stammtisch*, or table reserved for a group of regular customers, is at the best inn (hotel to strangers). They are the small-town elite, the town notables. Among them you will find the mayor, the parson, the superintendent of the high school, a representative of the leading industry on which half the town subsists, the editor of the local daily paper, two doctors and a lawyer. Finally a Mr. Something-or-other. No one knows exactly what he does, but he is a protégé of the mayor.

One thing often overlooked in this little microcosm where all things seem to be in order, is interesting because we may refer to it as typically German: Since the superintendent of the high school is present, none of his teachers may be. And the representative of industry, the richest and therefore probably the most-respected man in the group, would be reduced to as good as nothing if his boss, the *Generaldirektor*, or president of his firm, should suddenly turn up at the table. Other examples: for the citizens of a university town, the *Herr Professor* is a man to be respected, even if he is only an *aussenplanmässiger* professor, which means that he is not a member of the faculty, but has the right to lecture at the university. In a group of professors, however, there is no room for the man who is "only a lecturer." A *Regierungsrat*, or low-grade upper civil servant (but he has to have a degree!) could associate with men such as Adenauer and Krupp rather than with an official above him in rank. Of course there are exceptions to this rule (there are always exceptions, that is why we have life), but the rule undoubtedly is: The physical presence of a superior lessens one's social prestige drastically.

These examples of the fact that social position is not a constant in Germany can also be used to demonstrate the admiration for the so-called free professions, or professional men, even in Germany. Personal freedom and independence alone do not decide a person's position in German society, as they do, for instance, in England. We are still far removed from anything like that. In Prussian tradition, rank and position are valued much more highly than individual freedom; officers and civil servants are admired more than any other type of professional men. But the social standing of a doctor, lawyer, or writer will not be lowered by the appearance of a superior on the scene. And finally, an example of the looseness of social classifications in Germany, which comes to mind as we look at this Gusselbach circle: if one of the small-town notables were to move to a neighboring city, he would take none of his social prestige with him. That's good only in Gusselbach!

The factors that determine the position of a citizen in West Germany today are easily demonstrated by a formula that keeps coming up in discussions about schools and universities. A young man on his way to reaching the goals in his life is seen as a freight train. The question then is: where do the switches lie, the switches that will guide this human freight train to happiness, honor, and dignity—in short, to all those things which he happens to think worth striving for?

I can see five switches: (1) family, (2) school, (3) university, (4) career, (5) a very important switch—undeterminate or chance influences.

1. To choose his procreator carefully is much more important in Germany than it is in the United States; less important than in England. Let us assume that the goal is to have a good position in society; then it helps a lot to be born into a good family. (An aristocratic family is an exceptional case of a "good family.") If you are a girl, you should be pretty; if you are a boy, intelligent. When this switch is in the right position, nothing much can go wrong.

2. The second switch, unlike the first, may be manipulated. To enter any of the better professions is almost impossible without a high-school education, which in Germany gives the student scholastic standing comparable with second-year college in the United States. Many pedogogic efforts are poisoned by the very understandable desire of parents to leave nothing undone in their efforts to see their children pass the *abitur*, or final high-school exams. Toward this end, a bitter battle toward social prestige is fought year by year on the nerves of children and teachers.

3. The universities don't like to be responsible for choosing a social elite from their not always completely top-drawer scholars. They would prefer to be an end in themselves, not a steppingstone for social advancement. All they are really prepared to do is select the top students in particular academic fields for scholarships. However, there can be a switch here, too. Swindlers and snobs, those Geiger counters of social prestige, have been found calling themselves "doctors" without justification. There was, for instance, an apparently extremely competent psychologist named Schneider, who would never have been given a key position among the Bundeswehr officers if he hadn't called himself "Dr." Schneider. When it was discovered that he had no right to the title, there was great indignation; his capabilities were forgotten.

The leaders of society emerge full force in professional life (switch four), via all sorts of imponderables (switch five). Sociologists write thick volumes about the extent to which a society with a class system (whose upper class is automatically its elite) still exists. Briefly, they say: Of course we still have levels of society as a humus of good intentions, of happy starting conditions. But after this, and above such ground, we find no more social strata, only pyramids; and their structure is more or less strictly hierarchic. We find a number of them in our economic, political, and cultural life, and we have the old traditional pyramids of government bureaucracy and army, standing firm, steeled by time.

Let us build—as an example of all the others—an economic pyramid. At the bottom we find unskilled labor; above it the white-collar worker and skilled labor; next step up—the employee, in various ascendant stages of responsibility, to departmental head, manager, director. And at the very top, a man like August Thyssen, who may reject the title of *Herr Generaldirektor* with the words, "I am *not* a *Herr General-direktor*. I *have* a *Herr Generaldirektor!*"

Here there can be no doubt whatsoever as to who is at the bottom and who is at the top. German society consists of thousands, hundreds of thousands of such solidly grounded pyramids. A few are a little shaky; some are still in the process of being built; some tower above everything around them. Between them wander erratically criminals, vagabonds, journalists, unmarried women, artists, doctors, and lawyers.

The problem of German society is to establish contact between the pyramidic empires of economy, politics, and the nation's cultural life. Of course they are constantly crossing each other, and wherever they do, you find the power figures, the men in key positions: union leaders and management where economy and politics meet; directors of cultural institutions and various departmental heads where politics and culture are tangential; distributor and producer in the borderline areas between culture and economy. Such power has to be paid for by the renunciation of a secure position in the firm body of the pyramid and with exhausting efforts to bring together two systems of values that are not attuned to each other. Men in these positions enjoy the highest social recognition, but they also suffer from the most extreme social uncertainty. No one will recognize tomorrow the manager who fails today because he wasn't really big; he only looked big from where he stood.

He may retain one form of power, a form that is valid in the pyramids of West German society as the lowest common denominator: the power of money. And it is a power only because, beyond the firm classifications of a small town or great pyramid, we have no other binding standards. And the simplest way of using this ultimate power is to let everyone see that you have it.

We only seem to have turned our backs on the question of social order in bringing up the subject of power. Whoever fails to grasp the extent to which power and social standing fall together will not understand Germany.

3. THE GERMAN UNIVERSITIES

Germany has 24 universities, with 175,000 students. Not quite 30,000 of them live in East Germany and are state students; in West Germany 24 categories of students may avail themselves of student aid sponsored by various organizations. Far more than half of West Germany's students finance their education themselves.

As might be expected, the largest German Länder have the greatest number of universities. Only the Hanseatic city of Bremen, the smallest German Land, has at present no university, but that may soon change. Since the centuries tend to lend an aura to a university, let us group the German universities according to their age: Heidelberg, founded in 1386; Leipzig, 1409; Greifswald, 1456; Freiburg, 1457; Tübingen, 1477; Marburg, 1527; Jena, 1558; Würzburg, 1582; Kiel, 1665; Halle, 1694; Göttingen, 1737; Erlangen, 1743; Münster, 1780; Berlin-East, 1810; Bonn, 1818; Munich, 1826; Frankfurt, 1914; Hamburg, 1919; Cologne, 1919; Mainz, 1946; Saarbrücken, 1947; Berlin-West, 1948; Giessen (reformed), 1957. We could also group the German universities according to size, according to religion—separating Protestant from Catholic—or according to their worldly foundings by prince or citizenry. But everyone draws back, justifiably, from the question that interests foreigners most: Which is the best?

How am I to classify the German universities? I think I can justify the following order: Munich, Hamburg, Freiburg, Heidelberg, Göttingen, Tübingen, Marburg, Bonn, Cologne, Frankfurt, Münster, Berlin-West, Würzburg, Kiel, Erlangen, Giessen, Saarbrücken, Mainz—Leipzig, Berlin-Ost, Jena, Rostock, Greifswald, Halle. The dash preceding Leipzig is important. If you were to ask the question east of the Harz Mountains, all those after the dash, i.e., the six socialist universities, would have to be mentioned first.

The reputation of a university in Germany stands or falls according to a fairly useful indicator. *From* where and *to* where may a university professor be successfully offered a chair? Naturally personal considerations play a part when a professor accepts a call to another university, but this doesn't change the fact that, generally speaking, a professor from Mainz would accept a call to Hamburg, whereas the university of Erlangen would hardly dare to invite a professor from Munich to take one of its chairs unless the faculty happened to be collecting rejection slips.

This prestige list shows a trend new in German university history and deplored by many, namely a trend toward the big-city universities in which purely economic factors prevail. Universities such as Munich and Hamburg have more to offer: higher salaries, guaranteed lecture fees, better outside earning possibilities for students, finer institutes and research possibilities, or a more congenial atmosphere. This in turn has its effect on the reputation of a university; the big-name personalities—and we still have them—are concentrated in the universities of the larger cities.

"Can you give us an example?" my friends wanted to know. But I felt this would be an unnecessary humiliation for those great scholars who have stuck it out in the smaller universities. One could try to give a picture by listing Nobel prize winners. We have only ten today—a come-down for the German universities which once were studded with them—and they can be divided pretty evenly among the larger universities: Munich (Butenandt, Heisenberg), Göttingen (Hahn, Windaus) Heidelberg (Kuhn), Freiburg (Staudinger), West Berlin (Warburg), Leipzig (Hertz). But all such groupings are artificial. One could spend days, weeks, in lecture halls and institutes and have exactly the same experiences in Freiburg and Frankfurt, in Marburg and Mainz—but, of course, not at all the same experiences in Leipzig and Rostock! There is a uniformity about German universities, or I should say there are two uniformities: a standard Type East, and a standard Type West.

Once upon a time the German universities were proud of their students' freedom. Some still are, but then it is an anachronism. Today it is unthinkable for an East German Leipzig student to study in Göttingen, just as a Göttingen student wouldn't think of studying in Leipzig, but even within the *de facto* countries, very few students still enjoy an independence that allows them to change their university. Any such change brings with it the necessity to find new lodgings (difficult), the necessity to matriculate all over again (tedious), the search for new outside earning possibilities (a necessity for the majority of students), a time loss (probably), and new professors (undiplomatic). And whoever wants to round out his college years with a state examination does best to study at a Länder college because a student who has graduated from—let's say—Bonn University, won't find it easy to get a teaching job in Bavaria. Year after year, more than 20,000 German students take the state examination. About 17,000 pass; 6,000 want to go on for their doctorate and 6,000 make it. The fact that in spite of these statistics, the promotion to "doctor" still counts in orthodox university circles as a difficult and creditable thing, helps explain to a foreigner the German "doctor" inflation he finds so amusing.

Such decisions as, "I want to study Medieval History so I'm going to Professor X in Munich," or, "I want to study gynecology under Professor Y; that's why I'm going to Hamburg," are not heard very often these days. The universities are losing their individual, immutable faces more and more. All practical considerations seem to plead for a uniform type college. That a great many values are lost in the course of this development can be proved; still it may be justified. I am probably just being sentimental. . . .

4. PROFESSOR IN HEIDELBERG

A professor in a West German university has more in common with a professor in East Germany than one might think. Both enjoy great social prestige. A survey in 1958 asked the question: What do you think the monthly earnings of a university professor should be? The average answer gave him 1,194 marks. Only the manager of a factory was granted a higher income, 1,198 marks. A member of Parliament was allowed only 646 marks. The actual incomes are much higher than this "representative cross section of the population" seems to realize.

On this side as on the other side of the border that divides Germany, science has increasingly usurped the place once occupied by religion with the result, paradoxically yet typically, that the strongest religious impulse—at any rate in Protestant spheres—today comes from theology *professors* such as Karl Barth, Helmut Gollwitzer, Rudolf Bultmann, and Helmut Thielicke. The highest ambition of every intellectually professional group is to be recognized as a "science": social science, literary science, political science; now we even have a newspaper science! In a century in which atheistic Marxist-Leninism will not admit to any limitations of knowledge, "science" is the remorseless magic formula.

Thus the German professor, as high priest of the sciences, is a sort of super guiding star, a powerful symbol from which radiates freedom of research and learning. But he is at the same time a high state official and in duty bound to be loyal to whoever happens to be in power. "Art and science, research and teaching are free. Freedom in teaching does not absolve from loyalty to the constitution." (Statute of the Federal Republic. Art. 5:3.)

In a democratic state this may lead to conflict, in a dictatorship to imprisonment. Since only one man in a thousand feels called upon to be a martyr, it is understandable that the German universities under dictatorial rule were not the centers of freedom the student dreams of during his first semester. In Germany this is not considered a subject for conversation, but foreigners see it all the more clearly. Davidson, in his book, *The Death and Life of Germany*, writes of the university professors that there were "few heroes among them." And English Professor Eliza Marianne Butler told her students in Manchester and Cambridge about "the regrettable paucity of [German] professors who had not bowed the knee to Hitler."

All this makes a few other things evident: that there is a lot of competition for professorships; that the way to a chair has become more and more rigorous; that a professorship, normally a career closed to all outsiders, may open up for the outsider when the state system changes, as it did in 1933 in all Germany, in 1945 and 1946 in East Germany and—less incisively—in West Germany.

I had told my friends who couldn't get there about my friend Professor George Schmidt in Leipzig, and it was Dick's special wish that we stay longer in Heidelberg than in any other West German university town. For just as the English feel drawn to all things Hannoverian and therefore consider Göttingen half English, most Americans feel— at least they did until 1945—that there is only one German university —Heidelberg. The place is so famous that small towns in the United States, Australia, and Africa have been named after it.

Sober citizens of Heidelberg don't attribute this fame entirely to the arts and sciences. To be sure, philospohers such as Spinoza, Hegel, Kuno Fischer, and Karl Jaspers, have helped to bring the name Heidelberg to the fore. Quite a few people also connect Heidelberg with its triumverate of great natural historians: Bunsen, Helmholtz, and Kirchhoff. George Friedrich Creuzer, classical philologist, taught there; so did historian Heinrich von Treitschke; Ludwig Curtius (archaeology), and Friedrich Gundolf (history of literature) were professors at Heidelberg.

"I hate to say this," Dick remarked, "but when I hear the word 'Heidelberg,' I don't think of professors. For me Heidelberg is German romanticism." And of course he was right. Up to Heidelberg, the Neckar valley is truly beautiful in the gentle, dreamy way often accredited to the Rhine and the Mosel valleys. Beyond Heidelberg, the Neckar turns into a busy industrial river that flows into the Rhine at the inland port of Mannheim. High above the town, towers Heidelberg Castle, a last "romantic" jewel of the Neckar valley; and romantic in the same sense is the classic Heidelberg Goethe period of Marianne von Willemer, the Suleika of his *West-Oestlicher Divan:*

An vollen Büschelzweigen,	See the bushy, full-bloomed branches,
Geliebte, sieh nur hin!	Beloved, let me show you their fruit. . . .
Lass dir die Früchte zeigen. . . .	

written as he was waiting for her in the castle. Old Heidelberg is truly romantic, and this image was exported into the world by a not very learned or literarily demanding work, a story called *Karlheinrich,* by Wilhelm Meyer-Förster, which was dramatized and translated into English and created a sensation at the beginning of the century in the United States as *The Student Prince.* Even before that quite a few German emigrants had been sending their sons back to study in Heidelberg, but after *The Student Prince,* no other college existed for any young Amercian wishing to study in Germany. And Dick O'Connor was such an American.

There is a widespread belief, which has not been contradicted to date, that the American bombers of World War II spared Heidelberg until the very end for just such romantic reasons. It is a fact that the American artillery commander who opened negotiations for the capitulation of Heidelberg knew the town only from *The Student Prince.*

Only a few German towns of comparative size remained as unscathed, and today they pay for their old-world beauty with modern-day problems because the roads above the ground and the sewers below it are still as medieval as the towns: Regensburg, Passau, Bamberg, Constance—all smaller than Heidelberg. The forbearance granted Heidelberg could, of course, have had other than exclusively romantic reasons. In 1945, the town became the headquarters of the United States Armed Forces, and when we visited it in 1960, Dick could still meet his compatriots everywhere, in America Town (South Heidelberg), or Little Wall Street, where you could see almost as many Buicks and Chevrolets as Opels and DKW's, but above all in the bars and night clubs that looked a little out of place between the modest houses of respectable citizens. Saddler-master Ebert, who became the first German President after World War I, lived in one of them.

And now I must create a synthetic Heidelberg professor, just as I

Königsberg

OST-

Danzig

PREUSSEN

M M E R N

Stettin

DEN-

R G

Breslau

SCHLESIEN

MECKLENBURG · POMMERN · DANZIG · OSTPREUSSEN

SCHLESWIG
HOLSTEIN · NIEDER-
SACHSEN · BRANDEN-
BURG

SACHSEN
ANHALT · THÜRINGEN

HAMBURG · BERLIN

SACHSEN · SCHLESIEN

NORDRHEIN
WESTFALEN · HESSEN · RHEINLAND
PFALZ · SAARLAND · BADEN
WÜRTTEMBERG · BAYERN

Outside boundaries of the Federal Republic of West Germany.
West boundary of the territory presently administered by Poland (ie. Oder-Neisse Line).
Dividing line between Polish and Soviet territory.

created a synthetic Leipzig professor some pages back. Every word spoken in the conversation that follows was uttered somewhere, at some time or other, but tactless efforts to get to the bottom of things must be abandoned when an abuse of personal confidence might be involved. This isn't a question of decency but simply a rule without which the journalist can't operate, and one which sometimes puts him in the paradoxical position of having the least to say about the people he knows best.

So let us say we visited my synthetic professor, the type of whom the English lady previously quoted wrote: ". . . their exponent parts are popularly supposed to be spectacles, indifference to the ordinary sublunary affairs of life, and an unlimited faculty for evolving camels (or anything else) out of their inner consciousness which furnishes the owner with a never-failing supply of happy abstractions." Eliza Marianne Butler was feeling less charitable when she referred to Bonn Germanics Professor Litzmann as follows: "His main function was to discourage the love of poetry and to bar the door to literary research against all comers. . . . Nearly all our teachers, with the honorable exceptions of Meissner on Old High German and Clemens on Art, were indeed almost incredibly dull . . . the obsequiousness shown [to Litzmann] was nauseating."

"You must forgive my compatriots, Herr Professor," said Ralph, who was embarrassed by these quoted aspersions because we had been so amiably received in the simple, slightly old-fashioned apartment which took up the ground floor of a villa built in the 20's. "But that's the way they saw it. Perhaps everything's different today."

"I wouldn't say that," said our host. "One thing certainly hasn't changed: to group us together as 'professors of higher learning' is still highly questionable, or as my colleague in the sociology department would put it—in a profession that still depends so much on individual achievement and personality, you will find few correlative behavior patterns."

"But outwardly," said Yvonne, "the professors do represent a definite group, perhaps even the elite?"

It is true that in all German-speaking countries—and Pierre Spälti corroborated this for the Swiss universities—the college professor enjoys a prestige that would be unthinkable in England, France, or the United States. I don't mean the scientific reputation granted to a single authority—this is found anywhere—but the prestige of a professorship per se.

"What would an American opportunist pretend to be?" I asked Dick.

"A millionaire."

"And an English swindler?"

Ralph hesitated, but only for a moment. "A lord."

"And a French one?"

"A writer . . . maybe," said Yvonne.

"And a Swiss?"

"Well," said Professor Spälti, "I'd say there were two possibilities
. . . either a ski instructor or—yes, probably a university professor."

"The same would apply to us," said Andreas von Hattesdorf.

"Why do you suppose the college professor enjoys so much prestige in Germany?" Yvonne wanted to know.

"Unfortunately I'm not a sociologist," I told her, "but I wonder if
even a sociologist could answer that. If you promise not to quote me,
I'm ready to risk a perfectly dreadful simplification: because you can
find, in the reputation of the college professor, the prestige of the
former Prussian government official combined with that of science;
and it is fortunate that what the one lost in esteem was the other's gain.
To this you may add that once a profession is accorded so much honor,
many seek it, which in turn gives the universities the chance to be
extremely selective. And this selectiveness again heightens the reputation of the professor." Then I asked our host, "Do you really think,
Herr Professor, that our universities choose the best professors?"

He grinned. "Let me tell you a story," he said, "and since I don't
want to offend anybody, I shall borrow a few Latin terms from my
medical colleagues. There are three possible ways for a man to get to
be a university professor in Germany:

"1. *per animum:*
    a) *sui*, in that he thinks up something profound.
    b) *alius*, in that he is a clever copier.

"2. *per membrum virile:*
    a) *sui*, in that he marries a professor's daughter.
    b) *alius*, in that he is born a professor's son.

"3. *per posteriorem:*
    a) *sui*, in that he applies seat of pants to seat of chair.
    b) *alius*, in that he is an ass-kisser."

"And which would you say was the most common procedure, Herr
Professor?"

"The sequence is fairly obvious: 1a is far in the lead. Then, perhaps—
3a. I don't think 2a and 2b play as important a part in West Germany
as they used to, but 3b—yes, 3b has always been strong and still is
today. Perhaps we should give it second place."

Once we had him started, the professor put on a good show and
turned out to be a pleasant contradiction to the picture of a German
university professor which Ralph and Yvonne, especially, had had
until then. Worthy of note is his observation that, "Seen from the inside it all looks quite a bit different. Here it is the women who cling
to a strict hierarchic order. They're the ones who have to worry over
it because every now and then they give a party and must seat their
guests, and then all professors aren't equal. As a matter of fact, a full
professor isn't really acknowledged unless he is head of a department or institute. The others have to do all their work themselves.
And scientific reputation, department, number of students, seniority
also help to establish rank." All truths that remain true as long as the

mood is blithe, as long as far-reaching conclusions are not too seriously drawn.

As we were bidding our host farewell, Ralph came up with some unfinished business. "But what do you have to say about the attitude of my two countrywomen?"

"Taking first the reproach for our leaning toward abstractionism—yes, the language spoken at German universities is highly abstract, especially in the philosophy department, more abstract than is necessary."

"I think we are dealing here," interposed Pierre Spälti, "not only with a form of expression but with what lies behind it, a spiraling up to heights and a digging down into bottomless depths, the 'ivresse des grandes profondeurs,' as Austin calls it."

"But think how many scientific achievements are based on this passionate plumbing of depths!"

"To be sure, to be sure," said Pierre Spälti, "but think how much chaff is being threshed at the same time. . . ."

"As for Professor Butler's 'nauseating obsequiousness' of the students," our Heidelberg professor concluded, "that exists; no doubt about it, that still exists. *Per posteriorem alius,* remember? There are plenty who try it. The fact of the matter is that the student tries in every conceivable way to reach his goal, which is the passing of his final examinations. Of course we like attentive pupils; maybe we grow so accustomed to them that we interpret as perfectly normal an attentiveness that may look like nauseating obsequiousness to the outsider. And that may be your answer. As for my own pupils—I wouldn't call them obsequious. But every professor may think along these lines. Why don't you ask the students?"

5. UNDERGRADUETTES

The traditions of German university life go back to the Middle Ages and have been violently disturbed four times: in the sixteenth century by the Reformation and Humanism, with their new viewpoints of "science," and the freedom of teaching and learning; in the eighteenth century by the "era of enlightenment," which did away with the supremacy of theology as the scholar's discipline, and Latin as his tongue; in the nineteenth century by Wilhelm von Humboldt's reforms of the Prussian universities, with the foundation of the professorship as a powerful official position in which research and learning were combined to "educate" in the sense of "character development"; in the twentieth century by the admission of women to the seats of higher learning, and ever greater stress on "academic freedom" as that freedom shrank.

Oh alte Burschenherrlichkeit, wohin bist du entschwunden? "Oh where are thou gone, old student glory?" There can be no more question of student glory today. The inheritors of the old student corporations try to inject life into antiquated customs. Quite a few find this ridiculous, others see democracy endangered in the arrogant beer-and-hurrah patriotism which tends to be found wherever the "colors" are worn, toasts are made, duels are fought, and freshmen are bullied by their fraternity elders. Most of the students who are *korporiert, i.e.,* belong to one of the uniformed corporations—in Marburg and Tübingen they comprise a third of the student body—wear their colors and fight a duel if it can't be avoided. These corporations have succeeded in reforming their ranks against opposition where others failed. But there can be no thought of a true *universitas,* a community of staff and student body at the German universities today. Any efforts to restore it by the initiation of joint living quarters or dormitory life according to the example set by Anglo-American universities hasn't even been tried as far as the staff is concerned, and in the case of the student body never went beyond a few encouraging efforts.

At most German universities, the students have great difficulty in finding a room unless they are prepared to spend half of the 200 marks granted them by the government in 1956 as a monthly budget. Many of them do. Their uncertainty as far as future profession is concerned is great. Only very few freshmen have any idea what they are going to do when they graduate. A few fraternities—especially the Catholic ones—have won the students' confidence by showing great understanding of their needs. They help them to find a place to live. They often have hostels with communal living rooms, libraries, even living quarters. They help to relieve a student's loneliness by offering him a form of community life which the critical person may find unreal; still, many feel that it is better than no community life at all. And finally, alumni organizations are in a position to help the student get a job after he has passed his examinations. The Catholic CV is famous, one might almost say notorious, in this respect. Perhaps not unjustifiably, they stand accused of influencing the filling of political positions in West Germany.

Since April, 1951, therefore, we have had an AGA in West Germany. The letters stand for *Arbeitsgemeinschaft Andernach der mensurbeflissenen Verbände,* or Duel-Enthusiasts' Association Community Workshop Andernach, and in the future foreigners won't have to do without what seems to have become for them the main characteristic of German academic life, the dueling scar. For the time being, however, duels are still being fought with reticence.

"They say that Tübingen is again a center for dueling corporations," said Yvonne, "but we haven't seen a single student yet with a fresh scar." We didn't see any during the rest of our stay either. Yvonne was a little relieved, yet quite a bit disappointed.

Tübingen is a university town that really meets the romantic ideas of a German university town more than halfway and is ringed by fraternity houses as if fortified by them. After the ups and downs of its almost five-hundred-year history, the university blossomed forth again during the first postwar years. The horrors of war have left few traces in Tübingen. Lecture halls and institutes stand undamaged. But the formation of Land Baden-Württemberg put an end to Tübingen as a Land capital. Some of the larger university institutes disappeared as quickly as they had come into being. The number of world-renowned scholars was drastically reduced; some died; others reached the age of retirement or transferred to larger and wealthier universities. The jurisprudence professors moved to Hamburg with their Max-Planck Institute; the biochemists followed their teacher, Adolf Butenandt, to Munich.

In Tübingen nearly everybody still knows everybody else. People still meet on the Rennbahn between Old and New Aula, but here too the Stammtisch where the professors of the "upper town" met the *Gogen* (vintners) of the "lower town" has become a rarity. Once a truth and now a legend is the statement that you could divide the population of Tübingen into two groups: *Gogen* and academic men. Today, according to statistics, only three families in the whole place still live off their vineyards.

We accompanied Lilo Braune, student of medicine, to a colloquium on Thomas Mann that was being held by philologist Walter Jens, well-known novelist and critic. Fräulein Braune was a very charming victim of our thirst for knowledge. She was living in a large pleasant room overlooking the Neckar, thanks to the fact that she had chosen her father carefully and had an income of 300 marks at her disposal, to say nothing of frequent packages from home and the 20-mark bills that found their way into letters from her parents every now and then.

Prototypes of this young lady could not have been found at a German university fifty years ago. For fifty years now, female students in Germany have been trying to compensate erotically for the contempt in which they are held academically, according to Fräulein Braune.

"You're not going to write that!" she protested, as I made a note of it.

"Why not?"

"You'll be sorry. I wrote an article once—I was naïve—about the various types of female students. It caused an uproar!"

I think her article is apt enough to be quoted in part. According to Lilo Braune, female students may be divided into four groups:

1. The compulsive student who devours science with dedicated thoroughness and suffers the resultant bellyache.

2. The student who rejoices in her beauty. She makes no demands but attends the university exclusively for her own and everybody else's amusement and uses up more perfume than ink.

3. The experimental student, numerically the largest group. She is looking for a man, a husband. Studying is something to fall back on, just in case. She is really very determined and studious but rarely with outstanding results in either endeavor.

4. The female student who is already married.

"And this caused a furor?"

"I'll say!" said Lilo Braune.

Let us try some cautious documentation. Academic contempt for the female can be proved. At first the universities were semimonastic institutions. In the eighteenth century they became more worldly; in the nineteeth century it was the women who became more worldly. The first logical consequences were drawn from this in Switzerland. In 1864, the first woman matriculated at the University of Zürich, followed by the United States and England in 1880, the Scandinavian countries and Italy in 1890, Belgium in 1896. Of all the civilized countries, Germany was the last to permit women to study, and between the most liberal German administrative areas, Baden and Hamburg on the one hand, and least liberal Prussia on the other, lay an interval of eight years. Until August, 1908, the daughters of Berlin who wanted a university education had to find it in Switzerland.

The objections to giving women the right to study, which were raised at the time, are not as outdated as one might imagine. As late as the ninth decade of the nineteenth century, the question of admitting women to the universities was on the agenda of the Prussian Parliament, but the gentlemen seemed to find it more important to settle the problem of poaching. In the Allgemeine *Zeitung* of 1892, one finds the following: "Of course there are exceptions. Now and then you do come across a really attractive girl with a brief case under her arm, but in general it is not the fairer members of the fair sex who embrace the arts and sciences, which is understandable." And at the end of the nineteenth century, a deputy of one of the provincial governments declared: "A woman really gains knowledge only from the man she loves, and she learns what and as much as her beloved man, through his love, delights in having her know." In its awkward German, *und es lernt dasjenige, was, und soviel, wie der geliebte Mann durch seine Liebe als ihn erfreuend haben will,* this sentence expresses what the patriarchal families in Germany—and by no means only the male members—feel is right. And the most patriarchal institution in a country that has always been strongly patriarchal, is the German university. The most important man attending to the creation and fostering of new academic blood is rather significantly called *Doktor-Vater* (Doctor-Father), and it must be clear to everyone that it would be extremely difficult to replace him with a *Doktor-Mutter* (Doctor-Mother), even if everybody has admitted long ago that Professor Dodel was right when he expressed in an article the opinion that: "The presence of women students has not only *not* harmed the male student body's attitude and seriousness of life and learning habits, but has greatly furthered them."

Oh, dear me, yes, we have quite got over the days when Germanics Professor Roethe and anatomy Professor Waldeyer wouldn't allow female students in their Berlin lecture halls. Even Ernst Robert Curtius, that snide (*nota bene* grand) Bonn Romanist, didn't have much to say against the female student, but shamelessly preferred those who were exceptionally pretty. When they married, he sent them a wire: "My heartiest congratulations for the optimal ending of your college education."

The first part of Dodel's article is still not generally accepted at the German universities, the part that reads: "Many of them [he was referring to the female student in Zürich] belong to the elite of those who are capable." Or let us say that the German universities have done very little toward tapping the resources of this elite. On the one hand you hear that new chairs cannot be created because they can't be filled by sufficiently qualified candidates; on the other, the course of female education looks statistically like this: Of 100 students, 25 are female. Of all doctoral candidates, 25 per cent are female. And what happens after that? Most female doctors hit the peak of their scientific careers watering plants or filing in the institutes, with quasi-nursing duties in the clinics. Among a hundred of those achieving their doctorate, only 4 are female; and of the hundred who become professors, only one half of one (not to be taken visually!). To be more precise: in a recent survey, only 13 professors out of 2,421 were women. You won't find another ratio like this, not even in the next most-inimical-to-women profession: law. Of our 11,502 judges, 301 are female.

In East Germany things are different. The example of Hilde Benjamin, Minister of Justice in East Germany, who is feared because of the rigorous harshness with which she carries out her duties (no feminine mercy there!) may not be exactly encouraging, but they take total male-female equality seriously over there when it comes to manual labor, as well. . . .

Yes, academic contempt for the female student in Germany is irrefutable. Only hypocrisy and exceptions contradict the words of the Freiburg student, Christa Meyer-Quandt, who wrote: "The goal of today's female student is marriage and motherhood," and the order in which they are placed should be adhered to, if possible.

It would be nonsense to decry the female student as more marriage-mad than other German girls; on the contrary, with progresssive intelligence, the urge to get married diminishes. Students just happen to also participate—and why not?—in the very natural desire to have a family, which is no weaker in Germany than it is anywhere else. A married woman is more highly respected than a spinster. On the lowest level of the pyramid this is absolutely valid; in the middle, exceptions are reluctantly recognized; only at the top, where independence and sovereignty of the individual make themselves felt, does the wedding ring no longer count.

A girl of good family—and I am quoting Lilo Braune again—doesn't have such an easy time in Germany to get to know young men other than her brothers. There really are only two respectable ways to go about it: to meet the friends of her brothers and the brothers of her friends. But what of the poor girl who doesn't have any brothers? Then only the sons of family friends are possible, that is barring one of those happy accidents that don't quite seem to go with good breeding.

But if a girl goes to college, all this is changed. The duty toward science calls, and for the first time she finds herself surrounded by potential marriage partners. Who can possibly be surprised if this results in complications? The statistics on virginity show a sharp decline, and the fact that a lot of people take no cognizance of the fact, others accept it as a matter of course, and practically no one is indignant about it in a country where they are quick with their indignation said Fräulein Lilo, "Is rather nice," and all of us agreed with her. I think I am right when I say that the tensions which, according to the analyses of Professor Freud, dominate the world in a complex-creative way while repressed, are evident in Germany to a much lesser degree than in England or the United States. In spite of which no one could say that we lack neuroses. . . .

6. A GENERATION RICH IN ATTRIBUTES

Peter is the oldest of the Liebner children. He is twenty-eight, and just got his degree. He wants to be a journalist. His twenty-three-year-old sister, Renate, is studying psychology, sociology, and philosophy. Her stated goal is to be an industrial psychologist; her secret goal— to marry a well-to-do man and have children who will love their parents more "than the children of today love their parents." Claus is still going to high school. He is seventeen and a senior. He is the black sheep of the family and has already been in trouble with the police for damaging the seats of a concert hall after a jam session. To round out the family I must present Cornelia, age twelve; and Gabrielle, age three; but in the course of our conversation they did not have as much to offer as the others. No, that isn't quite right either. It was actually Cornelia and little Gabrielle from whom we got the unvarnished truth.

"Papa, you've got to buy a television set," said Cornelia.

"I do? Why?"

"Because I've got to write a composition on my favorite television program."

"You," said little Gabrielle, addressing Dick, the only one of us who seemed to register with her, "have a neat car. What did it cost?"

Dick, slightly taken aback, "About seven thousand dollars."

Gabrielle: "That's an awful lot of money. Did you have enough?"

This question was probably asked quite often in the Liebner family, although the children didn't look as if they lacked for anything. Herr Liebner is *prokurist*, something akin to a fairly high-ranking employee with the right to sign checks for the firm. *Pro cura* is what he has, and what makes him a *prokurist*. Herr Liebner works in a small but flourishing business and probably earns 3,000 marks a month, perhaps more. But he has to have a Mercedes (prestige), a maid ("My wife can't manage the household alone"), a large apartment ("I have to do a lot of entertaining"). He also has to be well groomed and carry a lot of insurance and . . . and . . . and . . . buy a television set for Cornelia.

The German postwar generation was known as *The Skeptical Generation*, which was the title of a book of very revealing essays by sociologist Helmut Schulsky (Eugen Diedrich Verlag, 1957). In it he finds the objects of his loving efforts accommodating, realistic, helpful, and assured. Others found other pertinent traits: they were a practical generation, an elastic generation, a flexible generation; then someone else came along who found so many contradictions in the characteristics listed here that he decided on a "generation without attributes."

This certainly shows laudable caution and a dread of too daring generalizations, still it is less than satisfactory. A German author who just managed to absorb the last war years, wrote an article for *Die Zeit*, entitled *Nüchterne Jugend*, "Sober Youth," or more freely translated, *"Youth with No Illusions."* His name is Eckart Kroneberg, and his novel, *Der Grenzgänger*, is the best portrait I know of the young generation. In his article, he makes five points about the young people of Germany today:

1. They take "almost blithe pleasure in their own bodies," and see in sex "a possibility that is not to be neglected, or—more bluntly—that is to be used."

2. "Love of one's parents" they think is a cliché. There can be no question of love or hate, only indifference, an indifference that does not exclude a certain benevolence.

3. They consider a profession a means to make money, nothing more.

4. They feel no need for religion.

5. They accept the state as an apparatus for law and order, but they have no feeling of patriotism.

He comes to the following conclusion: "In spite of all this I can see a new type of human being emerging whom I can accept unreservedly: free of prejudice, free of preconceived principles, unrealistic ideas and ideologies, free of the conventions and political resentment, free therefore for every new approach at any time; a human being ready to say yes to his fellow men, free and full of promise as never before."

His theories were interesting, but even more so were the letters to the editor that resulted from his article. Out of a hundred, 30 were written by adults, 70 by young people, by which I mean those under twenty-two. The overwhelming majority of adults (90 per cent) rejected Kroneberg's ideas angrily: "Our children are not like that!" A majority of young people (70 per cent) agreed with him coolly: "That's what we're like; at last somebody's come along to say so." One outcome may therefore be considered certain: parents tend to have illusions about their children. You may see them day after day in the children's courts: father, mother, staring down at the floor, or sobbing, face in hands, while their offspring stands accused of something stupid or vicious such as vandalism or assault. Generally speaking though, and contrary to general opinion, juvenile delinquency is no greater in Germany today than it used to be, and the children's courts have a reputation for being lenient and understanding. But it is relatively new that in the case of children of so-called good families—which in many parts of the country is synonymous with "well-to-do" —the reason for the delinquency is very often, "I was so alone. Nobody cared about me, I couldn't talk to my parents."

The lack of understanding between generations is a basic fact of world history and therefore also a favorite theme in world literature. Side by side with the Freudian father-son power struggle, we find the love-struggle of mother and son. America has its hoodlums, England its Teddy boys, Germany its *Halbstarken*, or "half-strong ones," in a way the best name of all.

All this is true, but it is not the whole truth. These angry young men, by whatever name you call them, or however they choose to designate themselves, are eminently suited for all pictorial purposes and therefore attract a great deal of attention. But they are at best symptomatic, and an infinitesmal, not at all typical, minority. The unprejudiced observer sees more than these few rebels against the not-always-admirable background of their parents' way of life; he also sees the mass of young consumers, guided indirectly by a partially state, partially economic "industry for the young." They have a good time, adapt themselves well, have good jobs, and don't want to attract attention.

In Germany another problem has to be added to the general problems of youth. Even for a nation which, lying as it does in a magnetic field of conflicting interests, has always led a rather stormy life, a lot has happened recently, perhaps a little too much. Whether we are conscious of it or not, what we are, feel, and think today continues to be influenced by the manner in which we experienced Hitler's Reich, the war, and the catastrophe that followed it. And for all of us the decisive factor was: how old were we when it happened? According to this we may differentiate between a prewar and NSDAP generation, a Hitler Youth or war generation, and a postwar generation. And between them we find abysses, not of *mis*understanding but of the impossibility to understand. There is no way of jumping across these abysses; at best they may be bridged; but we Germans were never very good at bridging differences; that presupposes a readiness for compromise, and compromise we have felt always to be slightly lacking in character. . . .

The prewar generation in Germany encompasses those born between the years of 1912–1918. It is the generation which consciously experienced Hitler and the Third Reich, conscious especially because they knew there were other things: a world before Hitler, a world beyond Hitler. Of every ten members of this generation, nine—reckoning kindly—sooner or later recognized their country as National Socialist, by far more *nolens* than *volens*, with less personal sympathy than the denazification commissions ever realized, and with much less insight into the murky corners of a regime than seems credible today when all such corners have been illuminated with floodlights. They were followed by the Hitler Youth and war generation of the years from 1918 to 1931. For them there was the National Youth Movement; the only form of government was *"der Führer,"* the only source of information the Reichs Propaganda Ministry, via press and radio. This generation had the most war casualties, and after the war, was torn between the inertia of its elders and the pressures of youth. Whenever you hear talk of a lack of postwar cultural impulses and new blood to fill professorships, of feeble postwar literature and no young leaders in politics and business, this "missing generation" is involved. The survivors do what they can, but the common people are justified in their blanket statement: the best were killed.

And finally those born after 1931, with which we get back to Peter, Renate, and Claus Liebner, to say nothing of Cornelia and little Gabrielle. They have heard a lot about the Hitler era, but grasped very little of it. They had to endure its finale: starvation, ruins, occupation, without really experiencing them as the effects of a cause. For that not even better history lessons than they are getting, or the most painstaking reporting on Germany, would suffice. And, of course, they don't have the least understanding of the fact that some of their idiotic elders have tears in their eyes when there is talk of Königsberg or Dresden. As if Marl and Mainz weren't enough to make one happy!

Peter, Renate and Claus had read Kroneberg's article. Peter said, "It's the best thing I've read in a newspaper for a long time." Claus: "It's all right with me." Renate: "Every word is true."

"For heavens sake, Renate, do you 'use' your sex?"

"Of course I do. And don't you have any illusions about it. I don't. If only you old men weren't all such hypocrites!"

Bull's-eye!

Peter: "Frankly, I don't know what he means by 'use.' He may be referring more to girls. They certainly know their way around. Wasn't it like that before?"

Claus: "If I'm supposed to find pleasure in my own body, then it's when I'm playing football."

According to Kroneberg, for this generation love of parents is a cliché. There can be no question of love or hate, only of indifference.

"That's a tough one," said Claus. "My old man's fine, but I don't understand why he has to drive a Mercedes yet doesn't want to give me a piffling three hundred marks for a trip to England."

"I don't want to talk about my mother," said Renate, "and I won't have a word said against my father."

Peter had more to contribute than the other two, "I don't know why my father made such a secret of it. All right, so he was a Party member, but then all of them were. A few months ago I said to him,

'Look here, in your place I'm sure I'd have joined the Party, too.' Since then we've been on speaking terms again and get along fine. And now I understand that he has to work pretty hard with five children, and all of them wanting to study. I could have slapped Cornelia when she brought up the television set. But mother's difficult. I just don't know how to behave naturally with her."

A profession offers a chance to make money, nothing more.

"You can't apply that to me," said Peter. "If I had nothing on my mind but making money, I'd have gone into my father's business. But here I am, of marriageable age, and only earning three hundred marks a month as a trainee. I want a profession I can enjoy. Of course if I should happen to make money, too, I wouldn't object."

"Oh, yes, I want money," said Renate. "Lots of money."

And Peter, "By which she means she wants a husband who makes a lot of money, and looking the way she does, it shouldn't be too difficult."

Claus: "The man's right. Of course I'd rather not work at all. I'd like to travel. I'm sick to death of school. Maybe they'll allow pros in Germany soon, then I'm going to be a football player. In the end I'll probably go into Papa's business, but only because I want to make as much money as possible. After all, that's all that counts when you're grown up."

As for Kroneberg theory number four: They feel no need for religion.

Peter, Renate, and Claus agreed: "That's right."

Did young people ever have religious needs? . . . Once they had a better religious education than the guidance and example most of today's adults can give them, but I wouldn't say that they ever had religious needs.

"Our director certainly dishes out plenty of platitudes," said Claus, "and when he gets confidential with the dear Lord at Monday-morning service, I tell you it's unbearable!"

Fifth and last theory: They accept the state as an apparatus for law and order, but they have no patriotism.

"I think we object to words like 'patriotism' and 'fatherland' wherever they are used in vain. But if it ever came to the point . . . I don't know. Of course we wouldn't mind being Americans or English, but we'd rather not be Bulgarians or Soviet-Zonal."

"Soviet-Zonal" is what Dr. Peter Liebner, age twenty-eight, said, and this is the fruit of the so-called reunification policy.

"I have no idea if this has anything to do with patriotism, but I'd much rather marry an Australian or an American than a German," was Renate's contribution.

"I suppose they want to talk me into patriotism as an excuse for the fact that I'll soon have to spend part of my life in a barracks," said Claus, "and I'm dreading that right now." But then, Claus is the black sheep of the family. . . .

7. A WOMAN CALLED ELIZABETH

Germany is hell for statisticians and lexicographers. Scarcely a figure holds good for more than ten years, and it is impossible to make the most conservative statements without letting oneself in for highly undesirable political discussions. Altogether, Germany is no unmixed pleasure for any type of reporter, for it has the treacherous quality of a kaleidoscope: you've just steadied the pattern, but give it the slightest tap, and everything looks different. And God knows, we've been treated to plenty of taps! What I am trying to do is describe the small pieces that constitute the whole, and for that we can't always do without statistics.

The 53½ million inhabitants of West Germany, plus the 17 million living in East Germany, give us a total of 70 million Germans. Every thirty-seventh inhabitant of this earth is a German. Among them we have more women (37 million) than men; more Protestants (39 million) than Catholics; more small-town people (33 million) than inhabitants of cities or villages; more employees . . . but here the possibility of seeing both Germanys together ceases abruptly because the statistics available from East Germany suffer from the doctrine that classifies these desirable elements of mankind not as employees but as "workers and farmers."

Two-thirds of all Germans rise at 7:00 A.M. and go to bed at ten thirty at the latest. Most Germans consider two children the ideal number to have. The men in Germany are preferably called Hans, Karl, or Willi; and if the English and French take pleasure in lumping all Germans together under the heading of "Fritz," I have news for them—Fritz is only fifth on the list of German men's names, right after Heinz. The women are called for the most part Elizabeth, Maria, or Anna, though not many are so christened today. But our Cornelias and Gabrielles, if the fad lasts, are going to have to wait at least twenty years before they will have the majority in any statistical survey.

The typical German (who doesn't exist) would therefore have to be depicted in a way never before shown in caricature or cartoon: a Protestant employee called Elizabeth, living in a small town. . . .

In the aforementioned May 31, 1954, issue of *Life* magazine, you may read the following about the new German girl, whose name was given as Edda:

"Reckoned by U.S. standards, the life of Edda Liss, a 26-year-old German girl who works as a secretary for a big chemical company in the West German city of Hannover, is not very easy or independent. But in Germany, where, traditionally, proper young ladies were expected to stay at home and obey their fathers, the fact that Edda has a secretarial job and handles her own money, represents a big change in the status of German women. . . . She has worked up to $94 [a month], a high salary for a woman. Brought up conservatively, Edda thinks it is unladylike to be interested in politics, keeps out of the current controversy over giving women equal rights in society. But in her own way she is branching out, tasting freedom and making decisions which would have been unusual before the war. She wears lipstick but no powder. . . . She wants to get married . . . it seems likely she will soon settle down to happy domestic servitude, staying home and obeying her husband."

"So what do you say to that?" said Dick.

"Well, first of all I consider it improbable that a young lady who was twenty-six in 1954, and must therefore have been born in 1928, would be called Edda. That's a name which became fashionable five years later, during our Nordic Renaissance, especially when Hermann Göring named his daughter Edda."

"But what about the rest?"

"The rest of the story is rather like Edda—improbable."

"What's wrong with it?"

"Let's go see. We'll visit Edda, only our Edda will be called Elizabeth."

She is two years older than Edda, and married. The average age for marriage in Germany is twenty-six for women, thirty for men. Elizabeth has a job as secretary in a large concern. In West Germany there are five million married couples with man and wife working. Frau Schneider (as we now have to call Edda, alias Elizabeth) received us in the living room of her pleasant, modern, three-room apartment. Somehow the six of us managed to find room in it. She was a woman and German, yet she was not "a German woman" as American and French books would have it—the Wilhelminian type who was born at the onset of the nineteenth century, poetically glorified by Kleist in his *Kätchen von Heilbronn*, made visible for all to see in the person of the *Landesmutter*, Queen Luise, praised, side by side with German 'fealty' in *Deutschland, Deutschland über alles*, made simple by Chamisso: "Let me bow before my master in devotion and humility."

One finds little devotion and humility nowadays, a development that predated 1945. Even if in 1933 state propaganda was urging a mother-hen ideal of womanhood, there was no stopping the emancipation of women, not even in Germany.

"I think 'emancipation' is a dreadful word," said Frau Schneider.

Eyebrows were raised. Yvonne said quickly, "But don't you want equality?"

"E-qua-li-ty?" Frau Schneider said slowly, and you couldn't fail to get the implication—Do you want to rob me of my privileges?

In many respects, German society is what it always has been, patriarchal. The family revolves around the father, but how it turns is decided by the mother. In professional life, the men often have "better pay for the same work," but when the money gets home, it is the women who take charge of it. It is certainly easier for a man to reach a prominent position, but how often it is the woman's ambition that gets him there! In the society generally called high, the men who have made a name for themselves may be the most sought after and their wives mere appendages. Granted. But who decides who is to be invited in the first place? Generally a woman. What would a party be without a "hostess"? We recently borrowed the terminology (only) from the American idiom.

" 'I am a German Hausfrau,' is the ultimate paean of pride which these patient spouses know . . . the life of the ordinary German woman is little better than that of an upper servant. She is a soft, sentimental creature, all sensibility and adjectives, weaving 'heavenly roses' into this earthly life; melancholy, *schwärmerisch*, blue-eyed and pensive, swimming somewhat vaguely in vast seas of sentiment. . . . Poets paint them helpless, and their husbands like them subjugated."

Our English lady, whose reflections were published in 1884, wrote home in this vein. I suspect her of trying to make a bit of an effect even then, but if this picture of the German woman has remained alive ever since in England, America, France, and Switzerland, it cannot be only because the world is blind. Of course some things observed by foreigners in Germany tend to corroborate the picture. The three K's *Küche, Kirche, Kinderstube* (kitchen, church, nursery) still play their part; and yet. . . .

"I never go to church; my husband helps me in the kitchen; and we can't afford children," said Frau Schneider.

But Dick wanted to know exactly how big the difference was between *Life* magazine's Edda and Elizabeth Schneider. "May I ask you something? If you could be born again, which would you rather be, a boy or a girl?"

"If I was pretty, a girl."

"Then you have nothing to regret," said Von Hattesdorf gallantly.

"But if I was intelligent, I'd want to be a boy."

"Why?"

"Because boys have a much better chance of advancement."

The term "chance of advancement" plays an important role in the world of the employee, and four-fifths of the West Germans are employees. In this chance of advancement, we find expressed a view of life which may be the result of hierarchic ideas, but it recognizes the established classifications only as long as diligence and ability, combined with a little good luck, contribute to working one's way up step by step. People who concentrate on working their way up are not always sympathetic, but West Germany has them to thank, more than any others for the fact that fifteen years after the catastrophe it can be fêted (and fleeced) as a prosperous country, a country in which the prosperity of the individual is not as great as might at first be imagined, but where the kind of want and misery that may be eliminated by money alone no longer exist.

The ruling attitude toward life in such a world of employees is fundamentally optimistic. What's the best way to go about it? When shall we achieve it? When shall we be able to afford it? Such happy-future questions don't go very well with the dark, pessimistic picture of our times that artists and intellectuals like to paint. Strife? Atomization? *La nausée?* Not a trace of them in this society which is hopeful of succeeding.

8. IS THE GERMAN FAMILY STILL INTACT?

This is a question sociologists like to ask, and it has the peculiarity that the most straightforward answer, "That depends on the family," doesn't satisfy.

"The total disintegration of family life" is announced with almost the same persuasiveness as the opinion that the family has withstood change better than any form of communal life tried in Germany during the last decades. The truth is that often it has, often it hasn't, and more than half the German families fall into the in-between category of so-so.

From the outside, "close corporations" tend to look (to those who don't belong to them) either ludicrous (like the Bird Watchers' Association), or dangerous (like the German Refugee or Veterans' Associations). But this can't be said of the Industrial Family as a group even if on its yearly outings it may appear threatening and ludicrous at the same time! When the farsighted leaders of industry recognized that it would diplomatic and humane to make the just demands of their employees their own, thereby avoiding power conflicts with the unions, the "industrial family" was created, and disposed of all the beautiful theories that concerned themselves with "exploiters and exploited."

We were sitting in the small but comfortable apartment of a "typical German," according to the statistics: Elizabeth Schneider, Protestant, married, living in a small town. The name of the small town is Velbert. It lies in an industrial area, in the hills above the Ruhr valley, which became the forge of Germany about a hundred years ago when man discovered that he could combine coal with iron to make steel and many useful side-products, from gas to fertilizer. In more heroic times, this forge was known as the *Waffenschmiede*, or armament forge. . . . But Velbert was never an armament forge. Like so many other towns in this area, it has its industry to thank for everything. A hundred years ago it was a quiet little village, belonging to Cloister Werden, after which it became the property of Count von Berg who gave his name to this *Bergisches* Land. Under Napoleon, Velbert was incorporated into the French Empire, like the rest of the Rhineland, and that didn't do it any harm. After the Congress of Vienna (1815) it was handed over, still a village, to Prussia, although Napoleon's governor had conferred upon it the status of "municipality" in the meantime. The population count was 1,040.

On July 13, 1827, with a population of 5,000, it really became a town, one of the many industrial towns administered by Prussian lieutenants. It prospered late and slowly, but steadily. At the turn of the century it had 15,000 inhabitants; before the beginning of World War II, double that number. Meanwhile its big neighbors, Essen in the north and Wuppertal in the south, were being smashed by a rain of bombs; but Velbert continued to develop. It acquired 50,000 inhabitants; today it has almost 60,000. Velbert is therefore a quite typical German small town. Or I should perhaps say medium-size town. Whoever wants to understand Germany must understand Velbert, even if he has never heard of it, which is probably the case with nine out of ten Germans.

Whoever does know Velbert, without having friends or relatives there, knows it as the German lock town, and that explains its slow but steady development. Nothing spectacular was manufactured in Velbert, no cannons for World War I, no tanks for World War II, nothing but locks and metal fittings. Locksmiths and foundry-men made the town famous. The grandfathers of Velbert hammered out nails and screws; today their grandsons own small factories. If you want to belong to Velbert's high society, you must own a small factory. But Velbert also boasts the largest lock factory in Europe. The first safety lock (BKS) was made in Velbert.

The small factories absorb only one-fourth of those employed in industry, the rest work in plants with a personnel of over a hundred. Elizabeth Schneider has been working in such a plant for six years. Every day she travels half an hour to Essen, and half an hour back, in a bus that is an auxiliary of the railroad. Velbert was late in getting a railway line, even later in making it pay. The road was just giving Velbert's evolution as an industrial city a boost when it became unprofitable, like so many branch lines which could not keep pace with the cheaper auto highways.

Dick wanted to find out what a woman's place was in such an industry. "When you do have children, Frau Schneider, what will happen?"

"Well, first I get the legal twelve weeks' vacation, six before the event and six after." Which just goes to show how nature can upset the calculations of the best lawmakers with their fine ideas of equality! In Germany many other customs, traditional rights, and obligations stand opposed to it, too. A statute of the Basic Law (Article 3, paragraph 2) states clearly: "Men and women have equal rights." This goes a step further than the Weimar constitution which stated that they were to enjoy "basically the same civic rights"; family and economic rights were not included.

"The ideas some English people have of the patient, humble German household slave are really grotesque," Ralph admitted.

Professor Spälti added, "German women, unlike our women in Switzerland, even have the vote."

An American illustrated magazine, we explained, had stated that in Germany it wasn't considered proper for a woman to be interested in politics. What did Elizabeth Schneider have to say to that?

"Not proper? Nonsense! But I must admit I'm not particularly interested in politics."

"Why not?"

"Oh, politicians are swindlers. They talk about 'the West,' and 'social justice,' but all they have on their minds is their own advantage. I may be wrong. I don't know. But it leaves me cold. Anyway, I can't change anything that's decided higher up."

Her last words throw light on the political indifference prevalent among women in Germany today. But we should not be hasty in concluding from this that the women's vote doesn't count for much. On the contrary, as long as daily life runs smoothly, the women tend to re-elect the incumbent. Thus they become the strongest supporters of conservatism. This was quite clear to those running the election propaganda of the CDU/CSU, and on the strength of it they coined the brilliant election slogan, "No experiments!"

"At the plant it's different," said Frau Schneider. "There I can see what's going on, and I know a few of the people in charge. There I do have a certain amount of influence."

"You'd go back to work even if you had children?" asked Dick.

"Of course. . . . Well, I don't know . . . if Richard was earning more . . . but right now there can't be any question of my stopping work."

The Schneider family income is about 1,000 marks monthly, of which Richard Schneider, bank employee, contributes approximately half. The amount just about pays expenses: rent 120 marks; light and heat 50 marks; household money (food, laundry, cleaning, etc.) 250 marks; acquisitions (they have just finished paying for their furniture; they still have four installments to pay on a record player, and are saving for a car) 120 marks; federal housing savings account 50 marks; employee insurance (medical care and old age insurance) 150 marks; clothing 40 marks; pocket money for Richard (lunch, newspapers, modest amusements) 60 marks; pocket money for Elizabeth (lunch, fares, hairdresser, cosmetics, lipstick for state occasions, eyebrow pencil, very little powder) 80 marks. . . .

Frau Schneider was going to tell us about their vacation budget when I drew her attention to the fact that she had accounted for their monthly income quite a while back.

"I know, but that's the way it is. We don't have enough to cover expenses, so we eat a little less, or we don't save anything—the car has already waited a long time. Sometimes I work overtime and that brings in extra money, but of course that's *my* money."

Should Elizabeth Schneider stop working, there would be drastic changes in her daily life; and any woman who is more or less content, shies away from drastic changes. A great deal would change for Frau Schneider not only because the money she earns would be lacking. The plant relieves her of quite a few worries. If she is ill, she goes to the plant doctor; if she is very ill, the plant arranges for her to stay in a sanatorium. In the canteen she not only eats a whole meal for what a plate of soup would cost in a restaurant, but she can buy anything from bananas to nightgowns considerably cheaper than anywhere else. The plant gives her a birthday present, and 500 marks at Christmas. It has a nursery school that would care for her children. She can spend her vacations in one of its holiday houses in the mountains or at the sea-shore, as she pleases. She works with many people who have the same worries as she, and know how to give good advice and aid. But above all, the plant is an established order in which she has a secure place and her chance "to get promoted." Rain or shine, more important than the weather is the "plant climate." Most big industries have a professional psychiatrist who has been hired to keep this plant climate at an even temperature.

9. THE RUHR: BETWEEN COAL AND GARDEN

Elizabeth Schneider of Velbert works in a model plant. Salaries in such a plant are not very high; sometimes they are even below average. Far more important are the "social benefits": the canteen where one can buy many necessities as cheaply as possible; nurseries, doctors, cheerful workrooms, Christmas bonuses and rest homes; a firm name one can mention with the pride with which so many natives of Essen say, "Krupp." All these things are worth a few marks less at the end of the month.

Of course less model plants exist, but as long as it remains difficult to get good skilled labor, the number of model plants increases steadily. In the Ruhr they are especially numerous because its big industries are rich and have to be exemplary. For, although it may hurt the feelings of five million people, there is no denying the fact that the Ruhr is not the prettiest part of Germany in the eyes of those who find a tree more beautiful than a smokestack, a meadow lovelier than a slag heap, or for whom the most modern steel-and-glass architecture is ugly. But one can't expect visual beauty from the largest industrial region in Europe.

Here 11 large cities harbor more than 3½ million people. To these must be added the smaller towns, among them Castrop-Rauxel and Marl, which have sprung up around large chemical works, and are on their way to passing the 100,000 mark. In the same class are Hagen and Wuppertal, on the outskirts of the Ruhr; and sociologically speak-ing even Düsseldorf, which is counting house and social center for this gigantic industrial area.

In the Ruhr itself—a monster metropolis, 100 kilometers long and 30 wide—there are really no more villages or true small towns. Every year 24,000 tons of dust fall on every one of its 11 big cities; 70,000 Bundesbahn freight cars are required to cart away the 1½ million tons of dust that sift down on the Ruhr yearly. The sun shines less over the Ruhr than elsewhere. So it is not surprising that we find more distiller-ies, breweries and taverns here than in any other part of Germany. You pass from foundries to slag heaps, from blast furnaces to workshops, from business to residential district, and in between, every now and then, there is a bit of green. One can't tell where the borderline between Duisburg and Oberhausen lies, where Essen stops and Bochum begins. The highway running between Unna and Duisburg, straight through this industrial area, is the most heavily traveled road in Germany; the contractors called it with pride, "the Ruhr Speedway" (Ruhrschnellweg). Irate drivers have renamed it "the Ruhr Crawlway" (Ruhrschleichweg).

This area exports more than half the coal for the nations belonging to the European Iron and Steel Community, and converts Swedish and Lorraine ore into more than one-third of their steel. Experience has taught us that steel production is more than just one industry among others; it is a fairly reliable measure for living standards. North-Rhine Westphalia is therefore the richest of the West German Länder. Here, once a month, a new millionaire is born, in spite of the fact that labor costs more here than in any other part of Germany.

It remains to be seen whether this development will continue as coal is displaced by atomic energy. But inventiveness has always been a strong factor in the Ruhr, and not always indigenous inventiveness. In the Ruhr, industry is wide open to outside influences; its people watch what their neighbors are doing and learn from them. The most important inventions for blending coal and iron ore into steel, and in the coke and coal-mining industries are English: coke ovens, Bessemer converters, the steam engine, the locomotive. When an overwhelming amount of scrap literally threatened to choke the life out of the steel industry and poison the essential water supply, that industry was on the verge of a crisis; but engineers found solutions, and with constantly diminishing scrap, made reality of the magic formula of economics: There is no such thing as waste.

Everything was utilized: the escape gases of the coke foundries were piped along a broad network to heat whole cities; fertilizers were produced from the residue of steel production; and once it had become possible to reduce the especially troublesome coal tar (in quantities sufficient to pave every road in Germany with asphalt once a year) to its hundreds of chemical parts, it didn't take the experts long to concoct something from these parts, i.e., to create synthetically such viable products as rubber, benzine, enamel, and other synthetic materials.

As for the waters of the Ruhr, the life elixir of this area, aptly named after its river—the Ruhr is cleaner than most German streams; much cleaner for instance than the Rhine, and it manages to provide this whole colossal area, this coal and steel world, with fresh water in spite of the fact that every one of its 5 million inhabitants requires approximately 300 liters daily, and that 20 tons are needed for the production of 1 ton of steel. A technical library could be filled with what the engineers of the science of water had to think up to achieve this.

Three major and highly complicated interferences with nature were necessary to save the Ruhr. So that it might live, another river had to die: the Emscher, flowing into the Rhine farther north, into which all poisonous sewage had to be channeled. So that the water of the Ruhr might not run out, it was stored: the river was rebuilt into a staircase of seven reservoirs. So that they might not be dependent on the sources of the Ruhr in Sauerland alone, the sewage had to be purified and channeled back into the Ruhr. A system of pipes and pumps was constructed in such a fashion that it would be technically possible to let the Ruhr run backward and uphill from its mouth at the Rhine to its source in Sauerland!

The coal deposits of the Ruhr are rich and far from exhausted. There is very little native iron ore, but it can be imported fairly cheaply from Lorraine and Sweden, since natural waterways have been augmented by the Mitteland Canal, the Rhine-Weser Canal, the Dortmund-Ems and Rhine-Herne canals.

But the Ruhr doesn't have steel alone to thank for its industrial power. It was helped to riches and fame by the insight that steel and its by-products had to be worked where installations and workers were available, and where energy was cheap.

10. THE GERMAN FACTORY WORKER DOESN'T STRIKE

We drove from Velbert to Duisburg to get to know the German factory worker. The Stadt Montan, where almost a third of Germany's steel production is concentrated, where every fourth man of the 500,-000 inhabitants lives by the iron or metal industry, seemed a promising territory.

There are at least four ways of looking at the German worker: (1) romantically, (2) statistically, (3) as a class member, (4) as an individual. It is necessary to draw this larger framework before we get to Jochen Warczinsky and his family in Duisburg.

The romantic vision of the worker is a relic of the early days of the industrial revolution: strong naked muscles under a layer of sweat-glistening soot; a little social misery limned decoratively in the background. If a few molders, formers, and firers didn't still exist, especially the miner underground and those irreplaceable smelters who tap the blast furnaces, reporters and photographers would be in despair. Even the assembly line, traditional symbol for the enslavement of mankind, is threatened by automation. In spite of all this, heavy industry is still the best setting for worker romanticism. It is a sober fact, however, that the physical strength exerted by the average worker in a modern factory is less than that expended by a hairdresser, and few industrial workers get as dirty in the course of their working day as the motorist who has to change a tire. Today's factories are comparatively clean and put horsepower before manpower whenever they can.

According to statistics, every second German is a male worker, a worker's child, a working woman, or a retired worker. At the beginning of the century, they worked 60 hours a week; in 1925, only 50; and finally, in 1953, 40 hours. Agricultural and nonunion workers are not included in this tabulation. According to the statisticians, therefore, in 1976, contractual working hours in industry will be 30 a week. An outgrowth of this is the justifiably controversial "free time," which, again, according to the statisticians, is 3 hours 4 minutes a day for to-day's worker. Employees and clerks have 3 minutes more; land laborers get only 1 hour and 33 minutes; professional men 2 hours 4 minutes.

The factory worker earns 60 to 250 marks weekly. The only thing that differentiates him from his white-collar brother is the fact that he is paid weekly, on Fridays, and that his social security differs from that of the white-collar worker. In many of the bigger industries, the traditional weekly wage has been replaced by a ten-day wage, but in any case, the skilled factory hand draws more pay than the clerk or minor office employee. However, since white-collar salaries fluctuate between 140 marks monthly (office help) and 15,000 marks monthly (managerial employees), comparisons are not very revealing.

Just as we no longer find powerful symbolic images in today's worker-world, we no longer find a clear-cut worker's class in modern society. In this respect the border between East and West makes less difference than one would think. A poet from Duisburg is as little to be envied as the workers' poet of Socialist realism. The symbols which poetry needs are lacking on both sides of the Iron Curtain. The poets of East Germany were able to adopt only one symbol from their Soviet Russian colleagues, the tractor, and rather significantly the tractor does not come to us from the factory world. Of course, compared with the middle class and the leaders of industry, the workers still form a recognizable group, but what makes them recognizable are ideas that coincide less and less with everyday reality.

There is, for instance, "uncertainty," the worker's traditional fear of unemployment. But during recent years, whenever a firm encountered difficulties, the factory and office workers were equally hard hit, and it transpired that the stronger protection which the office worker was supposed to enjoy was no longer valid except in cases where separate benefit contracts had been made. And then we have the low social status of the industrial worker in West Germany. Of a hundred work-ers interviewed, sixty said that it was of greater importance to them to be more highly respected than to make more money.

Of course there are worries, lifelong customs, platitudes, that still apply to many workers. But as a result of individual proficiency, an improvement of their lot is often just around the corner. The same situ-ation prevails as in the white-collar world: the chance of promotion. A big business-machine factory could turn all its blue-collar into white-collar workers overnight, the social situation is that fluid. But com-plications result from the fact that workers are treated differently by the federal social-security organizations; it is therefore only bureau-cratically difficult to make a white collar man of a worker.

Whenever the German worker is dissatisfied, he holds management responsible; or he abuses the administrative bureaucracy, and finally the government. In this he does not differ in any way from his white-collar brothers. In general though, statistics show that the worker is not dissatisfied. The customary demands for salary increases have led slowly but steadily to a rise in income, and have always been one step ahead of inflation. The discipline of the German workers, seen from England, France, or the United States, is still exemplary, and this is not only because the Germans were always disciplined—as long as they felt they were being watched. No other country in the Western world has had so little production loss because of strikes as Germany.

The forced-labor methods in East Germany, with their idealization of "the norm," are not very inspiring, but the many tears shed over the fact that the workers in East Germany can't strike are crocodile tears. Strikes were more often than not forbidden in all Germany, and they were never popular.

In 1959, West Germany lost 62,000 working days through strikes, as much as if 240 workers had done nothing for a year. In comparison England lost 5,251,000 working days in the same year, almost one hundred times as much; the United States and France lost even more than that.

There is no solid working class in Germany. Leaders of industry tend to meet any reasonable demands of the workers more than halfway, and strikes stand opposed to that general social prestige which is more important than money. The result is something that never ceases to astonish the Americans, English, and French: that the numerically large and seemingly powerful German unions, with their 6 million members, do not play a decisive role in the republic's political and economic life.

The first German unions were formed in 1848, in line with the first serious efforts on the part of the Germans to introduce democratic rule. But these beginnings of worker solidarity disappeared again as such things tend to disappear in Germany: they were forbidden. In 1863, Ferdinand Lassalle founded the *Allgemeine Deutsche Arbeiterverein*, or German Workers' Union, one of the germ cells of the future Social Democrat Party. But its development, too, was retarded, this time by Bismarck's Socialist laws. When they were abrogated in 1890, the unions for the first time had an opportunity to form a *Generalkommission*. In 1933, that was forbidden.

In the Soviet Occupation Zone, a Free German Workers' Union was formed in 1946. In 1949, a German Workers' Union, the DGB or *Deutscher Gewerkschaftsbund*, was formed in the three West Zones without any irritating stress on freedom. Seventy-four-year-old Hans Böckler, a great man, was its chairman. He had been a parliamentary deputy of the Socialist Party, yet he raised the political independence of his union to the ranks of a principle; and although the unions are naturally closer to the Socialist opposition than to the governing party, this principle has never been violated.

This peaceful and generally happy development in the Federal Republic of Germany would not have been possible if the unions had been opposed to government or management. But regardless of whether one is looking at German history from 1848 or across the present borders of East and West, it is fairly obvious that the less the unions participate in public life, the more questionable is that free play of power we call democracy. The strongest, the Anglo-Saxon democracies, have the strongest unions.

"Are you a union member?" Ralph asked crane operator Jochen Warczinsky, when we visited him in his three-room apartment in Duisburg, where he lives with his wife and two children, Ingrid, age seventeen, and Horst, age twelve.

"I should say not. Why should I be?"

Herr Warczinsky leaned back in his massive dark brown upholstered chair. There was a matching sofa and imitation Oriental rug. The whole apartment—the living room we were sitting in, an elegantly furnished bedroom, Inge's little room plastered with film-star photos, a cosy kitchen—was spotlessly clean and would have been perfectly adequate for a small clerk and his family at the turn of the century. In that it was obeying a sociological law of taste, apparently valid universally: people find beautiful what those socially above them found beautiful thirty years before.

Jochen Warczinsky went on to explain much of what I have already stated. His income and expenses showed a budget astonishingly similar to that of the white-collar Schneider family in Velbert. The main difference lay in the fact that the Warczinsky's have a little more money, 270 marks a week, of which he earns 130, his wife and daughter 140.

"Girls don't go very far here," Jochen Warczinsky said, "not factory girls."

It was the only time he implied in any way that he thought of himself and his family as workers.

"And what are your plans, Fräulein Ingrid?"

Embarrassed silence.

"Well"—her father helped her out—"someday somebody's going to have to marry her."

Have to? In a slightly coarse way, Ingrid was very pretty. Why "have to"?

The deeper meaning of the nonchalant way Jochen Warczinsky used the auxiliary verb became clear to me when I recalled a conversation of long ago with Mary Wilson, a London working girl. She told me that virtue was probably a good thing, but anyone like herself couldn't afford too much of it, or she'd never get into that half-dreaded, half-hoped-for condition in which a decent fellow would "have to" marry her. But perhaps Jochen Warczinsky didn't mean it that way. I recall that Ingrid didn't blush.

"The unions"—Jochen Warczinsky picked up our topic again—"were very important when we still had unemployment, when we were having a bad time, under the Weimar Republic. But today we have a good life. I don't know what more we could want. When I work, I'm paid well enough. . . . More money? Oh, yes . . . but what I'd rather have is more time. When I'm sick, I get paid. 'Sick leave pay,' they call it today. And when I'm sixty-five, I'll get a pension. Until then, I can improve my position. And we have lots of possibilities for promotion."

11. DOCTORS ARE NOT SAINTS

Jochen Warczinsky's family pays approximately one-fifth of its income to the *Allgemeine Ortskrankenkasse*, or Federal Medical Insurance plan. This, as is the case with 85 per cent of his fellow countrymen, provides him with free medical examination and when necessary, hospitalization, full-pay compensation at first, partial compensation later, and assistance in cases of birth or old age (after sixty-five).

The West German worker, as explained earlier, does not strike; or, let us say, he rarely strikes. But he goes in for a less obtrusive and more personal form of protest: he gets sick. And he does this sort of thing more often than his colleague in the East, where sickness is called sabotage; or in the Western world where the idea of shirking seems to bother people more. Out of 4 Germans, 3 go to the doctor every year.

"But when you travel through Germany," said Ralph, "you don't get the impression that so many people are sick."

Are we so sick?

Conservative circles say it's all the fault of social security, which encourages all forms of shirking. If only sickness still meant financial risk, and if only the responsibility for those who were sick fell on the healthy members of a family, things would be a lot better.

Perhaps.

The fact is, though, that the families which could shoulder such responsibilities, families with a grandmother, mother, children, and a male breadwinner don't exist any more. It's not their fault that they no longer exist, and there's no point in trying to bring them back with "if's" and "only's."

No, social security is not to blame; at least it can't be solely to blame, because the risk of getting sick is no greater in other countries than it is in Germany, and in some countries (England and France, for instance) it is less. Complaints that socialized medical care fosters malingering are international.

In Germany, two things must be added: we are really not as healthy as the French, the English, and the Americans. We have Hitler behind us, and that wasn't healthy for quite a lot of us. The six war years didn't help either. They were followed, for the inhabitants of the big cities especially, by an era of general German hunger and cold (1945–1948) and we are probably still suffering from that. And finally, the wild chase after good fortune: catch as catch can, the devil take the hindmost; use your elbows; work overtime; work day and night; get along in the world and make a name for yourself; he who stops, rusts. . . . One can't live like that for any length of time without sacrificing physical and emotional strength.

According to a survey, only half of those asked to describe their general health replied that it was good, or excellent. Even among those under thirty, there were many (one-fifth) who said they didn't feel well. As was to be expected, health conditions deteriorated with age; in this respect city and country showed little difference. The best report came from career women under forty-five. More than a quarter of them declared that their general health was very good. Of the housewives in the same age group, only every 7th one gave the same answer; and out of those over forty-five, only every 33rd. Those who answered that their health was poor were: field workers, 15 per cent; farmers, 10 per cent; laborers, 10 per cent; clerks, 8 per cent; professional people, 8 per cent; office workers, 5 per cent; yet 60 per cent of all Germans swallow pills! In two weeks, 26 out of a hundred Germans take something for headaches, 18 for colds, 15 for poor circulation, 14 for indigestion, 9 for insomnia, 8 for stomach and gall-bladder conditions, 7 for rheumatism, 4 for toothache, 2 for overweight. To which should be added a specific sort of worry over health which is cultivated nowhere else as it is in Germany. At best it can be compared to the passion for cleanliness found in the United States.

As children we longed to eat just once something that *tasted* good. What our parents and grandparents served us was always dished out with the admonition that it was good for us. Eat more fish and stay healthy. Eat fresh fruit and be strong. Whenever an advertisement can convince people that what they are promoting is healthy, they've scored a hit. Health-food shops and restaurants, fruit juices, and filter cigarettes started on their triumphant world tour from Germany. Anyone with any self-respect whatsoever doesn't go on a vacation; he takes a cure. Various institutions dedicated to health flourish: sanatoriums, Kurhotels, mud baths, massage emporiums, Kneipp baths (hydropathic establishments named after the German parson, Kneipp, who founded the first one at Bad Wörishofen in Bavaria). Indulge in more sport, and you'll be healthy. Even those who know no Latin, know *mens sana in corpore sano*. And an American friend of mine, who spent the postwar years over here in the Army of Occupation, when referring to the seducibility of German girls, said, "All you have to do is tell them it's healthy."

It is the doctors who have to bear the brunt of all this. Except for university professors, no other profession in Germany is more highly respected, and none is so *überfordert*, or "over-demanded," a very fashionable expression in Germany today. The average life span of German doctors is a lot lower than, for instance, that of clergymen. According to statistics, there is one doctor for every 800 West Germans. Compared with other countries, this doesn't seem too low, but for us, with our damaged health and our complex about it, it isn't adequate. As a result of the superhuman demands made on our doctors, this highly individualistic and most humane of all professions suddenly developed 'professional interests' and created a *Standesinteressen-Vertreter-Organisation*, or a Professional Interests Representation Association, the duties of which were foreign to everything humane.

To give one example: a well-known journalist wrote a story about a doctor who, like many of his colleagues, collected all the sick slips from the families of the workers who were his patients. He also collected the payment that went with them, 10 to 15 marks per slip, regardless of whether anyone in the family had been ill or not. The journalist was promptly sued for libel by the president of the German Medical Association!

"Well, and how do things really work out with these sick slips?" I asked a doctor living in a small town. I can't repeat what he told me or I'd be hauled into court for libel myself. Instead I'll describe this doctor's life for you.

He gets up in the morning at seven-thirty, and a half hour later is on his rounds. From nine to eleven, he has office hours; the last patient often doesn't leave until twelve-thirty. His midday break usually doesn't allow time for further calls he has to make, much less for lunch. From three to five he has office hours again. It is always six, sometimes seven, before the last patient leaves, and his office is in order again, his paper work done. "Actually, during the week all I can do is jot things down; the rest has to wait for Sunday." An evening entirely free of patients is a rarity, and at least three times during the week he is called at night—unexpected complications, a premature birth, a car accident.

Fifteen working hours a day, sometimes more. Let's take for granted that all of his patients have government medical insurance, which they have in nine cases out of ten, and that all of them are really sick, in which case we can fairly concede 150 minutes per patient for diagnosis, house calls (often involving a lengthy trip), ambulatory care, and the necessary paper work—all over a period of possibly several weeks.

Formerly, when the doctor used to come, he stayed an hour; when someone was dying, he stayed the night. But that's a thing of the past. No doctor can afford a family visit and a cup of tea any more. People don't die at home, but in hospitals. Just the same, 150 minutes to cure somebody who is sick may still be accepted as an average case.

This being so, Dr. Dahn (let's call him that) could take care of 390 patients and account for 390 medical slips. Calculating an average of 12.50 marks per slip, we get a monthly average gross income of 1,625 marks, from which he has to pay rent, light, heat, instruments (X-ray machines run as high as 20,000 marks, a simple heat ray therapy lamp, 500 marks), office help (with tax and insurance, not to be had under 500 marks), and a car, which is of course indispensable. But I had stopped calculating, because my friends had already grasped that in the end little more than 300 marks would be left.

"But, Doctor, that's impossible!" Ralph said.

"Of course it's impossible," said Dr. Dahn, "if I had only three hundred and ninety patients every quarter."

"So how many do you have?"

Dr. Dahn pursed his lips and looked up at the ceiling. "Well, let's say five times as many. And you can quote me on that," he said, turning to me, "because there's nothing unusual about a doctor's charging for two thousand medical slips every quarter. You can check that at the local medical insurance office if you like."

Two thousand a quarter makes eight thousand a year. According to the statistics, a doctor in West Germany has 800 patients?

"I suppose I shouldn't accept a slip if all I've done is prescribe a few pills," said Dr. Dahn, "because the three minutes it took to do that are obviously not worth 12.50 marks. But only by doing so can I take some sort of care of those who really need it. I'm a doctor, not a saint. And unfortunately I have hardly any private patients."

Private patients are those who are left over when you subtract 85 government insured patients from every hundred Germans. A doctor charges them for one visit about as much as he gets from a government insured patient in three months, often a lot more. Some people pay this out of their own pockets; others carry some sort of private insurance which refunds on the average of 65 per cent of the patient's expenses. This doesn't always work out too well. To illustrate: A man whom we shall call Meyer was on his vacation, when he came down with a rather unpleasant rash. He went to the resort doctor, and for 30 marks got a wrong diagnosis and was advised to consult a specialist. Meyer paid without rancor; the resort doctor had done what he could. Meyer's private insurance paid *two-thirds* of the doctor's fee.

Meyer got home, and since the rash showed no signs of disappearing, he went to a specialist. The examination lasted five minutes. The specialist diagnosed a dreadful disease and the necessity for six months of treatment, "If you're lucky . . ." Meyer was to come back the following week.

Now as luck would have it—but the specialist couldn't know this—Meyer had studied medicine in his youth, not enough to know for sure, but sufficiently to sense that his symptoms didn't indicate the dread disease. He did what he should have done first: called up a friend of his who was a doctor and asked for the name of a reliable specialist, went to him, was examined thoroughly, paid (happily) 104 marks, and was glad to find out that he had been right: the rash was harmless. However, toward this specialist's fee, his insurance paid 25 marks, or only *one-quarter*.

Politely but not very cordially, Meyer wrote to specialist No. 1 that he would not be coming in for the treatments because he didn't have the disease. A few days later he got the man's bill: 20 marks (for a wrong diagnosis? Shameless! thought Meyer).

Meyer was a businessman and realized that one had to pay for one's mistakes, but that somebody should be rewarded for making a mistake was something else again. Surely, he decided, his insurance company, being equally businesslike, would be glad that he had spared them their share of the expense for six months treatment of a non-existing ailment (which might have run to as much as 26 times 20 marks) so he wrote them a letter, informing them that he didn't even feel like paying his share of the 20 marks for a diagnosis that had caused him nothing but vexation and would have burdened them quite unnecessarily.

After an appropriate lapse of time, he got a letter. Someone with an illegible signature informed him that the insurance company had no right to interefere in the confidential relationship between doctor and patient. Herr Meyer could file a complaint, if he liked, with the Medical Association. But they wished to call his attention to the fact that beside the word diagnosis were the letters 'z.B.' *zur Beobachtung*, for observation (Oho! thought Meyer, at 20 marks a weekly visit!), the doctor therefore could not be pinned down to his diagnosis. And this professional solidarity was upheld by an insurance firm that had been perfectly willing to pay two-thirds of the cost of a wrong diagnosis, but had come forward with only a quarter payment for the expert examination that had led to the correct one!

So Herr Meyer paid the last bill, too, and decided he'd rather be a little poorer than more seriously ill. He was no saint either, and he wasn't going to demand saintliness from anybody else on this sinful earth, not from doctors or from insurance companies. The officers of the German Medical Association might, of course, hold a different opinion. . . .

12. WE MUST HAVE LAW AND ORDER

The latest German fairy tale runs as follows:

Once upon a time there was a man named Heinrich Meier. He lived in a small town in the province of Westphalia, and since he was an admirer of law and order and the powers that enforced it, he became a policeman. He was an officer with a strong sense of duty, and in his private life, a devoted family man. Suddenly a terrible disease broke out in the little town in the province of Westphalia, as it did in all Germany. The name of the disease was National Socialism. Heinrich Meier caught it, as did many of his compatriots, and since it was his job to see to it that there was law and order, he had a rather worse case of it than some of the others. And there was law and order throughout the entire epidemic, no doubt about that!

So it came to pass that Heinrich Meier, like so many other policemen at the time, became attached to an organization called the SD (*Sicherheitsdienst*, or Security Service)—he didn't have much choice—and in this capacity he saw to it that there was law and order not in the little Westphalian town, but in the "eastern territories" where the disorder was very great and it was not always possible to avoid drastic measures. They say that a few disturbers of the peace were shot while trying to flee. . . . Fortunately, however, all this lies far back and can no longer be proved with any exactitude.

By 1945, the disease had spent itself. Heinrich Meier was able to convince the new authorities that he had not joined the SD of his own free will, and was therefore given the choice of again becoming a member of the police force, or of the Security Service. But he wanted no part of the latter, even though it now had a different and less sinister-sounding name, and was guaranteed to be a democratic organization. Heinrich Meier preferred to become a member of the regular police force of the newly formed western Land: North-Rhine Westphalia. Most of the unpleasant events connected with the years 1933 to 1945, which had been unavoidable, fell from him like ashes from a phoenix. Now he is Obermeister, or chief inspector, a good democrat, an officer with a strong sense of duty, and in his private life, a devoted family man.

The fairy-tale quality in this almost-true story is provided by the gentle light of such phrases as "see to it that there is law and order," or "shot while trying to flee"; the blissful forgetting of all disorderly corpses, and the complacent but nonsensical interpretation of National Socialism as a scourge from some metaphysical world that was visited upon the German people.

"When you converse with Germans," I. F. Stone reported to his countrymen after a trip through Germany, "you get the impression that there are still many among them who are capable, in an officious bureaucratic way, of perpetrating the most cruel crimes. When they come home, they take off their uniforms and are good husbands and fathers. 'Duty' is a word that plays an important part in the German's idealized idea of himself. . . . Two hundred years ago, Madame de Staël, who admired the Germans, made fun of the discrepancy between their bold philosophy and their political submissiveness. Even then she noticed that they obeyed their superiors *comme si tout ordre était un devoir*, 'as if every order were a duty.' "

Madame de Staël understood the philosophy of German idealism very well, but she knew too little about the intellectual father of this philosophy, the most German of all philosophers, Immanuel Kant, who wrote: "The characteristics of a child must include, above all, obedience. This obedience may be obtained by force—then it is absolute; or by confidence—then it is voluntary. The latter is important, but the former is an absolute necessity, because it prepares the child for adherence to the laws he will have to obey as a future citizen, whether he likes them or not."

All you have to do after that, is eliminate the supreme court of moral law, and you arrive at Heinrich Meier, and the minor German official, Prussian in character, who—let's not fool ourselves—might again be a reliable, obedient, and dutiful servant to any new leader who came along with fresh plans for world salvation.

With Kant, moral law is already an abstract conception. We find very little concrete opposition to its elimination. And we hear the same overtones through the centuries: "Obey your superiors, and let others quarrel about them."—Matthias Claudius.

"When Paul said, 'Obey the authorities for they are appointed by God,' he gave expression to a monstrous tradition that probably could not be established except under Christian rule."—Goethe.

"Obedience and labor are the two mainstays of human society."—German poet, Leopold Schefer.

"The development of a man with character is inconceivable without an education in obedience."—Friedrich Adolf Wilhelm Diesterweg, one of the most influential German pedagogues.

"If reasons are given, I don't know how you can call it obedience."—Guiding principle of member of the board of education and parliament, Lorenz Kellner, who was renowned as a nineteenth-century Catholic "spiritual pedagogue."

"There is a strong mixture of Slavic and Teutonic elements in the Prussians, which is one of the main sources of their political usefulness. They have inherited some of the submissiveness of the Slavs combined with the virility of the Teutons."—Bismarck.

"Today, when no one really believes any more in the grace-of-Godness of the ruling class, their former pre-eminence is expressed all the more strongly in external manifestations, because appearances have their effect on the heart."—Hermann Graf von Keyserling in his *Diary of a Philosopher*.

"The Germans are too obsequious, and adhere too closely to the letter of the law."—Stalin, to Roosevelt and Churchill.

"The German family and the German schools are more authoritarian than equivalent institutions in other countries; German respect for force, titles, and function is more automatic . . . the German laborer is more servile; the German philosophy is less intelligible . . . the German attachment to liberty is less deep."—*Life* magazine article, May 10, 1954, for which Chancellor Adenauer wrote the foreword.

"I find this excess of exterior and lack of inner discipline a little frightening. As long as it is only a question of traffic laws, it is at best ridiculous and does no harm. But if someone were to come along and use this fear of the authorities for other purposes, the results could be dangerous."—Peter Grubbe, for years English correspondent for the German daily, *The World*, on his return to West Germany.

Let every man interpret these quotations in his own way. The six of us discussed them heatedly and in the end were agreed on one thing: that we had arrived at one of the points where the secret of "the Germans" could be found, the reason for their extraordinary successes and miserable defeats; for much of the reliance they inspire, and for the hatred and scorn that is rarely directed against them individually but again and again collectively.

But isn't Kant supposed to be admirable? Isn't Goethe right? Would unconditional disobedience be preferable to unconditional obedience? And now I got a surprise. To the last question, my five friends answered "yes." Of course my alternative was wrong, since it left no room for the power which is the source of all free communities: conditional obedience.

The famous-notorious quote from Paul's Epistle to the Romans, 13,1: "Let everyone be subject to the higher authorities, for there exists no authority except from God, and those who exist have been appointed by God," has created frightful confusion in Germany—even among its theologians—in the last four hundred years. Perhaps every German Bible should add a note: "No one is forced—on the contrary, it is forbidden him—to obey prince or master, or to keep an oath to the damnation of his soul—that being against God and right."—Martin Luther.

Whoever could get a law passed describing under what conditions a law was *not* to be obeyed would be benefiting the German nation because only a law could protect these most faithful-to-the-law citizens from the edicts of their authorities.

Every group, every nation, has to demand that individuals give up part of their individual will to the collective will. *Where is this demand to halt?*

I see three possible barriers: faith—religious or Kantian philosophical —in a moral law above all human laws. Apathy, as a human protest against the inhuman abstractions of the letter of the law. Common sense, as long as it sees in individual man the reason for all human order, and desires to protect him. But . . .

We have just as little obligatory faith in West Germany as anywhere else, and the diminution of Christian faith has left a vacuum which has not been filled, as in England, with a humanitarian agnosticism. As for apathy—an indifference that would suffice, let us say, to ignore the whole Iron Curtain—it has to be eliminated as a totally un-German concept. All we have left, then, is common sense, and I can see no reason why common sense should not one day be restored in Germany. You may see promising beginnings toward that end everywhere. Why shouldn't they one day unite and create an "informed public opinion" to stand guard so that no government and no office would ever dare abuse the beautiful belief in the *positive* values of obedience. Ah me, yes—why not?

Obermeister Heinrich Meier, a little astonished and quite honored, received his six guests from six different nations—an impressive group— in his spotlessly clean three-room apartment complete with bathroom, television set, spotlessly clean wife, and three immaculate children. He was a big man, but he appeared smaller than his visitors. There were three armchairs in the living room, and one sofa. He had chairs brought in from the dining room.

Dick, on his best behavior, inquired about the children, then about Meier's chances of promotion, with which he immediately conquered host and hostess. They were proud of their children and worried about the future, as people are the world over.

"Anyway," Heinrich Meier concluded his report, "they're not delinquents. They obey, and that's the main thing."

"The main thing?"

"Yes. *Ordnung muss sein*," for which classic German cliché there is significantly no English equivalent. "We must have law and order," is what Meier was implying.

It came as a bit of a shock. There he sat, in a gray flannel suit, but he sounded as if he had just clicked his heels.

Promotion turned out to be a rather unsatisfactory theme. *Obermeister* was apparently something of a dead end for policemen as far as promotion was concerned.

"This is such a pleasant little town," said Dick. "I don't suppose you have much trouble."

"Law and order are threatened," Heinrich Meier declared politely and precisely, "by our juvenile delinquents, Communists, and drivers."

He went on to suggest that all juvenile delinquents be drafted, the death sentence be re-enacted for Communists, and much sterner measures be adopted for drivers. "There was a fellow the other day," he explained, "who came up to me and asked me how to get to the expressway. He'd been drinking. I could smell it at once. I took him straight to the station."

"I beg your pardon," said Dick. "The man asked you for directions, and you took him to the police station?"

"Naturally. It was my duty. I gave him an alcohol test. Of course, positive. So I sent for the doctor . . . blood test . . ."

"I see," said Dick. "You did your duty. But tell me something: are you supposed to haul as many people as you can into court?"

"A policeman who does his duty," said Heinrich Meier, "and does it with the necessary zeal, will always come across disorderly conduct that has to be reported."

Now it was my turn. "I've heard something about a point system whereby the policeman who brings in the most reports may hope for a reward: bonuses, promotion."

"I don't know anything about that," said Heinrich Meier loftily. "But we have to put up with a lot, too. Now, as I was going to say, about this drunken fellow——"

"Who asked you where the expressway was," said Dick helpfully.

"Yes. Now they tell me the case has been dropped."

"Why?"

"The test showed only 0.7. That's not enough."

"The man was on his way somewhere, I guess."

"Yes."

"So how did he continue his journey?"

"By train, of course. You don't suppose we'd let a man like that——"

"But then you're going to have to pay him damages," said Dick, "since he was evidently innocent."

"That's all we need!"

Heinrich Meier was right. No one he reports can claim damages for time lost, bodily injury, or any inconvenience, even if the case is dropped for lack of sufficient evidence. If, on the other hand, the man reported is influential, it could be embarrassing for Meier. Fortunately not many influential men pass through the little town in North-Rhine Westphalia. . . .

13. THE CREDO OF A STUDIENRAT

Dick was upset. Until now he had praised the German police as models of politeness and circumspection. We had had the few brushes with the law which are unavoidable on a long car trip, but as soon as Dick was recognized as an American, everyone was all smiles and ready to be helpful. Now, on our way back to the hotel, he exploded. "Good heavens, what difference does it make if they call it a monarchy, a democracy, or anarchy? With a police system like that, it's always going to be a police state."

I tried to calm him down. Things were actually much improved, I assured him. We have quite a few model, polite, restrained policemen, completely free from all duty-mania. In fact, in my opinion, they are in the majority. The police have their problems, too, beginning with the difficulty in recruiting men for such a strenuous and poorly paid profession; more difficult than it used to be because today the police force has to compete with the army for its recruits.

Policemen are civil servants and like to be considered as such. Perhaps they are not typical civil servants, because every now and then they have to carry out unpleasant duties against peaceful citizens, which doesn't help to make them more popular. Of course very few have enjoyed a higher education, nor are there many in high social positions. Civil servants of this sort are to be found almost exclusively in the department of education, and while we are considering what part obedience plays in Germany's everyday life, it's only fair to take a look at them, too.

The basis of all German officialdom is obedience to one's employer (meaning the state) and the right to be taken care of by this employer quite naturally goes with it. When an otherwise complicated relationship is simplified to such a degree, it is easy to understand why it should become a model for other working relationships as well, in the realm of laborer and office worker, for instance, and in a so-called free economy. What the entrepreneur offers is security; what he demands is reliable service. In this give and take between obedience in work on the one hand and guaranteed social security on the other, we never hear the word that is so popular in our public vocabulary: freedom.

"Let's face it," said Ralph; "where everything depends on achievement and security, any kind of freedom can only be a deterrent."

During the rise of German bureaucracy in the eighteenth century, and especially in Prussia in the nineteenth century, things were clear and unequivocal. The civil servant swore to serve his provincial lord "humbly, loyally, obediently." In 1933, it was not difficult for the Führer to step into the position of this provincial lord, a place that had remained vacant for fifteen years. The National Socialists were therefore able to call the measures by which they took over an entire professional category, boldly and with little opposition, "a law to restore the professional civil service."

In the Federal Republic, the Länder provide various rights for their civil servants, but all of them are based on obedience and security. In the other German Lands, belonging to that part of Germany which we are not supposed to recognize but which exists nevertheless, the German Democratic Republic, the rights of the civil servant have been abrogated as "typically capitalistic." Of course there are civil servants even in East Germany, the difference being that the greatest possible political restraint is *not* demanded of them; on the contrary, as in the former National Socialist state, they are expected to reaffirm constantly their faith in a one-party system. The civil servant in East Germany is called a "co-worker in the state administrative system." As in the days of the Kaiser, and as in the Federal Republic, he has his own disciplinary rights, is duty bound to be loyally submissive, may be fired only if he has stolen the proverbial silver spoon or made himself unpopular politically, *i.e.*, hasn't shown enough humility. As in the days of the Kaiser and in the Federal Republic, he gets compensation via state aid, petty favors, and privileges, and all sorts of public recognition for sacrificial services that enrich no one.

"But what sort of freedom *does* the civil servant have?" Ralph wanted to know.

We were at the next stop of our journey, in one of the larger cities of North-Rhine Westphalia, and we were to be the guests of a high-school teacher, a *Studienrat*, to give him his title.

The whole thing started off rather amusingly. I had asked Dr. Beyer a few days before to invite the superintendent of his school to join us because we wanted to discuss the German educational system; surely the superintendent would have plenty to contribute. Our telephone conversation had run along these lines:

DR. BEYER: "I'd rather not."

LEONHARDT: "But I've heard he's very nice."

DR. BEYER: "Yes, yes, but . . ."

LEONHARDT: "Have you had trouble with him?"

DR. BEYER: "Of course not!"

LEONHARDT: "Should I ask him? I've met him once."

DR. BEYER: "No, no!"

LEONHARDT: "Mr. O'Connor could invite him. He's American. That always goes over big."

DR. BEYER: "That's not the point. It just isn't done. I can't invite the superintendent to my house, and nobody else can either. That would be even worse."

I was unable to steer my foreign friends' mixture of amusement and dismay over this attitude into those reasonable channels where resentment and prejudice may be allowed more or less to dissipate themselves. Authority-free Ralph's question, "But what sort of freedom does a civil servant have?" could therefore also be applied to Dr. Beyer.

"He has lots of freedom," said Beyer. "In fact, he is committed to our democratic Basic Law."

"But what sort of democratic order is that," Dick wanted to know, "which forbids you to invite your boss to your house?"

"That isn't a question of democratic order," said Beyer, "but of tact."

"What on earth does tact have to do with it?" asked Yvonne, who was accustomed to letting herself be invited only by the people she wanted to be invited by. "Would he invite you to his house?"

"Why should he?" said Beyer. "We see enough of each other in school."

But Ralph was persistent. "I don't know . . . where I come from nobody's committed to unconditional obedience to any liberal Basic Law. Altogether, we don't talk so much about freedom; perhaps that's why we still have quite a lot of it."

"Don't you get the impression, too," asked Dick, addressing Ralph, "that people talk most about what they have least of?"

"Of course. Poor people talk about money."

"And men talk about love," said Yvonne.

"And the whole world talks about peace." With which this topic came to an abrupt end.

Meanwhile the two Beyer children were demonstrating what freedom could mean—a six-year-old boy and a three-year-old girl, absolutely undismayed by rank or honors of those present. They included in their wild games the living room in which we were sitting; in one door, out the other. They had a lot to say and they said it loudly, to us, to each other, without ever using the word freedom. . . .

Frau Dr. Beyer—not only her husband's mate but also his colleague—apologized for the disorderly behavior of her progeny.

"Please don't," said Ralph. "I'm so glad to see that a lot of German homes have apparently ceased to be the drilling ground for children that I remember with horror from former visits. When they get to school, there'll be an end to their freedom anyway. . . . I'm sorry"—he turned to Dr. Beyer—"I wasn't referring to you. I know you are committed to a liberal Basic Law, but I can't find anyone who can explain to me just what that means."

To which Dr. Beyer replied, "I think you will understand my inhibitions in talking to an Englishman, of all people, about freedom, but that's not all there is to it. I, too, have to listen to too much talk about freedom. And what's worse, I have to read sophomoric compositions on it, with all the dreadful phraseology and clichés of which the German language seems to have a vaster store than any other.

"My freedom begins in the morning with that famous freedom that still guarantees (since I am not a Communist) that if the doorbell rings before seven o'clock, it is only the milkman or a telegram. And whoever has had experience to the contrary, knows what that means and will do everything in his power to preserve this state of affairs. At seven I am so unfree as to have to get up, although I don't want to. Punctually at eight—again most unfree—I have to be in school. Punctuality is one of the charms of a civil servant. Besides, it would complicate the study plan considerably if everyone were to arrive when he felt like it. Then I am entirely free again to tell my pupils in German or English what I consider right. We do have a so-called class goal, but it isn't too narrowly defined, and it's up to me to reach it in any way I see fit.

"I don't want to exaggerate. It would not be advisable, for instance, for me to take up Apitz and Strittmatter in my German class. These are two leading writers from 'over there.' Nor would it be wise if I were to say a few friendly words in praise of the Soviet Zone. And I'm pretty sure it wouldn't work out at all well, in the long run, if I were to read 'Hitler Youth Quex' by Schenzinger in one of my classes, and follow it up with a justification of Hitler's Reich. It is fortunate, therefore, that I don't look upon any of these prohibitions as a curtailment of my freedom. Similarly, I can't take a stand of my own against church or religion in this town, which is predominantly Catholic. Of course, any atheistic colleague of mine may consider this as ominous interference with his freedom, but I feel you've got to grant the children's parents the freedom not to want their children's faith violated in the schools.

"In my senior class, I have read Ernst Jünger and Bert Brecht, with no worse consequences than having one of the members of the Board of Education ask me, in the case of Brecht, whether I felt it was necessary. It's quite possible that some of my colleagues think Brecht (rather than Jünger) could get them into trouble, and that they therefore restrain themselves more than is necessary. Who can tell? After all, there are plenty of good reasons for leaving Brecht out of the school curriculum, but to forego Brecht entirely seems to me more honest than to evade the issue by choosing one of his less controversial works so as to spare oneself the discussion of how a man like Brecht could be a Communist. . . .

"After school, the only things encroaching on my freedom are those I brought upon myself when I chose to be a teacher and decided to have a family: papers to correct, study plans to prepare, interviews with parents, screaming children (my own) . . . things like that.

"Briefly, I lead the life of a more or less free man, at any rate a life which has fulfilled more promise than I could have hoped for in 1940 or 1945. I think the government in Bonn is more often right than wrong, and I see no reason for making things more difficult for it. Don't hesitate to look upon me as a strange example of a species which you may feel is condemned to die out, or is perhaps already extinct— a human being who is free, content, and quite often happy within the framework of what is possible." And with the word "happy," I thought I saw him glance at his wife and children, or perhaps I just imagined it.

"All that sounds very idyllic," said Ralph, who had grown a bit impatient, "but it's not enough. It sounds—please forgive me, but I can't find a better word—it sounds a little too complacent."

"What Stevens means," said Dick, "is that in your school everything seems to be in good order; in your family everything seems to be in good order; but what are you doing personally toward seeing that everything in your country is in good order?"

We left Studienrat Beyer owing us an answer to this. He might have pointed out that a country was pretty well off even if nothing but its schools and families were in good order. . . .

14. WE ARE LEARNING NOT FOR SCHOOL BUT FOR LIFE

"Germany is the land of the schoolmaster," wrote James B. Conant, scholar, president of Harvard University, High Commissioner and first postwar ambassador to Germany, a man therefore whose intellectual judgment is irrefutable, and whose attitude toward Germany has always been benevolently unbiased.

"The lowering of teacher prestige is catastrophic," wrote Helmut Becker, one of Germany's leading pedagogues. His father was the famous Prussian Minister for Culture, Becker.

Thus two competent people make their own observations without coming to the same conclusion. One man has it that a certain type determines the character of a nation, the other that the same type's prestige has suffered catastrophically.

To what extent is Germany a nation of schoolmasters? Is this supposed to mean that it is a country of birch rod-obedience? True, the tradition of the Prussian corporal who actually beat the rudiments of learning into a fearful group of children still lies in our speech and blood. But today we no longer enforce obedience by such primitive methods. Certainly not in the schools. On the contrary, a teacher can be hauled into court for administering a box on the ears, however well deserved. Or is the "nation of schoolmasters" supposed to mean what German soldiers of World War II summed up bitterly in the words, "This war can't end until the last elementary schoolteacher has been made an officer," which was intended as criticism of the ascendancy of a type? This type was ostentatiously diligent and semi-educated, had little judgment and many prejudices, wore glasses; bowed low when he was looking up and stepped hard when he was looking down; couldn't see himself as anything but a dictator in a small Reich, whether this Reich happened to be his family, his class in school, his office; a type which has certainly achieved some prominence in Germany, but which is surely too narrowly described as schoolmaster or teacher. The same type is to be found in every profession, but in the schools, although still present, it is undoubtedly on its way out. This type distinguishes himself in that he functions, and is therefore best described as a "functionary."

Germany is a nation of school reformers, and school reform. Yet according to Helmut Becker, the prestige of the teacher has suffered. How are we to reconcile this?

The prestige of all civil servants has suffered since World War II. When Germany was to be restored, there were two alternatives: either to leave in their positions those who had always been civil servants, and—something that was quite unjustly overlooked—who had preserved a "civil servant ethos" throughout the Third Reich; or to put in their place people who would normally not have become civil servants. One choice was as controversial as the other.

A nation's reservoir of talent for specific professions is limited. That is why, in 1945, people were given civil-service jobs who were not suited for them, people who were not prepared to pay for their civil-service rights the price of loyalty, restraint, and reliability, but who thought worth striving for other things than prestige and security —above all, power and wealth. Wherever these were not to be found in the line of duty, devious ways became enticing. Some succumbed to bribery; quite a few didn't get away with it.

The public heard about it through a long sequence of bribery cases. Apparently the average citizen is willing to grant a civil servant the advantages he enjoys only as long as he can believe such advantages are justified by self-denial. Thus, a civil servant who can be bribed is, in Germany, the object of the most merciless scorn. A survey asked "a representative cross-section" of the German people: "Do you think that, generally speaking, the German civil servant cannot be suborned or corrupted?" The cautious formulation of the question betrays the hope that the answer will not be too derogatory, otherwise it might have read: "Do you think we have corrupt civil servants?" Anyway, if there was such a wish behind the question, it was cruelly denied. Only 35 per cent of those questioned felt that the German civil servant was incorruptible. Especially sceptical were the men: 33 per cent decided for incorruptibility. More confidence was shown by the women: 37 per cent, and by government and party members: 44 per cent. Civil servants came up, rather naturally, with 60 per cent. Just the same—25 per cent of the civil servants considered the civil servant corruptible, the remaining 15 per cent held no opinion. And that is shocking. To grasp just how shocking it is, you must perhaps be a German with a shot of Prussian, and still fairly closely linked to an earlier generation. If my grandfather were not dead, the results of this survey might have killed him. But as I remember the gay old gentleman, he would simply have preferred not to believe it.

The reputation of the civil servant is obviously not what it used to be, yet the image of the civil servant has become more and more the model for all working relationships. The trouble is that such things are more difficult to categorize than they would seem, and whoever is writing about them really should apologize to his reader on every second page for the fact that such complicated matters can only be treated abstractly (academically) or in a simplified fashion (journalistically). I happen to be a journalist.

I don't think it is quite right to call Germany a nation of schoolmasters. However, if we talked about a "nation of frustrated schoolmasters," we might come closer to the truth. Foreigners, for instance, have noticed that German drivers seem absorbed primarily with teaching the other fellow how to drive, and there are quite a few teachers who say a lot of people think they know how to teach better than the instructors. I don't believe it is quite right either to say that the teacher's prestige has sunk catastrophically; personally, I don't think it was ever quite so high.

Household tutors and governesses—the predecessors of today's teachers—were considered members of the staff and did not eat with their employers. All were pitifully poor; often they had to perform other duties as well, such as ring bells and wash linen. If they weren't in the service of the aristocracy, then they were in the service of the church, and rated far below the minister. Until the middle of the nineteenth century, they were called "school servants." But when Prussia started filling these posts with retired army men, the school *servant* became a school *master*, and a man who had been trodden underfoot for a long time became a formidable treader underfoot. That gave his reputation quite a boost.

Studienrat Dr. Beyer, though, was more inclined to trace his intellectual origin back to the doctors and schoolmasters of the universities. Both ancestries run together since, under Humboldt, the profession of a state-licensed high-school teacher was created in Prussia, which raised him to the rank of an academic man. The two seem to coincide in such general expressions as "school" and "teacher," and in the public educational system where all teachers may be lumped together under the heading of "civil servants concerned with the profession of educating." But such abstractions are deceiving. In a modern army less separates the private from the general than the lowest member of the teaching profession from his top-ranking superior. At every level, the differences in status are embarrassingly stressed. The *Mittelschule*, or polytechnical school, had barely been created when the teacher employed there was no longer satisfied with being just a plain teacher, but proceeded to call himself *Mittelschul*teacher.

All efforts to bring about a change in these ridiculously sad conditions have so far been unavailing. Efforts were made in several of the German Länder to fill the gap between *Gelehrtenschule*—a higher high school intended for the education of future scholars—and the university by granting teachers in the former the coveted title of professor. This resulted in instructors in the latter calling themselves *Universitätsprofessoren*. A few of the Länder tried to fill the abyss between elementary-school teachers and those at schools of higher learning by demanding a university education from the former as well. But what was the use? After passing the necessary examinations, only the instructor at a school of higher learning may call himself *Studienrat*, or Study Councillor. The SPD governments of Hamburg and Berlin actually succeeded in equalizing the designations between elementary school and high school; suddenly all schools (as in East Germany and, *mutatis mutandis*, in England) were called *Oberschulen* or Upper Schools, and classes were neatly numbered from 1 up to 13. To no avail. The difference between "teacher" and *Studienrat* stood firm!

So the teacher whose prestige might have suffered doesn't exist. The reputation of the university professor has risen, if anything; that of the elementary-school teacher couldn't sink much lower. The reputation of the high-school teacher has suffered from the fact that the old-style high school, which was a small, easily surveyable island of humanism, no longer exists; but the Studienrat has become a freer spirit because of it. He is no longer in as great danger of being "typed" by his surroundings.

In twentieth century Germany, a teacher can't be distinguished from an engineer or dentist, and there can't be very much wrong with his prestige because in most cases it doesn't seem to worry him. In the more progressive German Länder, it has even become customary for children to say "Herr Muller," "Frau Schmid," "Herr Schulze," rather than Herr Lehrer (Mr. Teacher), Frau Studienrätin, or Herr Direktor.

Herr Professor and Herr Doktor are of course sacrosanct, to the amusement of some foreigners who think nothing of calling a man sir, or letting themselves be so addressed. There is a lot to be said for titulatory address as long as the titles are simple. "Ministerialdirigent" (for the highest type of civil servant, just below Under Secretary of State) is terrible; "Count" is fine. At least it helps you to address a person whose name you don't understand when you are introduced. But there's a lot to be said against it, too. At a faculty session, with only professors attending, a university janitor would create chaos with the outcry, "Herr Professor, your house is on fire!"

"I don't think," said Studienrat Beyer, "that my colleagues worry too much nowadays about forms of address."

"So what do they worry about?" asked Professor Spälti.

"If you want to know the truth, the demands made on our profession are horrifying for anyone who is conscientious. On the one hand we're supposed to be extremely selective; on the other, parents will stop at nothing to get their children promoted, and when it comes to a showdown, the parents are nearly always right. We're responsible for the young people's physical-fitness, but if one of them breaks a leg, which can easily happen during sports, then we're personally to blame. Individual study courses are supposed to treat subjects 'in depth,' and we may have just succeeded in convincing a colleague who teaches geography that his subject is so unimportant it has to be dropped because we have to concentrate on fewer subjects when—bang!—we are presented with a new super-subject consisting of history, politics, sociology, and philosophy combined, and called 'Civics.' Whenever something goes wrong, the schools are supposed to find the solution. And that goes back to the oldest problem in the world, the one that began with Adam and Eve. In the schools we call it co-education."

"I'm afraid we started that," said Ralph.

"No," said Dr. Beyer. "Don't look so crushed. We only got the word from you. The nonsense it stands for—namely to make a philosophical issue of whether or not a boy and girl should go to school together—we can provide very well ourselves."

"So what kind of a question would you say it really is?"

"First of all, a question of educational practice and habits of thought. We have apparently become accustomed to thinking that there are no sex differences during elementary school; in high school the sexes are separated; at the universities there is again no difference between them."

"And do you think that's right?"

"Just as right as the attitude toward another big issue which unfortunately doesn't touch us so much in the high schools: parochial versus public school? In the elementary schools, religion is all-powerful. The separate faiths have their separate schools. In high school religion is represented only in periods of religious instruction, according to the various faiths. At the universities it plays no part at all."

And so we have arrived at a subject that deserves a chapter to itself.

15. THE GRETCHEN QUESTION IN CATHOLICISM

> "Tell me—how do you feel about religion?"
> —Gretchen to Faust, Part One. Goethe

Among the questions foreigners ask over and over again, those concerning National Socialism before 1945 or after 1960 are the most frequent; next comes anti-Semitism; followed by the Gretchen question. In the language of the twentieth century, and adapted to our situation, it reads: "What part do religion and the churches *really* play in Germany today?"

This suspicious "really" is, I suppose, the price we have to pay for the fact that we apparently behave in a crassly materialistic fashion yet have a governmental party that carries Christianity in its crest. The question doesn't become any simpler when one realizes that politically Protestants and Catholics seem to be in complete harmony; theologically all efforts toward a rapprochement are being constantly rebuffed from both sides; practically speaking, daughters and sons are still being disinherited if they marry someone of a different religion; children aren't allowed to go to the same school if they are not of the same faith. . . . Do they *really* have that much faith?

Religious questions are difficult to answer in any country. Even Faust squirmed when he had to answer Gretchen, and said evasively: "*Erfüll davon dein Herz, so gross es ist, und wenn du ganz in dem Gefühle selig bist, dann nenn' es wie du willst . . . ich habe keinen*

Namen dafür." ("Let it fill your heart wholly, and when your rapture is complete, call it what you will . . . I have no name for it.") And the man who wrote these lines refused to be pinned down to the extent that today some claim him as a Christian, others as an atheist.

In his speech to the Reichstag, February 6, 1888, Bismarck spoke the famous words, "We Germans fear God but nothing else in the world." A few years ago, Wolfdietrich Schnurre, in his tale, *The Burial*, wrote, "Loved by no one, hated by no one, after a long period of suffering borne with heavenly patience, God died." Of course we find "God is dead," as a literary motif in Nietzsche, and it turns up again in German literature immediately after 1945, in our first postwar drama, Wolfgang Borchert's *Outside at the Door*.

That Christianity survived the skepticism of natural science unharmed is the wishful thinking of the faithful; the opposite can be proved. That nothing is so greatly feared in Germany as God's wrath was a rhetorical rather than a sociological statement, even in Bismarck's day. That nothing much has changed since then, that atheism has triumphed just as little as the religious renaissance that was expected by so many as a result of the Second World War, is as valid for Germany as for most nations of a once-Christian world. Still it is difficult to rid oneself of the feeling that things are somewhat different in Germany, and any long stay outside its borders, any conversation with foreigners on the subject of religion, serve only to strengthen this feeling. How do the facts go with it? What was Andreas von Hattesdorf's opinion?

"Our Austrian proportional system [he was referring to the equal representation of one Catholic and one Social Democrat in all government offices] wouldn't function in Germany, where there are Catholic Socialists, where Protestants occupy key positions in the Catholic Christian Democratic Party, and where Freethinkers are divided fairly evenly among both big parties. And the Socialists don't seem to feel right any more either among purely atheist Marxists."

"Do you find the position of the Christian faiths different in Switzerland?"

"In many ways it is similar," said Professor Spälti. "We also have two—in a way three—denominations of comparatively equal strength, but in most of our cantons, one predominates. Anyway, our various faiths do not participate in public life to the extent yours do."

"In Germany," writes historian Golo Mann, "the religious strife of the 16th century split the nation into two halves. This did not happen anywhere else."

Would it be desirable for the borders of the Länder to coincide more sharply with the religious borders? A futile question. Only in the Länder that can boast a historic development does the *cuius regio eius religio* of the Peace of Augsburg (1555) still provide for fairly unequivocal conditions. In such large and important Länder as North-Rhine Westphalia, Hesse, and Baden-Württemberg, the denominations are mixed. Are these Lands worse off as a result? The postwar rapprochement of Catholic and Protestant politicians, which led finally to the formation of the CDU, took place mainly in North-Rhine West-phalia. . . .

What had Yvonne noticed before anything else?

"The abysmal hatred which still exists between the religions. Hatred is perhaps too passionate a word. Contempt? Distrust? You know what I mean. Remember what your friend Heinrich told us."

Heinrich had told us how his father had been transferred from Munich to Potsdam, and he, little Heini at the time, was thus moved from a Catholic to a Protestant school. In a recess period his class-mates enlightened him. "The Catholics are hypocrites, liars and cheats." Heini had heard this before; only one thing was wrong. "No, no!" he cried. "That's the Protestants!"

In the children's section of the Trier diocese periodical, *Paulinus*, the following interesting contribution appeared on July 19, 1959, on the question of religion in Germany. The little ones were instructed: "Surely all of you know a lot of other children with whom you play football and eat ice cream and go to the movies, and you get along with them very well. And all those little children want to go to heaven one day, just like you. But they are Protestants. Now that is a dreadful thing. . . ."

The author may quite possibly not have been praised by his bishop for displaying such undiplomatic zeal, yet in his own way he spoke the truth, because in those families which take their religion seriously, such concepts as "It is dreadful to be a Protestant" (or "a Catholic," as the case may be) are not as anachronistic as their more enlightened contemporaries like to think. But if you could ask a hundred average Christians what the difference really is between Catholic and Protestant Christianity, you might not get a single completely correct answer.

"And that's what I find so strange," said Dick. "I know all about these petty and often malicious prejudices, but in Germany very real dogmatic questions also separate the two religions. In the United States we try to keep them out of politics entirely. President Kennedy's elec-tion might have been helped by the very fact that a few Republicans felt they had to use his Catholicism against him. In Germany though, Christianity is constantly being made a political issue. Yet a theological rapprochement such as the Una-Sancta (One Faith) Movement, doesn't seem to come into question, in spite of the fact that the two religions can hardly be told apart in the realm of politics. And in the schools, in family life, in religious magazines, petty heckling and gross enmity seem to be rampant. How do you explain that?"

How, indeed!

I see four possible answers. First: that the churches have put aside their individual claims to a unique fulfillment of God's will and have joined forces to protect the Christian Occident from the common foe—communism. But this explanation won't stand up. The churches, since their founding, have never joined forces against a common foe. The "enemy position," to use a military term, isn't so clear-cut either. The devout Catholics in Poland; common interests of dyed-in-the-wool

Christians and old-style Communists; free thinkers and atheists in their own ranks, must give a highly confusing picture to anyone looking for a clear-cut front.

The three other possibilities are at least imaginable:

1. Superficially, parties and public relations conceal the truth that Catholicism and Protestantism are as irreconcilable today as they were in the sixteenth century, and the truth could burst forth any day in an eruption that would blow the German government party sky-high.

2. The people who really count, the one hundred or one thousand of those in power agreed in the cynical belief that Christianity and some of its dogma and commandments are still quite useful as a façade, but they don't believe in a Judgment Day on which they will have to answer for what they have done in life.

3. Under the pressures of necessity, the political men have hurried far ahead of the theologians, and especially far ahead of that weirdly conservative thing called public opinion. A CDU of theologians and dogmaticists lies ahead of us, if it can be said that anything very much lies ahead of us. . . .

"Fascinating," said Dick, with as much mockery as admiration. "But which of the three do you think is right?"

I didn't bite. The use of organized systems of belief on historic reality has never had very good results. To subject the lives of nations to the laws of logic is evidently just as unsatisfactory as applying them to the many private lives of which, in the last analysis, a nation's life is composed.

Ralph still had to have his say, and what he had to tell concerning the difference between Christianity in Germany and England seemed to me most pertinent. It ran along these lines:

"In Germany there evidently was and is such a thing as a church ethos, namely of the Catholic Church. There also was and is a national ethos, but it is a Protestant ethos. The two have fought and weakened each other. But that is only one side of the question. They have also complemented each other marvelously, and not let any third element arise. However, what you lack in Germany, or let us say I have come across it only as an exception, is a condition independent of church and state, a condition of acting decently for the sole purpose of acting decently. If you want me to use big words, I'll call it a humanitarian ethos, something like what your Kant taught. But in the end Kant remained a Prussian and a Protestant, especially once he fell into the hands of Hegel and German idealism. A humanitarian ethos—don't misunderstand me—that is not opposed to church or state. And I don't mean the opposition-humanitarianism of the intellectual Left, which you find in Germany as everywhere else. No, I mean the desire to be good, to be decent, as a rather indefinable feeling to be interpreted biologically rather than metaphysically, not meaning much more than 'It would be desirable,' yet very desirable. You'll find it in England. Church and state couldn't possibly feel jeopardized by it; on the contrary, they simply incorporated this a-religious urge for decency in their teachings. Now this hasn't resulted in the English becoming better than other people, although some Englishmen like to think so; the result is simply that anyone in England, who is in opposition to the governing party and at the same time feels that the laws of the church don't apply to him, is not thrown into the dreadful moral vacuum which I seem to feel so often in Germany."

For many foreigners and for most Germans, West Germany is a country in which the Roman Catholic Church is dominant. Actually, though, there are three million more nominal Protestants than Catholics. But there are only three million regular churchgoers among the Protestants of West Germany as opposed to eleven million Catholics. Add to this the fact that the Catholic Church is united and the Protestants split among Lutherans, Reformed, and United Protestants, and finally, that for the time being the Catholic religious still constitute an invaluable moral and intellectual backbone of the Roman Catholic Church. I say "for the time being," since learned padres have informed me that it is becoming more and more difficult to find suitable new blood. But there are still 100,000 women in Catholic nunneries who, as welfare workers, teachers, governesses, and nurses, represent an unparalleled reservoir of loyalty and consolation; and we still have over 130,000 friars and padres: Dominicans who attend to social misery, missionary Franciscans, cultured Benedictines, terrifyingly clever Jesuits. What can the Protestant churches offer in comparison?

16. PROTEST-WEARY PROTESTANTISM

The renaissance of Germany's spiritual life, if not through Protestantism, then through the Protestant parsonages, may be expressed statistically. "Since the Reformation, there hasn't been a noteworthy German who did not have his roots in a Protestant parsonage," wrote Gustave Freytag, who came from one. "Scarcely one," said Felix Dahn, whose father was an actor.

They were exaggerating, and yet: Gottsched was the son of a minister; so were Gellert, Fleming, Gryphius, Hölty, and Bürger. Matthias Claudius and Lenz, Wieland and Lessing, the Schlegels and Schelling, Jean Paul and Nietzsche; Geibel and Gottfried Benn; historians such as Mommsen, Lamprecht and Ranke; naturalists such as Linné, Euler, Brehm; Friedrich Naumann and Albert Schweitzer, and Turnvater Jahn, father of the science of calisthenics in Germany.

It was not a Protestant, though, nor a clergyman's son, but a Roman Catholic who, simply by studying a compilation of *German Biographies*, established the fact that of 1,600 Great Germans of the seventeenth, eighteenth, and nineteenth centuries, 861 came from parsonages, as follows: 24 per cent of all naturalists, 30 per cent of all famous doctors, 40 per cent of all famous jurists, 50 per cent of all famous philologists. "The entire intellectually productive and culturally creative power of the German people sprang from this milieu," wrote Gottfried Benn in his article, "The German." I have him to thank for many of the assertions made here.

In the twentieth century we are not so dogmatic. Available reference books no longer contain such thorough information about the origins of our great men. But no one could suspect that the Protestant parsonages play a part today as "heritage milieu," as Benn called it in 1933, that could be compared in any way with the role they evidently played in the seventeenth, eighteenth, and nineteenth centuries.

It is probably no coincidence that the Protestant parsonage has lost its significance; German Protestantism can deplore the same loss of importance. And whom could this possibly surprise in a country where any protest, as long as it doesn't remain nicely metaphysical, is not considered genteel; where "protesting," "opposition," "pamphlets," "polemics," and similar words are used derogatively if not abusively in nine cases out of ten? When German Protestantism ceased to be the religion of the state (against which it never protested), it ceased to play a decisive role.

I can recall very well that in 1935, when the church was a matter of indifference to me, as is normal for a fourteen-year-old boy, I began to hear rumors that there were Christians who refused to be German Christians. Whoever hasn't lived through anything like this must learn to differentiate between *deutsche* Christians, written with a small "d," and *Deutsche* Christians, adjective capitalized because part of a provocative title, a new breed. The Deutsche Christians could boast Länder bishops and a Reich bishop. They were supplemented by the *Deutsche* Faith Movement, founded as a rival firm, for whom Christ was an Aryan superman whose teachings had found their fulfillment in Hitler.

In those days the interpretability of the Protestant religion was quite far-reaching. The first deserters to National Socialism were Protestants: the most vehement opponents were Protestants. Did the Protestant churches therefore suffer a loss of strength or prestige? Our English lady of 1884 had this to say: "Of church going there is, in Protestant Germany, no question." In the solemn act of confirmation she saw, "nothing of 'recollection' or piety. . . . It simply means to those whom it most concerns a long dress, visiting cards, a bouquet, a lace-frilled pocket-handkerchief, the '*du*' of childhood to be exchanged for the '*Sie*' of young-ladyhood. . . . The Protestant religion in Germany is a dead letter. . . . The very links that bound it to the things 'protested against' are broken. It has ceased to have any distinctive entity of its own. . . . Protestant clergymen in Germany are *nowhere*, and their social influence is absolutely *nil*. Go to the churches of Protestant Germany, and what will you see? Vast and gloomy edifices, empty— the huge cold shell of what once had life. It is Sunday. A sprinkling of women scattered few and far between is spread about the gloomy building. Perhaps two or three men will be there. They look infinitely bored and wearied. There is no poetry, no passion, no grace, no attraction about the services. It is cold of comfort."

What happened in 1933, seems therefore to have started long before that, but there must have been exceptions—there always are—which our English lady, generalizing and deducing from her own life, just didn't happen to see. The exceptions, after 1933, were the ministers and the faithful of the *Bekennende Kirche,* or Confessional Church. The only one I knew was Pastor Pfeiffer, and he was unforgettable. I only half-grasped what he was trying to tell us, and this via a school-mate, his beautiful daughter, Helga. But I did live to see the dignitaries of our town snub him. Whoever protested in Germany in those days didn't have an easy time. Professor Pfeiffer died in a concentration camp.

While the Roman Catholic Church in Germany stood back and waited, did not expose itself, and to the end did not feel that the little dictator from Austria should be taken seriously, even went so far as to think he might be used as a tool; while the spiritual leader of this religion (to the best of my knowledge) became the first foreign potentate to sign a treaty—the Concordat—with the Führer of the German Reich and People, a few lonely Protestant pastors were shunted off into concentration camps.

In those days, through the Pfeiffers, I heard mentioned over and over again, two names on which the Protestant Christians in Germany were pinning their hopes. I mean those Protestants who had not become capital "d" *Deutsche* Christians or *Deutsche* Faith Movement followers. The names were Karl Barth and Martin Niemöller. Their sermons were printed and passed from hand to hand in that small circle that called itself the Confessional Church and was tolerated as long as none of its members stuck out their necks too far. Barth was Swiss; Niemöller survived the concentration camp; the little Pfeiffers are never mentioned. . . .

When it was all over, I saw and heard Karl Barth and Martin Niemöller for the first time (until then they had been simply revered names), Karl Barth as guest professor in Bonn; Martin Niemöller on one of his many world-wide lecture tours. Barth won you over with the brilliance of his formulation, the dialectics of a Mephistopheles, all in the service of God; Niemöller was a tower of strength in miserable surroundings. In a way, he seemed to be aware of it. . . .

Barth and Niemöller, and the small group that called itself the Confessional Church, went the way Martin Luther had gone: they withdrew from a state they could not recognize Paulinically as "from God," into the pure dogma of positive Christianity, into a dialectic theology. It seems to me that in those days far too many Protestant Christians forgot the Ten Commandments and with them their entire catechism. Their Christianity had always been a mixture of faith in God and faith in the state. They preserved a little of their faith in God, but they feared only the state, nothing else. In the end the strongest "protestants" against Hitler's Reich were the Catholics, after Hitler had kept very few of the promises he had made in the Concordat; and after Pope Pius XI, on March 14, 1937, "with burning sorrow," issued an encyclical letter on the position of the Catholic Church in the German Reich.

And now something typically German took place. You would have thought that the survivors of the Confessional Church, who had behaved so admirably, and whose viewpoint had been so definitely borne out by events, would have been the focal point around which a new community could be formed; and at first it looked as if this was going to be the case. Karl Barth was recalled as guest professor to the University of Bonn, where he had taught from 1930 to 1934. Martin Niemöller received office and honors in the *Evangelische Kirche Deutschlands*, the German Protestant Church, which again combined Lutheran, Reformed, and United Protestants, each carefully guarding the nuances of their faith.

Soon, however, there was no denying the fact that it was their attractive white shirts (in contrast to brown, and therefore highly sought after) that were being singled out for honors, rather than the belligerent Protestant attitude they had displayed. Barth and Niemöller were being honored because they were clean, not because they had rebelled. That very period of protest against Hitler had apparntly left them with an aura of eccentricity, with the onus of being "difficult," cranks, sectarians. . . .

Men like Barth and Niemöller never stopped being awkward personalities. A few years ago, the Peace Prize of the German book dealers, one of the most important awards in West Germany, was to be given to Karl Barth. Influential objections made it impossible. And Martin Niemöller . . . whisper-whisper-whisper . . . isn't he a little on the pink side?

This suspicion is just as grotesque as it would have been if directed at former U-boat Captain Niemöller, who made it quite clear in more than words how he stood on the subject of dictatorships, whether of proletarian or capitalist origin. This sort of thing is beginning to be as disturbing in West Germany as it was in the United States in Senator McCarthy's day, and I can see no Ed Murrow among us to oppose it.

Niemöller and others, who in an exaggerated state of lonely opposition may sometimes say or write foolish things, have to take such suspicions upon themselves because they still believe in a German oneness instead of in the "reunification" of two separate German states. Actually the Protestant church in Germany is the last big collectively German institution. If it could be in any way compared in strength to the Protestant church of the seventeenth century, if the Protestants in West and East Germany were really protestants, if dismal experiences had not made them protest-weary, then there could be no talk any more of a divided Germany, or let us say, in that case the political division would not be great enough to endanger this spiritual unity.

But we still have our protestants, and they are again called nonconformists. They are also called liberals. We find them in the Protestant and Catholic churches, and outside the big denominations. There are a lot of cranks among them, and quite a few visionaries. I hope this won't be considered sufficient reason for exterminating them. For a free state that can no longer afford a protesting minority ceases to be a free state.

17. THE ACCUSED IS AS GOOD AS GUILTY

The most powerful, most influential, most important man in German penal law is the district attorney. There are a lot of good and bad reasons for this. One of them seems to be decisive, and it is one the district attorney does not always like to admit.

The climate of a constitutional state is determined not so much by how the courts treat its thieves and murderers—they are really far more a concern of the police. But apart from the controversial death penalty (no longer possible in West Germany under the Basic Law), which may be discussed morally rather than judicially, there is far-reaching international agreement on how each individual society may best and most practically defend itself against the obvious criminal. I am here concerned with the comparatively normal and peaceful citizen. The climate of a constitutional state has to agree with him.

German law gives the district attorney a top-ranking position. He has to answer the decisive question, often of greater importance to the average citizen than a court sentence, the question of whether a charge is to be made. The more complicated our lives get, and with them our laws (think of the legal complications the invention of the automobile alone brought with it!), the more pluralistic and shaky the general feeling of right and wrong becomes, the more decisive is this question of the prosecution: Must I bring charges against this man?

In our grandparents' day it was still considered a disgrace to come into conflict with the police, and I can well imagine that a policeman would have thought twice before trying to pin anything on a man like my grandfather. In the meantime we have become drivers and parking delinquents, and can't afford to be so sensitive any more. But I still think that among those who have honorably passed forty, there are many for whom having to stand accused in a courtroom would be a far heavier punishment than a year in jail would be for the hardened criminal. The law doesn't help much here, but the district attorney may, by dismissing a case because of its negligibility. The concurrence of the judge—a formal necessity—may then be taken for granted. The judge may, of course, dismiss a case, too, and for the same reason; but he is psychologically in a more difficult position because he can do so only after the district attorney, evidently not convinced of its negligibility, has brought the charge.

By a liberal interpretation of the articles of law, the district attorney is immensely influential in seeing to it that undisgraced citizens remain undisgraced. As long as no dire offense or crime is involved, he may save people from being brought into court, for whom acquittal would no longer come as salvation after highly embarrassing hearings had taken place. Whose way of life is so exemplary that he wouldn't mind seeing every corner of it illuminated for every one to see? In the case of a man accused, this doesn't have to happen, but it can happen—and very easily when someone is interested in seeing that it does. There was a professor accused of a political offense. The hearings resulted in material for a new charge, this time for misconduct with a student. The thought of what could happen if every high-school teacher and university professor who married one of his pupils had to furnish proof that he had entered into intimate relations with her only after marriage makes one shudder!

So we enter a wide area, overgrown with articles of law: the twilight zone of the unknown quantity. There are a lot of misdemeanors and quite a few crimes that do not fill our jails for the simple reason that they are rarely prosecuted. If, for instance, 576 cases of misconduct between males according to Article 175 have been tried in Germany in the last ten years, it means something quite different than if the 576 cases had been murders. In the case of murder, the unknown quantity is low; very few murders remain undiscovered; in the case of homosexuality it is high, because very few cases are known, or let us say, officially recognized.

Among these sub-rosa characters we find homosexuals, procurers, abortionists, adulterers, traffic-law breakers (scofflaws), and those charged with complicated trade and currency misdeameanors. In the case of the scofflaws, the figures become obscure because, in spite of the most zealous prosecution, only a fraction are punished.

Must I bring charges? In the district attorney's answer to this question of conscience you may read what differentiates the constitutional from the unconstitutional state, the practice of law from its abuses, especially where these sub-rosa characters are concerned. For three reasons:

1. A judge, even if he wanted to, would be unable in the case of these minor offenses, to acquit an accused who is guilty. The district attorney therefore passes sentence as soon as he brings charges.

2. The degree of punishment is not crucial (traffic offenses excepted) since the public trial itself, whatever the verdict, is enough to damage the accused socially or professionally.

3. To all this must be added the fact that in German jurisprudence there is a school of thought that has almost entirely disappeared in the rest of the world. Its adherents see the purpose of punishment in intimidation. The offender must be made an example of. But in a state where out of 100 misdemeanors committed only one is prosecuted—when this one case is singled out as an example—we have not justice, but injustice.

In Germany—and here I believe we differ from most other nations of the Western world—there is among a great majority of the people (but fortunately among only a minority of jurists) a readiness to look upon any respect for the unprosecuted as reprehensible laxness, if not corruption. This rigorous adherence to the letter of the law, which probably springs from decent and honorable motives, overlooks the fact that it is just this respect for the unknown quantity that keeps an administration of justice from being an administration of judicial terror.

It is not a coincidence that certain sexual practices, for which measures that are almost one hundred years old no longer suffice, are classified among these rarely prosecuted misdemeanors. Public opinion has changed considerably, and the religious and church laws on which these statutes were based for the most part, have become unsuitable for a society no longer firmly rooted in church or religion. Similarly, we find here the misdemeanors for which there are no old laws because the offenses became possible only in our motorized world of expense account and currency laws.

The lawmakers can't possibly do justice to every fresh social situation by passing new laws or changing the old ones. All they can do is see to it that they don't practice the conservative rigor which is still very often the quickest path to popularity in Germany. Yet they must start with the theory that human beings have to adjust to the law, not vice versa. A wise jurist knows that this theory is impractical, history teaches us that—we no longer hang sheep rustlers—but there is no point in making an issue of it. Respect for the twilight zone of the unknown quantity makes possible a constitutional state in which interpretations may develop and change, even if the letter of the law has to remain rigid.

A dictatorship—and this is overlooked by the rigorists who mean well but only do harm—does not require flagrant lawbreaking in order to practice terror. Long before he stopped at nothing, Hitler began by not respecting the unknown quantity. It might be proved, or rumored (guilt is never easy to prove in the case of such misdemeanors) that a political enemy was homosexual. There was no death penalty for homosexuality, but death for the accused was what Hitler was after. All that was needed was to add some "code of honor" elements, and a little "folk fury" to the indictment, and soon quite a lot of people could see the death penalty as a "stern application of the law" when in fact it was a flagrant miscarriage of justice.

With the first law suits against our Jewish citizens, spies were hired to violate the twilight zone. Great interest was taken suddenly in the business practices of this specific group, in the relationship between boss and secretary, man of the house and maid of the house. How many enemies of Hitler's Reich were convicted for "currency crimes"? And how many of us shuddered when we heard that in the Soviet Union, Olga Ivinskaya, Pasternak's lifelong companion, and her daughter, both of whom had made themselves unpopular several times, had been condemned to years of hard labor for currency offenses?

In the twilight zone it is always open season for the demagogue, and the *profanum vulgus* is for punishment (as severe as possible). If the prosecution can't find anything, it can easily invent something. It wouldn't be easy to prove that I was homosexual; but it would be quite impossible for me to prove that I was *not* homosexual.

Must I bring charges? The German district attorney who takes this question seriously, as it should be taken, is not to be envied, for the reasons already mentioned and for one that stands before all the others: because the accused, once the trial has begun, is as good as guilty. Anyone accustomed to an English courtroom, sitting in on a German trial, must often find it hard to control himself. The way in which some German judges bully the accused whose guilt is by no means proved as yet, would result, in an English court, in the judge being dismissed. In an English court he doesn't have the right to interfere in the trial in such a manner, and in any American or French court the effect would at least be furious protest from the defense lawyer.

In Germany it is almost impossible to dismiss a judge, and that he considers the accused guilty before tried would certainly be no reason for doing so. "The conduct of the trial, the interrogation of the accused, and the hearing of the witnesses, are the concern of the presiding judge." If he didn't consider the accused sufficiently suspect, he wouldn't have opened the case against him in the first place. And the powerlessness of the defense is so obvious in a German trial that even the President of the German Law Courts deplored it at the thirtieth German Lawyers' Convention.

The completely innocent accused who is found guilty is, of course, an exception even in German courts. Still, one gets an uncomfortable feeling when one recalls some cases of the past. Many terrible things have happened in our administration of justice which don't seem to be explained sufficiently by the metaphor, "the plague of National Socialism broke out among the German people." How could it happen? How can we see to it that it never happens again?

"The thing that strikes coldest in the heart," Theodore Haecker wrote in his *Day and Night Notebooks,* under the date February 15, 1940, "is the spiritual condition and behavior of the German judges. They would send a person who buys a Pole a glass of beer to jail, and that is dreadful."

The plague of National Socialism? No. Not at all. Similar sentences are handed down today by German judges in East Germany. A student fled to West Germany after two years in jail for criticizing the regime. "But you know," he said, rejecting all sentimental compassion, "that means no more over there than a warning with fine means here in West Germany."

So are we to call what goes on over there, "the plague of communism"? *And why are we so susceptible to plagues?*

$$4$$

QUESTION PERIOD

1. A CAPSULE HISTORY

Point Zero (1945):

Hitler's death on April 30, and the unconditional surrender of the German army on May 7 and 8, separate the twelve years of our *unbewältigte Vergangenheit*, or the past we haven't overcome, from the eighteen years of our most recent history, 1945–1963. Let historians decide, from the safe perspective of the twenty-first century, how decisive the years 1933–1945 really were. The view that 1933 ushered in a completely new era, and that 1945 did the same thing, seems convenient rather than right.

The patent solution—to make good German democrats out of bad German Nazis—was called denazification. The Allies issued an order for everyone to have himself denazified, and the worst cases were tried by Allied military courts: in the American Zone 169,282; in the Soviet Zone 18,328 (later the Soviets reproached the Americans—of all people!—for letting too many Nazis go free;) in the French Zone 17,353; in the British Zone 2,296.

Each occupational force had its pleasant and unpleasant aspects. The English made themselves unpopular with their dismantlings (the Americans didn't think much of this); the French with their plundering (no other zone suffered so much hunger); the Russians by raping women and treating prisoners badly (in this respect the English were the best behaved); the Americans by their denazification efforts which weren't funny for those affected by them although the rest of the world soon found them amusing.

This summing up is not a reproach ("War is a brutish, powerful

122

thing." *Wallenstein*, Schiller), but the truth. Otherwise some of the resentments which are still smoldering would be incomprehensible.

What a Nazi truly is remains undefinable. We children of the so-
called middle class heard the word used for the first time in the late
twenties as a term of invective. We feel that little changed in this
respect during the thirties and forties (clandestinely) or in the fifties
and sixties (openly). Denazification therefore meant de-undefining the
undefinable. Nothing very sensible could possibly have come of it.
There was a party in postwar Czechoslovakia that called itself National
Socialist. After all, there is nothing criminal about nationalism or socialism. Those with the power to judge were consequently thrown back
on the simplest solution, not necessarily the most intelligent one: "Were
you a member of the NSDAP, or one of its organizations?" Today
every one knows what we knew then: not every member of the
NSDAP or one of its organizations was a dangerous Nazi. But that
apparently doesn't stop a lot of us from looking upon every member of
the East German SED or any of its organizations as a dangerous Communist. That's the way people are. Or are they that way only in Germany?

The chronicler can't be spared the effort of assembling a few con-
cise articles of the Nazi faith of, let's say, the year 1941:

1. This war must be won. (Militarism?)
2. Germany is a bulwark against the East. (Anticommunism.)
3. The Jews are our misfortune. (Anti-Semitism.)
4. The German Autobahns are the best, and *am deutschen Wesen
soll die Welt genesen* . . . "the world shall be restored by the German image." (Nationalism?)
5. It is better for one man to make the decisions than for many to
bicker and argue over them. (Antiparliamentarian totalitarianism.)
6. Right is what benefits the nation. (No comment.)
7. German unity is a good thing; European unity would be even
better.

The last paragraph is met with incredulity by every foreigner who
hears it, and by many Germans. Actually, the passionate interest in
Europa on the part of young Germans was just as great in 1936 as
it was ten years later. Of course Hitler's Europa would have pleased
very few non-German Europeans, but Hitler's Europa was not what
the Hitler Youth was dreaming about.

Denazification therefore, and its less militant parallel, re-education
(a word fortunately never translated into German) meant getting rid
of *all* these articles of faith; not only nationalism and anti-Semitism,
but also anticommunism and militarism. (At first, no army officer who
had been decorated was allowed to study at a university.) Paul Sethe
wrote on this subject: "In those days (the postwar forties) a German
journalist who refused to work in the same office with Communists
couldn't find a job in Frankfurt. Two years later he would have been

fired for being willing to work with them. That's how times change. . . ." In 1945, George Shaw Wheeler was in charge of the department for denazification; in 1947, he fled to Czechoslovakia.

In the year 1 (1946):

Those living in the big cities, with no farm or black-market connections, were living on approximately two slices of bread a day. They learned to hate the word "calories." A number of people, members of the army of occupation especially, discovered that there were still quite a few surprisingly likable people among the Germans. During this year, in spite of the Morgenthau Plan and denazifications, the German love for the United States was born. In January, the American Commander in Chief, General Eisenhower, gave the Swedish Red Cross permission to do something for Germany's children. The number of American soldiers who, against orders, fed whole German families from their own generous rations increased. In this respect they were better off than their English, French, and Russian allies. And as the years rolled on, the stream of CARE packages from all over the world, but from the United States in particular, grew larger and larger, saving literally hundreds of thousands from starvation. All this lies far back, but thousands of us will never forget it. On September 6, United States Secretary of State Byrnes made his famous speech in Stuttgart, announcing a new American policy toward Germany: "The American people want to help the German people to win their way back to an honorable place among the free and peace-loving nations of the world."

In the year 2 (1947):

On March 10, the foreign ministers of the United States, the Soviet Union, Great Britain, and France—who were to remain allies only to the end of the year—met in Moscow. Soviet Foreign Minister Molotov's suggestion to create an all-German government and state after the old Weimar pattern, via free elections in Germany was understood as the Soviet Russian wish to extend its influence to the Rhine—above all across the Ruhr—and was rejected. British Foreign Minister Bevin declared that he didn't care if the future government was monarchistic, democratic, or Communistic—one thing it would certainly be, and that was—dangerous.

In December, the second big conference, this time in London, reaffirmed what the first had already indicated: the not-so-holy alliance of World War II was broken, and with it, Germany. From here on in there are two perspectives for viewing world history: the Eastern and the Western. The truth lies somewhere in between.

In the year 3 (1948):

On April 1, every approach to Berlin was blocked by the Soviet Union. This land blockade lasted until May, 1949, but was broken by the Air Lift of the Western Powers on June 30, 1948. Thus began the "Berlin crisis" which still exists. It is aggravated or alleviated according to which condition suits the prevailing political concept. Provoking a Berlin crisis as a means of putting on pressure at conferences became a weapon of Soviet foreign policy. Primarily, however, this latent crisis situation developed purely geographically as a result of the fact that the east-west division of the world was not prepared with sufficient care, and Berlin was unexpectedly thrust into the role of a Western bridgehead in the Eastern sphere of influence.

In the year 4 (1949):

On May 8, the Basic Law of the Federal Republic of (West) Germany was adopted; on May 23, it was officially proclaimed. For the second time in their history, the Germans tried to be pleased at being a constitutional democracy, again after a lost war and under the direct influence of the victorious powers who reserved the right of control.

Decisive for all future developments were Articles 65 and 67, granting principal executive power to the chancellor. This was intended to avoid a too-frequent change of government, a factor that had fatally weakened the Weimar Republic. It has resulted in there being no change of government in the Federal Republic since its foundation. . . .

There probably were at least two people in the parliamentary advisory council who saw quite clearly the power these articles would give to a strong chancellor. They were the leaders of the two largest parties: Dr. Konrad Adenauer (CDU) and Dr. Kurt Schumacher (SPD). Neither had any reason to protest, as might have been expected if either of them had seen the part he was to play as that of life-long leader of the opposition. Both, however, were sufficiently self-assured to presume that the power granted the German chancellor in the Basic Law would be to their advantage. On September 15, Dr. Konrad Adenauer was elected Chancellor by the famous majority of one, which meant that by this margin he had managed to squeeze in on the first ballot, with the required two-thirds majority. The straight majority required in later elections, he had pretty safely in hand from the start.

In the year 5 (1950):

At one of those spots where East and West are not cleanly divided, war broke out on June 25: at the 38th parallel in Korea. This was the month in which the law passed by the Allies to prevent German re-armament was ratified. A few weeks later the "German defense contribution" was an established fact. The only opposition, to it in Germany was an at-first-powerless and later even ridiculous "without me" movement, and one government member, Dr. Gustave Heinemann, who resigned his cabinet post as Minister of the Interior in protest against the government's rearmament policy. He has a place in German postwar history as the only cabinet member to resign of his own free will.

The "defense contribution" decision was probably correct; in any event, it was dictated by a world policy over which the German government had no control. The young German officer who had survived 1945, only to be treated like a "war criminal," and suffer "re-education," became a cynic. Again it was proved that a strong measure of opportunism is indispensable for those who want to survive in the center of a magnetic field of overlapping interests.

In the year 6 (1951):

On January 1, India became the first country to end the state of war between itself and Germany. On July 9, Great Britain and the other Commonwealth nations followed suit; France on July 13; the United States on October 19. The resolution of all controversial problems was put off until there could be a "peaceful settlement with a united Germany." If any more reasons were needed for *not* desiring a united Germany, the fact that it would then become necessary to confer on all sorts of highly controversial subjects (Germany's eastern boundaries, for example) would certainly be one of them. Peace treaties are always disagreeable for the country that has lost a war.

In the year 7 (1952):

On May 26, a "Contract with Germany" was signed in Bonn; "full sovereignty" for the Federal Republic became an established fact, but it was controversial from the start and was not enforced until May 5, 1955, due to French delaying tactics. In 1953, Professor Joachim Schoeps wrote: "In the last 40 years, we Germans have experienced Hohenzollern Kaiserdom, the Weimar Republic, Hitler's Third Reich, and now a divided Germany with governments that lack the sovereignty to make free political decisions." An editorial in the English weekly, *The New Statesman,* said on August 29, 1959; "In terms of *Realpolitik,* West Germany is truly a satellite; it depends on NATO for its very existence."

Since no nation may any longer call itself sovereign, and since no reliable criterion for sovereignty exists, the effort to designate any state as "more or less" sovereign is futile. And although obvious dependency has been a thorn in the flesh for many Germans, full sovereignty is of little concern to them.

In the year 8 (1953):

On June 17, there was a revolt in East Berlin. It was not an intellectually inspired revolt, nor were "remnants of the bourgeoisie" venting indignation. The pampered lap-children of the Workers' and Farmers' State, the skilled workers, the masons and carpenters started it on the Stalinallee (the name was, of course, changed later), which was supposed to be a showplace for the Soviet regime in East Germany.

The revolt proved three things:

1. That you can't always have your own way with Germans. The number of those who, in World War I, in Hitler's Reich, and in postwar East Germany, were willing to risk death for meaningful political freedom is greater than our generalizing critics would have it.

2. That only with Russian help can those governing in East Germany hold their own against those they govern.

3. That the Cold War will be a dubious battle as long as those waging it are willing to risk only lives other than their own.

It is certainly untrue that the Berlin revolt of June 17, and the Hungarian revolt three years later, were inspired by "capitalist warmongers," as the official Communist writers would have it. Revolutions are not imported. But there undoubtedly were powers outside East Germany, and three years later outside Hungary, that contributed directly to the tensions, and a few thousand Hungarians and Germans had to pay the price in the revolutionary explosions that ensued.

I can't help asking: What is so admirably harsh or so especially clever about someone barking who knows very well that he doesn't want to or can't bite?

In the year 9 (1954):

On the thirtieth of August, the plan for a European Defense Community was rejected by a large majority in the Paris National Assembly. It is difficult to estimate how hard hit were those enthusiastic hearts and active heads in Germany who had made German rearmament their cause because it was to be for the defense of Europe. This German Europa idealism has been abused, misunderstood, misinterpreted, and underrated over and over again. Adenauer, with his sober doggedness, seemed to be the man to convert into political reality a Europa image that had never gone very far beyond speculation, dreams, and literature. But then the English moved away. After the war, Churchill was the first to urge the formation of a United States of Europe, but after he became Prime Minister again in 1951, he seemed to have forgotten all about it. Now, in 1954, the French demonstrated that they, too, were in no mood to take Europa seriously. In that year the number of people in the Federal Republic who couldn't stand the sound of the word swelled into the thousands.

In the year 10 (1955):

On June 7, the Soviet Union suggested that diplomatic relations be established between the Soviet Union and Bonn. On December 20, Bonn accepted the invitation. How diplomatic all procedure between Moscow and Bonn was during this period, is stressed especially by those critics of German foreign policy who are of the opinion that in this year, for the last time, a politically united Germany might have been possible if the Federal Republic had been prepared to pay the price by refusing to join NATO. Members of the government, however, insist that the Russians would never have come forward with any concrete suggestions for reunification, and that their alleged readiness to discuss the matter had been nothing more than a nuisance action, directed against the Western Alliance, the Common Market, and the Paris Treaties. Be that as it may, Dr. Adenauer rejected negotiation with the

Soviet Union, declaring that Russia would come forward with concessions in due course if only Germany remained firm. To which Dr.
Paul Sethe had this to say: "The jubilation with which this explanation
was received made the blood run cold in one's veins. Were these the
same people who had been felled and lain stricken ten years before?
Did they already feel so strong that they could pass lightly over the
serious warnings of a world power? Are the Germans doomed to live
forever in extremes—either doubting themselves or being boldly presumptuous?"

In the year 11 (1956):
On August 18, the Communist Party was outlawed in Germany.
German anticommunism, which had been suppressed for only a short
time, thereby became law. The Weimar Republic may serve as an illustration for the fact that a state endangers itself if the liberalism of its
constitution protects the enemy of the state. And yet . . .
As a result of this Communist suppression, a slight feeling of uneasiness began to make itself felt in the more liberal wing of the government party. After all, it had never really looked as if the Communists
could gain influence in Germany unless Soviet power were standing
directly behind them. Was it wise to force them underground now?
Was it a responsible action to give political jurdisdiction in Germany
this fresh impetus? Did German democracy have to be more democratic than the English, French, Italian, all of whom tolerated the
Communist Party? And no one felt any better about it when they
saw the same people who had done time in Hitler's concentration
camps disappearing into the prisons again. Quite a few people couldn't
see much difference . . .

In the year 12 (1957):
The Federal Republic became a strong state. It was no longer considered the thing to point out that, according to the constitution, it
was a provisory state. As for its credo:
1. In order to have a minimum feeling of security against Soviet
military might, the German *Wehrkraft*—nobody liked to call it *Wehrmacht*—had to be strong.
2. Germany is a bulwark against the East. Three years later, on
January 22, 1960, Chancellor Adenauer put it this way: "I believe that
God has given the German people a specific function: to be the de-
fenders of the west against the powerful influences that affect us from
the east."
3. No one is to be at a disadvantage or favored because of sex,
birth, race, speech, native land, or descent, faith or religion or political
point of view. That is what the statute says.
4. The German highways are the best in the world, and Germans
are to be divided into West German human beings and East German
not-so-human beings. (East of the Harz Mountains, the terms have to
be reversed.)

5. It is still considered better, at least theoretically, for several people to have something to say in a state, than for one man to have all the power of government in his hands. (In 1957, 6 out of 10 Germans still felt this way.)

6. Whatever profits the state is right wherever state interests are directly involved, as, for instance, in political jurisdiction. But there are some people, especially among the jurists, who don't believe in this, and there is a Supreme Court that has its own ideas of right and enforces them.

7. German unity would be fine; European unity would be even finer.

This was the year in which Chancellor Adenauer's party, the CDU or Catholic Democratic Union, was brilliantly reacclaimed, and got a greater majority than ever before in parliament with its election slogan, "No experiments!"

In the year 13 (1958):

On March 25, the German Parliament voted to accept atomic weapons. Only such specific questions as "Where should the guns and launching pads be placed? Where should the missiles be stored? Who is to be in charge of the detonators for this form of armament? Who is to have the keys?" remained unanswered. To me, and to many like myself, a further question arises: "Are we bad Germans if we are afraid that one day a German general might gain access to the keys, be he in West German Cologne or East German Dresden?"

In the year 14 (1959):

President Professor Dr. Theodore Heuss's term expired for the second time. He was the German Federal Republic's first President, and had succeeded in giving the state a frank, Swabian, liberal outlook for ten long years. The Basic Law doesn't permit a third term. It also prescribes that the President may propose a candidate for the office of chancellor. It now turned out that this Article (63) could be reversed.

On the sixteenth of February, Chancellor Adenauer decided that he didn't want to be President. On February 24, he proposed Professor Dr. Ludwig Erhard, Minister of Economics at the time, as presidential candidate. On March 3, Dr. Erhard rejected the offer. On April 7, Dr. Adenauer changed his February-sixteenth mind, and permitted himself to be nominated as candidate for his party. "I may have come to this decision quickly, but I must say that I have thought it over carefully and feel that it is right." On June 4, the Chancellor changed his carefully thought-out-and-right decision again. On July 1, Dr. Heinrich Lübke, who until then had been Secretary for Agriculture, was elected President. At the time Dr. Marion Countess Dönhoff wrote in *Die Zeit:* "The feeling that the individual and his free will are safe in a democracy because its democratic institutions and laws are determining factors, seems shaken."

It has been pointed out that the totalitarian state rests on the author-ity of one person, the democratic state on respect for its democratic institutions. From this point of view, Germany was not a democratic state.

In the year 15 (1960):
The year began with the excitement resulting from the fact that young vandals had smeared swastikas on a synagogue in Cologne. On May 4, Cabinet Minister for Refugees, Theodore Oberländer, an expert in "eastern affairs" during the Third Reich, was let go, "at his request." On May 20, according to the Sixth *Strafrechtsänderungsgesetz,* or Penal Law Alterations Edict, anti-Semitic manifestations became punishable by law. Thus fifteen years after the war, National Socialism was made equivalent to anti-Semitism, which is understandable, but mistaken.

In the year 16 (1961):
According to the judgment that had prevailed in the DDR for a long time, and was now being forced on the Federal Republic more and more, the political reunification of Germany would have to begin by a disappearance of the West German population into East German prisons on the one hand, while on the other the West German courts would need years to sentence the functionaries of the SED. For the first time "official contacts" with the East were prosecuted as punish-able acts by the West German courts. What "East," "contacts" and "official" were was to be decided from case to case. The division of Germany may therefore be considered sealed, and the German who ignores it has, in both parts of his country, to count on being made to answer for it in court as a political criminal.

In the year 17 (1962):
On October 26 the Spiegel Affair began. The editorial offices and apartments of editors of *Der Spiegel,* a weekly news magazine, were searched at night; papers were confiscated; editors, as well as the publisher, Rudolf Augstein, were arrested. Reason: suspicion of treason because of an article published eighteen days before, which dealt criti-cally with the defensive power of the West Germany army. All liberal Germans were uneasily reminded of times when such "under cover of night" actions were commonplace. Their uneasiness didn't diminish when it became known that Franz Joseph Strauss, Defense Minister at the time, whose personal vindictiveness might have been construed as being behind the whole action, turned out to be actually more involved than he had chosen to admit at the outset. Furthermore, the arrest of one of the editors of *Der Spiegel* had taken place in Spain on a "not entirely legal basis," as the Secretary of the Interior chose to put it. All this caused general indignation; because it was *not* by chance that the mode of procedure had aroused terrible memories—the action

was led by a police officer who had been a successful persecutor in Hitler's day; because the "morass of treason," which Adenauer had suspected in the offices of *Der Spiegel*, was actually located in his own chancellery, where one year later a leading official had to be arrested as an agent of the East; because an action, which at the time was considered so urgent has to date (1964) produced no results, not even the opening of legal proceedings against anyone.

In the year 18 (1963):

Three great nations of the West experienced a change of leadership. Three statesmen whose images were part of the general consciousness and lent themselves easily to the pens of cartoonists, disappeared from the political arena. The United States lost their president, John F. Kennedy, killed by an assassin; Britain's prime minister, Sir Harold Macmillan, fell victim to a "diplomatic disease"; the chief of the West German government, Dr. Konrad Adenauer, saw no chance of evading his promise to step down; not this time. Professor Ludwig Erhard, the CDU Minister of Economic Affairs, liked by everyone—except Adenauer—became his successor. However, even those who now hope for a more liberal course and less authoritarian handling of democratic institutions under Erhard, ask themselves, not without anxiety: Will his hand be firm enough to steer the ship of state through future crises? Not only the sun-spot experts—who go so far as to see "maximum danger" for the year nineteen, after Hitler—assure us that tempestuous times lie ahead in 1964.

Erhard owes his reputation for "being soft," symbolized by the metaphor of "the rubber lion," to his predecessor more than to anyone else. The life of a small shopkeeper's son in the Bavarian town of Fürth, who in sixty-six years has risen to top-ranking position in the West German state, tells a different story. From humble beginnings he managed to get a university education. Though an outsider, he managed to become a professor. Amid the sordid confusion of the Third Reich, he managed to keep his hands clean. And even if he did not think highly of heroic resistance as long as it seemed to lead nowhere, he made courageous decisions when he could see an aim worth striving for. Best known and typical is his arbitrary decision to lift rationing the day the currency reform went into effect—this against the advice of German politicians and without asking the Allies. When he was reprimanded by the U.S. Military Governor: "Didn't you know, Herr Erhard, that any change in the system of rationing is for the Occupation Powers to decide?" he replied, "I didn't change rationing—I abolished it." This is the kind of thing that inspires hope, even if any future political miracle should not succeed wholly in matching the economic one. The latter was certainly not achieved by Erhard alone, but he can fairly take the credit because there were times when it seemed to rest on his faith alone. But then, we don't always have to have miracles. . . .

2. "WHAT DO YOU THINK OF GERMANY'S DEVELOPMENT SINCE 1945?"

"I think," said Herr X, whose guests we were, "that much of Leonhardt's criticism of the eighteen years after Hitler is justified. But the liberalism he keeps holding up to us as a yardstick is unrealistic. There isn't a country in the world today that can afford it."

Ralph was puffing on his pipe nervously. "Forgive me, but I think that statement is as sad as it is wrong. If anything's to save us from the threat of totalitarianism, it isn't going to be a threat of counter-total-itarianism, but an intellectual attitude that, as far as I'm concerned, you can call liberalism.

The word "liberal" still comes pretty close to being a dirty word in Germany. "German liberalism," wrote the Frenchman, Joseph Rovan, in his book on Germany, "was never quite able to rid itself of the stigma of its foreign origin."

Liber, of course, means free. All combinations of the word "free" —Freethinkers and Free Body Culture (a rather pompous way of referring to nudism in Germany) excepted—enjoy the best reputation in Germany: freedom, free elections, freedom fighters, wars of freedom, free markets, freely; but the same thing can't be said of the word "liberal" and its derivatives. The LPD, or Liberal Democratic Party, for instance, was smart enough to rename itself the Free Democratic Party.

"But in England, too," said Herr X, "the Liberal Party isn't very strong any more."

"Not right now," said Ralph. "And that I happen to regret this, and want to do what I can to see it changed, won't necessarily interest you. What is interesting though is the question as to why the Liberal Party is so weak in a country as liberal as England. I think the answer is pretty clear. It is because the other two parties—the Conservatives and the Socialists—have adopted so many liberal ideas that the Liberal Party has lost its *raison d'être*. Too bad for the Party but good for the country. Can the same thing be said of the two big parties in Germany? Now there's a question that really interests me."

Actually it is hard to decide where "the liberal" may find a place for himself in today's Germany. There are no more *Weltanschauung* parties; but a party with a program consisting entirely of getting in and staying in is not going to be popular either. The CDU/CSU (Christian Democratic Union and Christian Socialist Union) is the government party, the only one beside the SPD, or Socialist Party, that may presume to have certain ideas on Germany's future, for the realization of which it needs the mandate of the German people. The German people gave the CDU/CSU their mandate in 1949, 1953, 1957, and 1961. At this point I can see only one possibility (short of nuclear war) that they might deny the CDU/CSU this mandate in 1965, 1969, 1973, and 1977—the possibility of the old hereditary enmity between Catholic and Protestant breaking out anew.

Critics tend to make things a little too easy for themselves when they say that the coalition between Socialist and Democratic Christians, as demonstrated by the CDU and CSU, is lacking in the Christian sentiment it so boldly professes on the party flag. This is not entirely true. In the state dictionary, published by the Görres Society (Herder Verlag) is the following definition: "The characteristic component of the name CDU/CSU is [*not the attribute 'Christian,' or even the attribute 'democratic,' but*] the word 'Union.'" (The italicized contribution is mine.) Very true. Yet the strongest common denominator on which the government party rests *is* Christianity in the broadest sense. On the day that Catholics and Protestants rediscover their three-hundred-year-old differences, the German government party will cease to be just that; and since the Catholics and Protestants in the CDU/CSU are fully aware of this, they will probably be very careful not to embark on any such voyages of discovery.

The Berliners and Rhinelanders quarrel about who invented the CDU. The name Christian Democratic Union dates back undoubtedly to the founding of the party in Berlin on June 26, 1945, by Dr. Andreas Hermes, former Reichsminister of the Centrum Party. From the start, the Catholic impetus was the stronger. Internal party politics therefore have to be aimed at strengthening the Protestant wing, because the fact that neither a Catholic nor a Protestant party would be powerful enough to win a parliamentary majority on its own may be read in the history of the Weimar Republic.

"We've been talking about the CDU for quite a while now, and the name Adenauer hasn't been mentioned—as if the Party were imaginable without him."

Dick took the bull by the horns and dropped the name, just like that. Not only would the majority of his countrymen agree with him— Dr. Adenauer would, too. Whoever wishes the Federal Republic continued political stability can only hope that Dick isn't right, and that a CDU will still be possible without Dr. Adenauer.

In all probability though, the CDU wouldn't have become what it is today without him; and he would certainly not have achieved what he did without the CDU. Before 1945, not one German in a hundred had ever heard the name Adenauer, although the man already had a full life behind him. And until 1950, Professor Ludwig Erhard, the present chancellor and "father of the German economic miracle," was certainly more in the limelight than the former Chancellor. Adenauer did not participate in the founding of the CDU, but he soon joined it and became its chairman. We have the story of how this took place from a reliable witness who was there when it happened.

Dr. Holzapfel, co-chairman of the Westphalian Christian Democrats, had called a meeting that was to create a new party out of a regional group. As the gentlemen were about to sit down, they found the chairman's seat already occupied. The mayor of Cologne had sat down in it with a friendly, "*Sie jestatten doch sischer*. . . . You don't mind, I'm sure," in his best Cologne dialect. No one had asked him to do so.

It is impossible to do justice to the request to "say something about Adenauer." When a definitive biography of him is finally written—until now we have had nothing but eulogies or political attacks—it will be a fat volume. Ten pages could be filled just with his titles and offices: Honorary degrees in law at Harvard and Yale, in engineering in Berlin, medicine in Freiburg, and apparently all the faculties at Cologne. Honorary citizen of the cities of Honnef, Cologne, and Bonn; Bearer of the Honor-Ring of German Crafts, and a Grand Cross for Service to the Federal Republic, cast especially for him. Honorary president of the Europa Movement and the German Horticultural Society; Man of the Year 1953 for *Time* magazine in the United States, and Knight of the Order of St. George in England, which gives him the right to be addressed as "Sir Konrad."

My foreign friends asked me again and again to tell them something about Adenauer, and my choice is a version of the story of how he came to be dismissed as mayor of Cologne for "incompetence."

I have heard the story from two sources: from one of Adenauer's relatives with whom I once studied, and from a colonel on the staff of the British commander, who later became a friend of mine. In several biographies the action has been attributed to General Barraclough. The man actually responsible, though, is General Templer, who called himself "His Majesty's only general ever wounded by a grand piano." (The instrument was hurled out of a truck by an explosion.)

Templer was one of those barrack types famous in the English army for having their men paint black coal heaps white to keep them busy, or to create what they consider "order and cleanliness." (Order and cleanliness have to "rule" in a barracks, or they have to be "created.") In a similar fashion, Templer wanted to create order and cleanliness in Cologne. There was obviously no sense in painting the ruins white, but people could be set to rearranging them in an orderly fashion. Civilian Adenauer didn't think much of the idea; he could see more pressing things to do. So he got a dressing down by Barraclough on Templer's orders, and this was something he could not tolerate. After all, he had suffered a lot more under Hitler than the English had. Besides, it wasn't the first occupation by British troops for him. He'd gone through it all before, in 1918, and at that time had told the English commander how a gentleman should behave. The dismissal for "incompetence" that followed relieved Konrad Adenauer of his position as Mayor of Cologne and forbade him "any political activity whatsoever . . . directly or indirectly."

Barraclough and Adenauer must have articulated pretty clearly what they thought of each other, and it couldn't have been very complimentary on either side. Mayor Adenauer went so far as to accuse the English general of finding himself in "fine company," referring, of course, to the Soviet Union. At a later date, Adenauer is supposed to have said, "I have meanwhile found out from a reliable source that my dismissal was due to the influence of the deputy of another [German] party." My English chronicler, however, considers this highly improbable.

So here we have four important factors at the hour of Konrad Adenauer's "birth": the anticommunism of a Catholic Rhinelander; the intolerance of a patriarch for strong men at his side, much less above him; the alienism toward all things English of the Carolingian with the English title, disciple of a Holy Roman Empire that covered more or less the same territory as "the Six" (EEC) do today, on a political basis that consisted mainly of unity between Germany and France; and his contempt for "the other" party.

When was Adenauer really born?

In October, 1945, he became famous overnight; there can be no doubt about that. One of the most capable civil servants in Germany, without a brown stain on his white shirt, had been dismissed for incompetence! The affair was worth an entire election campaign. All of us talked about nothing else. Adenauer had told the not-very-popular representative of a not-very-popular occupation force where to get off. In order that this "hour of birth" may create no false associations, I must add that this first and, until 1963, only Chancellor the Federal Republic ever had, had already passed the age of retirement by eight years when he was elected!

"Your Chancellor (he was by then eighty-five) didn't use any of these couches," the head of the Vienna Museum told me when I sank down on the cushions exhausted after a two-hour tour.

Anecdotes grow about Adenauer like ivy around an oak. I would like to tell two more:

This one is true. Editor-in-chief Tüngel of Die Zeit, had written in an editorial that the Chancellor went at politics as if he were in charge of a volunteer fire department, to which the Chancellor replied, "Der Herr Tüngel, der hat janz recht, aber er hat sicher keine Ahnung wie schwer dat iss mit der freiwilligen Feuerwehr. . . . Herr Tüngel is probably quite right, but I'm sure he has no idea what a time you can have with a volunteer fire department."

It was always one of Adenauer's sources of strength that, as mayor, he handled his city as if it were his family (he has seven children and twenty-one grandchildren, unless a few more grandchildren have been added by now), and that he ruled the nation as he had once ruled his city.

As for the second anecdote: A delegation from his party came to him with the complaint, "But you can't expect us to say yes and amen to everything you do, Herr Bundeskanzler," to which the Bundeskanzler replied, "But my dear gentlemen, nobody is asking you to say amen."

It remains to be seen how much damage the rather frail institutions of a not-very-solidly grounded German democracy have suffered at the hands of a man who hasn't been very considerate of them. Adenauer's successor may discover, if he tries to walk in the footsteps of this patriarchal autocrat, that the old man's boots are a few sizes too

large for him. It will then be up to the CDU to teach their party leader
the democratic rules.

After making the important exception, that ex-Chancellor Adenauer
never had much feeling for the necessary democratic divisions of
power, the American historian Gordon A. Craig writes: "Konrad
Adenauer remains the most impressive statesman in the western world."
A perhaps even greater compliment is what I heard two of his most
vehement opponents in the German press say about him, "There may
come a day when we shall long to have Adenauer back. . . ."

What was fair for CDU politician, Herr X, must also be granted his
opposite number in the SPD. Let's call him Mr. Y. My friends started
off by asking him the usual questions and got the usual answers: What
do you consider the most important internal political problem? Reunification, unless you want to call reunification a foreign policy problem. What do you consider the most important foreign policy problem? The strengthening of the Western world against the Eastern
menace. What do you think of NATO? I consider NATO an indispensable alliance to which we have to be extremely loyal. What do
you think of atomic weapons? One-sided atomic disarmament is impossible; but we are for American dispositionary rights to German
atomic war piles. And what are your social-political aims? To protect
our economy from crisis and to further an equal distribution of
wealth.

It is worth noting that we had received the same answers, almost
word for word, to the purposely same questions a few days before
from Herr X of the CDU.

The SPD may be referred to as the party which is not in power,
never has been. And in the end that's not good for a party. If a stable
is full of good horses that are never allowed to run a race, they'll be
ready to do almost anything to get a chance to do so; for instance,
assure everyone that they could run just as well and just as fast, yes,
even with the same fine form as the horses in the active stable, without
realizing that with these assurances there ceases to be a reason for
changing stables!

SPD and CDU differ in West Germany today far more because of
their reputations than because of their policies. The SPD is not more
socialistic than the CDU, which once had an extremely socialistic platform, the Ahlen program, while its sister party, the Bavarian Christian
Socialist Union, has socialism in its crest; nor is the Christian Democratic Union more Christian than the SPD. Two prominent Christians,
Protestant Gustave Heinemann and Catholic Peter Nellen, left the
CDU for the SPD because of their Christian convictions. Both parties
have rigorously orthodox cores (which have difficulty, however, when
it comes to a definition of dogma), a liberal minority of men who make
it possible for people like myself to believe in a political future for
Germany, and lots of foot soldiers marching along, ever ready to hang
their light coats in the wind created by the strongest man.

Both parties have, or had, their eminent mayors, prototypes of the German political figure if ever there was one, the most legitimate descendant of the provincial sovereign, to whom we are still strongly attuned. For the CDU—Adenauer in Cologne, Lehr in Düsseldorf, Heinemann in Essen; for the SPD—Brauer in Hamburg, Kaisen in Bremen, Heinemann in Essen (after his "defection" from the CDU). Both parties have made disconcerting about-faces on important political issues: the SPD, originally the party of international relationships and involvements, has, especially under the influence of its first postwar chairman, behaved more nationalistically than the CDU, which is dedicated to the nationalism of the German middle class, yet has steered a very strong pro-Europa course.

The CDU, originally the party which, with the help of the Allies, established German federalism, has accepted centralized government more and more during its fourteen years of rule, and had to be told by the Federal Constitutional Court that the Basic Law grants certain rights also to the Länder. The SPD, organized in a centralized way, and always more oriented toward centralized government than the CDU, learned to love the Länder because it has only them to thank for the fact that any of its deputies govern in Germany!

The Länder are further proof of the fact that the main difference (not the only difference, the main difference) between CDU and SPD lies in the fact that one party governs and the other does not. The same reproaches about patronage, one party rule, lack of respect for minorities, which the CDU has to listen to in Bonn, capital of the Federal Republic, are directed at the SPD administration in Wiesbaden, capital of Land Hesse. And a man would have to be bold or blind to declare that the SPD administration in Hamburg projected a Socialist-proletarian image, or the CDU government in Rhineland-Palatinate, a bourgeois-capitalistic one. The truth is that no one could tell merely by his experiences in any of the German Länder, which party was governing it. Not even the schools, which governmental ideologies often like to reform or contra-form, give any clear indication.

Perhaps there is a difference between those who vote SPD or CDU?

I'm afraid not. Any preferences shown are far more concerned with the two parties' reputations than with their policies. "The curse of the SPD is that it has a history," said Herr Y, "a history that doesn't go very well with our fine chromium world refined by references to Christianity."

In 1945, three parties were able to start where they had left off in 1933, when they had been forbidden: the Catholic Centrum Party, the Socialist SPD, and the Communist KPD. Only the SPD survived and may now be proud of being the only one of the new parties with a hundred-year-old tradition.

"You can have it," said Herr Y, referring to the tradition. "Of Schumacher's three great tactical errors, the greatest probably was that he didn't think of disaasociating himself from the history of the SPD by giving the party a new name."

Dr. Kurt Schumacher, the stubborn West Prussian who founded the SPD anew after the war and became its chairman, could have seen little reason for doing that. Wasn't his party the only one that had steered a course in opposition to Hitler to the end? The only party that had dared to vote against Hitler's Enabling Act, the law that gave him and his party full power to rule in a state of emergency, without the consent of Parliament? Hadn't all top functionaries of the party then been forced to emigrate, or like himself, been sent to a concentration camp? But Dr. Kurt Schumacher couldn't know that soon it would not be considered "the thing" to have emigrated or been in a concentration camp.

The phrase "to be considered the thing" must sound strange in such a connection, but it demonstrates what I was trying to point out when I spoke of the reputation of the SPD as something never actually defined and therefore difficult to contradict. Of course those who suffered in concentration camps are respected by a majority of the population. The overzealous electioneers of the CDU, who tried to discredit the SPD candidate for the chancellorship by referring to him as an "emigrant," were met with indignation not only by SPD voters. But emigration and concentration camp sentence (weren't there a lot of Communists in the concentration camps, too?) certainly do not belong to the imponderables that count as the thing. So what does?

I'd rather not answer that question. Such things are too undemonstrable and too mixed up with one's own prejudices. Although work is highly respected in Germany (at any rate, most foreigners think it is) I wouldn't call "worker" a prestige profession. The reputation of the SPD was, therefore, not enhanced by the fact that it has always been the workers' party. Besides, it used to be a Marxist party, and Marxism was never considered the thing in German middle-class circles. Who would be so stupid as to support the prophet who was prophesying one's doom?

Among the first prominent Marxist and Social Democrats, there were many Jews and, let's face it, Jewish origin is no advantage to anyone striving for social prestige in Germany. I'll have more to say on that subject later. But first of all, and apart from all racial theories, what was held against the Jews more than anything else was the fact that they were not Christians. And it is considered the thing, in twentieth-century Europe, to be Christian, or at least not anti-Christian. Nothing harmed the SPD more than its not-entirely-unfounded reputation as an un-Christian or anti-Christian party.

"In England things are quite different," said Ralph. "Not only are the Free Protestant communities—the former nonconformists—the core of the Socialist Party; but it is generally believed that 80 per cent of approximately 4½ million Catholics vote for Labor."

The policy of the SPD in questions of national defense has a long and alarming history of misunderstandings and tactical foolishness. After bearing the odium of being a pacifist party of "fatherlandless comrades," the Socialists voted for the issuance of War Bonds in August, 1914. After a Peoples' Army had been part of their platform for a long time, they suddenly refused, in 1927, to vote for the construction of pocket battleships, and this assumed the proportions of a scandal. The party polemics against Chancellor Adenauer's rearmament policy put the SPD in an unfortunate position, because their chairman was for rearmament, and in discussions concerned with this highly important matter, no one was interested in nuances. The SPD is not against national defense, still it has managed somehow to earn that reputation.

"And what were Dr. Schumacher's two other mistakes?" Dick wanted to know.

"His second mistake was that he overestimated his own chances to be Chancellor and therefore helped to make the chancellor as good as irremovable from office."

"And the third?"

"His third mistake was letting the SPD refuse to take part in the Economic Council of the Bizone. That was how the CDU was able to take over all government business, not in 1949, but practically speaking in the summer of 1948. The foundations of the state, that is, the top administration, could be made up of officials close to the CDU, and the SPD was forced into the role of opposition party from the start."

But a strategic error, for which Dr. Kurt Schumacher's character and personality were to blame, seems to me to carry even more weight than all these tactical errors. The same SPD which founded the First International and whose followers were described as "enemies of the state" under the Kaiser, the same SPD whose political men were denounced as "fulfillment politicians" under the Weimar Republic and called traitors when Hitler came to power, this same SPD discovered a nationalistic mission at the very moment when the German dream of nationalism was dead. "Are you a Chancellor of the Allies?" the chairman of the SPD cried out to Konrad Adenauer in Parliament. The little bit of popularity capital that might have been won by this approach melted away together with the dwindling resentment against the occupation forces. Opportunism doesn't suit a party that has done without it for a hundred years.

It is difficult to remain loyal to old convictions and still not become old-fashioned, and that is the dilemma of a party which already suffers from the fact that it isn't considered the thing in the good society that is still a hazy ideal for every lower middle-class housewife. The apparatus of a hundred-year-old party is cumbersome. Outsiders recognize this most clearly in the language of party pronouncements, and in its propaganda leaflets that are supposed to recruit new members. It is almost paradox: through their way of expressing themselves, which comes close to the old army instructions, the SPD betrays its Prussianism.

To find a way out of these and sundry other dilemmas, the SPD played its highest trump: it always did provide Berlin (and most German big cities) with a mayor. Now we have to realize that for those

Germans who have long ago written off the Eastern Territories (and there are many such Germans) Berlin remains a thing apart, something indispensable, something grandiose. I know few sacrifices which I can imagine any West German taking upon himself because of the Eastern Territories; on the other hand, I can imagine few sacrifices which any German would *not* be willing to make for Berlin. That may be less true in the south than in the north, still it remains valid.

It is good for a German political man to be a mayor, and to be mayor of Berlin is best of all. So the SPD put up their mayor of Berlin as chancellor against Konrad Adenauer. This was the beginning of a radical reorganization of the party according to an American pattern: opinion polls and brain trusts were mobilized to create the "Kennedy look" for Willy Brandt, who fortunately is not utterly dissimilar in type to the late American President, who was perhaps more loved and admired—nay, adored—in Germany than anywhere else, particularly by our young people, our intellectuals, our liberals, and Berliners. Finally, for a leading political figure, Brandt is young. To which we have, of course, to ask ourselves: is it the thing in Germany to be young? When the Germans were asked which of Adenauer's characteristics they thought of most highly, quite a few answered: his age.

Brandt would not be the smart man he is if he hadn't seen, by glancing at the statistics, that for the SPD everything depended on the female vote. So he had to shake off the sweaty, red-faced, church-inimical, service-entrance reputation of his party and become socially acceptable. All of which meant: away with Marxism, with nationalization of industries, with the pacifists, with all philosophical ballast. Away with everything that stood between the SPD and its goal: to become the party in power.

The tactics are understandable. The party that wants to be socially acceptable in Germany must do everything it can to become the party in power, because opposition isn't considered the thing in Germany. And this leaves us with one small difficulty: How do you convince the necessary number of citizens that they must choose an opposition party that is promising to do what the party in power has been trying to do, and not without success, for the past sixteen years?

3. ARE WE MILITARISTS AGAIN?

"You must stop thinking that fear of the German soldier is a Communist invention!"

Yvonne was really excited. Her voice was quite shrill. She, a burnt child of the German occupation of France, had just called the generals of the Federal Republic's army, "Hitler's generals," and all I had done was ask her not to take this expression of East German propaganda too literally.

The same thing could be said of our higher civil servants. Top-ranking officers and civil servants have similar traditions: both were mainstays of the Prussian state; both have their own disciplinary laws, the same scale of retirement pay and salary ratings (first lieutenant equivalent, for instance, to *Oberregierungsrat* or Upper Administrative Adviser), and in both cases the West German government decided that their advice could not be dispensed with even if they had had key positions in Hitler's Reich, as long as nothing could be proved against them from that time, which would be considered a punishable offense in Germany today.

I personally regret this decision, but I would like to understand it. If, as manager of a firm, I had the choice between a man who knows his business but is otherwise slightly suspect, and one with an irreproachable character who simply can't do what's required of him, I'm afraid I would hire the expert and tell myself that I could see to it that he didn't find any opportunity to justify the suspicions held against him. Perhaps, unless one is dealing with murderers, one should not judge people exclusively by what they did twenty years ago. What they are doing today is really much more important. And most important is the question: How will these people behave in a crisis that might become acute tomorrow or twenty years from now? The answer is of course entirely open.

"But you must admit it's a little suspicious," I told Yvonne, "that the East German government discovered its aversion to Hitler's generals just after the well-earned retirement of their own last representative of this type, General Vincent Müller, staff officer in the East German army (since deceased)."

"But we're not talking about East Germany," said Yvonne. "We're talking about the army of the Federal Republic. You can read all about it in *L'Express*, in this article by Michel Bosquet, and he's certainly no Communist."

I read the article in the September 1, 1960 issue. Five things trouble Bosquet:

1. The personality of Defense Minister Franz-Josef Strauss. His "ambition, hunger for power, and efficiency, fill everyone who knows him with admiration and anxiety."

2. The tenacity with which the West German government and its Defense Minister work for the arming of the Bundeswehr with atomic weapons, beginning with that day in February, 1957, on which Strauss is supposed to have told some assembled officers and correspondents that the Bundeswehr had to have atomic weapons, and would get them whether the United States liked it or not.

3. The strength of the Bundeswehr: when all plans have been carried out, it will again be (according to Bosquet) the strongest army in Europe, the Soviet Union excepted.

4. The rejection—not officially but certainly in fact—of the earlier idea of "a civilian in uniform." Two-thirds of the German army is made up of professional soldiers; and it has more than four times as many officers (17,000) as the old Reichswehr (4,000), and only a few

thousand less than the German army had at the beginning of World War II, in 1939—24,000.

5. The reawakening of German military preparedness, demonstrated by the fact that out of the first class drafted, only 0.3 per cent were conscientious objectors.

I think anyone who isn't worried about some of the things that seem to be taking place again in the Bundeswehr must be either unduly optimistic (and not many are) or insufficiently informed, with which you have the majority. Let's discuss German military readiness, or as it was called between 1945 and 1949, "German militarism," sometimes referred to as "Prussian militarism."

From Tacitus to the handbooks of the Allies in World War II, all voices are unanimous: the Germans hate peace, the Germans love war. Thus we still enjoy the reputation that there's nothing we'd rather do than march (preferably in boots and goose-step), stand at attention, click heels, wear uniforms, and die for the Fatherland. Our more recent critics, however, attest to the opposite: the Germans, they tell us, are so softened by luxury and fouled up by their own wealth that they aren't prepared to move a finger for anything outside their own little world of refrigerators and television sets.

Now both theories can't be right. It is a curse of day-to-day journalism to see—instead of actual developments which move slowly even in our hectic world—"leaps," "waves," and "sudden reversals of mood," that exist only in the fantasy of whoever is writing the editorials triggered by some event of the day. The true development of German militarism, as far as I can see, is a certain typically German pendulum motion swinging from euphoria (1914 and 1939) to sobriety (1918 and 1945). The pendulum never stops, but its motion has diminished. When we went to war in 1939, our élan—even when we were proud of our first Iron Cross—couldn't be compared with the enthusiasm with which, on November 11, 1914, hundreds of young German volunteers straight from school, with the national anthem on their lips, attacked the French in Ypres and fell like flies. And the martial spirit of our sons today seems lukewarm or sensibly muted to us, according to whether we look upon military preparedness as a virtue or a sad necessity. The hope that the pendulum will swing in the future only within a sensible range is not entirely without foundation.

"I wish I could share your optimism," said Ralph. "But I've heard German army officers say, on East German television, that in West Germany plans are already being drawn up for the next war. Now you can't tell me that was just East German propaganda. They were West German officers who had fled to East Germany. It was in the West German papers, too; only four lines on page five, but just the same . . . These men were convincing."

To defend the West German Bundeswehr is no simple matter. I felt a lot happier when you couldn't see any difference between the defense minister and the family minister, the days when the former was still being referred to as "the Chancellor's deputy for all problems resulting from the increase of Allied troops in Germany." And I liked it even better when, on Allied orders, all the shooting ranges at fairs were transformed into bowling alleys. And our former defense minister is supposed to have said, "Let the hand wither that ever touches a gun again," although he later denied it, so you can take it or leave it.

One shouldn't forget any of this or wave it aside; and to use the popular excuse, "They were Communists," for these West German officers, seems to me an indication of incipient softening of the brain. Whoever still wants to understand the world should forget none of the disasters which the German soldiers—and those of other nations, but in our century predominantly German soldiers—brought upon the world. But—and this is a big "but"—does it therefore have to be stressed week after week in army information bulletins? Should we expect the German soldier constantly to drag around with him grave doubts of his own profession? Should the subject be dealt with in officer's training?

I like to recall an old colonel whose pupils at the military academy in Halle on the Saale admired and respected him. I have him to thank for two expressions of military wisdom. One: "Life and love, gentlemen, are worth while only on the brink of danger." And the second: "Officer instruction is not academic instruction for intellectuals. It differs from instruction by noncommissioned officers in that it is meant only for semi-idiots." I think we may believe that this venerable staff officer only intended to characterize and not to hurt anybody's feelings when he used the expression "semi-idiots."

Of course we find instructions in today's Bundeswehr manuals that would seem intended for semi- or even full-fledged idiots if an intellectual were to start analyzing them. That evolves from the fact that a soldier has to know the answer to everything. "What would you do in the event of an atomic attack?" It was a young cadet in the Bundeswehr who assured me solemnly that in such a case, which he hoped would never materialize, I should lie down under the nearest tree and cover myself with a white coat. . . .

Actually we haven't digressed much from the West German officers who, on East German television, told the German TV audience, and probably quite a few foreigners beside Ralph Stevens, that the West German Bundeswehr was preparing for the next war. I don't think we need bring up such notorious excuses as brainwashing to explain it.

What is an army supposed to be training for except war? And as for the difference between "offensive" and "defensive" war, which is completely erased by pseudo-concepts such as "offensive-defense," over which scholars of international law are still squabbling inconclusively— who could possibly expect officers' or noncommissioned officers' instruction to resolve that? And even the most harmless maneuvers demand certain "positions." NATO maneuvers are certainly not just sport, and they can't possibly be carried out without realistic "enemy positions." Since there isn't a soul who expects an attack from Denmark, the hypothetical enemy for all maneuvers lies in the east. In high staff circles he is still referred to diplomatically, but the men simply

call him "the Russian," or "Ivan." What's more, the enemy was called
"the Red" in German maneuvers long before there was any thought of
the red flag of the Soviet Union. And one more point: whatever practical fighting experience the Bundeswehr may have was gathered for
the most part in Russia.

From all of which may be deduced without too much cogitation that
if anyone with a naïve heart watches a maneuver of the Bundeswehr,
he may very well come to the conclusion that war against the Soviet
Union is in the making, but I wouldn't be surprised if we had a few
commanders who would do better not to let their anti-Russian resentments, accumulated in years of war and imprisonment, run quite
so rampant.

"So you don't really mind that barely twenty years after the war,
the Germans are again the strongest military power in Europe? . . .
All right, with a few qualifications," said Yvonne. She couldn't have
been more wrong. I do mind. Above all, because one set of Germans is
quite evidently threatening to become the strongest military power of
the Western world (after the United States), and the other set of
Germans is threatening to become the strongest military power of the
Eastern world (after the Soviet Union). And because I shudder to
think of the day when these two sets of Germans fall upon each other.
No Indo-Chinese or Korean precedents will be valid then!

But once German rearmament was a *fait accompli*, there wasn't
much sense any more in being against it. Above all, there is no sense
whatsoever in reproaching the Bundeswehr for it. The men are practicing their profession with a lot of good will, a great deal of efficiency,
and decency. And if the German soldier—if there must be such—wants
to be as strong as possible, who is going to blame him for that? Here I
agree with ex-Chancellor Adenauer: When atomic rockets are being
used, there is no point in training fusiliers. War or no war? Even in
Germany the Generals can't decide that any more. That will be attended to by our statesmen.

"The old Nazi statesmen?"

Our little Yvonne had the last word.

4. THERE IS NO GERMAN ANTI-SEMITISM

"Adenauer and Heuss have erected a façade behind which reactionary
elements and true Nazis (not only opportunists) may infiltrate the
armed forces and the government to such an extent that they could
easily get control of them." An American, I. F. Stone, wrote that after
coming home from a trip to Germany. The *Frankfurter Hefte* printed
his article in July, 1959. Dick asked me what I thought of it.

The statement is made questionable by one expression. "Reactionary
elements"? Granted. "Opportunists"? I'll say! But "true Nazis"? What
are true Nazis? I thought we decided we couldn't define that quite a
few pages back. Or is a deeper interpretation of National Socialism

possible which would give us less trivial, pragmatic ways to decide who was "truly" a Nazi?

The Swiss historian, Gonzague de Reynold, sees and describes National Socialism as the freakish child of a vengeful pan-Germanism, born of the 1918 defeat and a facet of the German spirit still strongly influenced by Nordic myths and primitive paganism. As masters and philosophers of this Nazi Pan-Germanism, he quotes the theories of Spengler, Frobenius, and Spann: the culture of a people depends on political, economic, social, biological, and geographic events. This theory was expressed more specifically by Alfred Rosenberg: blood and earth decide all the manifestations of culture—religion, art, science, morality, economic, social, and political life. This was followed by the dogma of the German people as the Chosen People of all northern races. Spengler's *Decline of the West* was for Rosenberg a result of Germany's defeat in World War I. For according to him, only the Germans had a dynamic culture. Other nations, above all the French, had a civilization; but civilization was something static, petrified, a culture dying. The requisite for a rebirth of the Occident therefore was the rebirth of Germany, which was in turn dependent on a restoration of the purity of German blood and race. The logical result was anti-Semitism.

Since I believe in very little of this, I have tried to report it as literally as possible, and can therefore take no responsibility for style or terminology. Deeper interpretations subsequently led (with Reynold) to a list of "Forerunners and Pioneers of National Socialism," and here we find a curiously mixed group. The old High German poets of the *Muspilli*, an imaginative description of the Judgment Day (approximately 881 A.D.), the translator of the *Heliand*, Saxon version of the Gospel (830 A.D.), the Middle High German epic writers, Meister Eckart, Luther, Kant, Rousseau, Schleiermacher, Nietzsche, Wagner, Fichte, Hegel, Marx, Spengler, Heidegger. But such exercises in thought have very little to do with the historical truth as we witnessed it. I am not underestimating the romantic all-German, old-German idealism especially as practiced in Germanic studies. Somewhere along the line, their paths crossed National Socialism. But to say that such men as Bartels, Roethe, Nadler, Bertram, Naumann, Obenauer, Cysarz, Kindermann, Fricke, Fechter, Koch, invented Hitlerism, would be an absolutely crazy and presumptuous statement.

It is very unlikely that Hitler ever read a book in the field of Germanics. He couldn't abide Rosenberg. There are good reasons for doubting that he was ever very familiar with Rosenberg's *Mythos of the 20th Century*. Hitler's anti-Semitism didn't stem from that or from any Nordic-mythological Germanic philosophy. It was born in the lower-middle-class milieu of the Austrian provinces. Here a psychological explanation seems more plausible to me as a line of development than that of Luther-Fichte-Nietzsche-Heidegger. Witnesses have attested to the fact that Hitler was obsessed by the idea that, because of a slip on the part of his grandmother, Maria Anna Schicklgruber, he had Jewish blood. Anyway, he couldn't have felt too happy looking in the mirror after having listened to the race-theoreticians of the Third Reich.

"Is that the latest excuse?" Dick wanted to know, and he was almost angry. "So German anti-Semitism is supposed to be a trauma of Austrian lower-middle-class Adolf Hitler!"

Whatever may be said for or against this theory, it certainly is no excuse. Germany's crime is not anti-Semitism, but a sordid mixture of mass hysteria, opportunism, and cowardice which led to the murder of from 4,194,200 to 4,581,200 Jews, according to Gerald Reitlinger's *Final Solution* (Berlin 1960).

Hair-splitting? I don't think so. On the contrary, I think it is very important to differentiate: not all anti-Semites murder Jews (as is proved by English, American, and French anti-Semitism); not all Germans who murdered Jews were anti-Semites. In many cases they were simply executioners, some of whom may have enjoyed their bloody roles; but the vast majority did what they were told to do out of fear that they themselves might be the next victims. Above all, it is important to recognize as deceptive and dangerous (because so fearfully simple) the equation of National Socialism with anti-Semitism. For this equation leads automatically to the conclusion: If we can succeed in banning German anti-Semitism, we will have succeeded in ridding the world of the "German menace" which, via National Socialism, almost succeeded in destroying entire races, the German race included. Things are not as simple as that.

Willy Hellpach, psychology professor and politician, presidential candidate in 1925, and a great man came very close to the truth when he wrote: "Another deceptive facet of the young national consciousness which was awakened and fostered after 1871 . . . was the constantly less restrained anti-Semitism, for which Treitschke himself, in his search for a scapegoat for all things imperfect and undesirable, invented the slogan, 'The Jews are our misfortune.' " Treitschke was a very German historian, and this necessity to find a scapegoat was the most German thing about him. World history has brought its share of misfortune to Germans and Jews. They therefore not only share the comforting belief of being a "chosen people," which crops up again and again, but also the search for the Old Testamentarian scapegoat.

Since no one really believes any more in a red devil with horns and a tail, we have to find our devils in human form. For a while the Pope in Rome sufficed for the Protestants, and Martin Luther for the Catholics, but when those who were not so denominationally minded had settled down between Catholic and Protestant, a new scapegoat was needed, because the world was as far as ever from being perfect. Sometimes this vacant role fell to the Jew. In many medieval chronicles you may read how the Jews had to atone for plagues and famines. Heine's *Rabbi von Bacherach* uses this for a theme.

The National Socialists made the Jew a scapegoat programmatically.

This simplified world history enormously. "The Jews are to blame for everything; the Wise Men of Zion are conspiring against Germany." But this mixture of world-history simplification, religious spleen, political expediency, economic envy, and persecution, was not anti-Semitism. In the years between 1933 and 1945, I personally did not meet a single fanatic Jew-hater. Later, yes, and not only in Germany. Granted, I did not move in higher party circles, but I have been assured that it was no different there.

"So you don't think that German anti-Semitism can ever be a menace again?" asked Dick.

I consider it just as unlikely as that we should ever again burn redheads as witches. We don't have to be afraid that the Germans may go insane the same way twice. *What we have to fear is the German's search for a scapegoat!* "In no country in the world," a clever observer said once, "are those who think differently slandered to the extent they are in Germany."

"Just a minute," Dick interrupted. "I want to get this straight. Are you trying to say that there never was and isn't now any anti-Semitism in Germany?" By his tone I could tell he was wondering if I was a Nazi, or out of my mind.

"That's just about it. And to make it even harder for you to decide whether I am feeble-minded or a villain, I am going to add that until the end of the war, I didn't know what was really going on in the concentration camps, and that very probably nine out of ten Germans didn't either."

I could see that I was losing the respect and sympathy of my little group, and that the time had come for me to express myself more clearly. So I said, "You know your compatriot, Eugene Davidson, former director of the Yale University Press. You yourself told me to read his book, *The Death and Life of Germany*. Now you decide if Davidson is a Nazi or crazy. Anyway, you'll find these two sentences in his book: On Page 403: 'There is less anti-Semitism in Germany than in many other countries.' And on Page 304: 'Jews who were sent to Theresienstadt from Berlin reported even late in the war that they had heard rumors of extermination camps but did not believe them.' What is more, I feel that the murder of five million Jews is not a smaller but, if such a thing is possible, a greater crime when passionate hatred ceases to be a reason for it. I am not trying to excuse anything, only to explain."

There was no such thing as German anti-Semitism, but of course there was anti-Semitism in Germany before Hitler, as there was everywhere in the world where there was a Jewish minority; in northern countries more than in southern countries, for which Lagarde probably gave the correct reason when he wrote: "It is a great misfortune that the external aspect of the Jew is so instrumental in keeping alive in the German people the consciousness that the Jew is a foreigner." An intellectual like Nietzsche saw the same thing in a quite different light when he wrote: "What a blessing the Jew is among Germans!"

Nietzsche, who according to theoretical analysts of National Socialism such as Reynold, is a forerunner of Hitler?

Originally, anti-Semitism in Germany, as everywhere else, was religiously inspired, and directed against the people who had crucified Christ. The fact that Christ—before race research made an Aryan of him—was a Jew, didn't seem to worry the anti-Semites. In many German cities, Judengassen (Jew streets), where they have not been renamed in the last thirty years, remind one of the times when the Jews lived fairly poverty-stricken lives in their own narrow quarters or ghettos. In Munich, for instance, in the thirteenth century, they had to pay a tax of twenty kreuzers daily, they were not allowed to visit the baths or buy meat, and all professions except that of money-lender were closed to them. We know from *The Merchant of Venice* that in Italy, where the action takes place, and in England, where it was understood, similar measures were in force. In times of Jewish persecution, that unfortunate race had to hear its people reproached for practicing a profession that had been forced upon them.

In Germany, a more liberal way of life took longer in coming than in most other West European countries, but this is valid not only for the treatment of Jews in Germany. Religious anti-Semitism was kept alive in several sects, but was otherwise generally replaced by a social anti-Semitism. When Disraeli was Prime Minister in England, a Jew could still not become a Prussian civil servant or an army officer in Germany. We found out during the Dreyfus case that Jewish officers were not always popular in the French army either.

In my grandfather's day, the better German society still consisted mainly of civil servants and officers, categories that cover a much wider range in Germany than in most countries. To be a Jew meant being not quite fit to mingle in upper-class and aristocratic circles. This may imply arrogance and narrow-mindedness, but not necessarily malicious hostility. The picture didn't change very much until after the First World War, but then it changed rapidly, perhaps too rapidly. The Jews became prominent everywhere. For instance, almost every other Berlin hospital had a Jewish doctor as its chief, which gave rise to rumors (absolutely false) that any non-Jewish doctor would have a hard time getting a job there. During this time, economic envy of the Jew, the resentment of the debtor to his usurer in a somewhat sublimated form, created a fresh starting point for the anti-Semitic propaganda that erupted so forcefully in 1933.

Up to that point there is no history of any specific German anti-Semitism, only a history of anti-Semitism in Germany, another form of that world-wide anti-Semitism of which the English philosopher Hobbes wrote: "If the human being were truly humane, there would be no Jewish problem."

But quite another history of the Jews in Germany remains to be written, and that is the history of the Jewish-German intellectuals since the emancipation, *i.e.*, since the beginning of the nineteenth century. The words of a very prominent German (who naturally wishes to remain anonymous, and who would have every reason for rejecting the reproach that he admires the Jews) might serve very well as a motto: "Since they murdered the Jews, the Germans are becoming more and more stupid."

It would be a fat book, and it would include the upsurge of the German universities in general and natural science in particular, under Jewish influence. I would like at least to indicate the content of one of its chapters: The Jews in German Literature.

In 1812, Berlin became the first city in Germany to give the Jews equal rights as citizens. In the next hundred years, this capital city of Prussia became one of the three or four focal points of intellectual Europe, and the part played in this astonishing development by Berliners of Jewish origin cannot be overestimated. The first not wholly private encounters between Jews and non-Jews took place in Berlin's literary salons. These salons had evolved from the little reading circles of the era of enlightenment, when two powers missing in intellectual life until then could at last make their presence felt—women and Jews. Very often the two were joined. At any rate, Berlin has three Jewish women—three of the most fascinating German women—to thank for the first strong impulses of its literary life. Henriette de Lemos, a close friend of Schleiermacher (according to Reynold, a pioneer of National Socialism?) and wife of Dr. Marcus Herz; Rachel Levin, wife of Varnhagen von Ense; Dorothea Mendelssohn, daughter of the great Moses Mendelssohn, married first to the banker Veit, later to Friedrich Schlegel.

The most eminent men and women met in these Berlin salons. The guest books of the Herz and Varnhagen families read like an index to a history of German literature: Achim von Arnim, Ludwig Börne, Bettina Brentano, Johann Gottlieb Fichte, Friedrich Gentz, Franz Grillparzer, Friedrich Hegel, Heinrich Heine, Alexander and Wilhelm von Humboldt, Freiherr de la Motte-Fouqué, Jean Paul, Karl Wilhelm Ramler, Leopold Ranke, Friedrich Schlegel, Friedrich Schleiermacher, Ludwig Tieck. . . .

The number of great poets and writers in Germany was certainly no less impressive than in other countries; we had what was called Weimar Classicism and Heidelberg Romanticism, yet "German literature" was really nothing much more than a rather artificial collective expression. But in the years between 1810 and 1830, something very close to German literature was created in Berlin as a result of Jewish influence. Something very similar took place exactly a hundred years later, again in Berlin, and again under Jewish influence.

The fact that there was no politically united Germany at the beginning of the nineteenth century had an unfavorable effect on German literature, not directly, but in a rather complicated way. The desire for unity aroused the spirit of nationalism that erases the tolerance which any intellectual life, with its many necessary contradictions, has to have in order to flourish. At any rate, it is striking that after the death of Heine and Börne, no Jew played a leading role in German literature until the twentieth century. Then it was the Jews in Vienna: Kraus, Altenberg, Hofmannsthal, Schnitzler, Stefan Zweig; in Prague: Werfel, Kafka, Brod, Kisch; in Berlin: Harden, Kerr, Polgar, Alfred Neumann, Döblin, Arnold Zweig, Tucholsky, Kaiser, Feuchtwanger, Borchardt, S. Fischer, Jacobsohn, Kesten, Benjamin, Haas . . . until the year 1933, the emigration, the war, and the Final Solution of the Jews.

The Jew as a type suffers somewhat in Germany from the fact that the intellectual, as a type, is not valued too highly. The mistrust of the intellectual is countered, on the other hand, by great respect for the academic man and this results in a very curious cross-current of feelings. The facts which finally became known about such extermination centers as Auschwitz, Maidanek, and Dachau, sufficed to cure most Germans of an anti-Semitism that had been artificially fostered and was never very deeply rooted. To be sure, in 1952, every third German was still ready to declare that it was better for Germany to have no Jews, but no one spoke at the time of a rebirth of German anti-Semitism. That didn't happen until seven years later, when a few damn fools smeared swastikas on the walls of a synagogue. At this time, though, according to a survey, only every fifth German thought it would be better to have no Jews in Germany.

Twenty per cent. Is that frightening? And from that—to arrive at a fair ratio for Germany—we should subtract the percentage arrived at in other countries, the percentage of a universal anti-Semitism. What is left—and it isn't very much—can be spread across a still-shrinking remnant of incorrigibles and a few newcomers who have been encouraged in their feelings by the not-entirely-reasonable behavior of some Jewish emigrants.

"Do you really expect these people to behave reasonably after what they have been through?"

Certainly not. But I know that in the meantime we have acquired millions of young people who had nothing whatsoever to do with the gas chambers of Auschwitz. And some of them react sensitively when they are blamed for the last war by a Jewish emigrant, while they are being prepared for the next one by some other Jewish emigrant, William S. Schlamm, for instance, whose lectures to German students have been described as "warmongering," and I can see no reason for contradicting the definition.

Perhaps even more interesting than the steady decline of those who would rather see no Jews in Germany is the answer to another question: "What does anti-Semitism mean?" Half of those under thirty didn't know what it meant. . . .

5. IS THE GERMAN INTELLECTUAL ELITE LEFT WING?

The question was put to me more or less like that, and I feel it deserves a thorough answer, especially since it opens the way to a discussion of literature and art in Germany today.

Foreigners know shamefully little about German art and literature of the last fifteen years. Shamefully for us! It is often pointed out that perhaps art and literature don't exist in Germany today. The truth is that you can't get any sort of agreement on what writers, musicians, painters, sculptors, and architects, creating "art" in today's Germany, will still be considered important a hundred years from now. A banal, pragmatic definition, but it comes in handy at this point.

During a forum held as part of Dortmund's "German-English Cultural Weeks," I asked four prominent Englishmen: "What does Germany still mean to you today?" The answers included considerable mention of NATO, Berlin, the EFTA (European Free Trade Association), and the Common Market, but since we were supposed to be celebrating Cultural Weeks, I had hoped that the Germans would also be granted a certain importance in that realm of the intellect which lies beyond politics and economics. At last music was mentioned, but it turned out to be the music of Bach and Mozart.

"I may therefore conclude," I said, "that the German art, and literature of today have no reputation or meaning in England?"

That seemed to Lindley Fraser, one of the members of the panel, to be going too far. And he, whose profession it once was to fight fascism, and who was fighting communism at the time, tried to qualify this rather embarrassing fact by saying, "But the Brecht Berlin Ensemble made a great impression in London."

The Berlin Ensemble, for those who may not know it, is the show company of East Germany, which gives some really excellent performances at the Schiffbauerdamm Theater in East Berlin, and has made guest appearances with immense success in all the capitals of the world. They play not only Brecht but Communist-inspired dramas, or plays with an affirmative approach to Communist ideology.

In the British *Observer*, a recent article stated that but for an old sage like Ernst Jünger, no German postwar writer of international repute had appeared on the literary horizon. After which the following were named as on their way toward such acclaim: Hans Helmut Kirst, Heinrich Böll, Heinz Hüber, Hans Scholz, Gerd Gaiser, and Gregor von Rezzori. With all due respect to the humility so becoming in the literary observer who has seen his judgments of today become dubious tomorrow, that's a pretty mixed group. It reminds me of my favorite witness, the English lady of 1884, who wrote: "The German novel is usually a dull diversion, though Auerbach, Paul Heyse, Corvinus, and Marlitt have done much to redeem it from this reproach," and this at a time when Raabe was already writing as Raabe—Corvinus was a pseudonym—so were Stifter, Storm, Keller, Freytag, Fontane, in short, all those between Goethe and Thomas Mann who had something to say as novelists. According to German conceptions, it was a great era for the German novel.

Jünger's international reputation would be hotly disputed by most representatives of modern German literature (in all probability unjustly), and sagacity is certainly not the first thing I'd attribute to him.

Besides, he isn't a postwar author. As for the *Observer*'s list, it includes two writers I would also name: Böll and Gaiser, one who would come into consideration—Rezzori, one who isn't more highly regarded in Germany than the entire category of good escape literature to which he belongs—Kirst, another who is certainly no novelist—Scholz; and one whose name I have never heard before, in a decade of intense occupation with the new German literature—Hüber.

Another foreign observer said Jünger and Jaspers were the only two writers who still had a following waiting eagerly for their next books, a grotesque statement. I could think easily of ten other names to put beside Jünger's, and if we are going to include professors like Jaspers, I could come close to a list in three figures. But all this has nothing whatsoever to do with the literature of today.

Whose books are being eagerly awaited today by a readership of, let's say, three thousand literate people? This is not a bad yardstick, and among the West German postwar authors, at least a dozen should be mentioned: Alfred Andersch, Heinrich Böll, Gerd Gaiser, Günter Grass, Rudolf Hagelstange, Walter Jens, Wolfgang Koeppen, Siegfried Lenz, Arno Schmidt, Ernst Schnabel, Wolfdietrich Schnurre, Martin Walser. Since we may go beyond the boundaries of the West German Republic on our quest for German literature, the list should also include Friedrich Dürrenmatt and Max Frisch (Switzerland), Erwin Strittmatter (East Germany). But to get back to the opening question: Are these men left wing, and what does that mean?

Whoever invented the categoric statement: *Der Geist steht links* . . . "intellectualism stands on the Left," which, in the form of a question, was the title of this chapter in the original German edition, remains unknown. But he was evidently paraphrasing the words, "The enemy stands on the Right," with which Weimar Republic Chancellor Joseph Wirth very effectively closed one of his parliamentary speeches. The differentiation between Right and Left goes back to the British Parliament, where the conservatives, or Tories, sat on the right, the liberal Whigs on the left, but the terms have lost a lot of their original meaning. However, since they have been generally adopted, it is sometimes convenient to describe preservative, traditional, one might even say restorative powers, in a rather vague way, as being right; and all protesting, reformative, perhaps even revolutionary forces as being left.

The revolutionaries in art are represented by the avant-gardists. Seen thus every artist "stands on the Left," for there is no such thing as an artist who is satisfied with doing what has already been done. He at least wants to do something better; for the most part, though, he wants to do something different. In the case of the writer—unless he is a pure esthete or esoteric—and with the novelist especially, his material demands a close union with reality. Unable or unwilling to separate form and substance, the writer must be a critical observer of every day political life, an innovator, and in the last analysis a revolutionary.

In direct opposition to this stands the "Maecenas theory" of art, which runs, to put it as simply as I can: Maecenas (Emperor, Leader, State, or Party) does a great deal for the poet and writer and may therefore expect the poet and writer to do something for the Maecenas (Emperor, Leader, State, or Party). In East Germany this is the ruling concept in the most literal sense. Woe betide the writer who dares to find this Workers' and Farmers' State *not* absolutely magnificent. By that alone he would demonstrate his inferiority. For the Marxist-Leninistic doctrine lays claim to being the absolute truth. Not to acknowledge this can only be an error unworthy of an artist. There is no East German literary work which even attempts to question socialism and its achievements.

In West German literature, there are many works in which the republic and its government are violently attacked, by which I do not mean to imply that this beautiful freedom of literature is generally valued or admired where I come from. We would praise this freedom, some critics maintain, if only what came of it were not so poor. Well, complaints about the lack of admirable contemporary literature have been heard again and again in world history, with such regularity that we need not hesitate to count them among the literary platitudes of mankind. "Find me a man in Europe," wrote Nietzsche in the last century, "who counts, as our Goethe did, our Heine, our Hegel." *Ubi sunt . . .*

"Our Hegel" never did count; not literally. How could he? His German was execrable. "Our Heine" ran away to Paris and still rates only with a few people between Hamburg and Munich. As for "our Goethe," on whom we love to agree, and who is a measure for so many of our values—after his death, Friedrich Wilhelm III, then King of Prussia, forbade all memorial services in his honor in Prussia. Most foreigners moreover find him just as "dull and typically German" as they find our contemporary literature without it having occurred to anyone in Germany until now that this derogatory opinion could in any way damage Goethe. . . .

Is the new German literature left wing?

In the year 1947, a group of friends met, writers who had originally intended to launch a periodical. They enjoyed their meeting and found it useful in spite of the fact that the newspaper they had been planning had been forbidden by the occupation forces before it had had a chance to appear. Since then they have met again every year. Every publisher of any stature, every big newspaper that wants to keep its readers well informed, is happy to send an observer to "Group 47," a procedure that isn't as simple as it sounds because, in a desperate struggle against constantly growing attendance, Hans Werner Richter, the spiritual father of the group, insists that only those whom he has personally invited may come.

This "Group 47" enjoys a big reputation in literary circles, but not a very good one in more conservative quarters. It stands, so the latter say, on the left. This designation by the way is valid only as a reproach. The cultural functionaries of the SPD, for instance, haven't known for fifteen years what to do with a reservoir of intelligent and eminent writers who are apparently attributed to their party of the left. If therefore the Group does stand on the left, it is certainly not because its members were selected for their political affiliations, or because it was founded as a circle of Socialist intellectuals. With a few personal, nonpolitical exceptions, Richter has always invited to the meetings anyone from whom he could hope for any sort of contribution to postwar German literature. Three-fourths of this literature has been written by members of "Group 47." I put the name in quotes because it is not a registered organization or association, but rather a circle held together only by these yearly meetings, which last three days. By 'coincidence,' however, Böll, Koeppen, Jens, Lenz, Andersch, and Richter, Schallück, Johnson, Grass, Walser, and Enzensberger happen to be rather left wing. Could this be because the intellectual elite anywhere has a tendency to be left wing?

As soon as anyone tries to give color and form to the rather shop-worn expressions "left" and "left wing," he soon realizes that things are not so simple. If intellectual tendencies generally are left wing, and German postwar literature is representative of this tendency, then, again: what is left? That a younger generation is dissatisfied with what has has gone before in the realm of art? Yes, naturally. That the young creators are opposed to all restoration? In a country with a past that may hardly be considered worth restoring, this too, undoubtedly. But what else?

People are prone to indulge in such highly questionable grouping into right and left. Why? What meaning does it have beyond the obvious, trivial ones just mentioned? None, I am afraid; certainly no spectacular ones, and that is why these expressions are used so often. Because you have to be very vague (or very obvious) to find a common denominator acceptable to all. Let one of the best young German writers speak for many: "Yes, I suppose I am left wing. But I do not belong to the party that represents the left in politics. The SPD has made restoration its program. So what is leftist about men like Schnabel, Schmidt, Grass, and myself? I'm afraid that far too many faded inscriptions are to be found on this label. Perhaps it means to us simply certain forms of compassion and protest, to be able to say 'no' solicitously and at the right time."

In this sense, certainly, the German intellectual elite is left wing. But this is no different than in other countries. In this sense, Auden, Spender, and MacNeice, who gave English lyricism such a boost in the thirties, were left wing. For the postwar generation, the new voices in France were Sartre and Camus. Sartre went so far in an interview with English drama critic Kenneth Tynan as to declare that a modern drama that was good and rightist at the same time was unthinkable. The American Nobel Prize winner, John Steinbeck, who is apparently considered harmless enough to figure in the curriculum of German high schools, said publicly and outside the United States that the

American government had made being stupid socially acceptable! Until now most German writers haven't gone that far. . . .

Writers were never officially popular in Germany. They were too often in "opposition" and to be in opposition in a country like ours, as we have noted, does little for one's social standing or popularity. Heinrich Heine, who had quite some experience in the art of making himself unpopular via literature, expresses the following fascinating idea in his account of *A Journey from Munich to Genoa:* "Music is perhaps so exceptionally highly developed where the more articulate form of expression, literature, is too dangerous. . . ."

This might be a new angle for sociologists: to relate the musicality of a nation to its civic freedoms, and to draw some conclusions about, let's say, England and the United States on the one hand, and Germany and Russia on the other. Be that as it may, the fact remains that in Germany under Hitler, and in the DDR under Ulbricht, musicians had and have the least trouble. After 1945, the first primroses of cultural life to blossom in Germany were music festivals. And there would be no Wagner controversy if this powerful composer of pagan-Christian mythologies had stuck exclusively to music.

Germany was always considered a musical land, and there have been plenty of misunderstandings in this respect. "Every German man and woman is born with the musical instinct; in many it grows to be a passion," says my favorite witness, the English lady of 1884. If she was right (and it would sadden me if this were otherwise), then a lot of things have changed since then. Today we have statistics and with them the possibility of concrete information. Today only six out of a hundred Germans spend any of their free time making music. Those who listen to it are, of course, more numerous. But here too statistics give one pause. In the United States, 75 out of every 100 records are jazz; in West Germany, 88! And what jazz! To be sure, we have 40 opera houses and more than 60 opera companies with musicians employed by the city or state, almost twice as many as the rest of the world put together! And we are justifiably envied by friends of music the world over for such federal largesse, a last pleasant heritage of Germany's petty states of the past. But too far-reaching conclusions should not be drawn from this. Also in West Germany, 165 theaters, with 136,000 seats are subsidized, yet even an optimistic observer of today's German literature would find difficulty in naming one young German dramatist whose new play was being eagerly awaited.

But when comparisons are drawn with other art forms, then German postwar literature is suddenly not so badly off. How many German postwar sculptors and painters are known outside Germany? Or for that matter, inside Germany? How many architects? In the plastic and graphic arts we have had no miracles. Expressionism is still being discovered and exploited; Jugendstil and Bauhaus struggle with steel, concrete, and glass.

The fine arts are at two distinct disadvantages when compared with literature. They are much more dependent on the customer. When a building is to be erected, the ideas of the man who is paying for it, and who may be neither an expert nor an art connoisseur, are decisive. No artist has to suffer as much interference as the architect. Secondly, eyes and ears are more conservative than the intellect. Paul Klee, born in 1879, and Anton von Webern (1883) are only now, years after their deaths, breaking through the circle of their disciples to attain a larger following. Writers born at approximately the same time, such as Hermann Hesse (1877) or Hans Carossa (1878) have had their public and now seem almost a little passé, at least in their early works.

The music and fine arts of today, celebrated in small critical circles and as devoutly practiced as only art can be, yet still unable to reach the general public, may perhaps come to mean something to our children fifty years from now. I personally am skeptical about it, but I would gladly be proved wrong.

6. "WHY ARE YOU GERMANS SO HARD TO UNDERSTAND?"

We were in a Bavarian village, close to the Austrian border. A peasant sat down beside us and began to talk. My friends were very pleased to hear the truth about Germany from a Bavarian peasant for a change. And he told them a lot: about the Green Plan, through which the government in Bonn was generously subsidizing German agriculture, but that it was all worth nothing since it only helped to stop the gaps but didn't really guarantee "honest, decent earnings for honest, decent work"; that you couldn't get young people to work on the farms any more; and that you couldn't blame anyone for not wanting to work himself to death on a farm for nothing. A thankless job.

They heard all this, but they couldn't understand a word of it. If our Austrian friend hadn't been with us, I wouldn't have been much help either because I only understood every second word or so. I have Herr von Hattesdorf's translation to thank for what I have just reported.

It was a funny thing—we always called him "Herr von Hattesdorf," even when we had got to know each other quite well. We called our Swiss friend, Pierre Spälti, "Herr Professor," sometimes just "Professor." But Dick O'Connor, the oldest, most influential, and wealthiest member of our group, the one every waiter and hat-check girl made a beeline for, we soon called "Dick." Stevens was just plain "Ralph." As for Mademoiselle Yvonne Lefranc, there was nothing formal about our approach to her on our safari through Germany; everybody called her "Yvonne."

Dick, Ralph, and Yvonne spoke German very well, "But when it comes to understanding the language," said Dick, "I'm in trouble. I'm either listening to a peasant and don't understand a word, or I'm reading what some intellectual has written, and understand every word but never a sentence. Why are you Germans so hard to understand?"

Did the ambiguity of Dick's question, of which he was probably unaware, contain a certain amount of cause and effect? Is what we do perhaps so difficult for our neighbors to understand because what we say is often so incomprehensible?

Let's make a test. Take as an example the words of a doctor of philosophy and medicine, first in German: *Der Gefahr der Vermassung durch den Verstädterungsprozess mit allen seinen Gefahren vegetativer und emotionaler Fehlsteuerung und Fehlprägung kann ausser durch sinnvolle Steuerung der apersonalen psychosomatichen Einflüsse selbst nur durch Persönlichkeitsbildung und Ermöglichung der 'Bildung' von Gemeinschaften jeder nur möglichen Art begegnet werden, da von seiten der ärtzlichen Anthropologie als auf das bedrohlichste Zeichen einer Entartung des Verstädterungsprozesses hingewiesen werden muss auf die tödlich gefährliche menschliche Vereinsamung der einzelnen gerade im Zeitalter organisierter Massen.*

Translated into English and thereby automatically losing a lot of its murkiness: "The danger of overcrowding via the processes of urbanization, with all the inherent dangers of vegetative and emotional misguidance and misimpression, can—apart from a sensible guidance of the apersonal psychosomatic influences themselves—be offset only by personality education and the possibility of educating communities of every possible type, since from the side of medical anthropology it is considered necessary to draw our attention to the fact that the most threatening signs of a degeneration of the processes of urbanization are the fatally perilous human loneliness of the individual in this very age of organized masses. . . ."

We will now make a brief pause for station identification . . . but let it be said that this crazy style holds a tremendous fascination for the German who wants to write something in this day and age. You only have to practice it a little to find yourself suddenly capable of writing such gobbledegook with the greatest of ease!

The worst of it is not that we Germans actually talk and write like this—there may even be quite a few of us who don't—but that it is undeniably true that this way of writing is greatly admired! A young lawyer wrote to me a short while ago: "It's easy for you, but if I want to make a career for myself, I've got to write like that!"

So that's the way it is in Germany, and you may wonder why.

Some say the German language is at fault, and they are right to the extent that it wouldn't be possible to be quite so convolutedly pompous in English or French. But it wouldn't be fair to put all the blame on the German language; a language is not something fixed; it is created by the people who speak it. So why do the Germans express themselves this way?

Let's take someone who wants to say, "Cultural progress is handicapped in Germany because the Länder have cultural autonomy, but the Bund has the money. Constant disputes are the result." But he is writing for the Bund press bureau. If he wrote exactly what he meant, he would have trouble with the Länder, with his employer, with all those who have forgotten long ago that even unpleasant truths may be clearly and simply expressed. So the poor devil writes, "An exceptionally heavy burden imposed on all cultural-political work of Bund and Länder lies in the fact that, as a result of existing conditions, the questions arising from the polarity of both partners on a cultural level are as a rule transformed into problems of a financial nature, which govern the political controversy." And now let anyone pin him down as to what he's really trying to say!

This method of castrating a language, of letting the meaning disappear behind a blanket of fog, is not exclusive to Germany. Civilian and government offices the world over practice the art of presenting information so cloudily that it may be interpreted in various ways. The seal of this art-form is the illegible signature. There were always a great many bureaus and government offices in Germany, but Professor-German used to meet Bureaucrat-German more than halfway, for both had the same mother—caution. That is why we find a professor who wrote the voluminous paragraph on the perils of urbanization when all he wanted to say was, "Whoever lives in a big city has to count on losing his personality and becoming sick or crazy." But if he wrote that, he'd have twenty million big-city dwellers on his neck who think: Thanks a lot. We're still perfectly normal. Let's say our professor is a courageous man, which can happen. Then he wouldn't give a damn. He wouldn't fear the fury of those affected by what he had to say, but he would fear the damage to his reputation if his statement should be proved "erroneous by scientific verification."

The art of being scientifically irrefutable consists of being so abstract that the finally revealed idea loses all concrete controversial facets, and with that all color, all strength, and every practical meaning. Not that the big-city dweller therefore has to count on the quoted unpleasant-nesses—"urbanization processes" bring them in their wake. And who's talking about anything as concrete as being "sick," when it's nothing but a case of "vegetative misguidance"? Or of being "crazy," when he means "emotional misimpressions"? For it is an established fact—who would contradict it?—that "the danger of overcrowding via the processes of urbanization with all the inherent dangers of vegetative and emotional misguidance and misimpressions" exists, doesn't it? And that's what the fellow's trying to prove!

In Bureaucratic-German, the writer doesn't want to be the one who said it; in Academic-German, he doesn't want to stick his neck out.

"I notice you've dropped the expression 'Professor-German,'" Professor Spälti said laconically.

"I was afraid you might be hurt."

"Not really." Spälti laughed. "You'll find what you call professor-German in Switzerland, too, but I imagine it's more prevalent in Germany."

I hastily explained that I did not mean the language of any particular profession; that many professors speak and write better German than, for instance, a lot of journalists, but that I believed it was the universities, or—to be appropriately abstract—the sciences, from which this way of writing drew its prestige. And this is the language of which Martin Luther once said: "The German language is the most perfect of all languages, very similar to Greek." But in those days he had the right to say so, and he didn't say what would have sounded much more familiar today, "An examination of the syntactic conformities of the Greek and German languages leads us to the conclusion of an approximation which may be interpreted as the attainment of a maximum perfection in as far as the German language is concerned."

Two hundred and fifty years later, Herder was not so sure that the German language had fulfilled Luther's promise. "Our noble German language," he wrote, "has not developed as it should." Today this may be partly because in recent years we've had to express ourselves pretty circumspectly. We learned to write between the lines because if we had written with incautious frankness, we would have been risking our peace of mind; often much more than that. We found out that it was more advisable to write about the nature of things than about the things themselves; about the spirit than about the power (much less about those in power!).

But don't we have a saying: *Nun wollen wir mal deutsch reden?* . . . "Now let's talk German," the equivalent of talking turkey in the United States? We do. It must be kept in mind, however, that what we have been dealing with here is written German. Not that it is to be found only on paper. Official German, when spoken today, is in nine cases out of ten German that has been written first and then read aloud. Free speech isn't very highly regarded in Germany. But, of course, we still come across Germans who speak freely, rarely in "high" German, more frequently in North-German Plattdeutsch or in the West German dialects of Bavaria and Swabia, even in Saxony. In East German Saxony? Yes, in East German Saxony, still. . . .

7. "WHY IS THE GERMAN ABROAD SO UNPOPULAR?"

> Save us from gale and storm, O Lord,
> And from the German traveling abroad!

This is a seaman's adage. "Gale and storm" sound like a sailor, but you would think that on the high seas he wouldn't be very much concerned with "the German traveling abroad." Is a lot of what is said about the German abroad perhaps, like this old adage, untrustworthy?

"I wouldn't say so," said Yvonne, quite excited. "You should see them in Paris. They'll point to a little hotel whose owner was shot by their soldiers and proclaim loudly to all and sundry, 'This building was our regimental headquarters,' and then off they go to a girlie show on the Place Pigalle."

"In the Austrian Alps," said Andreas, "it's getting more and more difficult to find ski slopes that aren't crowded with them."

"But you can consider yourself lucky," said Spälti, "because you at least know they're going to go away again in a few weeks. In Switzerland—in the Ticino, for instance—they've built houses for themselves, and we're stuck with them for good."

"And you've managed to make so much money on them," said Ralph, "that real-estate prices in Switzerland have become impossible, even for the Germans. Now it's Ireland's turn. And I must admit," he added, "when the channel boat in Hoek van Holland is full of Germans, I take to my cabin and don't emerge until we've landed in Harwich."

I'm afraid that isn't all false accusation. The German abroad is often unpopular. For some ungodly reason, his yearning to communicate assumes loudspeaker proportions as soon as he crosses the borders of his native land. Could it be that we are like the little clerk Tucholsky used to write about, who in the office is submissive, but in the evening, when he walks in the park with his girl, can address his superior *in absentia* loudly and boldly? Or is it the other way round. Is it possible that our many little bosses, accustomed to everyone jumping to attention at their command in the little world they have created, can't imagine that there are other worlds? Obviously we are dealing here with cases of underdeveloped and overdeveloped German arrogance. Couldn't a perfectly normal majority lie in between?

Other complaints about German behavior abroad also contain an inner contradiction, pointing to the possibility that between two extremes there might be a sensible middle ground. From Switzerland, and especially from Austria, we hear voices raised against the occupants of big black automobiles, the Mercedes 300 type, also called the Volkswagen of the Ruhr, who put on a show that is extremely irritating, under the heading, "What price the world? We'll pay for it!" And then we get reports about young Germans who make themselves unpopular because their traveling plans exceed their traveler's checks. When they return, they boast about how they spent three weeks in Iceland without it costing them a cent. The longing for adventure can take strange forms, and these boys might be startled and disbelieving if someone were to tell them they had nothing to crow about. Just as their parents can't always grasp the displeasure felt—not only in Switzerland and Ireland—when the Germans buy up so much real estate. Happily they ask you, "Isn't this a much more harmless way of conquering the world than the one Hitler prescribed? We're not destroying anything. On the contrary, we buy up everything in sight and build on it. If only we could buy land in the DDR; then all Germany would be ours again!" And tomorrow the world? Every now and then those who can still hear the old song as it used to be sung are reminded of it.

I am sure no malice was intended when the results of a German survey on traveling abroad showed France and Russia as the countries most visited between 1940 and 1945. A war opens up the world to people who never before got out of their little village. And this they don't mind being reminded of. The idea that others might not like to be reminded of it evidently demands more imagination and tact than can be generally expected from us. It is therefore not wholly the German visitor's fault that he is welcome because he brings money with him, but otherwise doesn't command much respect. And it is an internationally recognized fact that the same people who attract attention are not very popular at home, either. Over two hundred years ago, in 1700, the English playwright, William Congreve, said: "I wonder there is not an Act of Parliament to save the Credit of the Nation, and prohibit the Exportation of Fools."

In the Federal Republic they are now pasting into German passports Twelve Golden Rules for the German Traveling Abroad. The items considered worth listing are quite indicative. The author, who confidentially uses the second person singular as he addresses the reader, is anonymous:

1. Never forget that in Germany you are one German among millions; in a foreign country you are *the* German, and the foreigner forms his opinion of your nation according to your behavior.

2. Don't deny the fact that your parentage is German, but see to it that the foreigner is pleasantly impressed by it.

3. If you are of the foolish opinion that everything outside Germany is worse, stay at home. If you think that outside Germany all things are better, don't come back.

4. Whenever you are traveling in a foreign country, see to it that it echoes with your silence. The quieter *you* are, the louder *others* will talk.

5. Dress so as to blend in with the natives, but don't wear a fez!

6. Be agreeable about singing when asked to, but only then!

7. Don't try to shine when a foreigner knows more than you; when you know more, let yourself be defeated with a smile; then you will win firm friends.

8. Keep in mind that only the names of virtues and vices can be translated into a foreign language; what they really mean you have to find out anew in every country.

9. Try to understand what seems strange to you in a foreign country; if you can't, then look for the reason first in yourself.

10. In a foreign country, lift your finger only to learn, never to teach.

11. Be frugal but not miserly when you are traveling; drink less than your host so that you may have that much more time to praise his hospitality.

12. You will come across the foreigner disguised in all sorts of national dress; in an emergency, don't forget that, like you, he is only human.

The temptation is great to beg the anonymous instructor to forbid those who are unmusical to sing under *all* circumstances, and not to invite adventurers to any further investigation of foreign vices; to ask him if his tenth commandment is only to be considered valid abroad, and who or what all is disguised in number twelve, but I have every intention of controlling myself. Perhaps, though, the fact that today every third German travels abroad if he possibly can (before the war it was four out of every hundred) should not be dealt with only from the angle of giving good advice, or as a cause for complaint and criticism. It also speaks loudly for a yearning away from provincialism, for the urge to explore what was shut off before, for the not-so-stupid decision to spend less time cultivating a world viewpoint and more time viewing the world. When "public opinion" was asked what the Germans would most like to do if they suddenly found they had more money than they thought, travel was in second place, right after "get things for the house." Of the young men asked, "If you had more money or time, what would you like to do?" more than half replied, "Go abroad."

If it suddenly became fashionable to study medicine, would that speak against the medical profession? In Germany today, traveling abroad is considered very fashionable; some Germans have an absolute thing about it. The travel brochures they bring home are far more important to them than the entire trip they plan to take, and they have to make sure that they travel in the right country. Italy? For heaven's sake, who wants to go to Italy? Spain? You certainly are behind the times. We've been there. Greece? Well, yes . . . that's a possibility. But Yugoslavia sounds better. In a way though, it's about time we took a look at North Africa—unless the Soviet Union makes traveling in that country easier, as they seem constantly on the verge of doing. India would be fine, of course, but for the average fashionable tourist, even if he's in the six-cylinder class, it's a little far away. The results of a survey show in first place, Capri, of course, 27 out of a hundred; a close second—Paris 24; not far behind—Rome 20; then come India 15, New York 15, Jerusalem 12, Egypt 11; and at the end, two more realistic goals—Greece 11, and England 11.

Tourism has grown in importance with the technical advances in transportation and the increase in paid vacations for those to be transported. Since further developments in transportation are likely, and the lengthening of yearly vacations is highly desirable, we may expect quite a few things to happen unless evolution is radically disturbed. Today the German civil servant has on the average of 25 days vacation a year, the office worker 19, the factory hand 16. But for quite a while now we have had civil servants and office workers with a 40-day vacation coming to them. A few years from now they will no longer be the exception. The argument of the medical profession that a vacation begins to have the desired effect only at the end of two weeks, is irrefutable. So we may perhaps see quite an increase in trips abroad in the future. A hundred years ago, a German from Holstein, Julius Stinde, who had made a name for himself with his popularizations of natural history, and become famous through his descriptions of the Berlin middle-class Family Bucholz, wrote: "It would be worth while for every German at least once to get away from home, to a foreign land, and to find out what has become of Germany, how unquestionably splendid his country looks when seen from a distance. Then he would learn to love it—not like the peasant his cow and pig, because of the advantages to be gained from it—but as the son loves his mother, as sacrosanct, unviolable treasure."

We have grown a little skeptical of the "unquestionable splendor" and "sacrosanct inviolable treasure," but many foreigners would willingly attest to the fact that to the Germans, Germany seems more lovable from afar.

8. VACATION PARADISE WITH A FEW FLAWS

"Why do so many Germans go abroad for their vacations?" Professor Spälti wanted to know, "when Germany is such an ideal vacation land?" The others were just as full of praise for Germany's holiday possibilities. "Unless you want to shoot a lion," said Dick, "you can find everything you could possibly desire right here in Germany: mountains and ocean, solitude and crowds, cosy little inns and grand hotels; theaters in every small town, and a lot of astonishingly nice people."

Andreas demurred. "You've got dollars to spend, in which case traveling in Germany can be delightful. But I find it too expensive."

This may be one of the reasons Germans go abroad. Because he who isn't satisfied with putting up for four weeks in an inn in the Spessart woods and simply enjoying the play of the wind in the treetops and walking, let him fill his purse! Let's take, for instance, the father of a family of five who wants to spend four weeks at the seashore. A small house may be rented on the Frisian island of Sylt for 50 to 100 marks daily, let's say 75. That's 28 times 75 just for a place to sleep, in other words—2,100 marks, the average German income for five months! A few kilometers northward, in Denmark, he won't find things quite so comfortable, but he'll spend only half as much. But probably another aspect plays a part in the German's urge to travel: in strange surroundings he is more likely to be willing to lower his standard of living, to forego comparisons and not care what the Schulzes and the Mullers are doing, or what is expected of him.

Apart from such considerations, which put more emphasis on vacationer than on vacation spot, Germany is neither particularly cheap nor excessively expensive. You can be lucky or unlucky wherever you go. But apart from that, vacationing in Germany remains cheaper than in the United States, England, France, Belgium, or Switzerland; more expensive than Scandinavia, Spain, Austria, Greece and Yugoslavia. Like all Edens since the loss of *the* Eden, vacationland Germany has a few flaws. Whoever is traveling with children should be warned. Germany is more unfriendly to children than any country I know. Dogs enjoy greater prestige. On the other hand we have a *Bundesfamilienministerium*, a Ministry for Family Affairs. Not a word against the minister, please; amid his much more powerful colleagues he doesn't have very much to say.

Otherwise Germany is neither undeveloped nor undiscovered as a vacationland. Not everyone is as enthusiastic about it as Professor Spälti and Dick, but a lot of people like to come here again and again. Ten million foreigners visit Germany yearly, and there are Germans who vacation in Germany too—two-thirds of the population.

The most popular vacation areas are the Black Forest, Upper Bavaria, and the North Sea. At quite a distance follow the Baltic, Lake Constance, and the Harz Mountains. An equally beautiful part of Germany unfortunately is out of the question for the Western vacationer, above all for West Germans. Passport difficulties are almost insurmountable; registering with the police is too tedious, monetary exchange too ideological, and the combination of vacation and politics too strenuous. The Baltic seacoast where it is most beautiful—the Mecklenburg and Pomeranian coast to the Danzig dunes of Oliva, the Königsberg beaches near Kranz—is therefore outside the vacation area for a majority of Germans; they also have to live without the Mark Brandenburg and the East Prussian lakes. No child from today's Cologne has memories of Saxony's Switzerland or the Erzgebirge or the Thuringian Forest.

Let's take a look at the West German vacation areas. The visitor to the Black Forest is looking for peace and quiet before anything else. In the summer, shady footpaths welcome him; in the winter, comparatively easy ski slopes. And you won't find as many inns and hotels each with its own special character, anywhere else. Bern Bohle, a Westphalian, composed a Geography of Hospitality in his book, *An Innkeeper's Guest* (Stuttgart 1957) in which he says: "The heart of German hospitality lies in the Black Forest." He favored especially the Adler in Hinterzarten; the Schwarzwald Hotel in Titisee, on that lake; the Haldenhof on the Schauinsland, a little mountain near Freiburg; the Adler in Unterglottertal; the Park Hotel in Triberg; the Selighof near Baden-Baden; Mönchs Posthotel in Herrenalb; the Hotel Funk on the Dobel; and the Post in Nagold.

There is nothing to be said against Herr Bohle's taste, but as you choose your bed, that's how you pay. None of the hotels he mentions —which offer their guests hunting and fishing, bars, in some cases have their own golf links—are cheap, and a few—primarily the Selighof and the Schwarzwald—are grand hotels and are priced accordingly, from 20 marks and up daily.

There are two kinds of hotels in Germany, sometimes you'll find them a rather successful composite of each other. One is a variation on private hospitality. A good example is the Adler in Bad Godesberg, a villa whose owner, in the last century, invited so many friends and acquaintances to visit him that he was in danger of becoming impoverished. In order to be able to remain the lavish host he was, and on the advice of his friends, he made a profession of it. Since 1860, his house has been an inn and today is one of the finest Godesberg hotels,

Königsberg

Zoppot
Danzig

Marienwerder

•Allenstein·

Stettin

•Küstrin

Frankfurt

•Guben

NEISSE

•Görlitz   ODER   ■Breslau

•Hirschberg

ittau

Glatz•   NEISSE   •Neisse

Outside boundaries of the Federal Republic of West Germany.
West boundary of the territory presently administered by Poland (ie. Oder-Neisse Line).
Dividing line between Polish and Soviet territory.

a "private hotel" in the best sense of both words. It has only twenty beds which are more often than not booked weeks in advance, and usually the same guests come back year after year.

This type of hotel still exists; you only have to know where to find it. On the Lüneburger Heide, in the Black Forest, on the Mosel, and in the Allgäu, they have preserved their character better than anywhere else. But places like that, by their very nature, have to be small. They are usually run by one family, and require as host or hostess a type that doesn't seem to flourish in our cold, scientific age. Anyway, they are dying out fast. The last representatives of the breed will probably be found fifty years from now in Scotland, in the Provence, in South Tyrol, and in Germany. A few hundred of them still manage to make a go of it, and it is a pleasure to chat and make merry with their owners. In some cases, it looks to me as if through their sons these houses might survive another generation.

The other type developed from the original hostel. With these caravanseries of the twentieth century, it is a case of the less personality, the better. They culminate in the wall-to-wall carpet-muted standard luxury of the German grand hotel which needn't fear comparison with those of other countries. Some are beyond reproach: the Hilton and Kempinski in Berlin, the Atlantic in Hamburg, the Breidenbacher Hof in Düsseldorf, the Excelsior Hotel Ernst in Cologne, the Frankfurter Hof in Frankfurt, the Graf Zeppelin in Stuttgart, the Euopäische Hof in Baden-Baden, the Römerbad in Badenweiler, or the Vier Jahreszeiten in Munich.

Wherever it has been possible to combine the grand tradition of personal hospitality with mass operations, without which—let's face it— a modern big city hotel can't survive, you won't go wrong. It seems to me that Germany comes up with more examples of the successful effort to unite the personal aura of a private home with the technicalities of a large hotel than any other country. The Park Hotel in Bremen and the Hessische Hof in Frankfurt can share equal billing with the Vier Jahreszeiten in Hamburg. But tomorrow a lot of other hotels might have to be included on the list. If I didn't hate abstract statements, I wouldn't give any concrete examples. Like human beings, hotels are too short-lived. A new owner or, in the case of the big hotels, a new manager, and everything may change. That is why hotel brochures have a way of becoming obsolete while they are being printed. Of course these first-rate hotels are accessible only to the wealthy traveler, if he is traveling at his own expense. At a cautious estimate, I would say that nine-tenths of all grand-hotel checks are expense-account checks. Their prices horrified Andreas. I suspect he isn't familiar with what it costs to stay in the big Austrian hotels where the prices are even higher.

The little man on vacation, who is paying his own way, is looking for small hotels and boardinghouses, and he won't have difficulty finding them in Upper Bavaria, which doesn't lag far behind the Black Forest in popularity. While the mature adult may be more attracted

to the serenity of the Black Forest, especially travelers from the Eng-
lish-speaking world for whom the Black Forest, the oldest touring
region in Germany, seems to be the *only* tourist region, young people
are more attracted to Upper Bavaria. The ski runs are steeper, the
mountains higher, the possibilities of fun greater in Upper Bavaria.
Munich isn't far away; in Garmisch, Berchtesgaden, and Tegernsee,
cosmopolitans meet. "Berchtesgaden has become fashionable," was
what it said in *This is the German's Fatherland,* as far back as 1897.
Any visitor would do well to book his room in advance, although the
lone traveler who doesn't care too much how or where he is housed,
may venture into this area without advance booking. Somehow, to
date, everyone has found a place to stay.

Six of the eight big German spas lies in Bavaria—three in Upper
Bavaria: Bad Reichenhall, Garmisch-Partenkirchen, and Bad Wiessee;
three in other parts of Bavaria: Oberstdorf in the Allgäu, Bad Wörishofen on the Swabian-Bavarian plateau, and Bad Kissingen in Rhön.
Outside Bavaria you will find only Bad Salzuflen (North-Rhine Westphalia) and Bad Orb (Hesse).

The beach resorts are at a sad disadvantage compared with the
Black Forest and Upper Bavaria. I personally can't think of a more
enjoyable place to spend a vacation than on the island of Sylt, with the
surf to pound me and the sand to laze on afterward, but you can unfortunately do this only three months in the year. You will therefore
find in these places what the hotel associations call "seasonal business,"
and all the less delightful aspects that go with it: the tremendous hustle
and bustle—in August you'll find more cars on the streets of Westerland
on Sylt than in any big city; exorbitant prices—and you can't really object to them when you stop to think that in three months enough has
to be earned to last a whole year; and the necessity for dismissing
personnel in the autumn and rehiring a new staff eight months later,
which doesn't make for a very reliable choice of waiters and chamber-
maids. These hectic three months and long winter sleep impose a
strange rhythm which the natives dread just as much as they look forward to it. A solution was found long ago, but the general public
seems loath to accept it, which is understandable. Hotel managers and
propagandists have done their best to explain to the vacationer that the
seaside which is fine in summer, is truly bracing, healthy, and rejuve-
nating only in winter. As a result a few rugged individualists are
regular Christmas and Easter guests on the civilized North Sea islands.
But it seems impossible, even with a hard sell, to tempt the thousands
who make these places financially successful in the summer to brave
the rigors of winter weather. So the North Sea bathing resorts will
probably have to continue to put up with the reputation of not having
the best hotels.

Have I said that the really good hotels in Germany are the best in
the world, and that you don't get gypped in the middling ones as you
sometimes do in England and Italy? I was ordered to say so by my
fellow travelers. In fact it was Dick who declared, "You told me the

Vier Jahreszeiten in Hamburg was the best hotel in Germany. I tell you it's the best in the whole damn world!"

Finally, after such praise, I want to mention the most frequent objection raised against German hotels. I do so as a warning to travelers, and to stimulate the groping imagination of the German hotel manager. The day begins with breakfast, and for a lot of German hotel guests this means it is off to a bad start. Years ago, the leading German hoteliers decided to give their guests a choice of having their meals at the hotel or elsewhere. However, the tendency of the small hotel managers to make up for a fraction of their losses at breakfast was not curbed by this measure. If you decide to breakfast at your hotel— and many do—you still pay, except in the really good hotels, three marks for bad coffee, rolls, not much and not always fresh butter, and canned marmalade. And the guest who refuses to partake of this breakfast in his hotel is penalized with a one mark fine.

The hotel manager can improve these deplorable breakfast conditions, but he is powerless against the second complaint: noise. In so far as it is being made by a poorly trained staff venting their early-morning indignation ("And they're still asleep while we have to work!" sort of thing) in loud morning jokes or by moving around as noisily as possible something can be done about it, but nothing can be done to counteract the evil effects of sound-porous walls. They were the only kind that could be built right after the war and quite a few builders found it profitable to go right on building them because to do otherwise would have cost more than leaseholder or hotel owner could afford.

No German big city and scarcely a smaller one exists in which no building is going on. Something or other is constantly in process of going up or down. The whole of Germany is one gigantic building site. And when the Germans don't happen to be building, a neighboring Federal Highway can provide similar sound effects. A truck for instance, starting up at 4:00 A.M., can drive an entire residential district to distraction. And where nothing else disturbs the peace, a few jets may be counted on to roar overhead. Anyone wanting to travel in Germany should take along some ear plugs,—Ohropax, if you're buying them in Germany. "Protector of the healthy and the sick against noise and sounds; the best tranquilizer," is what it says on the box. All of us ear-pacifists owe Max Negwer, the Bad Homburg apothecary who invented Ohropax, a vote of thanks.

9. RAILWAY PLEASURE; HIGHWAY GRIEF

As a traveler's land, Germany could be pure joy if the automobile had been invented before the locomotive. Everybody would have been enthusiastic about using the new invention, and the poor devils risking their lives in those smelly tin cans that chase each other on the road and are in turn chased by the police, would have been objects of contempt. About 1,100 are being injured in Germany daily, 36 killed, 5,000 hauled into court . . . *daily*. Compare with this the fact that the German railways have a broader and more closely knit network of convenient trains, prompt connections, and a more comprehensive customer service than any other railway network in the world. On 31,000 kilometers of rails (comparatively only Belgium has more), 23,000 passenger trains and 13,000 freight trains run daily. Approximately one-half of what is being transported in Germany today, human freight included, is carried by rail. The other half travels by car on roads that give little cause for the national pride that is revealed in the statistics of traffic bureaus and causes so many patriotic breasts to swell whenever the *Autobahns* are mentioned. They constitute only one-fiftieth of inadequate German highways. "Underdeveloped" was the designation of European experts for the roads in Schleswig-Holstein, East Friesland, the Eifel, the Hunsrück, Franconia, Upper Palatinate, and Rhön.

The substance of our traffic regulations can be formulated calmly and objectively only if you are in rigid control of yourself, which for the moment I trust I am. Here they are in a form that may be criticized as showing a lack of understanding but is at least understandable (I hope!):

1. The cabinet decides what is to be done with the billions collected in gasoline and automobile taxation. Every cabinet member wants money from the cabinet, and the Minister for Communications has only one vote.

2. From a legislative point of view, where traffic problems are concerned, the roads are never to blame. Of those who use them, 5,000 go before the courts daily; but never a road builder or a signposter! Whenever a road proves to be impassable without doing some sort of damage, the cause is always "human frailty."

3. There are only two obligatory ways of proving human frailty: the alcohol test and radar. Both are heavily used.

4. The German city or town is the supreme power when it comes to traffic regulations and posting road signs.

5. Trucks transport consumer goods, and the bigger the truck, the more goods it can transport. Any measures taken against such commercial traffic therefore tend to be frowned upon as contrary to the public welfare.

6. To drive in a disciplined fashion is synonymous with steering clear of the police.

A few sober facts should be added to each of these slightly exaggerated statements:

1. Statistics show that the money spent on road construction is a little more than the amount accruing from car and gasoline taxation; they even prove that Germany spends more on its roads than any other country in the world. Anyone traveling in the United States, England, Scandinavia, France, Holland, Belgium, Switzerland, must think: could the statistics be wrong (which can happen) or is there

more and less successful road construction in Germany than anywhere else, a viewpoint favored by my friends—they had never come
across so much road construction in their lives.

2. Do we Germans have a special tendency toward "human frailty"?
One thing I would like to refute, although many Germans have been
known to noise it abroad, is that in Germany there are notably *few*
good drivers. I don't see any signs of it. When old and young were
still enthusiastic about car racing, half the famous aces were German:
Bernd Rosemeyer, Hans Stuck, Manfred von Brauchitsch, Rudolf
Caracciola. And I consider it unlikely that there should be an unusual number of *bad* drivers in Germany, which doesn't come to quite
the same thing. Anyone driving in Europe soon realizes that there are
people in every country who turn into idiots or criminals as soon as
they are behind the wheel. But one thing has to be granted: the tendency to consider others as a matter of course is underdeveloped in
Germany. It's a beautiful luxury that we don't grant ourselves often
enough. Because to think of the other man means putting oneself in
his shoes if only for a few seconds. And in Germany, to have that
much imagination has sometimes been highly perilous.

3. We have the alcohol test and speed limits in common with most
of our western neighbors. Such subjugation of our fellow men by the
laws of technical progress may be sensible and necessary, but when
they are carried out with German thoroughness and organizational
ability, comparisons with other nations cease to be valid. Not much
juridical education is necessary to find 5,000 traffic delinquents a day a
trifle sinister. Of course it is still possible for considerate district at-
torneys and magistrates to temper the judgment of physiological chemistry with a humane sentence, but the perfectionists among the or-
ganizers find this irksome. A machine into which you can feed such a
marvelously computable offense and have the prisoner come out neatly
at the other end—that is their ideal!

4. I can only hope that the tricks played with street signs in German big cities amuse somebody. Anyone driving through Munich at
the prescribed speed of 50 kilometers an hour, which is much too fast
for the dense traffic on the Stachus Square but slower than would be
necessary on the broad highways leading out of town to the *Autobahns,* passes at least two and sometimes ten signs per second telling
him what to do and what not to do. Relieved of any judgment of his
own, he starts looking for orders to "Brake!" "Speed up!" "Shift into
first!" If signs like this aren't put up soon, I'll begin to think we're
slipping.

The men responsible for traffic regulations in the big German cities
are not to be envied. Hannover and Cassel excepted, there evidently
isn't a city that had an architect with enough imagination to foresee
the development of traffic and, while the houses still lay in ruins, create
space for the streets of the future. All he would really have had to do
was cast a glance across almost any of Germany's borders. But today
the powers that be seem at a total loss as to what to do. In Hamburg

all parking in the city has been rigorously curtailed in an effort to thin
down traffic; in Stuttgart they are making room for as many parking
lots as possible with the idea that city streets are primarily for automobiles. In Essen they have tried keeping all public transportation out
of the center of town; in Cologne they've given it the right of way.
With such contradictory goals, it isn't difficult to see how varied must
be the means to achieve them. In Munich the street signs are completely different from those in Hamburg. You may be an expert on
how to get through Düsseldorf, but your know-how won't do a thing
for you in Frankfurt. Not even the man who in every other respect
approves of the federalist structure of the Federal Republic can fathom
why it should be impossible to introduce something akin to a uniform
sign language and traffic-light system in all German big cities.

5. It is true that the mammoth trucks are the greatest traffic en-
cumbrance; it is not true that their drivers are inconsiderate; on the
contrary, they are the most disciplined and helpful users of our roads.
Oh, yes, if one could wish them off the roads, and also wish away the
streetcars, and the idiotic necessity to leave one's car standing in the
middle of the street following even the most minor accident, then we
would have done with traffic jams in cities like, for instance, Hamburg,
which with 300,000 registered cars may be considered the city with
the heaviest traffic. In the morning between 8 and 9, and in the afternoon between 5 and 6, things might proceed quite well. But the trucks
always have some sort of pressure group behind them, entrepreneurs
who approve of this type of consumer-goods transportation.

Not much can be said against the presence of these roaring monsters
on the *Autobahns*, except that their headlights are too high so that
they blind the driver of any lower car coming toward them, and that,
with all the "no passing" regulations, they can slow a whole column
of cars down to a crawl as they chug up a hill. The average city and
country road of minimal width is completely blocked by these ele-
phants.

6. We were driving in a leisurely fashion on the wide Elbchaussee
toward Hamburg. "Why are we going so slowly?" Ralph wanted to
know. The speedometer needle was wavering between 40 and 45
kilometers.

"Nobody's driving faster," said Yvonne. "Now there's German discipline for you!"

"Just wait a minute," said Andreas, who had sized up the situation.

The parade behind us got longer and longer. A few cars inched out
of line as if to do some passing, but drew their noses in again fast
because they had seen at the head of the column an elegant, green-
white "Peter-car" of the Hamburg police, a Mercedes 190. A community's prosperity can be measured by the cars in which its police
force rides, from the Isetta in the village of Lower Saxony—tiny, not
very fast, cheap, holds two—to the Jaguar-type sports car of the police
in North-Rhine Westphalia. The Peter-car drove slowly, but not
slowly enough to be passed without exceeding the speed limit. At last

it turned off to the left. I stepped on the gas to the speed limit, 50 kilometers, and every five seconds was passed by a car.

All worthy Germans are agreed that police regulations should be strictly enforced lest lack of discipline produce chaos. The six of us discussed this at length and came up with the following observations: The drivers who speeded up to 60 after their 40-kilometer crawl behind the police car were overcompensating.

"And I've noticed that cars never stop at the striped crosswalks," said Ralph. So much is forbidden; to drive on across a crosswalk is not. Overcompensation: that which is not expressly forbidden is allowed.

"Your pedestrians cross the street like herds of cattle," said Yvonne, startled at seeing an old woman nearly run over by a car turning a corner. Even if no car is in sight, you are not allowed to cross the street against the light. Overcompensation: nobody pays any attention to cars any more, but reacts to a green light like Pavlov's dogs, automatically.

But to get back to the joy of using the German railways; it is all the more glorious when compared with the misery the driver of an automobile goes through in Germany. Oh, yes, transportation by rail requires a greater expenditure of material, personnel, and organization. Ministers of Finance the world over therefore don't share my enthusiasm for traveling by train; you will find state subsidized railroads everywhere. They cost the German taxpayer 600 million marks a year, yet the government of the Federal Republic is well advised when it sees to it that such subsidies are passed. Of course if you want to be picayune about it, you could bring up the point that the excellent service accorded the customer in the big cities is not always quite so excellent in the smaller towns. And it isn't entirely clear why the railways should have to develop a network of buses as a subsidiary service. Shouldn't the state subsidies free the railways of having to be profitable? And the frequent checking of tickets—at the beginning of a trip, during a trip, at the end of a trip—is probably the result of internal personal-political reasoning rather than the fear that otherwise the companies might lose millions yearly. But aside from such minor reservations, it may be said that, in co-operation with the big travel bureaus, the Bundesbahn makes the traveler's life run as smoothly as possible. By telephone he can get information and advice as to how to travel wherever he may want to go; seats are reserved for him in smoker or nonsmoker, first or second class, sleeper or reclining-chair coach. The railway looks after his luggage, everything is organized to a T, and the system rarely breaks down, not even at Christmas or during the vacation weeks when the number of travelers increases enormously. The railways have even succeeded in persuading the car owner, spoiled by the advantages of the automobile—door-to-door transportation, his own timing, more privacy and intimacy—to use the TEE trains (Trans Europe Express). These fabulous diesel-engine trains are faster than the fastest cars, and in them you can write, eat, drink, or just sit back comfortably and doze. And if you want your car wherever you're going, there are special trains to carry them, too.

A few other small advantages of train travel: stations in Germany are focal points of sociability, "like a hyphen between me and the strange city," was the way a French visitor once put it. Clever building and renting concessions transform big-city stations into small business districts which, with the friendly co-operation of a sensible police force that doesn't take the slogan "For travelers only" too seriously, are open on Sunday when the rest of the city is dead. And the station restaurant is sometimes the best or one of the best in town. In Hamburg, for instance, and in Düsseldorf, but also in smaller towns like Lindau and Lüneburg.

And now I think the time has come (the reader may feel it came and went long ago) for us to stop moving sociologically, historically, politically, and questioningly across Germany, and start moving more geographically and systematically.

5

TRAVELOGUE

1. WE START TO TRAVEL BY CAR

Since only asses are consequent, and the trip was more important to us than the goal, we didn't travel through Germany by train, but by car. Our trip started at the Bodensee (Lake Constance).

"Please drive as you think best. We don't want to rush; unfortunately we don't have time to dawdle either, and, of course, we want to see as much as possible."

This rather vague program was the only one we had. It developed into a ten-day trip which I would like to describe in some detail. Anyone who has no better plan, and who has the time and inclination (which you have to have), a car and a little money (which you can borrow), could do worse than to follow our route. Starting at the Bodensee, we drove first in a northwesterly direction on a road numbered 33, which meant that it wished to be recognized as a Federal Highway. Aside from that, it was a narrow, gently winding country road.

At Singen we came to a peculiar landscape of bald, cone-shaped hills, burnt-out volcanos, setting of the late romantic writer Scheffel's medieval novel *Ekkehard*. Saeckingen, of the same writer's *Trumpeter of Saeckingen*, lies close by in this Swabian "*-ingen*" land where signposts point to Villingen, Schwenningen, Balingen, Tailfingen, Reutlingen, Tübingen, Böblingen, Nürtingen, Plochingen, Esslingen, and Göppingen. The road winds on past the Hohenstoffeln, with its double peak, through the little medieval town of Engen, at the foot of the Hohenhöwen (elevation 848 meters), the highest of these old volcanos which are typical of the Hegau.

Ascending gradually from the Bodensee, we came to the Danube, only to see it dwindle at Geisingen. Fifteen minutes later we were at its source in the princely town of Donaueschingen. Here ancient and modern art live in harmony side by side: paintings by Cranach and Holbein in the Karlsbau; the medieval manuscript of the *Song of the Nibelungs* in the Egon Exhibition Hall, and every year, the Festival of Contemporary Music.

We looked at a tablet in the Palace Park inscribed: "678 meters above sea level, 2,840 kilometers to the sea." But this Danube source makes only a small contribution to Europe's greatest river; actually it has its origin in two brooks that run down from the Black Forest and unite here, as expressed in the folk-rhyme, "Brigach and Breg, the Danube create." Another river, the Neckar, has its source ten kilometers to the north, and we could have followed that on our way to Stuttgart, but the road across the crest of the Black Forest mountains is more beautiful.

We continued along the Federal Highway into the realm of the giants among the Black Forest mountains, up the Feldberg, elevation 1,494 meters to the Titisee, which is famous the world over. But the little place itself, consisting in all of thirty houses catering to tourists, can't quite cope with its renown. Those who are looking for a quiet corner, will find it in the Schwarzwald Hotel, which is so distinguished that ordinary hustle and bustle doesn't dare to cross its threshold. From its terrace one has a beautiful view far beyond the clear mountain lake.

"An awful lot of trees," said Ralph. On the spot it sounded funny, but basically he was right. Despite the violent despoilation of war, Germany is still richer in woodlands than any other country in Western Europe. More than a quarter of West Germany is covered with trees, for the most part fir. Southern Germany is especially rich in forests, and the Black Forest makes the greatest single contribution to this treasure.

From Titisee to Baden-Baden is a spectacular drive. Our first stop was Hinterzarten, one of the most popular mountain resorts of the Black Forest, which has more of them than any other region in Germany. Then we turned right off the Freiburger Strasse and drove about 30 kilometers to the top of the Thurner, down again to Neuhäusle, into the ravine of Hexenloch (starred in the Baedecker), a steep climb up the other side to Neukirch, and through a magnificent forest to Furtwangen.

Furtwangen in the Breg valley has 6,000 inhabitants and the highest elevation of all the small towns in the southern part of the Black Forest. It lives by its clock industry; it has a clock museum and a school for clockmakers. Dick couldn't resist buying a cuckoo clock from a vast selection. But that doesn't mean that only cuckoo clocks are produced in the Black Forest region. In spite of its woodlands, Baden-Württemberg is the second largest industrial area in Germany, and first in the production of precision instruments. Half of all German musical instruments are manufactured here, nine out of ten German watches.

From Furtwangen, again a steep climb to the winter-sports village of Schönwald; down again to Triberg and the Hotel over the Waterfall, well worth a visit. But the most beautiful section still lay ahead of us—a road through lofty forests into the Gutach valley. First we saw the gay baroque tower of St. Mary in the Firs, a pilgrimage church propped against a slope. Then the little toy houses of the oldest Black Forest resort appeared one by one. Finally we crossed the Gutach bridge deep down in the ravine. The road descends in many curves, and the ruins of the castle greet you from the Homberger Schlossberg. Shortly before Hausach, we turned into the Kinzig valley.

Now the southern section of the Black Forest was behind us. In the north, the mountains are not so high and the ravines not so deeply incised. The Kinzig valley is the boundary between the two.

We drove on to Schiltach, Schenkenzell, and to the little town of Alpirsbach, the "jewel of the Black Forest." Art-history students come from far and wide to admire the Romanesque columns in its nine-hundred-year-old covent church. On through the Kinzig valley to Lossburg, and again through the woods to Freudenstadt.

There are people who maintain that Freudenstadt, rebuilt as if in a sandbox, with small houses and an enormous marketplace, is a beautiful town. Maybe they do so because they want to please its inhabitants. If so, I want to do so, too. Aside from that, the place can be described as a caprice of its high-minded master planner, Frederick I of Württemberg who, at the beginning of the seventeenth century, had the town built on a checkerboard ground plan, intending to put a large fortress in the center. First called Friedrichstadt, it was later renamed Freudenstadt, Town of Joy. Protestant refugees from Austria found a home there and were supposed to help mine the rich iron-ore deposits. However, the iron-ore deposits turned out to be not as rich as had been expected, the money to build the fortress was lacking, and the big square remained empty. In 1632, when the houses were burned down and the inhabitants became victims of marauding troops in the Thirty Years War, the fortress might have been a help.

The citizens of Freudenstadt rebuilt their town exactly as it had been before, with the checkerboard ground plan and the slightly megalomaniac marketplace surrounded by arcades which displayed an alien Italian influence. Thus the town stood quite joyfully for more than two hundred years, a small resort district developed along the slope. Then came Hitler, and on April 16, 1945, when the war was practically over, from a literally clear sky, a bombardment of French artillery which didn't stop until the following day and left the center of town a ruin. After that it was pillaged for three days, mainly by Moroccan troops. Nobody was permitted to lock his house and the women were compelled to yield to whoever wanted them. The responsible officer was Christian de Castries who became notorious later in the battle of Dienbienphu.

"Is it necessary to bring up all these old stories?" Yvonne asked indignantly.

"I'm afraid so," I said, "otherwise the history of the town is incomprehensible."

Again the survivors undertook to rebuild their town just as it had been before; checkerboard layout, big square, arcades, and in a corner of the square, the same old church—a curiosity because of its two naves built at right angles to each other, one section for the men, the other for the women. It has the same two naves today.

To rebuild a town from its foundations twice and still respect the peculiarities of a sovereign after more than three hundred years—that is truly Swabian, commented a citizen who had moved to Freudenstadt from Baden. Here I must mention an important event which we had viewed with the eyes of Europeans rather than as Black Forest natives, which means we had underestimated it. Ten kilometers before entering Freudenstadt we had crossed the border between Baden and Württemberg, and hadn't even noticed it. And this is surprising, because the Badeners (Aleman) and the Württembergers (Swabians) are poles apart in the "ideal-typology" of German tribes. "Live and let live," is the motto of the Badener; "Work, save, build a home" (with all sorts of additions; "buy a car," seems the most up-to-date one) is the motto of the Swabians. But the stranger who doesn't notice these differences, may be forgiven. Baden, Württemberg, and Hohenzollern were united by the referendum of December 9, 1951, under the heading of Land Baden-Württemberg.

We wanted to get to its capital, Stuttgart, before dark, so we drove on in the direction of Strassburg on the Black Forest Highway, a stretch that is rather dull until it turns right at the Zuflucht onto a plateau that reaches its highest elevation on the barren Schliffkopf (1,054 meters), winds in gentle curves through a wild-life conservation area, past Schweinkopf (1,014 meters) and Vogelkopf, down to Ruhestein, the old pass between Murgtal and Achetal. Up again to the ghost-haunted Mummelsee, with Hornisgrinde (1,166 meters), the highest mountain of the Black Forest, in the background. Then another gentle descent, around Hornisgrinde, past Untersmatt (the northernmost ski area of the Black Forest), Sand and Bühlerhöhe, and finally a steep downgrade and many curves to Baden-Baden.

The northern part of the Black Forest is not as famous and not quite as crowded as the southern part. Call the slopes of Schliffkopf and Hornisgrinde mountains and you elicit only condescending smiles from climbers. In the summer the crowd of vacationers is quite bearable, very much so in winter, and during the in-between seasons, which have been unjustly neglected, one can be downright lonely there. In fact, anyone who has the will and energy to walk a few hundred yards into the woods may be by himself at the height of the season.

Guests are very well taken care of along this amazing Black Forest Highway. Owners of the hotels on the Black Forest Highway can even afford to appreciate each other and praise their establishments in joint

advertising campaigns. For persons who are ailing and need the supervision of a doctor, Bühlerhöhe is famous not only because of its excellently run sanatorium but because a refined tranquility surrounds the
Kurhotel too, a tranquility that might spell boredom for the youthful
vacationer. The average age of guests at Bühlerhöhe is, in my estimation, fifty or over. People who have to earn their daily bread could
hardly afford to stay there at an earlier age.

Healthy young people who want to ski, hike, and have fun are
much better taken care of at a mountain inn called the Schliffkopfhaus.
There they can get a (very small) room for about 4 marks (less than a
dollar) or a mattress for the night for 1.50 marks. With their breakfast they can enjoy a panorama of the Black Forest range all the way
to the Swiss Alps, from a terrace furnished in rustic style: the "pleasantest dining room on the Black Forest Highway," which ends in
Baden-Baden.

One of the people who made Baden-Baden famous during the last
century was a man who held the concession for its gambling casino.
His role was similar to that of today's Kurdirektor, only he had far
greater means and power. Jacques Benazet was the uncrowned king of
the palaces of the Lichtenthaler Allee, where princes, emperors, and
cocottes lived splendidly, and a little notoriously, thereby giving the
splendor added luster. He is the originator of the saying; *Ces choses-là,
il faut les faire grandement ou ne pas les faire du tout* . . . "Things
should be done on a lavish scale, or they shouldn't be done at all." The
town name, Baden-Baden (translated Bathe-Bathe), recommends the
use of the salutary waters with a double imperative; but Baden-Baden
suffers from the fact that, in a Europe threatened, if we are to believe
its puritans, with ruination by luxury and decadence, it is simply not
possible any more *de faire grandement ces choses-là*, to enjoy yourself sans regrets and limitlessly, to live lavishly, to go on a spree.

Many roads lead from Baden-Baden to Calw, the little town on the
Nagold, where Dick wanted to pay his respects to Hermann Hesse's
birthplace; but none of them lead there uninterruptedly. Again we had
to cross the boundary between former Baden and Württemberg, and
the road builders had not done much to facilitate our crossing. We left
Calw and the Black Forest behind us and in less than an hour had
reached Stuttgart.

The best German cars are made in Stuttgart, and more wine is grown
here than in any other major German city. It is moreover the seat of
the Baden-Württemberg administration. The city has more than half
a million inhabitants; very few streets run horizontally; the well-to-do
people live outside the city proper, preferably on one of the hilltops
overlooking the Neckar, where you find street names such as "In
Paradise," that seem to disassociate themselves from the city below
which is very pretty to look at from one of these hilltops, especially
when the lights are on. We did just that while we were having dinner
on a hill called Bopster. Here a young playwright called Friedrich
Schiller read part of his first drama, *The Brigands*, to his friends; and

the pride of Stuttgart, the new television tower (211 meters high) is up here, too. As is proper for modern towers, it fans out near the top to form a panorama restaurant. Food and drink are not cheap, since everything has to be transported up so that you can look down while enjoying your meal, but for those who can afford to spend 20 marks, dinner at the restaurant in the Stuttgart Television Tower is a good investment.

At nine o'clock we set out in the direction of the *Autobahn*. We had a date with Munich for the following day.

2. MUNICH: CAPITAL OF THE THREE B'S

King Ludwig I promised to "make a city of Munich that would do such honor to Germany that no one would know Germany who had not seen Munich." Today's travel statistics corroborate the fact that he did it. Everybody wants to see Munich, especially the Americans. In one year, 100,000 Americans visited the city of which Thomas Wolfe said (in *The Web and the Rock*), "How can one speak of Munich but to say it is a kind of German heaven?" although he almost got his head cracked open with a stein when he was there. Only a few thousand less were attracted to Frankfurt am Main, which I think can be called the most American of all German cities. After that the curve falls sharply: 50,000 Americans a year for Cologne and Hamburg; 25,000 for Stuttgart and Düsseldorf. The statistics on Berlin are missing. I'd say it would be in third place.

Only historians of art, who are also experts on Bavarian history should guide visitors with a thirst for knowledge through Munich. Nobody else could identify all the churches and palaces and name the architects of its innumerable historic buildings. "Who did it?" Who is it?" I simply took to answering alternately, "Ludwig," and "Maximilian," and was quite often right. Whenever I didn't know, Andreas von Hattesdorf usually did. Andreas had a pleasant way of looking upon Germany as his native land wherever it was beautiful, but whenever the Nazis or other unpleasant contemporaries were involved, he was staunchly Austrian.

"All right, what must we see?"

An experienced guide is prepared for the question. I don't like to force my taste on other people, and I have a statistical bug, no denying it, so I asked fifty friends and acquaintances who traveled and kept their eyes open to tell me what sights they thought worth seeing in Germany. Here are the results: 1. The Zwinger in Dresden. 2. The Porta Nigra in Trier. 3. The harbor in Hamburg. 4. The Cathedral in Cologne. 5. The Television Tower in Stuttgart. 6. The Pergamon Altar in its own museum in East Berlin. 7. The Goethe House in Frankfurt. 8. The historic houses of the classical poets in Weimar. 9. The Old Pinakothek in Munich. 10. The Freiburg Cathedral. 11. The Hansa Quarter in West Berlin. 12. The Deutsche Museum in Munich. 13. The

Römer in Frankfurt. 14. The Riemenschneider Marienaltar in the Herrgottskirche in Creglingen (Franconia). 15. The Castle in Heidelberg.

So off to the Old Pinakothek and the Deutsche Museum! Enough for one day, not only because they lie at opposite ends of the city, but because anyone who can't give each place at least two hours of his time does better not to visit them at all.

The counterpart of the Old Pinakothek—the New Pinakothek—no longer exists. It was destroyed in World War II, and its treasures were divided among other museums. This proved especially helpful to the "House of Art," Hitler's monumental gift to the city, renamed in the folk-idiom, the "House of Kitsch," for which word an adequate translation is lacking. "Trash" comes closest to it. A travesty of art is implied.

It is utterly useless to try to describe in a few pages one of the five most famous art galleries in the world. And it is just as impossible to say more about the Deutsche Museum than that nowhere else can you see the history of technology and industry described so comprehensively and graphically as in this magnificent building, which it takes a good fifteen minutes to circle, walking briskly. In the Old Pinakothek we experienced Munich as most people see it, as a city of art; a city that contains the most valuable collections to be found in Germany; a city of which Thomas Mann wrote: "Art blossoms, art is sovereign, art waves its rose-entwined sceptre over the city and smiles. A reverent participation in its prosperity, a devotion and propaganda on its behalf, a faithful cult of line, adornment, form, sense and beauty prevail."

In the Deutsch Museum we received an artificial—by which I mean felicitously arranged—impression of the other Munich, the industrial city, home of the Bavarian Motor Works, Siemens, and Nymphenburg, one of the big German porcelain manufacturing companies; the city of machine factories, optical and precision instruments, rubber and textile processing; of the great publishers—Beck-Biederstein, Bruckmann, Desch, Ehrenwirth, Hanser, Kindler, Kösel, Langen-Müller, List, Nymphenburger Verlagsanstalt, Oldenbourg, Piper, Süddeutscher Verlag, Winkler. This is industrial Munich, Bavaria's capital, which invariably elects a Social Democratic mayor in spite of the fact that the old aristocracy sets the social pace in Bavaria as in no other German Land, and the Catholic government party, the CSU, rules with an iron majority.

Capital City Bavaria. That takes care of one of the B's. The next: Capital City Beer.

Almost as much has been written about Munich beer as about Munich art, one reason for not going into it too thoroughly here. With stein in hand, you'll get through Bavaria just fine. In Munich such minor contrasts as rich and poor, and such major ones as high-born and lowborn, disappear; even those of Catholic and Protestant, of Bavarian and non-Bavarian almost do. To quote Paul Heyse, an illustrious Municher by adoption: "The equality before this national

drink eases the pressures of social contrasts." Beer is the democratic juice in Munich's blood stream. Every year it joins city and
countryside on the *Wies'n* (meadow), and unites Germans and Americans every night in the Hofbräuhaus. And any stranger coming to
Munich with the urge to go native must grow accustomed to beer,
weisswürscht (white sausages), and the *föhn*—a sultry, enervating
mistral. It can't be too difficult because four out of every five Munichers are, in the local dialect, "*zuagroaste*," those who have moved
there, or the offspring of same. Which is why the city has grown so
rapidly, from 1,500 inhabitants in 1648, to 60,000 in 1800; 350,000 in
1890; 500,000 in 1910; in 1958 the millionth Municher was born, and
almost 200,000 have to be added to that figure to approximate the latest
census.

North Germans feel at home in Munich. One of the most prominent
ones said: "I did a good thing when I moved to Munich. This fine
city is the city of cities. There is something definitely southern about
its inhabitants and landscape. And to have the Alps so near! I can see
them from my window. I love to be here." That is what Prussian
Detlev von Liliencron of Schleswig-Holstein wrote to a friend in
1890. And someone who came from still farther north, Hans Christian
Andersen, called Munich "Germany's most interesting city."

The third B is Munich, Capital of the *Bewegung*, or Movement of
National Socialism, something Munichers don't like to be reminded
of. The title was bestowed on it in 1935 by the Führer. We who were
going to school at the time, learned this in a way we shall never forget.
On November 9, 1923, the first National Socialist revolt or Beer Hall
Putsch took place in Munich. "The vanguard of marchers was just
turning into the Brienner Strasse at the Theatinerkirche, when it happened." Shots . . . 14 dead . . . Hitler sentenced to the five years in
prison that enabled him to write *Mein Kampf*.

In the beer cellars of Munich, the Party assembled its psychological
equipment; in the Brienner Strasse you could find the first Brown
House, a classic aristocrat's palace, rebuilt according to Hitler's own
plans. From 1931 on it was the seat of the Reich's administration of
the NSDAP.

Munich is rich in such contrasts which seem irreconcilable to the
believer in a straightforward development. In Munich it was possible
for a dancer, the illegitimate daughter of a Scottish officer and a
Creole girl, to steer serious politics into liberal channels (the end of
religious supervision in schools, the lifting of press censorship) in a way
that made English Prime Minister Lord Palmerston and Bismarck admire her. The story of how she made her first impression on the
Bavarian king characterizes him, but also characterizes those who repeat the tale with a grin of approval.

Ludwig I was admiring the twenty-six-year-old young woman's
figure when he suddenly remarked that "a corset and the right clothes"
could do a lot for a person, whereupon the young woman is supposed
to have unbuttoned the bodice of her dress, "without a trace of co-

quetry," and with a curtsy said, "If it please you, Sire, convince yourself." The same Mrs. James (Mr. James was a lieutenant in the British Indian army), alias Lola Montez, was later banished as a "Babylonian whore" by the very professors who had been summoned by Ludwig I (in his pre-Lola days) to the University of Munich. She came to an early and sad end in Australia. The students of the Lola-faithful Corporation Alemannia were expelled.

In Munich, if I may be permitted the simplification, abstract painting was born. The artists of the Blue Rider period met in the Mandlstrasse, and Kandinsky said: "I painted my first abstract painting there. That was where I reflected on 'pure' painting, and 'pure' art." And yet . . . In Munich's House of Art you could look at the largest collection of sentimentally naturalistic monstrosities that any museum has ever tolerated within its walls.

In the introduction to his quite charming little *Munich Album* (Feldafing, 1958) Anton Sailer writes: "In other places you've got to live, here you are allowed to live, and what's more—you can live as you please."

In Munich's artist and student quarter, Schwabing, where, as in all such quarters in Europe today, art hides behind everyday life and tourist traffic, leading unkind critics to the conclusion that it does not exist—in Schwabing, a girl from the Lower Rhine called Gisela, in premises justifiably named after her, offers her conception of the freedom of the artist to an audience that fills them every night. To overflowing. Gisela's chansons are of the top music-hall variety. You'll find a lot of VIP's, very VIP's at Gisela's. The closer it gets to midnight, the greater the anticipation. And then at last—a muted spotlight, Gisela on the small stage singing the song about Novack, who doesn't let her down. The text is bold, often quite salacious, but she is allowed to sing it. It occurs to no one to protest. Live as you please! With one exception: when Gisela made a recording of the song, the police turned up at her house and confiscated it. *That* was forbidden. They say Gisela was surprised. In Land Lower-Rhine, where she came from, morality was more consistent. Another example: Liaisons are city-wide occurrences in Munich. Everybody knows it and doesn't give a damn. Live as you please! But then there was the case of a famous resident of Munich who was hauled into court and given a prison sentence because he had persuaded a friend to put his apartment at his disposal for an assignation.

Often it was the Catholic Church which gave the University of Munich the reputation of being a refuge for conservatism and a distorted example of academic freedom. In 1933, the university was *gleichgeschaltet*, an innocuous term for Nazified or brought into line politically, a transition that took place with comparative ease. But then again it was the Catholic Church that produced a few Munich students and one professor with the audacity to rise up against the "slogans and lies, with clean minds and the courage to speak the truth," as Theodore Heuss puts it in his introduction to Inge Scholl's book, *The White Rose.*

This book (S. Fischer Verlag) describes a radiant chapter in Munich's modern history; more than that, it is a most moving testimony on the revolt against Hitler. The frightful caricature of the German, for whose features we furnished the material, is canceled by the clean, frank, not-at-all fanatic faces of these young people who were condemned to death for treason.

On February 22, 1943, twenty-four-year-old medical student Christoph Probst from Munich, twenty-five-year-old medical student Hans Scholl from Ulm, and his twenty-two-year-old sister, philosophy student Sophie Scholl, were executed. On July 13, Inge Scholl's teacher, fifty-year-old psychology and philosophy professor Kurt Huber, and twenty-six-year-old medical student Alexander Schmorell from Munich were put to death; on October 12, 1943, medical student Willi Graf from Saarbrücken.

Take a look at their faces (the paperback mentioned above includes six good photographs), and listen to the words with which Professor Huber replied to the judges who had condemned him to death. They should make you lose your taste for some other faces and other words seen and heard daily.

"As a German university professor, I consider it my moral duty to fight what is quite obviously harmful. External loyalty has its limitations beyond which it becomes insincere and immoral, and this happens when it serves as a cloak for a cowardice that doesn't dare to stand up against a perfectly evident breaking of the law. I have reached my goal, which was to present this warning and exhortation before a responsible supreme court. You have taken my rights and rank as professor from me and have placed me on an equal footing with the lowest criminal. No charge of treason, however, can rob me of my honor as a university professor. I did what I had to do, and I take the consequences upon myself."

The story told in *The White Rose* impressed my friends more than anything else in Munich. We were there two days, and saw far too little of the city. Is a little better than nothing? I wouldn't have written this book if I didn't feel that the answer was "yes."

As I had done for my friends in Bonn and Berlin, I drew a map of the city for them, reducing its physiognomy to a few basic lines. Munich turned out to be rather like a cross—not unfitting—around the center of which numerous small crosses huddled as you may see on maps indicating churches. The long beam runs from the Sendlinger Tor to the Siegestor, or if you like you can run it on to the Feilitzschplatz. The shorter crossbeam unites Karlstor and Isartor, and may also be lengthened sideways in either direction. The two beams cross at the Marienplatz, which has always been the center of town. Around it you will find grouped Old Munich, with its famous churches, which are starred as obligatory for those who use a Baedeker: the Frauenkirche,

built by Jörg Ganghofer in the fifteenth century, a cathedral since
1821. Its hundred-meter-high twin towers, with their chubby capped
domes, can be seen for miles and have become Munich's landmark; the
Peterskirche, oldest parish church in Munich, with its tower called
Old Peter, which means to the Municher what Big Ben means to the
Londoner; the classic Heiliggeistkirche, begun in the fourteenth century, finished in the nineteenth; the former Court Church Sankt
Michaelis, built in the sixteenth century and a model of Renaissance
church architecture for all South Germany; the ochre, seventeenth-
century Italian baroque Theatinerkirche; the Asamkirche, dedicated to
Saint Nepomuk and built in the curious Bavarian rococo style which
is admired again today in a much gayer example—the Cuvilliés Theater
in the Alte Residenz. Our great-grandparents didn't think much of it.

In this little realm of churches and crosses, the tourist may find most
of everything else that might interest him, never more than ten minutes
walk away: Hofbräuhaus and Rathaus (City Hall), Feldherrnhalle
(General's Hall), and Hofgarten (Court Gardens), theaters, and big
hotels.

Munich is "the city on the Isar," yet the river doesn't flow through
one's picture of the town, in spite of the fact that Munich would
probably never have been founded by Henry the Lion if the Isar hadn't
been in the way of the Salzstrasse that led from Reichenhall to Augsburg and had to be bridged. The most suitable place for the bridge
seemed to be the monastery of Schäftlarn, where a few monks were
housed in huts. This area was therefore described in Old German as
"*zu den Munichen*," or "at the monks'." Thus the church played a part
in the very founding of the city, and the monks are commemorated
gratefully on its crest, on which can be seen the Münchner Kindl, a
little boy in habit and cowl. But if someone were to secretly remove
the Isar, very few tourists would notice it, and of the natives, only
those who live near the river. The Isar does as little for the physiognomy of Munich as the Spree does for Berlin, although both rivers
are evoked in such poetic efforts at terminology as "Athens on the
Isar" and "Athens on the Spree," for the two cities respectively.

At any rate, that is how my friends felt, and I have always been
similarly impressed. But, since a North German journalist wouldn't
dare say so without the backing of a Municher, or at least a man who
has lived in Munich for decades, I quote Wolfgang Koeppen, who
writes: "The Isar comes rushing down like a mountain child . . . but
river and city were never wed. Like a lass from the hills, the Isar flows
unwillingly under bridges, never making the slightest effort to appear
urban, with citified walls or cafés or restaurants along its banks, or with
rowboats, pleasure steamers. . . ." So you walk through the busy
Maximilianstrasse, finally reach the Isar, cross two bridges, and find
yourself in front of a colossal edifice, the Maximilianeum. Here you
have the administrative seat, not of the city of Munich but of Land
Bavaria.

3. BAVARIA—VACATIONLAND

For nine out of ten citizens who know Bavaria, it is a vacationland. For eight out of ten, Bavaria means Upper Bavaria, from the area south of Munich to the Austrian border. And here you find much that is good, expensive, and world famous: the Starnbergersee and Tegernsee, for instance, unapproachable because surrounded by private property. Here land costs a fortune per square meter, which keeps uninvited guests at bay. Ammersee and Chiemsee are more accessible. In the center lies Herrenchiemsee Castle, the Nymphenburg Versailles of Ludwig II. Herrenchiemsee is a historic site in the history of the Federal Republic. There, between August 10 and 23, 1948, the Herrenchiemsee Committee drafted the Basic Law.

Higher up in the mountains are fashionable summer and winter resorts: at the foot of the Watzmann, Berchtesgaden and Bad Reichenhall; under the Zugspitze, Mittenwald and Garmisch-Partenkirchen, where the rich—old and *nouveau*—of Europe and from overseas meet yearly, and a lot of fence-sitters manage to have fun, too. "I shall always count Upper Bavaria, with its rivers, lakes, and Alps, as the goal of my vacation dreams," wrote Baron Hervé de Gruben, Belgian Ambassador to Bonn. Many have the same dream.

From Munich we drove southwest, in the direction of the Starnberger See, on Federal Route 2. This highway runs from Berlin through Hof, Nürnberg, Munich, to the Austrian border. Since the Winter Olympics took place in Garmisch-Partenkirchen in 1936, this section of the road between Munich and the Alps has been called Olympiastrasse. We skirted the lake on the north and drove on to Murnau, a little town with many brightly muraled houses, not far from the Staffelsee, a section not yet completely spoiled by international tourism. After Eschenlohe, two tunnels, and we were in Oberau; in front of us the Wettersteinmassif with the Zugspitze in the middle. Here we turned off the Olympiastrasse onto the Deutsche Alpenstrasse. Effective names such as these, from an advertising viewpoint, are beginning to be the thing. The whole development was encouraged by the Bund railways which run scenic buses on such routes.

We already know several roads so christened; we are going to travel on quite a few more. The traveler may find it helpful to see them listed together, in the order in which they keep the promise of their attractive names.

1. Schwarzwaldhochstrasse (Black Forest Highway) from Freudenstadt to Baden-Baden.
2. Romantische Strasse (Romantic Highway) from Füssen to Würzburg (or Wertheim).
3. Alpenstrasse (Alpine Highway) from Berchtesgaden to Lindau.
4. Bergstrasse (Mountain Highway) from Darmstadt to Heidelberg.
5. Burgenstrasse (Castle Highway) from Mannheim to Nürnberg.
6. Salzstrasse, from Lüneburg to Lübeck.

7. Bayerische Ostmarkstrasse (Bavarian Eastern Marches Highway) from Bayreuth to Passau.

8. Weinstrasse (Wine Highway) from Monsheim to Schweigen in the Palatinate.

9. Nibelungenstrasse, from Worms to Würzburg.

10. Olympiastrasse, from Munich to Garmisch-Partenkirchen.

The last three are beautiful, granted, but the fact that they have names raises them undeservedly above some of their equally beautiful sister roads. For instance, the *Autobahn* between Munich and Salzburg, without being named Magnificent Upper Bavarian Highway, is hard to equal for its visual enjoyment. And I could name quite a few others: Coblenz-Trier, or Wiesbaden-Assmannshausen, that could be called Wine Highways with as much, if not more justification than the Weinstrasse.

The first four of the ten roads mentioned are unique in their way and fully deserve their attractive names. Number five is a rather artificial product and a good bit too long, but it does fulfill the expectations aroused by the name Castle Highway, especially in Hohenlohe and the Taubertal. The comparatively modestly named Salzstrasse disappoints only those who still expect to see salt being transported on it; aside from that it is a pleasant connection between two towns that are justly called the most beautiful in North Germany.

So we turned into the Alpenstrasse, which wasn't quite finished at the time, and was recognizable as such only on the map, but one thing was true about it—you could drive 500 kilometers and continuously have the majestic Alps as a backdrop.

We crossed the Ettaler Berg to the village it was named after which has a Benedictine monastery, founded in the twelfth century, to thank, not only for its name but also for its most important export article, Ettal Liqueur, and greatest tourist attraction, the rococo Ettal Church.

On to Linderhof, the fairy-tale castle of Ludwig II, and to Oberammergau, famous for its religious wood carving and Passion Play. The next Passion Play is scheduled for 1970, but the Oberammergauers are going to have to summon a lot of resistance to worldly pleasure if they don't decide, one fine day, that their vow made during the plague, 1633, to give a Passion Play every ten years, should be fulfilled more often in such hectic times as ours.

On to Saulgrub, Bayersoien, the impressive steel-cement arches of the Eschelsbacher Bridge across the Ammertal, toward Steingaden. But before that, an obligatory stop, for which we had to go two kilometers out of our way down a hill marked, "To the Wieskirche."

The first thing we saw was a huge parking lot and restaurants. Well, I don't suppose it's different wherever landscape and art are on sale, as they are all over Upper Bavaria. Some people get quite worked up about such commercialism. I can't see anything immoral about it, and a lot of it is very convenient. How grateful we were for the restaurants after we'd let ourselves be overwhelmed by the rococo miracle of Wies! Inconceivably beautiful and at the same time a little oppressive.

Such reverent merriment before God; such light effects, rhythm, harmony of color and form; such an almost casual blending of simple joy in faith with the most complex refinements. "Architecture is music petrified," said Goethe. If there is such a thing as an architectual correlative for Mozart's music, then this is it. But this is not our world! It isn't granted us any longer to create such playfulness in the presence of God. We know all about historical categories in art, we classify, we get carried away: "*Grossartig!*" "Wonderful!" "*Merveilleux!*" But that's about all we have to offer, and it isn't very much.

"Are we going to Regensburg?" asked Yvonne. "It's a place one's supposed to see. They say it has wonderful churches."

Should we have made the trip longer?

When a picture is to be printed, it is first broken up into dots. Any kind of dots will do as long as every one is sharp, and all are spread more or less evenly over the whole area. Then you get a photo-engraving screen that will make for a quite decent picture. What I am trying to do is give you a picture of Germany via such a spot-process. Most Germans would be of the opinion that any such picture shouldn't be too bright, but at every spot, anyone concerned with it personally pleads for a few rosy overtones. However, no one in the typographic business can tell you how to make a dismal picture out of a lot of rosy overtones. As for me, I can't see the picture so darkly nor its individual parts as so rosy.

Well . . . back to the Alpenstrasse and Steingaden, where you can see the styles of seven centuries in the Prämonstratenser Abbey. On a slope to the left, Hohenschwangau and Neuschwanstein were waiting to be visited, country residences of the Bavarian Maximilians and Ludwigs. They seemed more beautiful to us from down below. So, on to Füssen on the Lech, a town rich in antiquities. Just about here Upper Bavaria ends and the Alpenstrasse runs into that part of Bavaria which, for complicated historic reasons, is called Swabia, and for much more plausible reasons, the Allgäu, the second Bavarian vacationland.

The Pearl of the Allgäu is Oberstdorf, because it has so much to offer, a little something for everyone: easy and rugged mountain tours in summer; gentle and difficult ski slopes in winter; curing in the Stillachhaus; everything livened up with hotel life in the Allgäuer Bergbad; dancing, and fun in the Trettachstüble, at the Hirschen, in the Hotel Baur; elegance at the Wittelsbacher Hof and the Nebelhorn-bahnhotel; two ski jumps, hockey and ice skating in the Eisstadion; sight-seeing expeditions to Nebelhorn, Freibergsee, and above all, the Breitachklamm or gorge. There are so many gorges in Germany, but I really think this is the loveliest one.

The third Bavarian vacationland, overshadowed by Upper Bavaria and hence not sufficiently valued (and for the same reason not so overrun) is the Bavarian Forest, lying between the Danube and the Franconian Jura Mountains in the west, and the Czechoslovakian border in the east: Fichtelgebirge, Oberpfälzerwald, Böhmerwald, are part of it, too. Stifter was this region's poet. In the wooded areas there are no towns worth mentioning, but on the periphery lie Hof, Bayreuth, Regensburg, Passau, the latter the finest of them all.

Alexander von Humboldt, a much-traveled man, considered this old bishop's see, clustered around its late-Gothic cathedral, where the green waters of the River Inn mingle with the foam of the Ilz and the sluggish brown of the Danube, one of the seven most beautiful cities in the world, and a great many people agree with him. Not much has changed in Passau since Humboldt's day; the last war, for the most part, spared Passau and its 40,000 inhabitants.

Soon we were in Füssen. Here we left the Alpenstrasse for the Romantische Strasse, which is not an old or uniform road but an invention of travel bureaus, justified by every kilometer you put behind you. It starts in the district of the baroque Wessobrunner artists, the most important of whom was the mayor of Landsberg, Dominic Zimmermann (we have him to thank for the Wieskirche) and carries on from there into the Würzburger baroque of Balthazar Neumann. With that we enter the fourth Bavarian vacationland—Franconia, a half-historic, half-geographic makeshift designation, which means nothing more than that in the eighteenth century it was not yet Bavaria; it became a part of Bavaria only with Napoleon's friendly help at the beginning of the nineteenth century.

Wherever you may be—standing on the Segringerstrasse in Dinkelsbühl, or drinking the wonderful Franconian wine in the Deutsche Haus just around the corner (in Dinkelsbühl everything is just around the corner), you either feel that you have been shot back into the Middle Ages or that you are in a theater. Marketplace with fountain, renaissance Town Hall and late-Gothic church; town wall with moat; watchtower and narrow city gate—a set ready for the *Meistersinger;* Germany during the Thirty Years War in cinemascope.

This holds good not only for Dinkelsbühl but also for its even more famous neighbor, 50 kilometers to the north, which records its position astride the small River Tauber with the archaic preposition *"ob"*—Rothenburg ob der Tauber. (In our questionnaire: Which is the most beautiful German city? Rothenburg came first, remember?)

"And it really is marvelous," said Dick. "I've never seen a more beautiful city."

We had lunch in Rothenburg's most famous restaurant, the Eisenhut in the Ratskeller. The few places in Rothenburg that are not hundreds of years old, pretend to be.

"The kitchen," said Yvonne, "seems to be the only spot that indicates that we're not living in the Middle Ages."

"And the tourists," said von Hattesdorf.

Dick was offended by such cynicism. "Does one have to come from a country that lacks all magic of the past to appreciate this little medieval town?"

"I know what Yvonne means," said Ralph. "I lived in Cambridge for three years, in a college that was constantly being admired as a 'wonderful example of Tudor times.' Tudor churches are beautiful, granted, but Tudor bathrooms leave much to be desired."

"We really should be thankful that there are testimonials to the past so wonderfully preserved, so lovingly cared for," said Professor Spälti in his meticulous German.

"Bravo!" from Dick.

"But Professor," said Yvonne, "how would you like to spend your life in a museum?"

"I do," said Professor Spälti. "I am a university professor." His eyes twinkled happily, and Yvonne had nothing more to say.

The history that impresses itself so graphically on the twentieth century in Dinkelsbühl and Rothenburg is the history of the small German Reich towns in Franconia, and it has little connection with Bavaria. The same applies to that strange triumverate: Bamberg-Nürnberg-Fürth, which should be mentioned here, even though we did not visit them.

The old Reich city of Nürnberg, Germany's "chronicle in stone," the Mecca of all Germans with a feeling for medieval art, poetry, and architecture, "the most wonderful city in Germany" (positively!), merits more than a fleeting mention, even though it lost so much in World War II that can never be restored. Wherever German history is to be illustrated by memorials of the past, at least half of any chapter on Citizenry in the Middle Ages must be centered in Nürnberg. Watches, music boxes, air guns, firelocks, assay balances, were invented in Nürnberg, or were used there for the first time. Veit Stoss, Adam Krafft, the Peter Vischers, father and son, and Albrecht Dürer lived there; Martin Behaim stopped off in Nürnberg after one of his sea voyages and there invented the first globe; and Hans Sachs was "shoe-maker and poet" there.

We may have Hans Sachs to thank for the fact that Hitler chose Nürnberg as the City of the Party Rallies. For had there been no Hans Sachs, there would have been no *Meistersinger*, and it may well have been this work by a composer he admired so much that attracted Hitler's attention to Nürnberg. But, of course, it may also have been his race historians, who were in a position to draw his attention to the fact that even in those early days anti-Semitism had led to drastic measures in Nürnberg, and finally to the expulsion of that city's Jews, who moved to neighboring Fürth, which soon became a much more thriving industrial city than Nürnberg.

We have to view Bamberg, too, as connected with Nürnberg. Once it was called the heart of Germany. Two folk sayings corroborate this: "Grape vines, bells calling to mass, Bamberg—that is Franconia." And, "If Nürnberg were mine, I'd live on it in Bamberg."

Our goal for the day was Würzburg, at the end of the Romantische Strasse. "A merry city with merry maidens," a chronicler of the nineteenth century calls it, and "without doubt the pleasantest university town in Bavaria, toward which the vine hills contribute."

Well, now . . . "the pleasantest university town in Bavaria?" That's one of those phrases everyone uses who has to place city beside city in a never-ending row. This fellow says Würzburg is pleasanter than Erlangen and Munich. Who knows? Maybe it is. I noticed that the university doesn't seem to play the part in Würzburg that it might be expected to play in a small town. Freiburg, Tübingen, Marburg—you can still call them true university towns. But Würzburg is primarily a wine city, an episcopal see with tourism, with a university that lies not only geographically on its outskirts. Granted that it is gloriously situated, and that in this university area, the new architects of Würzburg have shown, in their amusing skyscrapers and boldly designed church, that Balthazar Neumann, who built the Bishop's Residence and the Summer Palace in Veitshöchheim (worth seeing for its baroque garden alone) has heirs he need not be ashamed of. Before the princely bishops moved into their residence in the center of town, they lived in Fortress Marienburg, high up on the opposite bank of the Main, which gives the town an imposing background. From here you get the best view of river and town. And Würzburg is quite spectacular when seen from a distance; individual parts of it are beautiful too, when seen close-up, but a medial distance does less for the town.

We were tired and thirsty once we had all the "duty sights" behind us. Dick was adamant that we see them all, so was Professor Spälti. But Ralph had read that there were 98 churches in Würzburg and 105 wine restaurants (there are only half as many today), and he wanted to be sure to get in all of the latter. "If necessary," he declared happily, "I'm ready to skip the churches."

He got what he was after that evening in the Bürgerspital zum Heiligen Geist. After a day like the one we had behind us, we didn't have to worry about getting a good night's sleep, especially not at the Lämmle, the solid middle-class hotel of the Würzburger elite.

4. FRANKFURT: A LITTLE GOETHE AND A LOT OF UNITED STATES

There isn't a city in the world about which you can't say something nice. Frankfurt is one of them. Guides praise its rich history and beautiful surroundings.

These surroundings, which can't be praised too highly, are called Taunus, Rhön, Spessart, Odenwald, Bergstrasse, Rheingau, or, assembled politically—Hesse. Never before was there a Land with exactly these boundaries, but after World War I an administrative province rather like it was established. A so-called tribe of Hessians, a Frankish tribe descended possibly from the Chatti, whose main characteristic is supposed to have been stubbornness, have just as doubtful a tradition. But the vitality emanating from Cassel, Darmstadt, Nassau, and above all Frankfurt, seems to have been sufficient, after the debacle of 1945, to permit the creation of a quite comprehensible Federal Land of Hesse, which can make regional demands as in the days of the Princes of Brabant; for the administrative district of Montabaur, for instance, which the French Occupation handed over to *their* creation: Rhineland-Palatinate.

Our American publisher, Dick O'Connor insisted that Frankfurt, as seen by five foreigners and explained by one German, be given a chapter of its own. For publishers Frankfurt is today what it once was for Kaiser, Goethe admirers, Jews, lovers of frankfurters, and American occupation soldiers—*the* German city.

There are several routes from Würzburg to Frankfurt; the most attractive one runs along the river that connects the two cities. It is not the most direct way, because between Spessart and Odenwald, the River Main winds until it finally reaches Frankfurt. Of course we left the famous part of the valley behind us in Würzburg—Franconia on the Main—a region cut out for a pleasant rest from hectic living, with gentle hills and medieval beauty spots such as Dettelbach, Kitzingen, Marktsteft, Marktbreit, Eibelstadt. I musn't forget to mention the city of Bamberg on the Upper Main, again, but this time for its cathedral and magnificent stone "Rider," and the most beautiful South German baroque church: Balthazar Neumann's Vierzehnheiligen (Fourteen Saints) near Lichtenfels. But the Lower Main to Aschaffenburg, at least as far as Wörth, may still be counted as the river on which small towns are strung "like pearls on a chain": Gemünden, Neustadt, Rothenfels, Marktheidenfeld, Wertheim, Stadtprozelten, Miltenberg. . . .

Two other roads—one famous, the other notorious—approach Frankfurt from the south, direction Heidelberg. They run almost parallel to each other: the Bergstrasse and the *Autobahn.*

The Bergstrasse runs along the valley on the west side of the Odenwald. The ancient Romans must take the blame for its misleading name; they were the ones who called this important route to the north *strata montana.* But when winter is scarcely over in other parts of Germany, the trees are already blooming here, because this happens to be Germany's largest orchard area, and because the mountains, containing the mild sea air from the west, protect the valley from the icy winds of the east. Thus not only vegetables and plums thrive here, but also such trees as cedar, fig, and almond.

The Bergstrasse ends in Darmstadt, which is a classic example for all those who want to compare the cultural rights of the German provinces with the leveling steel and concrete influence of big-city civilization. For here tradition, fortuitous circumstances, open-mindedness, and prudent administrative energy have succeeded in preserving a small German princely residence town for the twentieth century. Darmstadt manages to fulfill a lot of the promise which an American like Dick, more misled than oriented by Goethe's Weimar, expects from such a town.

Darmstadt still has an artists' colony, founded by a grand duke, and an Academy for Language and Poetry, which from time to time makes a name for itself. There are Darmstadt Music Festivals, and Darmstadt Debates, which usually bring together all sorts of prominent people. In 1956, a Darmstadt Anthology, lovingly and cleverly edited by a Darmstadt poet who also happened to be a town clerk, was published. There exists a documentary on Darmstadt, entitled *The City of Creative Encounters,* which offers a good deal more than the well-meant local patriotism of city tourist bureaus. There is a Darmstadt Theater, which has outranked much wealthier, big-city theaters.

The mayor of Darmstadt may point with pride to the fact that, "There were cities before there were states, and a city culture before all others. Today our greatest reserves still lie in our autonomous cities, and our culture is for the main part city culture. Bury it, and our spirit will die."

The United States, England, France, and Austria, as represented by our little group, were more than a little skeptical about this Darmstadt theory. "Are there any other cities that correspond to the Darmstadt pattern, I mean as far as this theory of city culture is concerned?" Dick wanted to know.

Thoughtful silence.

"Weimar perhaps?"

No. Certainly not Weimar. Not any more. One may say that the spirit of classicism has been embalmed in Weimar, artistically, lovingly, but since 1933 it has been serving a cultural policy that isn't city-bound but quite plainly nationally guided. So what cities could be named that live according to the theory that culture is still mainly a city affair? Göttingen, perhaps, and a few other university towns such as Freiburg and Tübingen; special cases like Bayreuth; a few admirable efforts of the big industrialists to create new cultural centers as in Marl (via the Hüls Chemical Works) and in Wolfsburg (via the Volkswagen Works). But these scraps of evidence aren't very convincing, certainly not convincing enough to silence all the voices raised against the culturally creative powers of today's German towns. But one thing is certain—in the turmoil of history, our towns have proved themselves again and again to be sociologically very hardy.

Away from this detour and back to the road to Frankfurt, the most notorious strip of the *Autobahn* in Germany, between the two American towns of Heidelberg and Frankfurt.

"When you call a German town American, are you disapproving, or what *do* you mean?" Dick asking, of course.

Disapproving? Not more than if someone were to say an American town was "German," implying that German cities were really best situated in Germany. To begin with, there are more Americans in Heidelberg and Frankfurt, the two United States headquarters, than in any other part of Germany; and since these Americans have apparently been infected by the national restlessness that is general over here, it means that there is just too much traffic on the highway connecting the two cities, and it is notorious for its many accidents.

During the first postwar years, Frankfurt had its American ghetto: a whole city quarter was enclosed by barbed wire across which natives and unwilling guests looked at each other with mixed feelings, and only certain types of girls and other light merchandise were allowed to pass through. These times have gone; the traces remain. The problem here, as with so many German cities after the war, was the manner of reconstruction, or as they say in Germany *Wiederaufbau*, "again-construction." In Frankfurt, American and German influences were strangely combined, and you really need a lot of local patriotism to banish your misgivings and not lose your faith in sixteenth century knight and humanist, Ulrich von Hutten, who saw "the flower of all cities, the pride of the Reich" in Frankfurt. But the Frankfurter was never short on pride. "How can anyone *not* be from Frankfurt?" asked Friedrich Stoltze, a local poet, not renowned outside Frankfurt.

After a trip to the United States, Jean Paul Sartre wrote, "For us a city's past has meaning before anything else; the first thing an American has in mind is its future." Applied to the questions arising when faced with a heap of rubble, this may be interpreted as "Now we will *wiederaufbauen* everything just the way it was," or, "Now we'll do things differently," in other words, "Now we'll build the city of yesterday," or, "Now we'll build a city of tomorrow."

For both these constructive principles, we have model examples: Freudenstadt in the Black Forest for loving reconstruction; Hannover for a bold plan of the future. And we have mixtures of the two; some more, some less successful compromises. It remained for Frankfurt to bow to both principles with equal deference—in the shadows of skyscrapers, the dome of the Paulskirche.

"I'm always skeptical," said Ralph, "when I hear a German word with *wieder* in it," and as he went on to explain his aversion to the German prefix usage of the word "again," we were at first surprised, then amused, finally thoughtful. "There are a lot more beside *Wiederaufbau* (to build up again). *Auf wiedersehen* can be horribly sentimental, especially when you hear it sung. Then we have *Wiedervereinigung* (unite again) and *Wiederbewaffnung* (arm again) and the people who always want to *wiederhaben* (have again) everything that belonged to them before the war."

"The *Wiedergutmachung* (make good again or restitution), too?" I asked.

"I'm sorry," said Ralph, "but I can't work up much enthusiasm for that either."

If there is such a thing as a sentimental need for *Wiederaufbauen*— quite possibly there is, and not only in Germany—and if such a need is expressed in a typically German way in the prefix *wieder*, then I would say that the German contributions to the restoration of Frankfurt were first and foremost the Goethe House and the Römerberg, whereas what the guide books, not altogether approvingly describe as "modern colossi" may be traced back to foreign influences.

But was the core of the old city rebuilt just as it had been before for purely sentimental reasons? After all, Römer and Goethe House were once the heart of political and spiritual Frankfurt: the Römer, a landmark of civic pride and Kaiser glory, from which the city had been ruled since the fifteenth century; and the unpretentious patrician house on the Hirschgraben had been a goal for all those countless pilgrims from all over the world who venerate Goethe as the greatest German poet. Can hearts be modernized without snuffing out all life? An alarming question. You could hear strongly contradictory answers in Frankfurt, particularly in connection with the faithful reconstruction of the Goethe House. In the end, the decisive word was spoken by Ernst Beutler, a modest but extremely determined man, director and top expert on Goethe research. He was willing to return to his post only if the Goethe House was restored as nearly as possible exactly as it had been before. Therefore anything that could be salvaged from the ruins was used.

"And he was right," said Dick. "Friends of Goethe are friends of tradition. No one is looking for contemporary life in the Goethe House. After all, the twentieth century has its own poets."

Altogether, Dick was touching in the way he insisted on defending Frankfurt, with not too spectacular success.

"The banks of the Main between Friedensbrücke and Ober-Main-brücke (Peace Bridge and Upper Main Bridge) are all right," said Yvonne. "As for the rest, I think it's ghastly!"

"The Frankfurters are not going to like that."

"You don't have to tell them."

But I decided I would. One Frankfurter parried with, "All right, so the city isn't beautiful. But it's beautiful to live in."

A feast for sore eyes it is not. The axis, around which Frankfurt's everyday life takes place, runs parallel to the Main and connects station and zoo. It starts rather indicatively with the once famous Kaiserstrasse. In 1945 it was hyper-democratically renamed Friedrich Ebertstrasse; ten years later it was re-established monarchistically and *wieder*-christened Kaiserstrasse. Two different powers pulling the street in opposite directions, and this may be read not only in its names. Things don't get any better on the second part of the stretch from station to zoo, the famous Frankfurter boulevard, the Zeil. Houses left standing, houses painstakingly renovated, houses still in ruins, especially on the side streets; rebuilt houses and colossal modern edifices or buildings that were meant to be colossal and loom larger as one approaches the square called the Konstablerwache. These buildings seem to irritate each other; they cover up the old picture of Frankfurt, but won't let the new one emerge.

"But you should see Frankfurt during the Fair," said Dick. Since he is a publisher, all that mattered to him was the Book Fair which takes place in late autumn. Since it isn't much of a moneymaker for the city, it is delayed to accommodate other conventions that might otherwise wander off to Hannover. Frankfurt, a fair town of old, not only for books, has actually succeeded in replacing Leipzig as a meeting ground for publishers, book sellers, agents, journalists. Of course there is still a Book Fair in Leipzig, but taking place as it does in a state with a rigidly conducted publishing policy that limits commercial possibilities and makes legal aspects, such as copyrights, dubious, it doesn't attract people who have definite ideas of "freedom" where their business is concerned, ideas that can't be shrugged off by propaganda or counterpropaganda. Leipzig publishers exhibit in Frankfurt too, without, however, being made to feel very welcome.

The Frankfurt fairground is situated as advantageously as possible, on the approaches of the *Autobahn*, on the Ring. If one visualizes Frankfurt as a big circle, with Main and the Ring of avenues as its periphery, it is quite easy to find one's way. For a fair or convention city it is important to lie in the center of a state, as Frankfurt lies in the center of the Federal Republic, almost exactly: 350 kilometers from Bremen in the north and Rosenheim in Upper Bavaria in the south; 150 kilometers from Trier in the west and Coburg in the east. The most important north-south and east-west routes meet here. Four highways converge on Frankfurt, and here you will also find Germany's largest airport.

The Federal Republic would be most easily governed from Frankfurt. Our statesmen didn't take advantage of the fact; our big industrialists did. Their offices and administrative buildings make up the greater part of the inner city. Frankfurt publishers enjoy the priceless advantage of not being dismissed in Bavaria as North German, or in Bremen as South German. S. Fischer, Suhrkamp, and the Frankfurter Allgemeine Zeitung are therefore among the most distinguished publishing houses. And the Association of German Publishers and Booksellers rules the German-speaking world from Frankfurt. Everyone who wants to experience this literary world, where Germany is still bounded by its language, and therefore so much broader, must travel once a year to Frankfurt. At Jimmy's Bar—Jimmy, now retired, was the famous bartender at the still-wonderful hotel, Hessische Hof—one may even forget that Frankfurt is a not-altogether-successful melange of Goethe and America, of Reichsstadt freedom and skyscraper concrete.

5. ABOUT FOOD AND DRINK

"For a German you don't really eat enough," Yvonne said to me.

"He's got to watch his figure," said Ralph. "All Germans have to watch their figures."

We enjoy a world-wide reputation as arch-gluttons. The special number of *Life* magazine, already quoted several times, featured a Munich carpenter George Bohler, whose obesity—remarkable even for Bavaria—the photographer had immortalized in six (no less!) different poses. Under the heading, "No Gorge like George," you read: "George . . . is not typical of Bavarians. Most of them eat no more than five meals a day. George eats six . . . the customary breakfast, hearty lunch, and a big dinner. But he also manages to get down three in-between meals, any of which would seem heavy to most Americans. In midmorning George drops into a delicatessen for a *frühschoppen* (morning beer) and fortifies himself solidly with *wurst* and pretzels. He fights off hunger in midafternoon by having rolls and a *wurstplatte* of ten kinds of sausages. After dinner he sustains himself until bedtime with platters of assorted cheese followed by some frankfurters. George, who weighs 277 pounds, washes down his snacks with more than a dozen big steins of beer a day. . . ."

Could somebody have been exaggerating a little?

Our English lady in her 1884 memories of Germany says: "Quantity, not quality, appears to be the motto of the repast," and what follows casts a dismal light not only on the greed of our ancestors, but also on their table manners. "To eat, if possible, twice of every dish, to splutter over the soup . . . to lap the gravy, to drink salad-dressing off knife blades, to scour the inside of the dish and platter with lumps of bread; to fill up the pauses in the interminable ceremony by picking their teeth . . . is a picture so true as to be trite, and so unattractive as to be scarcely excusable."

One has to come to the conclusion that the amount of food available in Germany must have shrunk in the same ratio as our table manners improved, because I must say I have never seen anything like that, although I will admit to having seen people, once used to more solid fare, attack oysters or lobster in a highly adventurous fashion. But even Frenchman Joseph Rovan's benevolent book on Germany says: "Every dish ordered in a restaurant seems intended as a whole meal. A serving of Roquefort can be as much as seven slices."

Evidently what we care most about when it comes to eating is to fill the stomach. And looking at what many Germans drag around with them between their hip bones, some frontally, others more to the rear, it becomes difficult to deny that statement completely. My friends, though, had a hard time finding any corroboration for this evidently popular impression of the German. Wherever we ate, to right and left of us, you could hear, "No soup, please." "No gravy for me." "Dessert? No thank you." Diet, diet, diet! As for the quality of the food, I'll let Yvonne, as representative of a nation with an internationally recognized cuisine be the authority. "You won't find a hearty yet digestible meal cooked as well anywhere as in Germany, but if you want to enjoy the variety of a fairly good French restaurant, you have to travel in Germany for ten days."

We traveled for ten days, and one possible way out of many of getting to know Germany in a pleasant fashion would be to orient yourself via menus. Seen gastronomically, German federalism is a downright blessing!

Who could possibly describe adequately and judge correctly all the regional specialties? Here reference books don't help much, for this is where folklore and smart tourist propaganda triumph. And you have to be very careful, because geographic adjectives can be misleading. We have Berlin to thank for Berlin "balls," Nürnberg for *lebkuchen*, Frankfurt for *würstchen*, but all three are so easily imitated that they can't really count as regional specialties any more. And we should differentiate between "typical" dishes and those "recommended." For a port city like Hamburg, *Labskaus* may be typical, but that's no reason for shocking landlubbers with this stew of mashed pickled meat with a fried egg on it which sailors find very satisfying. Hanseatic city folk like it, too. But Hamburg can be recommended for almost any kind of fish dish, especially its sweet eel soup cooked with dried fruit, pears and bacon. In Schleswig-Holstein try *Katen*ham. It tastes best with asparagus. Westphalia is also famous for its ham, but there you should eat pumpernickel with it. Typical only of Westphalia—you can't get it anywhere else—is *Pannhas,* made of diced bacon, pig's blood, and buckwheat flour, all cooked together. This was originally poor man's fare, as were most of these federalist delicacies. Their attraction at first was that they were cheap wherever they were made.

Rhine salmon used to enjoy a fine reputation before the waters became so polluted that fish no longer inhabit them. Mosel hake and eel, though, are still considered very fine eating. The Swabians contribute egg noodles, called *Spätzle,* to the Greater German menu, but these days you can be sure they are Swabian only if they are home-made. Whitefish swim in Lake Constance, a salmon-like fish that delights those who like to eat it in the Insel Hotel in Constance or in the Lindau restaurant Zum Lieben Augustin.

North Germans consider Bavarian cuisine exotic. With its *Kalbshax'n* and *Schweinshax'n* (calf and pig's knuckles) it meets the international German reputation for gluttony more than halfway. It also includes *Leberkäse* (calf or pig liver cooked in a box-shaped dish with pork, bacon, eggs and spices), dumplings, (super) radishes, and *weisswürscht,* little white sausages that don't taste like sausage and require sweetened mustard as a side dish. They are eaten only in the morning.

Hard to get hold of today, and according to a stern socialism, probably not always approved specialties, are Pomeranian breast of goose, Thuringian dumplings, Dresden Stollen—a fruit coffee cake baked only for Christmas and then in such quantities that, in a good Dresden household, it lasts until April, and improves with age!—Schlesisches Himmelreich (Silesian Paradise, even if the recipe does not sound exactly paradisiacal), a pork-prune stew, sometimes with carrots and peas added. Leipziger Allerlei, a canned mixture of carrots and peas, has found friends all over the world and has about as much to do with Leipzig today as *Casseler Rippchen* (smoked pork ribroast) has to do with Cassel, namely nothing at all.

But all over Germany there are hotels and restaurants that are famous for their cuisine and their own specialties. We don't have a classic handbook to show gourmets the way, like the Guide Michelin or Duncan Hines—not yet. But the *Varta Führer Durch Deutschland* (Mairs Geographische Verlag, Stuttgart) is coming along, and will be available to the United States reader, in translation, in 1964. It recommends "10 internationally famous cuisines," each one justified, and 60 "also well-known" eateries. And of course there are restaurants in Germany with menus as diversified as even a French girl like Yvonne could wish. In all the larger cities, you can find Chinese or Russian, Indian or Indonesian foods, sometimes a trifle pseudo, but that holds true in other countries as well. All things edible have become transportable, and most things don't deteriorate on the way, sweet water fish excepted. That's why it plays such an important role as a local specialty.

But epicures and hedonists are really happy only when they can have the right drink with the right meal, in the right surroundings. Mosel eel is a delicacy in its own right, but freshly hooked on the banks of that river, it tastes quite different, dished up perhaps by Trude Simonis in Kobern, and accompanied by a well-aged bottle of Koberner Uhlen.

You want to enjoy true Lake Constance whitefish with a glass of shimmering red Meersburger Weissherbst, while looking out on the calm waters of this lake, which has quite evidently been put just there for the delight of man. That's the way to do it, from the terrace of the Bahnhof restaurant in Lindau, for instance, or at the Shore Hotel Löchnerhaus on the island of Reichenau.

It would never occur to any comparatively normal person to eat *weisswürscht* in Berlin or Düsseldorf; that has to be done in Bavaria, preferably in Munich, and the right beer has to go with it. The proper setting, therefore, would be one of those Munich beer halls for which the Bavarian has so many affectionate names. In his *Journey from Munich to Genoa*, Heine writes: "The Arab has a thousand expressions for his sword, the Frenchman for love, the Englishman for hanging, the German for drinking, and the new Athenian [meaning the Municher] for the places where he drinks."

Yvonne took cognizance of her alleged penchant for a love vocabulary with an enigmatic smile; Ralph protested that he couldn't, so help him, think of three words for "hanging." Unfortunately we didn't have an Arab with us. But Heine could fall back on the solidly founded prejudice that not only stamps the German as fat, and a voracious eater, but as the goblet-hefting, stein-draining descendant of those legendary old Teutons who supposedly spent their lives sitting on the banks of the Rhine, drinking "just one more!"

The heavy drinker differs from the heavy eater in that he may be relegated to the a-social elements of society as an addict, where he plays a prominent role as a scapegoat in traffic accidents. And one's true character is supposed to be revealed under the influence of alcohol. Add to this the fact that liquor is supposed to be (next to cigarettes) the most health damaging of all vices, "according to today's scientific research," then consider the major role health culture plays in Germany, and you will understand why protests against alcoholic consumption grow louder daily. In Germany this is probably augmented by the fact that uninhibited characters and traffic accidents are more problematic here than anywhere else. Yet we have no strong religion-inspired prohibition group in Germany, as in the United States, where 42 per cent of the population protest drinking alcohol "as a matter of principle." German statistics on the same subject resulted in only 13 out of a hundred claiming to be teetotalers and this doesn't seem to be too firm a principle: the figure dwindles in a highly suspicious fashion with every increase in income. . . . Yet it was our American, Dick, who had hoped to get more enjoyment from German drinking habits than we were able to offer. At a formal party we attended, things were just that—formal. Dick, anxious to make sure that everybody had enough to drink, was disappointed when every other guest said, "No thank you. No more. I'm driving." And another time, in a Hamburg night club, we were served a bottle of nonalcoholic grape juice in a wine cooler.

"In our dry states," said Dick, "I've seen people drinking brandy out of coffee cups. This certainly is a crazy upside-down world."

So is everything to be said about German drinking habits a swan song before red-currant juice and Coca-cola? Or is Germany doomed to suffocate in a miasma of tobacco smoke and alcohol fumes? Sober statistics show that we have nothing extraordinary to hope or fear.

Compared with its western neighbors, Germany does not seem to be a nation of drinkers. Oh, yes, the German consumes his 80 liters of beer a year; but an Englishman downs 85, the New Zealander 100, the Australian 110, the Belgian 135. As for schnapps (more elegantly termed brandy) the German with 2½ liters (counted in pure alcohol) is in third place behind Sweden, 5 liters, and the United States, 4 liters. And wine? Socially and lyrically it may play an important role, but in France and Italy they drink ten times as much. Comparisons with our eastern neighbors, especially where brandy is concerned, would reveal a praiseworthy temperance on the part of the Germans *in alcoholicis;* unfortunately we have no reliable figures for Poland and the Soviet Union.

The German national beverage is, of course, not wine, as romantic souls would have it, but beer, and we have many fat stomachs because of it. Not only do the German breweries supply every German with his 80 liters of beer a year (some with less, some with more, goes without saying) but they have finally succeeded in passing Holland and reaching first place in beer export. The big names in the beer world come from Dortmund, Munich, and Kulmbach; but almost every self-respecting town has its own brewery; and it is advisable to drink the beer on tap of the town you are in. In the smaller taverns you don't have a choice; they belong to the brewery, and the devil would come and get the lessee who dared to sell any other brand.

Bock beer is double-strength beer, heavier, thicker, a little sweet. It is popularly named after local celebrities: "Salvator" in Munich, "Senator" in Hamburg. In Berlin they brew a special kind of light beer which serves as a basis for the popular *Berliner Weisse mit Schuss,* Berlin light beer with a shot of—brace yourself—fruit juice. Berliner Weisse tastes good to a thirsty man in Frankfurt or Stuttgart, but it isn't quite the right thing in either place. The crisp summer air of a garden restaurant in Berlin's Grunewald should go with it.

Brandy is the aquavit of Schleswig-Holstein, the Steinhäger of

Westphalia, and the whisky of the city barfly, but with what differences! *Aquavit*, rich with the proximity of Scandinavia; *Steinhäger*, all
"earth and groats and corn"; and whisky, with what the clever propaganda of one of our big cigarette companies likes to call "an aroma of
the big wide world."

On the seacoast we drink rum—tea with rum, grog made with rum.
For the Anglo-Saxon seaman, all these drinks are a disappointment because in Germany they dilute rum with a cheap type of brandy, and it
is poorer in alcoholic content as a result. *Bärenfang*, thick as honey,
was characteristic for East Prussia; and for the more delicate taste, not
quite so far east, you could get *Danziger Goldwasser*, in which something that really looked like golden plankton swam around. But the
farther east you traveled in Germany, the more the brandy began to
taste like vodka, and vodka certainly represents one of the purest and
most agreeable ways of enjoying distilled grain. But don't the textbooks
tell us that potatoes are the raw material from which vodka is made?
Hush! Don't tell a soul, because that's the *Dollpunkt* for vodka producers! Esthonian vodka, which connoisseurs say is the best, is still
distilled from potatoes, distilled twice, in the course of which it loses
all poor alcoholic taste, but four-fifths of the vodka production of the
world today undoubtedly consists of fermented and distilled grain.

The most German of all German brandies, and therefore the ones to
be most highly recommended, are the distilled fruit juices: prune,
cherry, and raspberry spirits. The most famous children of this race, it
is true, are raised outside Germany's borders: Swiss *Pflümliwasser* and
pear schnapps from Martigny, Yugoslavian *Slibowitz*, Lorraine *Mira-
belle*. The largest German fruit distilleries are in the Black Forest.

And finally the brandy distilled from the lees of wine presses and
vats are worth mentioning: *trester*, made from what is left of the
grapes after pressing, and *hefe* (yeast, barm, dregs) made of what is
left after the wine has been fermented. To the inhabitants of Germany's wine districts, they mean what *grappa* means to the Italian; the
most agreeable schnapps because the most closely related to wine.

German sekt can be a lot better than bad champagne; German
brandy better than cheap cognac. But the French product of course
rates as an unparalleled model, which is expressed clearly enough on
our labels. German brandy isn't labeled *Vom Garten* (from the garden) but the French equivalent, *Du Jardin*.

Fifty million sekt corks are popped in West Germany in a year, but
it isn't fair to see in this only the little man's yearning to live like a
big shot. Not everybody can be a connoisseur, and to become a wine
connoisseur takes a lifetime of dedicated study. Good sekt is in every
case better than poor wine, and with sekt you don't have to be a connoisseur; all you have to do is stick to a trade mark that guarantees
quality. Wine doesn't have such reliable trade marks; to be sure of a
good wine you have to know much more than a name, and for the de-
tails on that we have to get back in the car and get on with our trip.

6. THE RHYMING RHINE

"And now for the Rhine!" cried Ralph as we left Frankfurt behind us. Dick's favorite town was Heidelberg, but he had been perfectly happy in Frankfurt, too. Andreas had felt most at home in Bavaria, Yvonne in the Black Forest. Professor Spälti swore that Hamburg (still ahead of us) was the only German city in which he would like to live. Ralph was all for Hamburg, too, but his great love was the Rhine.

From Frankfurt, a broad highway soon gets you to Wiesbaden, seat of the Hesse administration, and just beyond it, to the Rhine. The Rhine is: 1. Germany's largest river, 695 kilometers from the Swiss border to Holland. 2. Germany's wine-wealthiest river. 3. Germany's most poeticized and lyricized river. 4. Germany's dirtiest river.

When the Rhine is mentioned, all of its 695 kilometers are rarely being referred to. Major interest in the river is concentrated on a bare quarter of the stretch, the 154 kilometers between Main and Bonn, which I suppose we could call the Middle Rhine. If you want to disassociate yourself from the taste of the masses, you would do well to praise the Upper and Lower Rhine. Certainly the patriotic songs about the Rhine which our grandfathers loved were referring to the Upper Rhine as "Germany's river, not Germany's boundary," because it was the boundary between Germany and France. A chronicler of the year 1897 writes: "What the sacred Nile meant to the Egyptians, the Ganges to the Hindus, the Jordan to the Israelites, we Germans feel to an even greater extent for the Rhine, which is the object of our deepest veneration, a very part of our being, the essence of our patriotism, our most priceless treasure, for which we are prepared to shed our blood and sacrifice our lives." If anyone seriously said this today he would be considered a ridiculous old fool by the younger generation.

The countryside of the Lower Rhine, where the river is much wider and flows in a leisurely fashion through green plains, has its own gentle beauty. Here Germany begins to look more and more like Holland. But the true Rhine enthusiast, wandering along its banks, or better still, sailing on it, has his good reasons for finding Upper and Lower Rhine a little sluggish and dull.

The Middle Rhine is distinguished by a much narrower valley, steeper banks, ranges of hills with castles on them, many little villages and towns directly on the water, and finally—the wine (which grows on the Upper Rhine, too, but not so luxuriantly and quite differently). There are people who think that the Germans are wine drinkers, even wine connoisseurs. Neither supposition is correct. In every other wine-growing country in Europe, more wine is drunk: in Switzerland three times as much; in Greece five times; in Spain six times; in Portugal nine times; in France and Italy, as noted, ten times as much. This misunderstanding could have arisen only because foreigners tend to favor certain German regions, for instance the wine-producing areas, and there meet innkeepers, vintners, or well-to-do natives who really like to drink their own wine, whether in Würzburg or Glottertal, on the Rhine or on the Mosel.

True wine drinkers are becoming increasingly rare; true wines are, too. An apparent (and purely statistical) compensation is supposed to be found in the fact that to drink wine (outside Bavaria, and of course outside the wine-growing districts) is considered elegant. "They can afford it. . . ." But since prestige consumption has gone over more and more to sekt, the flattering identification of wine drinker with wine connoisseur could be re-established, which prevents too much sugar water from seeping into our wines.

Nobody can tell you where the most popular Rhine wine is grown, probably not even the man who bottles it. It is called Liebfrau(en)-milch. Oh, yes, there are quite a few decent vineyards near the Lieb-frauenkirche in Worms, which gave this "impious milk" its name, but the hillside on which the vineyards once thrived fell victim to a land-slide. When this happened, a few vintners were given permission to name their wines, grown on neighboring hills, after Our Dear Lady; since then, "neighboring hills" are sometimes as far as a hundred miles away and today grow the wine that fills the cellars of second-rate hotels.

The Rhine wine that is best known in the Anglo-Saxon world doesn't come from the district that produces the best, the real Rhine wine; it doesn't grow in the Rheingau (Rhine district) but in Hochheim, on a level with Mainz, not on the Rhine at all. And the most curious thing about it is that the English and Americans now call all Rhine wines Hochheimers or "hock." Just the same, Hochheimer wine, particularly when it comes from the Domdechanei, is not a bad wine, and it has the correct Rheingau ending, "heim," which is a mark of the best Rhine wines. The Rheingau starts just beyond Wiesbaden with a village called Walluf, and belonged in the Middle Ages to the episcopal city of Mainz. It was fought over often, and protected by a wall with sixteen towers. Today wine villages and towns are strung along, one beside the other. You won't find another such concentration of them—Rauenthal, Eltville, Erbach, Hattenheim, Hallgarten, Oestrich, Mittel-heim, Winkel, Geisenheim, Rüdesheim, Assmannshausen—until you come to the banks of the Mosel.

Whoever hasn't time to go from wine cellar to wine cellar and try everything that flows together here from year to year and is poured into brown bottles (to differentiate from the green bottles of Mosel wine) is well advised to stick to the "-heim" wines. In Rüdesheim, a town of 7,000 inhabitants, more wine is drunk than in any other place of comparable size. The Drosselgasse, immortalized in many Rhineland songs, attracts drinkers from nearby Frankfurt and far-off Chicago. The Ewige Lampe (Eternal Lamp) and the Weinhaus Drosselhof are gay temples of Bacchus. Whoever happens to be in Rüdesheim should drink its wine. They have some very good locations: Schlossberg, Burgweg, Roseneck, Bischofsberg.

In the rivalry for the best Rheingau wine laurels, Rüdesheim must come after Geisenheim and Hattenheim. It seems fair to stick to the common denominator "heim," even if we are not referring to the actual town of Geisenheim but to Schloss Johannisberg, three kilometers away; and not to the little town of Hattenheim, but to Cloister Eberbach, four kilometers from it. Hattenheim, by the way, has a highly recommendable inn, Weinhaus Ress.

The decision between Johnnisberg and Cloister Eberbach, or Steinberg, wine, is an entirely personal one. With either, one probably comes about as close as one can get to drinking the best Rhine wine.

"You've been so explicit so far," said Dick. "Why stop?"

Because there is such a thing as the height of perfection when it becomes ridiculous to play Beethoven against Mozart, Shakespeare against Goethe, and *Fürst Metternich Cabinet Spätlese* (Johannisberg) against Steinberg Cabinet (Cloister Eberbach). Every now and then you'll find resentment against the Metternich Cabinet wines because they are so exorbitantly expensive and hard to find, as is often the case when something has been famous for a long time.

I am sure there are average, perhaps even below-average wines that are labeled "Johannisberger"; but if they really do come from Johannisberg, they are probably from valley vineyards. Where so much wine is grown, all of it can't be first-class. The same is true of Champagne. And in both regions, people are prone to ennoble what is actually inferior. You will come across not-very-laudable efforts to make apparently good wine out of bad with the help of chemistry and physics: the adding of suger, the interruption of fermentation, dilution ("for the city people who don't know any better"). Such efforts often come close to being unlawful, and the Wiesbaden, Coblenz, and Trier courts are kept busy coping with them.

Praiseworthy though, and blameless, are two other wine manipulations: the wine is heated and the alcoholic fumes are recaptured by cooling it again; or during the second fermentation it is poured into bottles and firmly corked, permitting the fumes to remain inside. When done in France, the results are cognac and champagne; in the Rheingau —*weinbrand* (brandy) and *sekt* (sparkling hock). You will find the most famous and biggest German sekt wineries in the Rheingau: Söhnlein and Henkell in Wiesbaden; Matheus Müller in Eltville; and, on the Mosel, Deinhard in Coblenz.

"You're not trying to say that champagne and sekt are as good as the same thing?" Ralph was indignant.

To him, as an Englishman, champagne and sparkling hock were two entirely different beverages. And actually we have the English to thank for the fact that the word "sekt" exists. Schlegel, while he was translating Shakespeare, came across the word "sack" (for Xeres wine or sherry), didn't know what to do with it and put down "sekt." When the actor Devrient, on stage as Falstaff, asked for "Sekt" (according to Schlegel), waiter Franz brought him what he always drank after performances: sparkling white wine, which from then on was called "sekt."

Sekt and champagne are produced in the same way; often they are made of the same ingredients because the German sekt distillers sometimes use French wines for their brewing. Otherwise sekt and champagne are to be differentiated in three ways: politically, sociologically, and gastronomically, and for just these three reasons, the differentiation becomes dubious.

In the Treaty of Versailles, France asked, as a small victory prize, that only its own sparkling wines and brandies, with their sometimes rather German-sounding names, like Roederer and Mumm, be called champagne and cognac.

"So what's unfair about that?" asked Yvonne. "Every firm protects its trade mark, and champagne should mean only wine from Champagne."

Everybody protects what he can. But names, and with them all trade-mark safeguards, are important only when products are so much alike that they can hardly be told apart. So what is the difference?

Whoever wants to know the answer should do what our little group did in Eltville's magnificent *Weinpump*, a blindfold test. Because all winegrowers and old taprooms despise sekt-drinkers, nobody there would take us seriously until we explained it was a bet, and the loser had to pay for the wine.

Place three French champagnes and three of the best German brands of sekt side by side, all six equally cooled. One of each should be extra dry (*très sec* or *brut*), one very dry (*sec*), and one dry (*demi sec*). Each contestant drinks blindfolded. Everybody takes twelve sips; twelve times he must declare what he drank. Important: no one samples the wines before the test, and no corrections may be made during it. When it was over, Ralph was subdued. He had given three correct answers. . . .

In category three—for no apparent reason called "dry"—sekt and champagne are easiest to tell apart. There is something fruity, aromatic, prickly about this mild, "dry" champagne, which even the best German sparkling wines can't seem to achieve. I think this is mainly because French champagne is controlled more strictly than German sekt. After the top-ranking German vintages, there are some perfectly dreadful wines. Rhine romanticism has no room for sekt. It came too late for that, and has another handicap—unlike wine, it doesn't rhyme with Rhine. . . .

Two kinds of mountains rise up between Mainz and Bonn as absolutely requisite settings for the romantic Rhine; one grows grapes, the other castles; some have both! Once Bretano and Arnim had set the fashion, there wasn't a self-respecting poet in Germany who didn't lyricize the Rhine, its wines, its castles, preferably all three. Rhenish drinking songs, some of poetic value, are, of course, much older than that. Hölty's "Father Rhine bestows on us a paradisiacal life," and Rhenish legend go far back, or so it seems. One of the first important examples of German literature, *The Song of the Nibelungs*, includes the river from *"ze wormse bi dem rine"* to Xanten, the home of Siegfried, and unites the sagas of the Walküre, Brünhild, the invulnerable Siegfried, and the Rheingold. The most renowned Rhine legend though is pure invention. In Bretano's novel, *Godwi*, we meet for the first time, on the Lorelei rock near St. Goarshausen, the fisherman-seducing Jungfrau, or virgin, who subsequently achieved world fame in Heinrich Heine's poem, *Die Lorelei*.

That Heine should be the first to see other aspects of this Rhine-wine romanticism, was to be expected. In *Le Grand*, he describes the Rhine as "that beautiful river where folly grows on green mountains, is picked in the autumn, pressed, poured into vats, and sent out into the world." On the Lorelei-rock especially, this Rhine-romanticism has worn a bit thin, having served for decades as the means toward an end for the tourist industry. An automobile road leads up to a parking field, and in an enormous restaurant, pretty Loreleis sit eating ice cream and pastry instead of combing their golden hair. The view on the opposite side of the river shows us a busy federal highway. Loudspeakers blare something about the rhyming Rhine. "Come, Gisela, we've still got to see the Drachenfels. . . ."

Ninety kilometers downstream, the same setup. "The castled crag of Drachenfels," which once enchanted Byron, is today a terraced restaurant, and it is less the castle's than the restaurant's fault that this hill, which slopes up about 300 meters above the Rhine diagonally opposite Bonn, is visited yearly by three million people, and so becomes the most climbed mountain in Europe. How it ever happened to become honored by having given sanctuary to Siegfried's dragon, nobody knows. But that's what they say. And that is why a "Drachen (or Dragon) burg," in which a stone dragon is housed, and a Nibelung Hall with Wagnerian pictures are there to attract the Drachenfels climber. If he wants to resist these temptations, he can have his picture taken in a cardboard airplane instead.

And so we arrive at the other Rhine, the *verkitscht*, in-poorest-taste Rhine, trying with every conceivable propaganda gimmick to hold the tourist who is elusive (perhaps for that very reason?); the river in which it is almost impossible to bathe any more (if you do, you need a bath afterwards); on which even a boat trip is a doubtful pleasure; a river that has no more fish to offer its visitors. The once-famous Rhine salmon, shad, and sturgeon, have been driven away, poisoned; mackerel, trout, pike, and perch, no longer run beyond the Upper Rhine, and even there they are becoming rarer. The few remaining eels taste of carbolic acid. . . .

This Rhine is the largest natural inland shipping lane in the world; 10,000 ships and barges travel on it daily. This Rhine holds so much sewage from cities and industries that for a long time its natural counterforces haven't been able to decompose and dispose of it. This Rhine is no longer the Rhine of the romanticists, the river celebrated by Goethe, Kleist, Hölderlin, Byron, Wordsworth, Thackeray, Longfellow, Melville, Cooper, Hugo, Madame de Staël, Chateaubriand. It is no longer the high spot of the trip from Mainz to Cologne, to which the first Baedeker was dedicated. The castles have crumbled, the wine is diluted, the Jungfrau combing her golden hair has . . .

Stop!

"The meaning of knighthood, the way the knights lived . . . I've never felt it so strongly as in the Marksburg," said Dick, "and it wasn't the least bit crumbled!"

The thousand-year-old Marksburg rises up out of a steep rock near Braubach, just north of Coblenz, the only castle on the Rhine which has remained inside and outside just as it must have been in the Middle Ages.

"And the Johannisberg wine we drank in the Schlossschenke, what was wrong with that?" Ralph sighed. Of course the wines of a distinguished vineyard are never diluted.

"And I don't want to hear a word against the Jungfrau," said Yvonne. "She gets treated much too harshly here anyway."

She may have been right. In Oberwesel, you'll find seven rocks, called the *Sieben Jungfrauen,* rising up out of the river. According to legend, they are seven sisters, seven princesses once, who were turned to stone because they would not say yes to the courtship of any man.

7. HOLY AND UNHOLY COLOGNE

Shortly after the end of World War II, André Gide, visiting his old friend, Ernst Robert Curtius, philologist and critic in Bonn, expressed the wish to see Cologne. Curtius went with him, and reported later, "As we got farther and farther into Cologne, Gide became paler and more silent, and we hadn't been in the inner city fifteen minutes when he begged that we might leave."

In the sad contest as to which of the German cities suffered most as a result of allied bombings, Cologne is easily the winner. But oddly enough it is only the non-Cologners who say that the city has been unrecognizable ever since. "Only the cathedral—Cologne's landmark—was left standing," said Dick, "as if by a miracle."

Since I happen to be a victim of Cologne Cathedral romanticism, and have never been able to put any perspective between myself and the overwhelming impression of this Gothic giant, I prefer to let the arch-Cologner among German writers of today speak for me. Heinrich Böll writes: "That it was so obviously spared by the bombings, while the magnificent Romanesque churches were not considered worth equal consideration, can be relegated to the sentimental errors of Cologne lore . . . the Cathedral is much less Cologne than the city's other churches."

These "magnificent Romanesque churches" were, and today, for the most part, fortunately are again: St. Gereon, erected in the fourth century, rebuilt in the thirteenth, bombed areas restored; the romantic Basilica St. Maria im Kapitol, eleventh century, destroyed in World War II, almost completely restored; St. Georg, eleventh century, only the tower left standing; Gross-St. Martin, twelfth and thirteenth centuries, destroyed in World War II, rebuilt; the Apostle Church, a late Romanesque, three-nave, pillar basilica, erected in the thirteenth century, restored in the nineteenth, destroyed in World War II, rebuilt; and the Dominican church St. Andreas, Gothic on a Romanesque foundation, built in the thirteenth century, destroyed in World War II, rebuilt. To which should be added, St. Kolumba. This old Romanesque-Gothic parish church was destroyed by bombs, but a stone figure of the Madonna remained upright, leaning against the east transept pillar, which had stood there for five hundred years. As "Madonna of the Ruins," she became a favorite of the Cologners, who built an octagonal chapel around her, truly a contemporary house of God.

For all non-Cologners, not only Americans, Cologne is and remains the city of the Cologne Cathedral. You can see it from far off as you approach the town, and always, like a gigantic signpost, it helps the stranger orient himself. When I asked fifty Germans whose taste in artistic matters was sound which were the most beautiful churches in Germany, of the Cologne churches only the Cathedral was among the first fifteen that were mentioned twenty times or more. Here are the results: 1. The Wieskirche near Steingaden in Upper Bavaria. 2. The pilgrimage church in Vierzehnheiligen (Fourteen Saints) on the Main, opposite Banz in Upper Franconia. 3. The Freiburg Cathedral. 4. The Bamberg Cathedral. 5. The Benedictine Monastery Maria Laach on the Eifel. 6. The Cologne Cathedral. 7. The Cathedral in Speyer. 8. The Ulm Cathedral. 9. The former Cistercian monastery Maulbronn in Württemberg. 10. The Cathedral in Naumburg, Thuringia. 11. The Cathedral in Worms. 12. The Benedictine monastery in Ettal, Upper Bavaria. 13. The Frauenkirche in Munich. 14. The Regensburg Cathedral. 15. The Marienkirche in Lübeck.

There was a time when the general enthusiasm for the Cologne Cathedral was greater, or it would still have no spires. At the beginning of the nineteenth century, romanticists saw in the edifice—which was not unlike some of the more famous French cathedrals—a monumental expression of a Gothic period that had just been discovered as the embodiment of the German Middle Ages. It therefore seemed to be a sign from above when the medieval plans were found, giving the new gentleman on the Rhine, King Friedrich Wilhelm IV of Prussia, the opportunity to do something for the city of Cologne, so close to the French border, on territory that had been French not long before. He sent his architect, Schinkel, to Cologne, and he reported that the plan to finish the cathedral was feasible. It took quite some time, but in 1842, Friedrich Wilhelm was able to lay the cornerstone for the cathedral's completion, and in 1880, the edifice which had been begun in 1284, was finished and consecrated.

Its many churches are a part of Cologne, a city that was once allowed to call itself, with Papal permission, the Holy City of Cologne. And it was very appropriate that there should suddenly be uncovered, under the old city hall, the foundations of a Roman palace dating back to the first century A.D. when the city of Cologne already existed under a more imposing Latin name, Colonia Agrippinensis. So today you can take an elevator in the City Hall and descend into Roman times. When twentieth-century Cologne was reduced to ashes, the much older Cologne suddenly became visible.

The churches of Cologne were certainly destroyed beyond recognition during World War II, and Ancient Roman Cologne consists after all of a heap of ruins which only an archeologist's eye can adequately appreciate. Still the Cologners don't like people to say that their city is not what it used to be. And it isn't only the native Cologners who won't hear anything said against their home town. Cologne apparently attracts proselytes, which can be said of few German cities. You'll find someone who moved to Cologne a few years ago from Saxony, or Westphalia, and today points to himself proudly as a citizen of Cologne. Not that the bona fide natives like this. In one of their famous carnival song hits they make fun of the "imi's," the imitators, the pseudo-Cologners who can be recognized by the fact that they can't properly pronounce the word for the sausage called *Blutwurst* (bloodwurst). By properly they mean *kölsch*, that inimitable mixture of Middle Rhenish with the *platt* of Northwest Germany. But if a city can attract proselytes, it proves that it lives its own typical life.

Before the war, Berlin was renowned for the fact that all Breslau Silesians soon became Berliners there. But today? How many German cities still have so much individuality that someone who has moved there suddenly stops feeling like an All-German German and feels that he is first and foremost the city's citizen? Munich, certainly; Hamburg, probably; Berlin can still say it has this effect on its inhabitants; Stuttgart, perhaps. As for Cologne . . .

When its natives say that nothing much has changed, anyway no more than anywhere else, what they really mean is, "The Rhine is still the same, and so are we," and there's very little to be said against that. Cologne clings to the Rhine. The ancient Roman section of the city forms a rectangle; in a semicircle around it lies the Old City, bounded by the Ring, where things are still kaiserly: Kaiser Wilhelmring, Hohenzollernring, Hohenstaufenring, Salierring, Sachsenring. Beyond this Ring, again in a semicircle, lies the New City, where a later Prussia dominates: Spichernstrasse, Moltkestrasse, Roonstrasse; and back of that is the living, breathing skin of this semicircular construction: the Grüngürtel or Green Belt, for which the city has to thank Konrad Adenauer, its mayor from 1917 to 1933.

From the Severins Gate to the Eigelstein Gate, parallel to the Rhine, runs Cologne's north-south axis, a part of the old Roman army road to the northern provinces. Between Gürzenich and Dom, the termini, it forms one long side of the aforementioned rectangle of the ancient city. There it is called Hohenstrasse, and is Cologne's oldest yet most up-to-date street. In May, 1945, not a stone was left in place on it. There is no trace of ruins today. However I don't call it up to date for that reason, but because it was one of the first business streets in Germany to be closed to automobile traffic during the day. In the narrow city streets of the old German towns, there simply is no other way of saving from sudden death the window shopper who occasionally has to take a step back to see that music box in the right light. News of this measure is getting around.

In the center of this ancient rectangle lies the City Hall, with the Roman ruins beneath it. The Cathedral Square forms the short north side; Gürzenichstrasse and Heumarkt (Haymarket) the south. The rectangle is clamped to the Rhine by the Hohenzollern Bridge (for the railway) and Köln-Deutzer Bridge (for automobile traffic). The bridges have been changed somewhat, in the course of which they have become more beautiful, and there are six of them now; the other four lie farther out of town. As for the Rhine, it's no cleaner and certainly unchanged.

And the Cologners haven't changed either. That has something to do with their Celtic-Roman heritage, and with the many churches of this Holy City. But whoever wants to draw conclusions beyond my "something to do with," could get involved in very misleading speculations. To be sure, Cologne was an arch-episcopal city long enough to rate as a good Catholic city, but the SPD, which is not exactly rated as a good Catholic party, has the majority in the Town Council; and the natives of Cologne really make more of a name for themselves with their carnival, with which, on the eve of Lent, they say farewell to all things carnal, than with the fasting and renunciation that are supposed to follow it.

During the carnival, Cologne becomes Germany's capital. Mainz comes next, then Düsseldorf, and Aachen, with their carnivals, in that order.

"But what about Munich?" asked Yvonne.

I suppose I should have put Munich beside Cologne, but in Munich they celebrate "Fasching," and even if the festivities are supposed to be more or less alike, having the same heathen (later Christian), origins, Fasching is not only a different word, but a different festival. A native of Cologne would be bored to death with Munich's Fasching, and to a Munich citizen, Cologne's carnival would seem horrifyingly vulgar. "Once a year," according to my favorite source, the special issue of *Life* magazine, "Germans turn all the Teutonic energy and thoroughness they usually devote to the solid pleasure of business, to the frivolous business of pleasure. The spectacular result, a combination of Mardi Gras and Beer Fest called Fasching, is the rowdiest and richest party in Europe. While it lasts, substantial merchants desert their desks and families dance all night in the streets with market girls and sensible citizens pawn household goods to buy fancy costumes."

Apart from a few exaggerations, the reporter made an unfortunate mistake: he lumped Munich's Fasching and Cologne's Carnival together, making of them one carnival which does not exist. Either Fasching therefore (that's Munich), or pawned furniture (that's Cologne).

Either frivolous (Munich can be all of that), or rowdy (that's more like Cologne). Either a party (Munich's Fasching is that), or dancing in the streets (which goes better with Cologne, unless the writer means the dancing of the market women in Munich's food market).

Munich's Fasching consists of a long, long series of festivals and balls, the most elegant ones in the Deutsche Theater, the Haus der Kunst, and the Regina Palast Hotel. Decorations, costumes, a "royal couple" (when it's over, he'll be a local business man again, and she a typist)—all can be assembled under the general heading of Fasching, whereas in Cologne such festivities are only a way of getting people under the influence of liquor, music, good spirits, and beautiful women. The *Bütten* speeches (delivered from the wine vat instead of the soap box) and, as the years go by, the growing repertoire of carnival song hits, the convivial swaying and jostling in taverns and streets, are very important, and the Rose Monday Parade, with all the preparations for it, is the climax of it all. There may be a few "better-class" Munichers who inform the visitor, with a mixture of resignation and contempt, "I never go to the Fasching balls; sometimes to a few private parties. They can be quite amusing," whereas any native Cologner, even if he'd much rather not take part in this public rumpus, would pretend to any outsider that the carnival was the high point of his existence.

And for many it really is, even today. Half the people who transform Cologne, in its last carnival week, into one huge amusement park, may be from the provinces, but the other half consists of Cologne natives, no doubt about that, and the carnival is their festival, a true folk festival still, in spite of the people whose main objective is to profit by it financially. They are a ridiculous minority compared with the hundreds of thousands who don't mind letting it cost them something.

My friends regretted that they couldn't see Cologne at carnival time, and swore they would come again some February. I consoled them. The Cologne carnival isn't everybody's cup of tea. You really have to be a bit of a Rhinelander, at any rate temperamentally, to enjoy this strenuous feast of joy, which is followed by the cross of ashes on Ash Wednesday.

8. IN COOLER NORTH GERMANY

Whenever anyone speaks about cool, harsh, severe and alien North Germany, he means Prussia, Protestant Northeast Germany. But the countryside surrounding the River Ems in the northwest is Catholic and today is a part of Land Lower Saxony, thereby contributing to the kind of paradox against which the conventional intellect rebels as against an Italian with freckles—a Catholic Lower Saxony!

Emsland is the most northern Catholic region in Germany. Until 1803, when it was secularized, it belonged to the Bishopric Münster. Surrounded on three sides by Protestants, the Emslanders remained true to their faith. In the districts of Lingen, Meppen and Aschendorf, four-fifths of the population are still Catholic.

And it is a strange country, so difficult to cultivate that convicts used to be sent there to make the land arable; and under Hitler, the Reichslabor Corps, girls from Bremen and boys from Central German industrial areas. They had never seen anything like it: a peat-brown desert, scrub woods, whole villages of huts, and a town, Papenburg, where the streets were canals. Otherwise it bore no resemblance to Venice. After the Reichslabor Corps, one of the most notorious concentration camps was located here; today refugees from East Germany have begun to settle in this area. With their influx, a lot of good work has been started in Emsland. You see more and more green between the brown of the peat bogs; and since crude oil was found in Bentheim, enough to pump 4 million barrels a year and run a big refinery in Lingen, this part of Germany, which was treated like a poor relation for such a long time, has even begun to be wealthy.

Of course Emsland wealth is a far cry from what is called over here "the economic miracle," even though other industries have sprung up around the oil area, progress has been made in swamp drainage, and towns and villages look much more habitable than they did years ago. Lingen and Nordhorn, once pretty but poor towns, are today called "industrial cities." But only a few kilometers from the giant plows and dredgers, from oil pumps and pipe lines, the bogs stretch bleak-brown as ever. You will see ramshackle huts, too big for sheep (the sheep-count has dropped one-twentieth in the last twenty years anyway); incredible that they could house people, yet sometimes they do; sometimes they just stand empty. You'd like to ask someone to tell you a little more about it all, but you don't meet a soul. On one of the good roads, built by the oil companies, and in a decent car, you can cross the district in an hour, and then? Then you're really in north Germany. It starts just beyond the River Weser.

My friends asked me to explain what was so special about North Germany as compared with South Germany? What made me stress so often the fact that we were getting to North Germany. I was not to worry about the fact that generalizations could be dangerous. Very well. I decided to start with myself as a factor I could be fairly sure of.

I feel better in the north; I love the south. "Now you know how I feel about it."

The north is cooler; the south warmer. That much can be proved. But I don't mean the temperature on a thermometer.

North German Willy Helpach wrote about the Catholic south as follows: "It is the sovereign gaiety of the Catholic world, its carefree proximity to life and—most surprising because of its inexorable dogmatic intolerance—its toleration of the slips and errors, the excesses and hedonism of human everyday life. What we like to call bigoted is almost completely foreign to practical Catholicism."

Johann Wolfgang von Goethe, from Weimar, wrote: "Most of the people in the north have more ideals than they know what to do with; that is why we have such peculiar manifestations of sentimentality, religious feeling, mysticism, etc."

North Germany is Johann Sebastian Bach, Johannes Brahms, Heinrich von Kleist, Detlev von Liliencron, Prussian classicism; south Germany is Wolfgang Amadeus Mozart, Christoph Willibald Gluck, Johann Nestroy, Jean Paul, Bavarian rococo. Forgive me for letting two Austrians slip in, but they belong here.

A North German and a South German were asked what they felt to be the most desirable human virtue. The North German replied, righteousness; the South German, love for one's neighbor. When North and South German, with their leaning toward these virtues, can't manage to attain them—which happens—then virtue becomes vice: for the North German, self-righteousness; for the South German, self-love.

We traveled across Westphalia from Cologne and the Ruhr: Unna, Soest, Paderborn, Brakel, Höxter. In Höxter is one of the most famous German Benedictine Monasteries, and whoever doesn't know the neighborhood too well—anyway, better than nine-tenths of the Germans—wouldn't dream that Cloister Corvey could possibly lie so far north. The monastery was secularized in 1803.

We crossed the border of Westphalia, which today is attached to North-Rhine, and the Weser into Lower Saxony, into Protestant North Germany, to Goslar, a purely Protestant Kaiser and Guelph town. As you drive through the Breite Tor (Broad Gate) on the Breitestrasse, you find yourself suddenly in a medieval town. The Middle Ages of the German Kaisers was an important era in the history of the Reich and of the Hanseatic town of Goslar, which had the copper and silver of its Rammelsberg region to thank for its wealth and reputation. Under Heinrich III (1039–1056) Goslar became the German Kaiser's favorite country seat. Barbarossa held court there magnificently. In 1219, an Imperial Diet met there, but by 1300 its glory was over.

The town's fate is reflected clearly in the history of its proudest building, the Kaiserpfalz, or Palace. It is the largest and oldest secular building of its kind still standing in Germany. In the eleventh, twelfth, and thirteenth centuries it was the resident of the Saliers and Staufers; in the fourteenth and fifteenth centuries it was courthouse and prison. In the sixteenth century it was a storage house and remained one until late in the nineteenth century.

At the beginning of the Second German Kaiserreich, the reputation of the First improved. The Kaiserpfalz was renovated, and in 1875, the Kaiser came personally, with the Crown Prince, to inspect what had been done. That is probably why his portrait, sitting very erect on his horse and surrounded by his faithful followers, was given precedence over all the other colossal paintings in the Reichshall depicting Germany's past. The skill of the artist who, at the end of the nineteenth century, painted this gigantic and highly illustrative picture-book mural, is evident in the fact that the heads of both the Kaiser and his horse face the observer, regardless of where he is standing. And in the same way the Kaiser's eyes rest amiably on the whole town, a town well aware of the debt of gratitude it owes its Kaisers. It keeps its past alive, as is customary today, with tours, guidebooks, and postcards in the Kaiserpfalz, in the Domvorhalle (once the north vestibule of the Cathedral of Saints Simon and Jude), and in the Huldigungshalle (Hall of Homage) of the town hall. In one of the fortress towers (Zwinger), there is an inn; in another one (Achtermann), a hotel, and a good one; and there is another hotel in the largest of the old Guild Halls, Kaiserworth. The Guild Halls are the special pride of the town.

That Goslar was always faithful to the Kaiser or *kaiserlich*—when there were no more Kaisers, this was called *Deutsch National* or German National—is self-evident. Its market square cries out for glee clubs to assemble on it and sing patriotic songs. And that's what they used to do. But today . . . well, today the glee clubs don't seem to have the following they once did; the patriotic songs don't either.

Whenever I think of Goslar, two other towns come to mind: Halberstadt and Hildesheim. I don't know why. The three have a few things in common. They are about the same size, and all three are beautiful in that stubborn North German way which never had any use for baroque or rococo. Here Prussian classicism followed hot on the heels of Romanesque and Gothic periods, which were adhered to as long as possible and sometimes mixed. Goslar lies between Halberstadt and Hildesheim, yet the trip to Halberstadt takes weeks; one must get a permit, if it is possible to get one, because Halberstadt lies "over there." As a matter of fact, much that goes with Goslar is "over there": the largest and most beautiful section of the Harz Mountains, for instance. The first station on the other side is called Elend . . . Misery.

So we drove to Hildesheim. It didn't take an hour and carried us straight through a rather weird town which lies between Goslar and Hildesheim: Salzgitter, Göring's never-realized dream of a super-industrial city. Next to Berlin, it is the biggest German city in area, consisting of one town and twenty-seven villages between Goslar and Wolfenbüttel; and it is the site of the largest foundries in Germany. Here ore is not transported to coal, as in the Ruhr; coal is transported to the ore that is here.

Salzgitter never did have many friends; not the peasants who had to give up their fruitful land; not the industrial magnates who distrustfully watched an apparently megalomaniac rival industry in the making; not the Germans who know hardly anything about it, and still don't. In 1950, there were a few days when all Germany talked about Salzgitter: here, for the first time, the civil population had rebelled against the occupation forces. Workers had defended their factory which was to be dismantled. But today? The factory is still being expanded, but Salzgitter, a struggling embryo, is still not a city.

Hildesheim was much harder hit in the war than Goslar, and only fourteen days before it was all over. Hans Egon Holthusen, from Hildesheim, wrote an essay on "the town that can never be brought back." "Close your eyes, and you can conjure up the living town once more as if preserved forever, like a constellation of stars on the nocturnal sky of remembrance, like a beloved of whose dear presence we have been robbed by time and fate and our own fault. Open your eyes, however, and you will see the other side of the coin."

Let us keep our eyes closed. . . .

The time has come anyway for us to reach our ultimate destination: Hamburg. To do that we have to cross a heath: the Lüneburger Heide, and once we have left the industrial areas around Braunschweig and Hannover behind us, we have three possible routes, all of them lovely. Federal Highway 4, in tourist propaganda sometimes called the Harz-Heath Highway, takes you from Braunschweig through Gifhorn, which became famous when it leaked out that the last chief of staff of the SA was sitting side by side with the son of anti-Nazi rebel leader Goerdeler in the offices of the district administration. (That's how confused things can be in the Guelph district.) Ülzen next, from where the road leads into Wendland, where you can still see on old courtyard gates the tulip of the Wittekind faithful who lost their lives in the struggle against Charlemagne. The district is really Wendic, or Slavic, as the names of places—Luchow, Grabow, Wüstrow—and of many families testify. (That's how confused things can be in the Guelph district.) And finally Lüneburg, one of the leading choices for the most beautiful town in North Germany, and although the title will in the end have to go to Lübeck, few tourist attractions can compare with the Lüneburg town hall, the square "Am Sande," the exemplary brick Gothic of its houses. Behind the façades, though, is a musty atmosphere, for hygienic fixtures don't seem to have developed here much since the Middle Ages. (That's how confused things can be in the Guelph district.)

Route 3 leads from Hannover through Celle, third (after Lübeck and Lüneburg) in the beauty contest; less stern, gayer, with a more southern atmosphere than either of its rivals. The Lüneburg dukes didn't live in Lüneburg but preferred Celle. The little town therefore still has a palace standing between two pretty frame houses. The Palace Theater that goes with it was built in 1685, and as such is Germany's oldest theater. Bergen next. For our generation hard to remember without a hyphen and the word Belsen after it. Where the concentration camp Bergen-Belsen once stood, in the southwest of this sprawling heath village, is a monument to which whole busloads of *Halbstarke*, "half-strong" teenagers often drive and, giving the lie to their derogatory title, swear to be stronger than their fathers. Soltau next. Here one should do what one might have done in Celle—leave the broad highway, detour a few kilometers, and drive through the Conservation Department Park. And after that—Hamburg.

9. HAMBURG: GATEWAY TO HALF THE WORLD

We proceeded to Hamburg via Lüneburg on Route 4. From Lüneburg we could have taken the Salzstrasse to Lübeck, highly recommended because it isn't yet jammed with traffic, and because of the places it passes through. The terraced Elbe town of Lauenburg, Schwarzenbek in the Saxon Forest, Till Eulenspiegel-Mölln on three lakes, and the island town of Ratzeburg need not shun comparison with the prettiest small South German towns. But we stuck to direction Hamburg, and therefore saw suddenly, on our right, just after we had passed through the little village of Bardowiek, a Gothic church which any big city could be proud of. And a big city might still be situated there, and Hamburg be only an Elbe harbor, if Henry the Lion, in his terrible rage over the unwillingness of this powerful Hanseatic town and bishop's see to pay its taxes, hadn't had the city that was there burned to the ground in 1189, down to the last house. Only the cathedral remained standing. On its south portal you will find a wooden sign with the words, *leonis vestigium*, the trace of the lion.

It was natural to invite my friends to Hamburg, the city where I live and am happy, the city which contains more of the world within its walls than any other city in Germany today; the city where it is easiest to comfort the timid souls who worry about the strength of German democracy, and to deceive them. . . .

"Within its walls" was not a slip into a pseudo-poetic description of a town. True, the town elders of Hamburg were among the first to recognize that protective walls had become obsolete as a means of conducting war, and since, as in Hamburg today, they had little regard for relics of the past, the walls were torn down in 1820, but the streets that lead around the heart of the city are still called walls: Klosterwall, Steintorwall, Gorch-Fock-Wall, Holstenwall, Glockengiesserwall. If you take a walk along the Jungfernstieg, starting from the center of the city—that is from the stock exchange and city hall—a narrow, elegant shopping street will soon open up on your left. If you continue to stroll down the Jungfernstieg for another hundred yards or so, you'll come to a street almost identical with the first one. Even old citizens of Hamburg have difficulty telling them apart.

The Jungfernstieg leads out of Old Hamburg to the Dammtor and the convent of Harvestehude, which practical citizens converted into a restaurant when it was no longer being used as a convent because Hamburg had become a Protestant city. Old Hamburg ended at the New Wall, and that is what the first street to the left of the Jungfernstieg is called. And when no vicious enemy happened to be laying siege to the wall (to tell the historic truth, none ever did!), then the housewives of Hamburg used to bleach their linen just outside it. The second street off the Jungfernstieg as you walk out of the city is therefore called Grosse Bleiche, or Great Bleaching Ground.

The temptation to tell some of the history of the Free Hanseatic City of Hamburg, which is so rich from various points of view, threatens to carry me beyond the limits of a short chapter. The temptation is the greater because, at first sight, Hamburg doesn't seem to have any history at all. Aren't we accustomed to seeing history manifest itself in beautiful old buildings, palaces, and sumptious patrician homes, in Gothic churches and old monasteries? Hamburg has very few such architectural testimonials to offer. Very few? Let's be frank—it has none! Wherever merchants play a leading role, monuments of bygone days are constantly forced to justify their present usefulness. Half the center of the city was ruined in a conflagration in 1842. Part of what survived perished in the air raids of the last war.

"There's a great resemblance between Hamburg and London," said Ralph, and he wasn't the first one to notice it. Eichendorff called Hamburg's way of life "a prelude to London." The inhabitants of Hamburg, like those of London or England, have a reputation for being formal and reserved. Fontane writes about the ladies of Hamburg: "Although they deny it, secretly it is their cherished desire to be mistaken for English ladies, and most of the time they come very close to their ideal." In Hamburg as in London, you can be preoccupied by the hour with the weather, and in both places for good reasons. The power of stock exchange and banks, shipyards, wharfs, and insurance companies has been equally great in both cities, and today is greater than may appear to the outsider.

"To draw parallels with foreign countries is always rather awkward," said Bismarck, an honorary citizen of Hamburg, who lies buried in Friedrichsruh in the adjacent Saxon Forest, and whose colossal statue towers high above the harbor, half impressing, half frightening the tourist.

Parallels or no parallels, close ties have always existed between Hamburg and London, business connections to be sure, but nonetheless hearty because of that. For in the city of Hamburg, as in the city of London, business and heart go hand in hand.

A story from the last war: During an air-raid alarm in Hamburg, people inside a shelter could hear the droning of a British plane, followed by wild flak noises, after which—silence. Into the silence came a voice from a far corner: "I hope nothing happened to him. . . ."

Even if the story isn't true, it is well contrived. It characterizes a mood that changed only in 1943, when the RAF not only destroyed four-fifths of the harbor, but with a rain of fire bombs created a conflagration that killed ten times as many people as the great fire that had destroyed half the city a hundred years before. "My poor Hamburg lies in ruins, and the places I knew so well, which form an integral part of the memories of my youth, are naught but smoldering ruins." Heinrich Heine, famous stepson of the Hanseatic City, wrote this in 1844; a hundred years later it was true again.

The British did not ingratiate themselves further when they dismantled what was left of the port after the war was over, for instance the proud wharf of Blohm & Voss. But the Hamburgers have one more trait in common with the British, and that is an aversion to resentments. When relations were resumed again, they were at first sober, matter of fact, simply necessary. But when Mr. Dunlop, the first British Consul General of the postwar era, left Hamburg in 1957, the many speechmakers didn't have to exaggerate as they spoke of the deep regret of the population. And then there is the story of the Hamburg merchant, who when his third daughter informed him that she, too, would like to marry an Englishman, said, "Well, I think it would be nice if *one* of you could stay in our country."

And that's the way it is again in Hamburg. About forty thousand foreigners live permanently in the city, augmented daily by the crews of the ships in harbor; by men passing through on business, who fill the Vier Jahreszeiten and Atlantic and other luxury hotels every week; by the tourists and visitors who, whatever they may be looking for in Hamburg, find something to attract and keep them there.

People who live inland often have rather fantastic notions about Hamburg. They still consider a city with a port adventurous in spite of the fact that seafaring has become far more sober and commonplace than in days gone by, when the Hamburg courts were busier sentencing pirates than traffic violators. On every sight-seeing cruise around the harbor, the Grasbrook where Claus Störtebeker, the most famous of these pirates, was executed in 1401, is pointed out to tourists. A distinguished elderly lady from Mainz, who visits Hamburg frequently, usually puts down the window of her car on the Lombard Bridge between the two Alster lakes, takes a deep breath and exclaims, "Ah, sea air!" in spite of the fact that she knows very well that the ocean is 100 kilometers away by car, and then it's the Baltic Sea! The North Sea is even farther away.

But there is such a thing as "sea air" in Hamburg, a damp smell of salt mixed with tar and diesel oil. Evidently this suffices even today to evoke Robinson Crusoe dreams. And there are sea gulls, especially in winter, when the tame birds, attracted by the food of the city, leave the coast. Stems of green bananas are unloaded here, as well as canisters of tea, sacks of unroasted coffee and stupefyingly fetid bundles of pelts. Locomotives and cars are shipped here, as well as agricultural machinery and even the equipment of entire factories. Every orange a German eats, every cup of coffee he drinks, has probably reached him via Hamburg (or Bremen). In the city proper, the adventurousness of world trade is felt rather than seen, because here it exists only on paper. In innumerable offices, innumerable pages are being filled with innumerable figures, which mean nothing to the layman but everything to the merchant.

Where to begin when you want to show the city to a stranger? What can you possibly show him when there are only a few hours (or pages) at your disposal and such an abundance of possibilities? What is familiar to one person, may be fresh to another.

"Let's do it this way," Dick suggested. "Let's each name one thing he wants to see, then combine them all into one program."

So that was what we did, and as an all-too-small selection, our program wasn't anything to sneeze at: the harbor, the Reeperbahn, the Alster, the Pressehaus, and the Elbe Highway.

If you visit Hamburg and don't see the harbor, you don't see Hamburg. Bustling yet picturesque port activity takes place close to the center of town. Like well-trained dogs, tugs and launches circle the metal mountains of 20,000-ton vessels which seem to glide effortlessly between pleasure craft and sight-seeing boats. Steel scaffolding towers high above wharves; cranes lower their long necks from the quay walls like herons. There is background music of electric machines and diesel motors, a slapping of waves against gliding metal, ship sirens, people shouting, all intermingled and constant throughout the busy day. At night all you hear is the "toot-toot" of the ships' horns. You can hear the sound all over the city, pleasant music to the Hamburger; sleep-robbing for the visitor who has lodgings close to the river.

There are four possibilities for viewing the panorama of the harbor. On land (stationary) from the windows of one of the numerous harbor restaurants; on land (mobile) strolling or driving along the Elbe, crossing the various bridges, or via the first underwater tunnel in Europe, 75 feet beneath the Elbe. On the water (stationary) in the restaurant-boat moored at the Überseebrücke, but this restaurant becomes mobile during the bathing season and takes off for Helgoland; on the water (mobile) in your own dinghy or on one of the vessels of the Hafen-Dampfschiffahrt A.G. which is more to be recommended to visitors. Lazy epicureans may enjoy a panoramic view from the quite expensive but very elegant rooftop restaurant of the Bavaria Brewery. We were nearly refused admittance because Ralph wasn't wearing a tie.

If you begin to take a serious interest in the harbor, figures start to buzz in your head. It has 35 docks for sea-going vessels, and 23 for river shipping; 1351 sea-going vessels make Hamburg their home port. It takes all day to walk around the quay walls (57 kilometers), and it costs approximately 10,000 to 20,000 marks to build a yard of quay wall. In addition, there are more than 46 kilometers of anchorage space in the dock basins on pile dolphins, and such a modern cluster of steel piles costs 5,000 marks. The turnover of goods shipped and unloaded here amounts to 30 million tons a year, but this is already beyond the layman's conception, even if he tries to realize what it means by telling himself that the average vessel holds only about 10,000 tons. Three thousand such vessels therefore take on cargo and unload here every year. Another interesting figure: it costs a ship of this size about 10,000 marks to spend a day in port, that is to say, about one mark for every ton of cargo space. Unloading one day faster saves 10,000 marks. On the basis of this calculation, the Hamburgers try to meet competition by making Hamburg "a fast port," where loading and unloading require a minimum of time. This is an effort on their part to compensate for the drawbacks (politically) of their geographical position, and to remain at least the fourth largest overseas port in the world, after New York, London, and Rotterdam. It is not easy to continue to be a world port after finding yourself situated suddenly on the brink of one world, on a front facing "enemy territory" that begins only fifty kilometers upriver. . . .

"And now we go to the Reeperbahn," said Yvonne.

The Reeperbahn is part of the harbor of Hamburg, just as the harbor is a part of Hamburg. During the day, you can't tell it apart from any other normal Hamburg street. But at night it poses problems that don't concern Hamburg alone.

"How did you like the show?" Miss Norway asked.

The question was part of the role this nineteen-year-old child with her painted doll face had to play. Her hair, blonde, long, stringy, fell down over her bony shoulders and smelled of tobacco. Her mouth was a strident orange, her silver-gray fingernails like claws.

The performance was over. Now she had an hour intermission. She could have spent it in her dressing room, but neither she nor her colleagues did that because it was dull and nothing came of it. So they switched roles: from nine to ten they were "models"; from ten to eleven they socialized, *i.e.*, they shared their company with anyone who wanted it, after which they became "models" again. Models, b-girls, models, b-girls, until they had worked their way through four shows, by which time it was 4:00 A.M. and the last customer had left, yawning or singing lustily.

Like the Montmartre section of Paris, Hamburg offers the tourist entertainment on the Reeperbahn, night after night. As in Paris? The names of a lot of the places indicate that they are modeled after French equivalents, but "a dangerous aspect of the French character is missing in the ponderous nature of the German—the attractiveness of vice. Whenever the German happens to stray along such paths, he becomes coarse and clumsy." That was written by Heinrich von Treitschke almost a hundred years ago; anyone visiting the Reeperbahn will find it apt.

"Where are the German nights," asked Bernard Dort, a young Frenchman, disappointed with a trip through the Federal Republic, "the romantic nights, the naturalistic nights, the expressionistic nights?" *Ubi sunt?* Clichés for world literature and dream fulfillment, not reality.

The reality of the Reeperbahn is neither so radiantly gay nor so horribly black as sometimes depicted. All Philistine attacks against this "Hamburg disgrace" could until now be countered by the city fathers with two solidly Hanseatic-pragmatic arguments: if a certain amount of night life is requisite for the life of a big city—and that seems to be the case—then it is better to concentrate it all in a few streets than to let it spread over the whole city. From their headquarters in the Davidswache, protectors of the law, chosen for their inordinate physical strength and great understanding of human frailty, appear to have the apparently very free activities firmly under control. The amusement area of the neon-glittering Reeperbahn seems to be the least of their worries. In the shadows of the side streets that run down to the harbor, vice takes on a more unmistakable and malevolent form.

The second argument would be hard to contradict, a city that lives on trade and shipping has to offer entertainment, because sailors fear a dull port (that's why they're so rare on earth), and I have not come across many commercial travelers who like to spend their evenings alone reading a novel or playing chess. If we want to see sailors and businesmen in our town, then we've got to offer them something amusing after dark.

Miss Norway helps attend to that. "How did you like the show?" *The show* is a linguistic concession to the Anglo-Saxon expression "show-business," in a honky-tonk world that tends otherwise more toward things French. But that is not the whole Reeperbahn. Another type of amusement, coarser, gustier, with a lot more jostling, is patterned more along Tyrolean lines with a shot of Rhenish atmosphere. *Zillertal* is what they like to call it.

What may actually be considered Hamburg's contribution to the Reeperbahn remains unclear. Certainly not the Catcher Tents where a wild style of wrestling takes place, *i.e.*, the art of being able to indicate absolute frenzies of brute strength without doing much damage. Ralph, our much-traveled English friend, declared there was one thing he'd seen nowhere else but in Hamburg, and that was women wrestling in mud. Very popular on the Reeperbahn, according to him. I pass on this bit of information with skepticism. I can find very little in the Hanseatic Lower Saxon folk character to suggest such sport. The tendency to sling mud at one another, even if in this case only to cover up illegal nudities, is so widespread, that I think it would be unfair to say it was typical of Hamburg.

Much more Hamburgian are places like Uncle Hugo's, where you can get an excellent supper or breakfast in the early hours of the morning. And then there are a few perfectly harmless dance halls, and some that are not so harmless. Once we took an English lady to one of the most famous ones. She was enchanted. "Oh, but it's just like a Lyon's tearoom," she said.

There are all sorts of bars, with and without music, with good drinks and bad drinks, with and without women. There are beer restaurants, frankfurter counters, and gambling halls, which seem to be gambling halls only because of the dull clatter of the slot machines; nothing very evil happens in them. There are conventional hotels and hotels with rooms by the hour, normal movies and abnormal movies called *Sittenfilme*, literally translated: moral films. They are called moral films because they are immoral. Sometimes they give the district attorney trouble; the man in the audience, too. To date I haven't been able to find anyone who enjoys them. Sometimes I get the feeling that these "moral films," contrary to their immoral purpose, have a quite moral effect. I watched one once for all of ten minutes and almost became a prude. In comparison, Miss Norway is downright lovable, and still quite easily recognizable as a human being.

"How did you like the show?"

Now of course I had to say something nice, because even a model has her pride and professional ambition. And why not? The wine was excellent and not too expensive. The service was good; the customers didn't look the least depraved. The girls weren't much better company

than they were models, but they weren't ugly or disagreeable. It gave
you food for thought. Some things that were meant to be amusing,
were saddening. . . . The show, for instance.

Through the dimly lighted room, a boardwalk, covered with red
sisal matting, moves slowly out from the noisy orchestra pit. The show
begins. You think you're in a bathing resort, watching one of those
democratic misnomers that call themselves, more succinctly than intended, "Miss" contests. Miss Norway, Miss Italy, Miss Holland, Miss
America, Miss Great Britain, Miss France, Miss Austria, Miss Switzerland, Miss Germany, and a few more misses get up on the catwalk
(no offense intended), and with barely concealed embarrassment, hurry
along it above the audience, about face, and disappear. With their last
steps, just before they reach the haven of the curtain, their faces relax.
During the brief performance they stare straight ahead and down a
little with the concentration that doesn't even permit a professional
smile to break through. This way they are able to avoid the obstrusive
stares of the audience, and at the same time make sure that they don't
trip off the walk. The only difference from the bathing resort is that
these girls wear tulle and nylon garments over their bikinis. In one
number they're called nightgowns, in another evening dresses. Such
nuances are explained by a master of ceremonies who manages to combine an artificial professional joviality with the hoarse voice of a
market crier. To prevent people from leaving too soon because the
"fashion show" hasn't come up to the expectations aroused by the
photographs outside and by the doorman's suggestive remarks, the
fellow tells you with oily insistence (he thinks he's being risqué) that
"You'll get your money's worth in a minute, gentlemen." This is probably the most embarrassing part of the performance.

The whole show is attuned to males. It is therefore astonishing that
in this still fairly decent honky-tonk atmosphere, the men barely predominate, at least not before 3:00 A.M. Down in the harbor it is, of
course, different; there the demand is quite clearly male, the supply
female.

"He wanted to clap, but she nudged him, so he stopped fast," said
one model to another when they were socializing again.

"That's the way it is," said her friend, "the women begrudge us our
applause. There's always something that doesn't suit them. They only
come here to disapprove."

If a woman really comes to the Reeperbahn with this in mind, ready
to pay a mark to get in and many more for drinks, she'll get her
money's worth, but whether the men feel that the master of ceremony's leering promises have been fulfilled is hard to say. What he
meant was made clear enough in one of the next numbers. A few of the
girls were literally half-dressed. Material covered their right shoulders,
but on the left side they wore nothing over their hearts. It looked odd,
rather like economy in the wrong place.

Were the men getting their money's worth? They clapped a lot,
loudly, if they had nobody with them to nudge them. "She's got a nice

face," one of them said, at the next table. Saint or hypocrite. The gentlemen at his table looked neither delighted nor disappointed; they had come to be amused, paid money for it, now they were amused.

As for the Misses . . . Sometimes foreigners get annoyed. A Finn invites "Miss Finland" to keep him company, and it turns out that she doesn't speak a word of Finnish; in fact her ideas as to where that country lies geographically are quite vague. Yet these "Miss-nomers" are further examples of German admiration for all things foreign, for what does the management expect to be the result? First and foremost, a big-wide-world atmosphere; and beyond that the quasi-moral safe-guard: how these exotic ladies behave is none of our concern. The customer, however, has little understanding for such subtle motivations, and complains, "I've been gipped!" As if what was being offered were a question of nationality!

But the girls are totally identified, for all practical purposes, with the land of their involuntary origin, and can therefore withdraw into an anonymity that leaves the spirit free. Not a soul in the place, not customer, waiter, not even the boss, knows who Fraulein Inge Krämer is. "Norway, come over here," they say. "Finland, you're wanted on number seventeen."

Fraulein Inge Krämer, alias Miss Norway, starts work here at 9:00 P.M. as "model." If she is asked by any official or non-Reeperbahn acquaintance what her profession is, she simply drops the quotes and *is* a model. Even her father, a decent mechanic living in a small Lower Saxony town, knows only that "Inge is working in Hamburg as a model."

In the course of each show, she appears nine times; nine times four, therefore, every night, of which six (times four) she is insufficiently clad. Since her dressing room is draughty, she often catches cold. At 4:00 A.M. she queues up with her colleagues for her pay. "Twenty marks a night," she explains. "With percentages, that's twice what I used to get as a salesgirl."

Her percentages are the 10 per cent she has coming to her from the money spent by the men with whom she "socialized." Sometimes they give her presents, too. But here she has to be careful. An attractively arranged package can be bought at the tables for just this purpose; it contains a box of candy and a pair of stockings. Inge likes flowers, too. (More percentages.)

"Some men ask me if I mind doing this. Idiots!"

Inge, like many of her colleagues, knows what she's after. "I'm going to do this for six months." Every afternoon she takes dancing and drama lessons. Who knows, one day she may make it.

In the gray dawn, her working day is over. Then she steps out to the café next door. It is still open, and a young man is waiting there for her. He wouldn't enter the place where she works, not even if he could afford it.

Inge likes money and many presents, but there's one present she won't accept, and that's money. She refuses it as a matter of principle, quite often with a heavy heart. She knows that this is the borderline beyond which lies prostitution. With very few exceptions, the girls stay this side of the line. The management helps see to it that they do.

And the exceptions? Well, they add up, and supplemented by a few other sources, become the rule in some parts of the Reeperbahn especially in its side streets. The older they get, the darker the places where they choose to stand. Throughout history, the prostitute has seesawed between highest honor and deepest shame: courtesan, meretrix, whore, doxie, harlot, strumpet, streetwalker, the woman of easy virtue. According to Egon Friedell, she guarantees "that normal, and one might say legitimate measure of immorality which probably belongs to the iron reserves of mankind." Noteworthy perhaps is the fact that one of the first human voices raised on her behalf was a German voice. In a fifteenth-century German law book one can read: "These free-living daughters are poor, dejected creatures, therefore they should be protected from power and injustice." And today's laws are relatively tolerant and generous toward these "free-living daughters," if not via the law itself, than in its interpretation. In their case, more often than not, the twilight zone of the unknown quantity is respected.

Next day, when at last all of us were up, we met at Michelsen's Coffee Shop on the Grosse Bleichen, which is famous, and justly so. Breakfast in Hamburg has, for visitors from the Reeperbahn, the pleasant peculiarity of actually being lunch. Our next project was the Alster.

Cities situated on rivers have certain advantages over riverless seas of houses. Hamburg is located on three rivers. "On the Alster, on the Elbe, on the Bille," according to Hamburg's "national anthem." The stranger will look in vain for the Bille, but he doesn't have to look far for the Alster because it can't be overlooked. However, if he doesn't take the trouble to go out to Wellingsbüttel, he'll never know that it is a river. In the city it looks like a small lake (*Binnen-* or Inner-Alster), plus a large lake (*Aussen-* or Outer-Alster). Seen topographically, Hamburg shapes up like a figure eight, with the Binnen-Alster forming the small top, and the Aussen-Alster, three times longer, the oval bottom. Almost tangentially above this eight runs the Elbe; the Old City lies in between. In Hamburg, all business faces the Elbe; for rest and recreation, its citizens turn to the Alster.

We walked around the Binnen-Alster in half an hour: Jungfernstieg, Neuer Jungfernstieg, Lombardsbrücke, Ballindam, stores, hotels, office buildings, no apartment houses. Hamburg has gone the way of all great cities to a greater extent than any other German city: hardly anyone lives in town any more. The rents are exorbitant. And like most big cities, Hamburg has good suburban residential districts: Harvestehude (also called Pöseldorf), Elbvororte, Wellingsbüttel, Uhlenhorst, where the "better," or let's say the well-to-do people live; and less desirable sections of course. Harvestehude and Uhlenhorst are on the Aussen-Alster, and to live in either of them is truly delightful.

The Aussen-Alster lies in the midst of a great city like an idyllic lake, bordered by green promenades, the two Lombard bridges at one end and the Krugkoppel Bridge at the other. From spring to fall, the Aussen-Alster is virtually covered with white sails that lend something akin to a permanent vacation mood to the peaceful scenery.

Of Germany's ten most representative newspapers, five are published in Hamburg, perhaps because today Hamburg is the only German city with that cosmopolitan aura on which newspapers thrive. We do not have one newspaper that you might say was representative for all of West Germany, and of course there is no one paper that is read in both parts of Germany. The government of East Germany threatens the import of West German newspapers with considerable punishment; the government of West Germany manages to keep East German newspapers almost completely out of its territory without invoking any special laws.

As a newspaper city, Hamburg has a two-hundred-year-old history. In the second half of the eighteenth century, the press began to be powerful in Germany by imitating the "moral" journals of the English gazeteers, Addison and Steele. Soon Hamburg had ninety-one such journals, some of which appeared daily and weren't so moral, among them the most famous ones, the *Vernünftler*, or The Rational Man, and The Patriot.

I was explaining all this to my five friends, as we were seated in one of those offices in Hamburg's Pressehaus, which the journalist finds so livable. Unfortunately, since all signs point to a highly gratifying economic upsurge, these offices are being replaced more and more by rooms a top executive could be proud of. Ralph interrupted my fine lecture on German newspaper history with the unexpected question, "But generally speaking the press doesn't have very much to say in Germany, does it?"

A sweeping statement like this is no more correct than the one issued by the Federal Republic Press and Information Bureau under—of all things—the heading *Facts*. "The Germans are assiduous newspaper readers."

Newspapers have an old, if not always venerable tradition in Germany. We even had a paper once which could presume to be the oldest in the world, the *Aviso* of 1609, probably founded, according to the latest research, by Duke Henry Julius von Braunschweig. There have been German newspapers with a world-wide reputation: the Hamburger *Fremdenblatt*, the Berlin *Vossische Zeitung*, the *Frankfurter Zeitung*, the *Kölnische Zeitung*; yet I don't suppose it is merely by chance that these papers have ceased to exist, and whenever a continuation is attempted, any expert can see the weak spots in the rigging.

I have the feeling that in no democratic country in the world are less newspapers read than in Germany, and as a basis for a feeling like that we have statistics on the amount of paper consumed: in West Germany, where it certainly must be greater than in East Germany, 10 kilograms per capita. In France, Holland, and Switzerland, the count is considerably higher; in the Scandinavian countries and Great Britain, more than double; and a citizen of the United States reads, or anyway buys, four times as much newsprint as the German.

Of course what is printed on the paper should also be taken into consideration, and the more you pursue that subject, the more depressed you can get about the state of German journalism. Far out in first place are the purely local papers that are delivered with the morning rolls, in which the creative processes seem to have been concentrated, with few exceptions, on the road work being done and the performance of the volunteer-fire-department band. Here the local editor is the important man, and he gets his political views in a package deal from some central editorial clearing house or other. All this is rather touching, almost idyllic, in an era of mass communications media; some even see something refreshing in it, a last remnant of indigenous individuality.

"But on what do papers like that subsist?" Ralph wanted to know. In England, the *News Chronicle* had to close down even though its circulation was more than a million."

Papers that print only 50,000 copies daily (often it is only 5,000) have to be cheap, and by that I mean cheap in every way. Some people may find them charming. I don't know anyone who would like to see all of them go. The truth of the matter is that the press was never very highly thought of under the monarchy; during the Nazi dictatorship and *gleichschaltung* (political alignment) it was hard hit; and the journalism of the provinces hasn't helped it to become any stronger.

"A really eminent personality would never write anything for a German newspaper, would he?" asked Yvonne. "As any famous scholar or poet would be glad to in France, and I'm sure in the United States and England, too."

Which is half true. Political figures—and who would deny that there are eminent ones among them?—often write for the big German newspapers. Among scholars and professional writers there is undoubtedly some opposition to the idea, but only in a few cases as a matter of principle. Anyone who has a reputation doesn't lose it by writing newspaper articles, but the impetus to do so doesn't happen to be very great. Fame and honor are sought in technical or scientific periodicals and books. You can't make much money with a newspaper article, and the urge to be read, which the newspapers can certainly satisfy, is still a little underdeveloped in a young democracy which, in spite of repeated good starts, hasn't progressed very far beyond the toddling stage. And yet, famous names are cropping up more and more frequently in the big German newspapers.

So there we were in the Hamburg Pressehaus where nearly all the papers are published that do not belong to the gigantic Springer Verlag: the Social Democratic *Echo*, the oldest Hamburg newspaper; also *Die Zeit* (Time), and *Der Spiegel* (Mirror), the *Morgenpost*

(Morning Post), and Germany's big illustrated paper, *Der Stern* (Star). Informative material was lying right there in front of us; we could pick up the papers we were talking about, look at them, make comparisons.

"But this wouldn't be possible in England," Ralph protested. "Look . . . on the same day, the most important newspapers in the country headline quite different items."

But that's the way it was. In the *Frankfurter Allgemeine Zeitung:* "Instrument capsule brought back from outer space." The Munich *SZ,* "The first UNO troops in Katanga." The *Welt,* "West declares Zone violates status of Berlin." Taking the other two of the five dailies that may be counted as among the ten biggest German newspapers, things got even crazier. Stuttgart: "Renewed attacks of the Federal government on the radio industry." *Bild:* "A mother reveals the secrets of her life." All on Saturday, August 13, a day like any other. And the German papers could prove that the German press wasn't very powerful, because the German press as a power factor doesn't exist. The minimum of solidarity that would be required is lacking. Whenever there is any talk about such a power of the press in the Federal Republic, it comes from dubious sources. At best it may be the result of ignorance; in some cases it springs from the obscure feeling that freely formed opinions, printed and distributed thousands of times, might make things more uncomfortable for the political, economic, and cultural potentates, than some people would like.

Of ten West Germans, three find the Basic Law of the Federal Republic good; one inclines to find it bad; one doesn't know what he thinks about it; and five admit that they don't know it. One of the less popular Articles is No. 5: "Everyone has the right freely to express and to disseminate his opinion through speech, writing and pictures, and, without hindrance, to instruct himself from generally accessible sources." Even the Basic Law, therefore, is not without restrictions: "From generally accessible sources," and after that: "These rights are limited by the provisions of the general laws, the legal regulations for the protection of juveniles, and by the right to personal honor."

Several attempts to restrict the freedom of the press have been successfully fought off so far, but there will be fresh efforts at restriction, and the German population can be counted on to consent to a majority of them. After all, they can fall back on crown witnesses such as Goethe: "Only when one hasn't read the papers for a few months, and then reads all of them together, does it become evident how much time we waste on them." Or Schopenhauer: "The newspapers are the second hand of history, which is not only frequently made of less noble metal, but also rarely goes right." And Bismarck: "The newspaper writer is a man who has missed his calling."

"And why is that?" Ralph wanted to know.

For the answer, let's turn back to the papers. Should we have great respect for a news enterprise that headlines as the most important item, "Mother reveals the secrets of her life," when, as happened to be the case that day, a man called Lumumba was fanning the fires in Africa; Berlin was again—or still—being threatened; England was taking important steps toward a union of sorts with the European continent; and outer space had been opened up a little further?

"But there have to be papers like that, too," said Ralph. "That doesn't mean anything."

I don't know. I know only that the Hamburger *Bild Zeitung*, in which that headline appeared, sells five times as many copies (3 million daily) as the three big serious dailies *together*. And I know that once, when I was traveling from Hamburg to Frankfurt on one of those super de luxe Bundesbahn trains that are used almost exclusively by the leaders of an expense-account society, nine out of ten of my fellow travelers were enjoying mother's secrets and similar fare. . . .

Last part of our program: the Elbe Highway. It runs along the River Elbe from Hamburg west to Blankensee, which was once a fishing village. Hamburg's residential section is located on both sides of the highway. The left side slopes down steeply to the river and is "the right side of the tracks." On the heights stand the mansions of the well-to-do; down by the river huddle the little houses of sea captains and river pilots, less elegant but much more charming. Here the captains can watch the ships pass by to which they owe their wealth or beautiful memories or both. The importers do the same thing from the upper stories of their villas above.

A stream of excursion traffic moves along the highway in the direction of Teufelsbrück, Jacob, Süllberg, to the Schulauer Ferry House with its "Welcome Establishment" for ships, or to many other fine restaurants. If you want to see more of the Elbe than may be glimpsed from the highway, you can walk along the river from St. Pauli to Wedel, a stroll of five hours on beautifully landscaped paths practically all the way. At the end of the road, at Wedel, you leave the Free Hanseatic City of Hamburg and enter Schleswig-Holstein.

10. THE PHOENIX THAT DIDN'T ARISE

"No, but he is really charming!" Yvonne could scarcely control her enthusiasm over the multi-colored stone figure in the marketplace of Wedel. "Yes," Ralph agreed. "If the *furor teutonicus* always appeared in such amiable Santa Clause guise, it would be much easier to believe in Germany's peaceful intentions."

The Roland of Wedel really doesn't look very militant and bears no resemblance to his famous brother in front of Bremen's city hall, who proudly calls himself "the Giant," and is a stylized, radiant Gothic hero. Of course Roland was a warrior and was even supposed to be an emperor. But when you look at the round cheeks and rolling eyes of Wedel's Roland, the word "*Blitzkrieg*," which Germany bequeathed to the world, doesn't come to mind, but rather a word that is just as typically German: *gemütlich*. The Roland of Nordhausen, in the Harz Mountains, wears cassock and cross and swings a sword, but he doesn't induce fear either. The one in Perleberg (Mark Brandenburg) might.

The relationship of all these Roland statues—Brandenburg, Halle, and Halberstadt claim him as patron—to the man who gave them his name, nephew of Charlemagne and hero of *The Song of Roland,* is still not satisfactorily clarified. According to the legend, he gave up his noble ghost in 778 A.D. at Roncevaux during Charlemagne's disastrous rearguard action in the Pyrenees. It is a fact though that many towns in the Reich of the Roland Statues, which I have just invented and which stretches from the Harz Mountains to Mark Brandenburg, and from there to Bremen, owe their existence to the great emperor of the Franks who was supposed to be Roland's uncle. Very likely the Roland statues indicated certain town rights, such as the right to a market center and their own court of law. It is a fact, too, that this Reich of the Roland Statues once overlapped another empire, which was nothing more than a loose confederation of cities and towns serving mutual interests: the Hanseatic League. History tells us that it was founded in the thirteenth century, flourished in the fourteenth and fifteenth centuries, declined during the sixteenth century, and was destroyed by the Thirty Years War which brought Germany to Point Zero not for the first but certainly not for the last time in its history. German history is full of such Point Zeros, and only three institutions have emerged from the debris and ashes time and again, like the phoenix, albeit a rather badly plucked phoenix: the Catholic Church, the universities, and the Hanseatic cities. Only two of these still exist today, and that is a sad story.

"If you should ask me what German city I consider the most beautiful, I'd say Lübeck," said Ralph, who felt particularly at home in the Hanseatic towns.

"I like Lübeck, too," said Pierre Spälti, lost in thought. "After all, it is the city of Thomas Mann." Whereupon an elderly lady of Lübeck's best society shuddered perceptibly. She was enjoying an opulent dinner with us in Lübeck's Schabbelhaus, one of the most excellent restaurants in Germany. Of course her shudder may have been noticeable only if you happened to know that the mercantile patricians of Lübeck were at first quite disgusted with Thomas Mann's famous novel, *Buddenbrooks,* which had for its subtitle, *The Decline of a Family.* Perhaps this sad tale of commerical decline and waning power hit so hard because it mirrored the fate of the city all too clearly. Lübeck was once the queen of the Hanseatic towns, more important than Bremen, more distinguished than Hamburg. But the Baltic Sea trade diminished; Lübeck lost more and more of its importance. In 1937, it even lost its status of Free City and became part of Schleswig-Holstein, a Prussian province. The Federal Republic was unable to revoke this decision and after the country had been divided into Länder, Kiel was still the Land capital. And for the old Lübeckers, Kiel is an unmentionable place. Hadn't the revolt against the Kaiser's Reich started in Kiel, a rebellion against the same Reich that had made Kiel a war port in 1871, and to which it owed its wealth ever since? As far as Lübeck's local patriotism was concerned, the situation had become unbearable. Now they might just as well recognize Thomas Mann since all was lost anyway.

This peculiar kind of local patriotism crops up in Germany in some very curious ways. The Swiss and the Austrians can understand this; the French and British (unless they happen to be Scotch) can't; and Dick, our American, took a dim view of it. But that's the way it is in Germany. Principalities, Kaiserreich, Weimar Republic, our unspeakable period—all have passed. Federal Republic and DDR, each in their own way, are artificial creations that don't go back far enough to "come naturally." But the cities have remained. No wonder there is such strong feeling for "my little town, my home town." Far more surprising is the fact that these feelings are not as predominant as one might expect and are really supported by only a few old families. But nowhere are they more pronounced than in Bremen.

Unlike Lübeck, Bremen still has vitality, and has therefore been able to retain its status of Free City; but unlike Hamburg, it is not a cosmopolitan city. "We stew in our own juice," was how the daughter of our Lübeck hostess expressed it rather unkindly. She had moved to Bremen after her marriage. "Believe me, the social incest there is terrible."

A strong word: incest. It is prompted on the one hand by the quite natural displeasure of the young generation with the foolishness of their elders; on the other hand, the old families of Bremen are undeniably pretty exclusive, and the outsider, even if he comes from Lübeck, has a hard time getting accepted.

"But the people of Bremen should be happy to have a lovely young woman come to live in their midst," Von Hattesdorf said gallantly. The lady from Lübeck thanked him, then explained; certainly loveliness and youth were valued by the old families of Bremen (in Hamburg and Lübeck, too), but to be the daughter of a local merchant was a priceless attribute.

Having pointed out some of the jealousies and local peculiarities of the Hanseatic cities, the time has come to emphasize something they have in common, which has outlived the political power of the Merchants' Guild. It was fitting that we should have discussed these Hanseatic characteristics in the Lübeck Schabbelhaus where today a room is set aside as a memorial to Thomas Mann. At the celebration of Lübeck's seven-hundredth anniversary, in 1926, he said: "If my style has been characterized as cool, lacking in pathos, and reserved; if it has been judged—approvingly or disapprovingly—as lacking the grand gesture and passion, and has been considered, generally speaking and individually, the instrument of a slow, sarcastic, and meticulous mind, rather than of a tempestuous genius, well then, I am fully aware of the fact that the Low German-Hanseatic linguistic landscape is being thus characterized." In the same speech, Thomas Mann called the Lübeck-

Hanseatic way of life "urbane" and "staunchly middle class" in contrast to that of Lower Saxony and Friesland.

This old urbane, staunchly middle-class culture, emanating from the temperament described by Thomas Mann, was a bulwark against the demonic and chaotic elements that have swept across Germany time and again; also when they erupted from within. The merchant was the first citizen of the Hanseatic towns. He reigned supreme in City Hall and stock exchange, which always stood side by side; in Lübeck they were in the same house. Here, and here only, he had to prove his worth. He married the daughter of a merchant who might just as well have been Dutch or English; if he had a taste for the exotic, he might even have brought home a girl from South America. But if his daughter married a Prussian officer, belonging to the very best society but outside the Hanseatic gates, that would have been considered a mesalliance and barely pardonable.

Well, these times have passed. Today the people of Hamburg don't think of neighboring Altona as "Holstein," "Danish," "Prussian foreign territory," and *"all-to -nah"* or "all-too-near." It belongs at last, and anyone who doesn't happen to know it would never notice where Hamburg ends and Altona begins. But in Hamburg they still like to tell the story of the man from Heiligengeistfeld; that's where Hamburg ends. This old man was crying bitterly, so the story goes, when a stranger approached him and tried to console him, without success. Finally the stranger begged, "Please tell me what your trouble is. Maybe I can help you because I am the Lord." For a moment the old man was hopeful. "I come from Altona," he said. Whereupon the Lord sat down and cried, too. . . .

Stories like this conserve the past, but are not entirely valid any more. And yet . . . while the other Länder have parliaments with ministers and minister-presidents, the Hanseatic City Länder are still ruled by a senate consisting of senators and a mayor. And while dinner jackets are once again weighted down with medals at festive occasions, in Bonn, for instance, it is part of a Hanseatic senator's code of honor not to accept a medal from "a foreign power" (such as the Federal government) as long as he is in office. The names of good Hanseatic families are Nottebohm and Godefroy, in Hamburg; Fehling and Eschenburg, in Lübeck; Marwede or Roselius, in Bremen. If someone is a baron or belongs to the nobility, you may rest assured that he is a "Quiddje"; that's what they call foreigners in Hamburg, in spite of the fact that they themselves often talk like Quiddjes; they *quiddelen*, which means they speak unclearly, or *not* the north German dialect: *Plattdeutsch*.

Of course all sorts of Quiddjes had moved to Hamburg before 1945, but after that they came in droves. When I look around me at my colleagues on the editorial staff of a newspaper, I find, beside three Hamburg natives, a man from East Prussia, one from West Prussia, one Swiss, two Swabians, one fellow from the Baltic, one from Berlin, a

Rhinelander, and a Lorraine Saxon. The Quiddjes owe Hamburg a lot, and Hamburg owes a lot to its Quiddjes.

11. SYLT, AND PROSPERITY

From Lübeck, a water-wind-cloud highway runs along the Baltic seacoast to Glücksburg on the Danish border, from there westward, and from Klanxbüll along the North Sea coast to Emden. This is no throughway, but a road thrown together, with some pretty rough spots and others that are excellently paved. If you enjoy water, wind, and clouds, you may even prefer it to Alpen- or Romantische Strasse. But those who have been spoiled by the Mediterranean should be warned: on this German seacoast you are always fully aware of the fact that the sea is nearby; usually you are only a few steps from it, but from your car you rarely see water. On the North Sea not at all (unless you're crossing the Elbe or Weser), and on the Baltic only on the stretch where, from Travemünde on, one bathing resort lies next to the other, and the highway runs along the beaches. We interrupted our coastal trek halfway; from Niebüll we took off for Sylt.

Anyone visiting the island of Sylt usually takes the train. Only railway tracks lead to it, no road, no path. Of course there are boats that dock on the south side of the island, in Hornum, but they come from Hamburg and Helgoland and the trip takes a whole day, three times as long as the train. Boats are therefore to be recommended only to the seafarer with a strong stomach who enjoys a voyage, not as a practical means of arriving in Sylt.

Since the German automobile driver does not like to do without what he pseudo-modestly calls "his mobile base," the railways do a land-office business during the summer months. For approximately 50 marks (less for very small, more for large cars) his car may take the train, too. In this way the big-city native can feel quite at home on the island. On a beautiful evening in August, there's not a street in Munich, Hamburg, or Düsseldorf with as many cars as the three main streets on Westerland on the island of Sylt.

Vacationers yearning for a little more peace and quiet, fled north- ward to Kampen, only to see the first traffic lights being installed there. These efforts at escape have by now created a quite active resort area south of Westerland, the former little village of Rantum, once hidden by dunes. It won't be long now, before visitors who want to swim will be able to get into the water only on a green light there too.

It is easy to paint the bathing crowds on Sylt in hideous colors; easy but incorrect. One could also report that little summer homes are renting there at a daily price equivalent to the average German's weekly salary; that for kilometers at a stretch you can't see any beach for bathers and their equipment; that transistor radios, bands, and jet planes overhead set the air in motion which is music to some people's ears but just plain noise to others; that you can't swim when it's windy or when it's calm, either because the current's too dangerous or the jelly fish too annoying; that you bathe first and clean off afterward the tar with which the ships of all nations are permitted to pollute the sea. Should anyone write all this and let it go at that, he would be giving an excellent example of how to tell the truth and still be lying.

Much is said and written to the effect that in the Federal Republic, affluence rules supreme and little else counts; that here the measure of a man is taken by the power of his automobile; that refrigerator, record player, and television set have replaced love, loyalty, and faith; that the Germans can't wax enthusiastic any more about anything except prosperity; that we have over three thousand millionaires while students and people living on fixed incomes can't buy enough to eat; that everything is directed toward Mammon, dependent on Mammon, and so on, and so on. True. And yet . . .

I don't think it was coincidence that just on Sylt, our conversation turned constantly in this direction. Because here money certainly was being worn visibly, and he who had a lot wore a lot. We were in the bar of the gambling casino of Westerland, and I must say I never saw a more successful mixture of vulgarity and respectability. By candlelight, black, coat-tailed waiters moved like shadows between champagne coolers; a black bow tie separated head from body.

"A little ghostly, isn't it?"

Actually, we were having a very good time, and had just finished trying to convince Ralph that German sekt was drinkable, too; yet each one of us in his own way felt what Dick meant when he said suddenly, "So this is how you Germans live."

The bar atmosphere was just as pleasant as in hundreds of bars between Shanghai and San Francisco. It was as un-German as elegant cosmopolitanism can be. But it certainly reeked of money. In the gaming room next door the bank was raking in a small fortune after every game, and was occasionally paying one out. And each game, according to the tempo of the croupier, lasted two or three minutes.

"Is it true that Germany has more gambling houses like this than any other country?" asked Ralph.

It is true. Approximately 5,000 gamblers visit 13 casinos in West Germany every night. The first of these postwar gambling spots was in Bad Neuenahr, near Bonn. It soon advanced to the second largest in Europe, after Monte Carlo. The smallest is in Westerland, since here the season, all efforts of the resort management notwithstanding, lasts only three months.

But one really should take a good look at these *vabanque* players, these amoralists, these Mr. Moneybags, and spendthrifts. They sit bowed modestly over their little pads, trying to construct some sort of system for the rolling ball which might double their stake of all of 2 marks. They may risk 30 to 50 marks; sometimes they even win. Of course there are others who satisfy the curious—Napoleons of the ivory ball, with rolls of fat at the napes of their necks, playing three tables at once, nonchalantly placing hundreds and raking in thousands, or vice versa. But the gaming tables prove nothing, at least nothing moral. They are just as controversial in Germany as they are in other countries, and the polemics against them are always directed against the same little bookkeeper who has embezzled the firm's funds, and who turns up every now and then in Germany as he does everywhere else. A few gambling concessions are not going to be renewed, so my count of 13 won't be correct much longer.

"Would you say that the pursuit of material pleasure was exceptionally strong in Germany?" Von Hattesdorf asked.

Everybody says so; many a German says so too, although he always sees himself as the exception that proves the rule. Nobody is going to deny that there is some truth in such a statement; but neither would I care to say it is the whole truth and nothing but the truth. I like to quote witnesses, in this case Friedrich Albert Lange: "The much abused quest for pleasure of our day and age is not nearly so startling as the quest for industry of our entrepreneurs . . . who sweep together the means for pleasure and then don't use them to have pleasure, but plough them back into further acquisitions. *That* is the ruling characteristic of our time." Thus Friedrich Albert Lange corroborates "the German economic mentality." The only trouble is, he wrote those lines in 1875. . . .

Ralph, with the doggedness of the journalist, said, "When conditions began to be normal again, I mean in 1948, the people first had to get their bellies full. That's understandable. After that they dressed themselves, furnished their apartments . . . bought refrigerators, TV sets, cars, on time. What next?"

Again and again it is our gross consumer-potential that troubles even well-meaning observers from abroad, to say nothing of the sterner German critics. I must say, I can't share their concern. I consider it improbable that people are going to get worse just because they are better off; that the programs of all political parties are therefore being aimed at making good hungry people satiated and bad. Besides, until now I haven't seen many signs pointing to the fact that the Germans are indecently well off.

They did eat their bellies full, granted; some couldn't let it go at that and today, to the joy of all caricaturists, drag more than two hundred pounds of circulation-threatened weight from their cars to their swivel chairs, and back again. They dressed themselves; some couldn't let it go at that and now have to model clothes for the rest of their fatiguing lives. They all have a great need to make up for happiness missed, and since many of them don't really know the meaning of the word, they sometimes go in for the hectic searching that leads to a rising consumption of sekt but rarely to a satisfying conclusion. In Germany most people work well, many earn well, but live well? No. The art hasn't reached such heights yet.

But there are practical criteria that tell another story. Let's take the oft-quoted television set. According to the latest statistics, 40 out of 1,000 Germans have a set. Compared as always with the population

count: the English own almost four times as many, citizens of the
United States, almost ten times. Or let's take the statistics for cars: 55
out of every 1,000 Germans are car owners; for Belgium the figures
are 71 out of every 1,000; 88 for England; 100 for France; 324 for the
United States.

After Point Zero of the years 1945 to 1948, this is a steep rise, but
it should cause anxiety only to those people who see prosperity as a
cause for anxiety. If one could assume that the curve would continue
to rise in the same proportion during the next ten years . . . but all
signs point the other way.

Anyone who tries to excuse Germany's prosperity finds himself in
a strange position, especially if he feels that German poverty would be
a much greater danger. He who has least to lose is always feared the
most. Statistics prove that the average German family income is about
600 marks, net. Then we have 22 in every 1,000 families whose net
income is over 1,800 marks. To say nothing of our millionaires. . . .

I happen to know three of them quite well. They have made their
millions in the field in which I earn my living, honestly and not badly.
All three are publishers. They live quite modestly. They own—all assets
taken together—millions. But they can't afford to lose three issues of
their publications, let's say because they're confiscated, or to have their
book business end up one year in the red. And there's a lesson to be
learned from this, not only for millionaires. The decisive prosperity
question is not: "What are you making?" but, "How long could you
and the people for whom you are responsible hold out without support, i.e., subsist on your principal?"

This question has never been asked. I can't, therefore, substantiate
with statistics a conviction that this survival period would be—in
Germany—on the average of four weeks, seen optimistically, certainly
lower than any other country in the Western world.

Ralph had asked, "So what do you do with all your money after
you've fed and clothed yourselves and have apparently succumbed to
the decadent luxuries?"

In this case a personal answer seems most fitting. "I have a refrigerator. My grandparents didn't have one; it hadn't been invented.
If you like, you can substitute a record player or television for the
refrigerator. I have a car; my grandparents didn't. But they had a coach
and horses, which were a lot more fun. If I'm lucky, if my family stays
well, if nothing intervenes (and in Germany we're rather accustomed
to the fact that things do), then I may, in a few years, reach the point,
which you, Ralph, and your countrymen of the so-called middle class
consider natural—and which was natural for my grandparents—where
I can call my house on its small plot of ground my own."

Real-estate prices have risen in West Germany during the last years
from 2 marks the square meter to 40, and whoever wants to buy
property in a big city may count on having to pay 100 marks the
square meter, and more. When I took out a building loan for 100,000
marks a few years ago, I was asked if I was contemplating buying a

feudal estate. Today you can barely purchase a one-family house in Hamburg with the money.

I can't see anything so terribly threatening in Germany's prosperity. Is it great enough to erase every consideration that does not concern money, buying potential, and new acquisitions? Here statistics help us again. Results of a survey to determine whether there was still a yearning for "ideals" in Germany, showed that only half the West German population felt that material prosperity was more important than anything else. The other half identified themselves with a man invented for this survey who declared, "I find today's political life much too materialistic. People have nothing on their minds but money. What we need are ideals for which people can work up some enthusiasm."

"People have nothing on their minds but making money." Half the German population admitted to that, but in the same breath 25 million said, "Of course, I'm not like that. The question also resulted in the discovery that men thought more of such ideals than women; college graduates more than those with only elementary and high-school educations; civil servants and professional people more than farmers and farm hands; those thirty to sixty years old more than Germans under thirty and over sixty.

A prosperity-swollen, economic-miracle land, and a noisy fair ground called Sylt are half-truths. Whoever conceals the other half for effect might be termed a good stylist, but he would be a poor reporter.

12. SYLT, AND THE EXPENSE-ACCOUNT MIRACLE (WITH NUDISM)

We had spent a very sekt-rich and informative evening in the bar of the casino in Westerland, but when I beckoned to one of the waiters and asked for the bill, he asked, discreetly, "You don't want it itemized, do you?" What he really wanted to know was, "Are you going to pay for this or let somebody else foot the bill?"

You can hear such questions being asked constantly all over Germany. "Do you want a receipt?" asks the taxi driver, and "What date do you want me to put on it?" (An especially popular question on Sundays.) "Shall I give you a receipt?" asks the attendant at the gas station. "For your tax statement," says the stewardess on the TEE train jokingly as she hands you a receipt for your opulent lunch. "Do you want me to put it all on one room?" the desk clerk in a very elegant hotel asks the gentleman who has just arrived with wife and children and doesn't look as if he wants to pay their bill himself.

According to cautious reckoning, half of all the costly automobiles, three-quarters of all TEE train and airplane tickets, four-fifths of the bills paid by Germans in luxury hotels, come under the heading of "expense account." Statistics on the subject of course don't exist. All you have to do, though, is watch the people and see how rarely they answer the question, "Do you want a receipt?" with, "No."

You see, Germany prosperity isn't a straightforward matter. A man earning 5,000 marks a month (and that's about as much as you can hope to earn honestly), who has family obligations and responsibilities, can hardly be termed a rich man. But if he can add a few thousand marks of expense account money to it—well, then he can really put on a show.

All this is no secret, and it isn't so very different in Germany than in the rest of the world, except that in Germany, as usual, it's wilder. And people will always come to the wrong conclusions.

To forestall the main argument—it is not true that here a few are leading a merry life at the expense of the general public. Have you ever ridden in a TEE train? Have you ever stopped off at a German luxury hotel? Did you find the people so merry? Much closer to the truth is the fact that three-quarters or more of the luxury which confuses the foreigner, or makes him envious or indignant, in German hotels, bars, and expensive places of amusement comes under the heading of "expense account." The German economic miracle, as expressed in champagne, caviar, and golf, is an expense-account miracle.

This has little to do with the German mentality, but a great deal to do with the German tax laws, and the thoroughness with which they are applied. Let's simplify the whole thing by giving an example that can't be proved (I'm not going to cause Herr Schultz any difficulties with the bureau of internal revenue), yet is valid.

Herr Schultz is a salesman, a big-time salesman, almost an executive. We met him on Sylt. He was staying there on his expense account and not doing badly. The Frisian Islands were a part of his territory, so why shouldn't he do the rounds at a time most agreeable not only for him, but also for the firm he represented?

"The revenue department allows me forty marks a day for board and lodging," Herr Schultz explained, "so that's forty marks I don't have to account for. But actually I need a hundred to a hundred and fifty marks daily to get along, because I've got to stay in first-rate hotels, drive up in a decent car, entertain my customers royally. So you can see I couldn't do without receipts. And while I'm collecting them, I might just as well get them for everything. Who can check whether they are business necessities or not? I can't. With receipts I manage to build the whole thing up to about two hundred marks daily (and nightly). Actually I'd much rather pay for the bit of personal fun I have myself, but if I did, I couldn't possibly make it come out right. For instance, I'll stay here two weeks; I imagine I'll make about five thousand. And I'm allowed five hundred and sixty for expenses, forty a day, right? That would leave me with approximately four and a half thousand taxable income, and I'd end up with less than three thousand marks. But I'm spending around two thousand here, so—net profit, one thousand marks. But if I add my receipts, I come up with around three thousand marks expenses and only have to pay taxes on two. So I finish up with fifteen hundred marks clear profit. Do you think that's too much? For two weeks? You have to take into consideration that it's the season. In the winter it's going to be less anyway.

I'm doing all right; I can't complain. But I wouldn't mind living more simply if such modesty didn't cost money."

Herr Schultz was the man so many people find "typically German": wobbly fat, several chins, at first sight not very prepossessing. But once you've summoned up enough imagination to see life as it really is, then suddenly he's not so unsympathetic any more. Anyway, he's not a type anyone need be afraid of; he's got a lot to lose.

Willy Helpach, usually a very moderate, dignified old gentleman, called the North German tax system "perverse." Weimar Minister of Finance, Johann Wolfgang von Goethe (1785) thought differently: "Taxes are tribute levied by the land rulers and protectors of the state, to be used for the general welfare and to further the general good, and should therefore be levied with equality." And in the oldest German tax listings (Trier 1363) it says quite simply, that "Kunz, the shop-keeper's boy . . . for himself and Metze, his concubine . . ." had to pay 20 schillings.

In those days everything was simple and clear; you could see what they were aiming at. Today Metze would have to be listed as "employee," in which case she would be tax deductible, or Kunz would have to marry her, in which case she wouldn't be. Instead of the ruler of the land, we have all sorts of tax profiteers—Bund, Länder, districts—that thrive on German respect for the authorities and don't have to account to any great extent for how they spend the taxpayer's money. The thought that they might be duty bound to give such an accounting is not considered advantageous for the state and is therefore not "the thing" to press. That duty is left to querulants. . . .

And nobody pays 20 schillings any more. The sums are less round and much higher. The amounts paid for income tax, wage tax, corporation taxes, sales tax, depreciation tax, occupational taxes, and real-estate taxes, is fixed by hundreds of laws with thousands of constantly changing articles. We have a complete "encyclopedia" of tax-deductible and non-tax-deductible items that is 204 pages thick and has gone into its second edition (Luchterhand Verlag). The tax-bureau personnel must have the patience of Job, the justice of Solomon, and the memory of an epic-writer before printing was invented. He should also have a sense of humor, like the examiner who notified a member of the German Bundestag as follows: "Your account is in order. However, we may deduce from it that, during the last month, you sat behind the wheel of your car for 48 days and nights, driving at an average speed of 140 kilometers an hour. . . ."

The German tax laws are the best illustration for the sort of injustice that occurs when the lawmakers try to please everybody: the state, with its many public handouts, its obligation to the fixed-income groups, its constantly expanding personnel; and the German taxpayer who, however much his willingness to work is praised or abused as a national virtue or vice, does like to expend his energy only where it will be worth while. The workingman in West Germany pays more taxes than anywhere else in the world. This statement, which can be proved statistically, is somewhat obscured by the fact that the number of tax-evasion artists who know how to shake off the onus gently, yet always "within the framework of the law," is high. If we were to subtract from all the ostentatious behavior, which isn't making us popular or happy, everything being spent on expense accounts, German modesty might yet become world famous.

Beyond the bars and restaurants, beyond the noise and roulette tables, lies the true island of Sylt: 40 kilometers long; 40 kilometers of sand and dunes in the west, from Hornum to the Elbow; 40 kilometers of open sea, sea breezes, and surf; an incomparable German island. On the other side, the east: the peace of the Wattensee between island and coast, calm, shallow, scarcely ever ruffled by the wind. North and south require only minutes to traverse on foot, from sea to Watt. In the center, the island rises; 15 kilometers lie between Westerland and the Hindenburgdamm.

Unforgettable pictures: the revolving beacon of Kampen's lighthouse in the late evening; the Red Cliff at sunset; the view across beach and waves from the Westerland Seenot, a little restaurant on the island's rim; the Wattenmeer in the afternoon, as seen from a chaise longue in the garden of the Kupferkanne (Coffeepot); the shifting dunes near List in the moonlight; the Morsum Cliff; in Keitum, the most beautiful village on the island, the old Romanesque St. Severin Church; the Vogelkoje near Kampen, for a change, in the heart of a woods that is small yet is an important source of shade for this sunny island.

The bathing resorts are the unexpected contradiction to the old adage that there is nothing new under the sun. For centuries, for thousands of years, people lived apparently without having it occur to them that it might be pleasant to bathe in the sea. And this in spite of the fact that associations between "bath" and "pleasure" go far back. In ancient Roman times, they were more pronounced than they are today, and bathing was immensely popular. But even then, when natural springs were used, there were only artificially installed baths. What could have happened to humankind that in the nineteenth century, and apparently never before that, they suddenly got the idea of bathing in the sea? All the big German bathing resorts were founded then: in 1885, North Sea resort Westerland, by Wulf Manne Decker and Dr. Ross. And it took even longer for people to become accustomed to bathing outdoors anywhere else. The first Public Bath was opened in Berlin-Wannsee in 1908.

Moral scruples probably played their part as an argument against bathing in the open, although—or perhaps because—the bathhouses, as we know already from Roman times, were often hard to distinguish from bordellos. Moral scruples were also responsible for the touching efforts of the first bathing resorts to get a woman's legs, which had only just left the cover of her skirt, covered by water as quickly as possible. Male and female were strictly separated from each other, and the bathing machines were wheeled far out before anybody went in the water. Behind their protection, the ladies got into the water unseen, or so they thought. Moritz Niese reports to the contrary from Helgoland (1837): "Although they undress in these bath houses on wheels, and although the ladies go to the left and the gentleman to the right . . . both sexes often get so close to each other that you can see without binoculars more than may be considered respectable. . . . At seaside resorts things are not taken very seriously."

Moritz Niese and his contemporaries would be slightly horrified were they to wander along the coast of Sylt today. From Hornum to Westerland or from Westerland to List are beautiful but quite strenuous walks, not only because they take six hours, but because the territory switches constantly from areas where the bathers wear clothes and those where they don't. Formerly these sections of beach where people disported themselves with their bodies fully exposed were called "Abyssinias," until the diplomatic service of that African state intervened, pointing out that the so-called underdeveloped states were not that underdeveloped, and they wished such insulting designations to cease. The protest came at a time when the authorities on Sylt (as in other bathing resorts) had begun to organize and administer nudity, and had bestowed on these areas, now fenced in, the well-sounding bureaucratic initials: FKK, for Freikörperkultur, or Free Body Culture.

The six of us walked through an FKK reserve, which happened to be on our way. We felt a little ashamed of the fact that we were dressed, and looked more dutifully at the sea than the foaming surf demanded. Suddenly a man loomed up, like us most unsuitably clad, and told us that walking through there was forbidden. Apparently it is no longer officially possible to walk the whole coastline from Rantum to Westerland. Too bad.

"Now that's typically German," said Andreas. "Even where all good middle-class conventions have been lifted, they manage to get in a *verboten.*"

"Well, I think it's great that anything like this can exist at all," said Dick, beaming. "Wouldn't be possible in the States."

"It reminds me of the Reeperbahn," said Ralph. "Strip tease."

"A little too much strip and too little tease," said Yvonne. "But, of course, I may be no judge of that."

"You know," Professor Spälti said in conclusion, "after you've walked through it, you're not quite so pleased any more with Mother Nature."

13. UP THE RIVER MOSEL, WITH CANAL WORRIES

I feel at home on the Mosel; that's why the last lap of our trip through Germany took us up that river. Besides, this had the advantage that we could gallantly escort the only lady in our group to the gates of her homeland.

In a country of beautiful river valleys, the Mosel valley is beyond compare. I insist on that, although today I suppose I should say was beyond compare. . . . Irrationally, in Old World fashion, the river winds between gently rising hills, 195 kilometers from Trier to Coblenz; as the crow flies it would be half the distance. If necessary, a lover of the Mosel valley would be willing to forego the 15 kilometers after Trier, and the last 20 kilometers before Coblenz.

The Mosel flows through poor country, true. There are no treasures underground and the fields are not richly fertile. On its summit, the Hunsrück range is bare, the Eifel desolate; yet somehow none of this detracts from its beauty. There are no big towns, yet one can live there, modestly, quietly, contentedly.

Compared with the mountainous country beyond the banks of the river, the Mosel valley was once not poor at all. The fields produced sufficient quantities of rye for the bread that was to be consumed with the wine; sheep grazed in the damp meadows along the shore; an abundance of fruit ripened in the mild climate, but above all the Riesling vines grew on the sunny slopes and brought to the valley riches that could not be measured in money alone. Johann Wolfgang von Goethe, who knew what he was talking about, wrote: "No doubt about it, wine bestows a freer character upon the regions where it grows and is consumed."

The vintners of the Mosel were a free and stubborn people, serenely stolid, with a peace of mind that was never rigid, piously devoted to a bacchanalian Catholicism. A few individuals like this are still around, but many look at their sons with misgivings: "All this is going to change. . . ."

The vintage Mosel wines start at Trier. Thirty kilometers downstream begins what the connoisseurs call the Middle Mosel, the most intoxicating wine region in Germany, beside, before, or after the Rhineland. The preposition is a matter of taste. Thörnich, Klüsserath, Trittenheim, Neumagen, Dhron; Piesport with its *Goldtröpfchen* (little drop of gold) and *Lay* (in my estimation Mosel wine number three); Wintrich, famous for its *Herrgott;* Brauneberg, home of the *Juffer* (Mosel wine number two, if you want my opinion); Bernkastel, and its world famous *Doktor* wines, for which year after year the demand is greater than the supply; Graach, with its *Himmelreich;* Wehlen, with its *Sonnenuhr;* and Zeltingen, with its *Schlossberg;* Ürzig, finally, with its *Würzgarten*, and Erden with *Erdener Treppchen*, my number one choice of Mosel wines, after *Doktor*, which is financially out of reach for the average wage-earner.

As the fame of the Middle Mosel spreads, so does the region. More and more places would like to belong to it, "just a little." Farther down the river, efforts are made to counterbalance the advantages of the Middle Mosel, its specific earth and slate and sunny slopes, with intensive propaganda or grape harvest festivals, as in Winningen. Those who love the delicate acrid flavor and taste of slate—the chief characteristic of Mosel wine, which has the richest bouquet and the lowest alcoholic content of any wine in the world—will find bottles that need no apology even below Enkirch, where the Middle Mosel definitely ends for the expert, at the very latest!

People who know and love the Mosel valley will not consider it mere chance that a man from this region discovered the principle of *coincidentia oppositorum;* contrasts may be great, but just when they are thought to be infinitely great, they become identical within God. Thus taught Nicholas von Cues, "the first modern philosopher," "Plato's greatest disciple of the Middle Ages," son of the most beautiful town on the Mosel: Bernkastel.

The marketplace of Bernkastel looks exactly as it did four hundred years ago: the fountain with its Michael column in the center, the Renaissance town hall on one side, top-heavy frame buildings with protruding balconies all around it. The Spitzhäuschen peers out of one of the little side streets; all this nestled between the vineyards of the Doktorberg on the one side and the Mosel on the other. And on the banks of the river stands the nearly seven-hundred-year-old Michael Tower, the slightly leaning landmark of a town with a disinclination for right angles.

Many roads lead to the Mosel, quiet little roads down the Eifel or Hunsrück. The road from Coblenz to Trier, which runs along the river, sometimes on the right, sometimes on the left, is not a fast superhighway. People in a hurry don't drive 195 kilometers to reach a goal only 100 kilometers away: the big Federal Highway from Coblenz to Trier runs across the Hunsrück. We drove up the Mosel on the right bank, always close to the river. On the curves there are signs: "Attention, Mosel!" Here the road has already lost some of its charm.

Castle Thurandt, above Alken, once a dreaded robber baron's castle, was our first stop. No art historian would consider it particularly interesting, and it really isn't very impressive. But it is in a good state of preservation, and seen from below, stretched across the mountaintop with its two towers, it commands respect. For Dick the trip suddenly became twice as attractive as before. "Oh, there are castles on the Mosel, too!"

I haven't counted them, but in my estimation there are nearly as many as on the Rhine: Niederburg and Oberburg near Kobern, Schloss Gondorf, the Ehrenburg above Brodenbach, Burg Bischofstein near Hatzenport, and so on upstream: Wildburg, Treis, Koraidelstein, Winneburg, Cochem, Arras, Montroyal, Landshut, Veldenz, Schloss Bekond. Most of them were destroyed by the French in the seventeenth century; only Burg Eltz, an hour's walk through the woods from Moselkern, was spared. It can therefore claim to be one of the most beautiful German castles extant.

When I asked people who still know all of Germany (there are fewer and fewer of them around), to name the most beautiful castles and palaces, they gave Burg Eltz seventh place. Schloss Sansouci came first; the residence of the Bishops of Würzburg next; then 3. Heidelberg Castle; 4. the Marienburg of the Grand Masters of Prussia; 5. the baroque palace Pommersfelde in Upper Franconia; 6. the Wartburg near Eisenach; 7. Castle Eltz; 8. Schloss Nymphenburg in Munich; 9. Schloss Schwetzingen, renowned for its park; 10. Castle Glücksburg on the Flensburg Ferry; 11. the Marksburg on the Rhine; 12. Schloss Brühl between Cologne and Bonn.

What can you do with a castle nowadays? Only a few big industrialists can afford such a luxurious way of life and therefore most castles are uninhabited ruins. Some serve as museums, others as youth hostels. The first attempt to make these defiant relics of a chivalric past profitable converted them into Burg Taverns and Castle Restaurants. The next step was the Castle Hotel. The reasoning probably ran as follows: city people and Americans love nature (castles are usually surrounded by a lot of nature) and a romantic past. Consequently they will want to stay in castle hotels. However, not all the hoped for swarms of well-heeled guests have materialized. Half of the fifty hotels of this type existing in Germany today joined in a combined advertising campaign with the slogan, "Be a Guest in a Castle." One of these castle hotels is Schloss Zell on the Mosel. It was once the castle of the Elector of Trier, and today has only one drawback: it is located in the center of town like all the other hotels. But it is pleasant to stay there, the food is excellent, and you may rest assured that the inevitable "Black Cat" stored in the cellar is really a product of the grapes grown in Zell.

The advantages and disadvantages of castle hotels are no secret, and they are all the more valid the more a castle is truly a castle, the older it is, the farther away from the city, and the higher the mountain on which it stands. Then its main attraction is a delightful tranquility, and in the Federal Republic, which must be the noisiest country in the world, that is saying a lot. Here anything going on in adjacent rooms remains mercifully unknown to you. The old knights evidently had very sensible ideas in this respect; anyway, they built very thick walls.

Where there is a castle, there is sure to be a park close by. Usually a vast estate goes with it, and this can provide the guest with warbling birds and ozone. The monotony of hotel routine blends in rather well with this enchanting backdrop so that you don't feel like a room number, but rather like an individual, surrounded by a world that has style, frankly speaking—a style you don't really know what to do with, yet you understand it vaguely and it gives you pleasant sensations.

The castle hotels, to sum up their drawbacks in a sentence, charge the prices of a luxury hotel without the luxuries. And these prices evidently are a handicap the founders of the castle hotels had not reckoned with. Based on a general opinion of widespread prosperity among Americans and Germans, the hoteliers had figured that nothing would be too expensive. True, the luxury hotels in the big cities are filled to capacity with guests who don't care whether they pay thirty marks or even a hundred for a room, but then they're not paying these prices themselves. Just the same, for the commercial traveler, the castle hotel is usually too far away from his business; and even if it takes less time to drive twenty kilometers on a highway than it does to cross a city from one end to the other, the traveling businessman fears that the office, checking his expenses, may say, "Listen Mr. Muller, was it really necessary for you to spend the night at a castle?"

Balancing the advantages of the castle hotel against its disadvantages, the results will depend, as in the case of every hotel or enterprise, on local circumstances and above all on management. As far as my experience goes, castle hotels offer well-to-do private travelers unusual, stylish, and very pleasant accommodations.

We didn't reach Zell on the first day of our trip along the Mosel, but stopped in Beilstein instead. "Along the Mosel, between Coblenz and Trier, there isn't another place with two hundred inhabitants as attractive for the tourist as the little town of Beilstein." The man who wrote this has a great future; he shows exemplary German caution. To be truthful, he would have had to add that Beilstein is the *only* place with two hundred inhabitants between Coblenz and Trier. But casting all such commendable caution to the winds, I would say that the following three Mosel towns are the most rewarding for the tourist: the big town of Trier, 87,000 inhabitants, because of its Roman monuments, above all the Porta Nigra and the thermes; the little town of Bernkastel, 6,000 inhabitants, because of its wine, its marketplace, and its immediate surroundings; and the tiny town of Beilstein for its own sake, for the sake of every single house in it.

Johann von Braunshorn was granted two things by Emperor Henry VII for the houses lying at the foot of his castle: urban privileges, and the permission to settle ten Jews there. This was in 1319, and must have been one of the earliest cases of Jewish emancipation in Germany. The reasons, however, were not to be found in enlightened humanitarianism, but in healthy egotism. People were needed who knew how to translate into cash the tithe delivered in produce.

The castle passed into the hands of the Seigneurs von Metternich, and began to deteriorate in the seventeenth century, but the Metternich of the Congress of Vienna was still the owner of the Beilstein estate. The town proper has hardly changed since then: the old church has become a community hall and the tithe storehouse, a warehouse; the Carmelite Convent and the Amtshaus Metternich were converted into hotels. The main street is actually a staircase which leads from the marketplace, probably the smallest marketplace anywhere in the world, to the church of the Carmelites. To right and left, two small parallel streets, really more like footpaths, lead into the Hunsrück. All three run at right angles from Beilstein's most impressive street which, coming from Cochem, leads to Senheim along the Mosel. If big cars meet on it, they have to maneuver a bit to get by.

Beilstein is rich in curiosities, the most conspicuous ones being the Black Madonna in the church above the town, and the Jewish cemetery on top of another hill behind the ruins of the castle. "Here hardly anything has changed since feudal days," one chronicler writes. As far as the scenery is concerned, this is correct, but otherwise . . .

We were sitting on the terrace of the *Alte Mosel Weinstube,* and my friend Alfred Beermann, vintner and Jew, was with us. Anyone who tries to bring up racial theories on the Mosel only makes himself ridiculous. For thousands of years, Celts, Franks, Romans, Jews, and later Germans and French, have intermingled here, and the vintners got accustomed long ago to not paying much attention to what "those over there in Coblenz," or "those over there in Trier," cooked up. They didn't change their ways in the Third Reich, and since my friend Beermann looks like every other vintner on the Mosel, perhaps a little more robust and a little smarter than average, no one bothered him. At first. But finally someone must have denounced him to "those over there in Coblenz" (or to "those over there in Trier"). Anyway, *agents provocateurs* came to Beilstein, two SD men in civilian clothes, and in Beermann's tavern started to speak derogatively of the Führer.

Two things must be explained at this point: Beermann's tavern lies high up above the Mosel and has a steep staircase leading down to the river, and Beermann had been warned. (I would also like to establish something else, namely that there were a lot of completely normal little people in Germany who certainly were not "resistance fighters," yet they often warned and helped their Jewish compatriots at the risk of their own lives.)

Alfred Beermann, therefore, listened to this Führer abuse for a while, then he walked over to the men and with the words, "This is what happens to people who insult the Führer," bounced them down the steep staircase. The two are said to have been badly hurt. Beermann, nevertheless, decided to wait in his vineyards for the Allies.

So there we were, sitting on the terrace of the *Alte Mosel Weinstube,* drinking Beilsteiner *Klosterberg,* a wine you can drink only where it is grown; not enough is available to make selling it commercially worth while. "Hardly anything has changed here?" Beermann couldn't get over his astonishment. "I'd say that except for the houses everything has changed."

Like all vintners, Beermann is conservative, and for a long time the conservatives had the upper hand in the Community Council. They were content to be far away from the mainstream of traffic. Only a few years before, busloads of office workers on outings had not been very welcome in Beilstein. Now all this has changed. Almost every second house has opened a restaurant. The castle has been leased to a man who has decked it out with garlands and lights, put a wire fence around it, and asks an admission fee of 75 pfennigs. The buses drive up the narrow street along the bank of the river, or on the other side where the street is wider, in which case their loads cross the river by ferry. Finally, when movie producers discovered that Beilstein offered ideal scenery for Mosel romanticism, it inevitably became a tourist attraction. Now, on Sundays during the summer, you hear lusty singing all over Beilstein, just as in other wine villages along the Mosel, only in Beilstein it sounds a little louder because the place is so famous and the space so limited.

The rhythm of life of a true Beilstein citizen was determined by the cultivation, gathering, and pressing of grapes. But this has changed, too. Nobody wants to work in the vineyards any more. The young people go to the city on their mopeds (a bicycle with a motor); they make more and easier money in the factories. The highest terraces, which means those with the best yield, are often not cultivated at all any more. Up there you can't simply run the plow through the rows as you can on level ground where far too many vines have been planted in recent years. The grapes that grow below are of poorer quality, but if fermentation is stopped in time, as the law permits, you get the kind of wine that is in greatest demand: sweet and cheap.

Old-timers of the Mosel valley are firmly convinced that only real wine connoisseurs are real human beings. If you can prove to a vintner that you can tell a Longuicher from a Bernkastel, and a Bernkasteler from a Calwiger, and wouldn't easily mistake the vintages of '59 and '61, then you are *persona grata* on the Mosel. But true wine connoisseurs are getting rare. A big world is reflected in little Beilstein.

It was the governments of Bonn and Paris, however, that shattered the peace of the Mosel valley. "Hitler couldn't have cared less than the gentlemen in Bonn about the people who were affected most." That was how the Jew Alfred Beermann put it.

When the French government renounced its claim to the annexation of the Saarland in 1955, it asked instead (in addition to some economic concessions) for the canalization of the Mosel to facilitate the transportation of coal from the Ruhr to the iron ore in Lorraine, thereby making it cheaper.

"I don't want to hear any more nonsense from those fine pedagogues and politicians about the loss of tranquility and simplicity, the disappearance of a natural way of life, about their concern for the leisure time of the industrial worker, and twaddle like that. When it was a question of preserving the most peaceful river valley in Germany or sacrificing it to industry, nobody lifted a finger."

This bitter accusation of Mosel vintner Beermann was uttered quietly, resignedly, which made it sound all the more convincing. Persons who have a conception of what the Ruhr region looked like before coal was discovered there, who knew the Rhine when it was not an industrial river, the Upper Rhine before it was "regulated," the Neckar before it was "graded," will understand what Alfred Beermann dreads: the death of a landscape.

"True," he admitted, "right here on the Mosel, the protests weren't as loud as I would have wished, but, of course, there are a lot of people who hope to gain greater influence by puddling up the region. [*Vertümpelung* is what the vintners call the canalization.] The people of the waterways control, who have nothing to do but check the pontoons once a year, are proud that now more important jobs are coming their way. In Coblenz and Trier, the chambers of commerce hope new factories will spring up out of the dirt. Ambitious mayors and local civil servants see greater power for themselves; they're not vintners!

Quite often they're not even from around here! But they know how to get publicity for their ideas. The Mosel region has lived off its wines for two thousand years. Frankly, I'm glad I'm too old to witness the industrialized Mosel Puddle Region."

Fourteen dams are being built, slowly, with obviously waning enthusiasm, because the day will come when the coal of the Ruhr, replaced by atomic energy, will no longer be important enough to justify the "puddling" of the Mosel. But the dams will be there; nobody ever tears down dams once they have been built.

What the vintners mean by puddling is that the waters of the Mosel will not flow freely any more. Insects, soot, and diesel fumes will not only affect the people but the vines as well. And the dams don't even promise the one thing that would have been in their favor from the winegrowers' point of view, namely protection from the catastrophic floods that engulf the Mosel villages every few years.

Next morning, driving up the Mosel from Beilstein, we came upon one of these construction sites, as we had twice before at regular intervals. The barren countryside is studded with barracks; ugly metal frames are being driven into the river bed; streets are torn up, covered with debris, made practically impassable for the time being. The noise of machinery echoes through the peaceful valley. Even my foreign friends were saddened by it, although it was hardly their concern. Certainly this project is not adding to the beauty of the Mosel valley, and if it has been undertaken without thoroughly weighing all arguments for and against, if the winegrowers, who are the ones mainly affected by it, were not given a decisive vote in the matter, then it isn't easy to be proud of it.

At the end of the day we reached the region for which the Mosel has to be canalized, but, of course, you can't blame the Saarlanders for it. Oddly enough, the same politicians who had protested against any annexation of German territory in the east [and rightly so] had written off the Saarland when suddenly it fell into their laps again. The Saarlanders simply didn't want to be written off.

Iron ore from Lorraine and coal from the Saarland belong together. This is one of the axioms of those realistic politicians who believe they are being very clever when they think in terms of industrial potential. This meant that either Lorraine had to become German (as it did in 1871) or the Saarland had to become French (as it did in 1918 and 1945). Persons who mentioned shyly that a few human beings happened to be living around the iron ore of Lorraine and the coal mines of the Saarland were dismissed as dreamers and visionaries. When the Federal government could not succeed in persuading the various French governments to return the Saar, it decided to combine a utopian political concept with renunciation of the Saarland: they claimed that the "germ cell of a United States of Europe" was located there. This was the tenor of the referendum that the population of the Saar was to vote on on October 23, 1955. But the Saarlanders didn't want to be renounced; they didn't want to be a "germ cell" either. Almost 97 per cent went to the polls; 67.7 per cent rejected the European Saar Statute. When the French government recognized this decision and consequently returned the Saar to Germany, it did more toward a French-German rapprochement than the "germ cell" could ever have accomplished. Perhaps they could have done without a Mosel canalization, too?

14. THE WORLD AS SEEN FROM GERMANY

In the Land which for centuries has been a cause of strife between Germany and France, which according to the will of a few idealists and opportunists was to have been the germ-cell of a united Europe, but whose population preferred to remain German; in the tenth and youngest of the German Länder, the Saar, our trip through Germany came to an end. The last two chapters of this book are dedicated to the conversation that took place on our last evening. We were the guests of a book dealer, and were finding out that there wasn't anything wrong with Saar wine either.

To be the guest of a book dealer is a good thing. Constant association with books results in a distinct and especially lovable type of person: too familiar with the commercial value of a book to slip off into purely intellectual estheticism; too accustomed to the written word's power of projecting beyond every day life to put business proficiency above everything else.

"Now we have seen quite a bit of Germany," said Dick, "and have found out a lot about it. We have told you [meaning me] politely I hope, but I think always clearly, what we think of Germany. How would it be if you were to tell us tonight what the Germans think of us?"

Unfortunately his suggestion was received with enthusiasm. I was therefore again forced to speak as "the" German, which is pure fraud. So again I fled into statistics, without which I would have an even greater feeling of guilt than I do about everything I have put down here.

In October, 1959, a survey asked a representative cross section of the German people, "We hear conflicting viewpoints about which nations Germany should work with most closely. What is your opinion?" The statisticians probably had good reasons for adding a list of nine countries to the question. Austria and Switzerland didn't figure in the answers because they were not on the list. Some of the other countries wouldn't have been mentioned, I am sure, if they hadn't been on the list.

The hierarchy of our friends, or rather—of the countries with which Germans wish their government to be closely associated were: 1. The United States, 81 per cent. 2. England, 49 per cent. 3. France, 48 per cent. 4. Japan, 32 per cent. 5. Italy, 31 per cent. 6. Russia, 31 per cent. 7. Spain, 27 per cent. 8. Poland, 25 per cent. 9. Israel, 19 per cent.

Totally unexpected to me was that Russia with 31 per cent was ahead of Poland. Even the Catholic Rhenish publication *Mercury* is sometimes inclined to forgive the Poles for being Communists. I am sure opportunism plays a major part in the Russian figure. If there is to be any "working together," then rather with a big than a small enemy. But that doesn't explain everything. The timing of the question is probably important, too: October, 1959. Khrushchev had just visited President Eisenhower, and the two had apparently got on very well at Camp David; some papers were already conjuring up "the spirit of Yalta," and quite a few got on that bandwagon, until the next stop. It may also be considered astonishing to find Japan and Italy in such high positions. The suspicion arises that the old Berlin-Rome-Tokio Axis is not quite dead. But apart from such surprises, the list sounds correct: the United States way up front, England and France close rivals for second place; the smaller countries as also-rans, then the absolute nadir, where sympathy and antipathy are balanced. (This is about where Poland lies.)

Differences of sex, birth, politics, and age, played astonishingly little part in our evaluation of our neighbors; the only real discrepancy in percentages: the Americans seem to be very popular with sexagenarians (75 per cent), but they are even more popular with the twenty-five-year-olds (85 per cent).

"That's very flattering for Mr. O'Connor," said Professor Spälti, "but as a neutral, and since Switzerland isn't even on the list, I may perhaps voice the suspicion that America's place at the top might have something to do with the fact that they happen to be the leaders of the Western World, or anyway"—and his eyes twinkled—"we think they are, and the Germans always did have a weakness for leaders."

That's one explanation, certainly. A nation that feels threatened by the greatest power in the East would tend quite naturally toward the greatest power in the West. But it doesn't explain everything. The fact should also be taken into consideration that the Americans were the first to banish all vindictiveness from their German policy.

"That's easy!" said Yvonne. "All they had behind them was a short, successful war. They came, they saw, they conquered!"

Possibly. But it should also be noted that the Americans didn't stop at not kicking the enemy when he was down, but quickly began to help him to his feet again.

"You were richer than we were," said Ralph. Dick nodded; all probably true. But many Germans have visited the United States since then, and I don't know one who hasn't come back a friend or at least an admirer of the United States.

That's the way it is. And why is it like that? J. B. Conant, the first American Ambassador to Bonn once said that more than one-sixth of the American people could lay claim to one or more German ancestors. Most of us like to hear explanations like that. Even if the Germans were able to achieve only promising beginnings in their own country, which invariably ended in this or that catastrophe, yet they are, like the Jews, to some extent "the salt of the earth."

Let those who are better versed than I in historic-ethnographic subjects decide how much truth there is in all this. It is certainly not meant to be interpreted as a justification of West German government policy. Such a neutral observer as Lord d'Abernon, first English Ambassador to the Weimar Republic, writes in the introduction to his memoirs that admiration for the United States is greater in Germany than in any other European state; and he found the strong sympathy and instinctive understanding between the two countries difficult to analyze and explain. Historian Golo Mann moves the effects of such a relationship still further back when he writes: "Since the beginning of the 19th century, German history has been characterized by a surrender to things new . . . to materialism, to that which is called Americanization, to such an extent that some parts of Germany seem to want to look more American than America."

Here a note of criticism can be felt. There are Germans who are not very happy about their relationship to America, especially about this wanting to be more American than the Americans. But on the whole, the German attitude toward the United States is positive, and above all, unproblematic. This becomes particularly evident when compared with the attitudes toward England and France.

When the survey asked with which nations the Germans would like to be closely associated, they of course hoped that several of the nine countries given would be named, and those asked did name on the average of three and four. Unfortunately the statisticians let a highly interesting revelation of their survey escape them: Which of the nine countries were named together? Probably all combinations. I can even imagine some naïve, slap-happy optimist listing America and Russia. But I have the feeling that England and France were rarely mentioned together. Anyway, you come across it all the time: an amiable little circle of Germans is assembled (perhaps in Cologne); the conversation is about France and everybody is pleased with everybody else's broad viewpoint, until suddenly the topic of conversation is England. . . . Or: an amiable little circle of Germans is assembled (perhaps in Hamburg); the conversation is about England and everybody is pleased with everybody else's broad world viewpoint, until suddenly the topic of conversation is France. . . .

Oh European misery! At some time or other in their long history, every European nation has once been the enemy of every other, and these are the periods that some people will never forget. The English and French of course were frequently bitter adversaries. As long as the North German and South German states were nicely separated, the English marched with the Prussians and the French with the Bavarians. In 1914, when Prussians and Bavarians marched together for the first time, England and France saw themselves forced into an obviously unnatural alliance.

I can see historians turning gray over such historic oversimplifications, so I hasten to quote a historian. "Between 1890 and the [first]
World War," writes Gonzague de Reynold, "it was fashionable to declare that the Teutons were superior to the Latins, or certainly that the
Anglo-Saxons were superior to the French. In those days, the political
inferiority of France and certain symptoms of dissolution in that country disturbed the best men. The French themselves liked to speak of
their own decadence, and the Germans always listened attentively.
Sociologist Edmond Demolins published a book in 1897, which attracted some attention: *Anglo-Saxon Superiority: To What Is It Due?*
Leadenhall Press, London 1920)."

Today you don't hear much talk any more about Anglo-Saxon superiority; not in France; not in Germany either. What we like and
admire about the English—if we like and admire them—is, I suppose,
their sense of fair play, in sports, in politics, in daily life; their dry
sense of humor; and in spite of everything, over and over again, their
reliability. "John Bull may be the coldest friend, but he is the safest
neighbor and the most straightforward and generous enemy. He guards
his own castle like a pasha, but he never tries to break into anyone
else's." (Heinrich Heine.)

"And what do you like about the French?" asked Yvonne, rather
enchantingly piqued. "When you like them?" To which, of course,
there was only one answer, "French girls!"

"I'm afraid we're not going to find out anything about Austria and
Switzerland," said Professor Spälti, "and only because they weren't included in the survey."

"If you won't quote me . . ." I had been waiting for a long time
for the opportunity to use just once this phrase which I get to hear
daily, and which makes my work so difficult. "If you won't quote me,
then I'd like to say that most Germans don't like to consider Switzerland, much less Austria, as foreign countries. By which I don't mean
that I think the old *Anschluss*, or a new one, is threatening. But for the
average German citizen, a foreign country really begins only where
he can't understand the language. We look upon the Austrians—in a
way the Swiss, too—as Germans who have been a little luckier in history, by which I don't mean that they haven't also done a lot to merit
their favorable position."

"Fair enough," said Dick. "I think all of us would agree to that. But
I think Germany's relationship to the East Bloc states is even more interesting because it's so controversial."

Of course he was right. It is a curious relationship, and certainly
much more complicated than it appears to be. It isn't stable; on the
contrary, it is very unstable. This instability however is not peculiar to
Germany's relationship with the Soviet Union (which after all determines Germany's relationship with the other East Bloc states). It
wasn't so very long ago that you could hear quite friendly opinions
about Russia coming from the United States. Eugene Davidson, above
all suspicion of communism, writes in *The Death and Life of Germany*:

"In general, he [Cordell Hull] thought Russia had been peaceably inclined, and Roosevelt said he agreed entirely. Stimson said the Russians were 'in their own strange way' . . . magnificent allies." And in the same book, Joseph E. Davies, former American Ambassador to Russia, "thought that what they were practicing in Russia was close to real Christianity. . . . Even Churchill wondered how far his power went, and in a letter to Eden, written in 1944, still referred to him [Stalin] in a hopeful moment as 'that great and good man.' " And to Acheson's statement that there was no greater opposition between the United States and Russia "today" than in the time of Jefferson and Tsar Alexander, Joseph Davies added (according to Davidson), "that no government or people has had a better or more consistent record of effort to preserve peace and security for mankind than the Soviet Union."

On the heels of this positive phase came Korea (negative); Stalin's death and Camp David (positive); Khrushchev's meeting with Eisenhower in Paris and with Kennedy in Vienna (negative); the Test Ban Treaty (positive). It isn't a very pleasant thought that the world may one day fall victim to such phase fluctuations.

So what does determine German-Russian relationships?

Perhaps the time has come at last to separate the people of the Federal Republic from those in the DDR. The survey was intended, of course, for West Germany only, but whenever I can, I speak of Germany as a whole, and I can see few reasons why the results of the survey couldn't be considered representative also for East Germany. "But in East Germany they think much more highly of the Americans and English and French because they are equivalent to their hopes for freedom," someone who had fled East Germany assured me. "But they think much less of the Americans and English and French in East Germany because they threaten world peace," said someone who had stayed there. And this is valid in reverse for the Soviet Union.

In East Germany, Russia is hated as the protective power of a not-generally-very-popular regime, yet respected as the leading power in the part of the world in which, after all, these people live. And one would do well to not underestimate this second factor. We Germans enjoy a reputation, which I fear we have merited, for being able to adapt ourselves very quickly, perhaps too quickly.

The relationship between West Germany and Russia is clouded by three circumstances which make it impossible to see clearly. The first lies in the past, Stalin's revenge, which sent Soviet troops bursting into what is today called East Germany, plundering and raping, truly impossible to tell apart from the "Asiatic hordes" of Goebbels' propaganda; and which kept German soldiers prisoner in the Soviet Union for so many years after the war. Such things have their aftereffects and are not easily forgotten. It is so much easier for us to forget that in World War II no country in the world suffered so much from the Germans as the Soviet Union.

The second originates in Germany. In this case the Soviet Union is not seen as Russia, but as the greatest Communist power in the world.

Nine out of ten Germans are convinced that the peace of the world could not be endangered in the next thirty or fifty years—*i.e.,* until China is an industrial power—if the Soviet Union did not exist.

And the third is the point where we see red: East Germany, the DDR. We blame the Soviet Union for this bastard in whom we hate ourselves. It is not clear if and since when it was the will of the Soviet Union to create this state, but it becomes increasingly clear that without the Soviet Union it would not exist. And with that we have come to the chief question of Germany's political life: When a German in Hamburg is looking at "the world as Germany sees it," does he see Leipzig as "outside" or "inside" Germany?

15. GERMANY'S PLACE IN THE WORLD

"But don't the Germans tend to overdramatize the partition of their country?" Ralph wanted to know. "Wouldn't it be possible to see it more soberly? Something like this: We started a war and lost it; now we have to pay for that. The Eastern Territories and East Germany, or if you like, East and Middle Germany, are the price. So let's make the Federal Republic a state we can be proud of."

Sounds very sensible. Formulated honestly though, it would have to run like this: "We lost a war and for three years atoned for it fairly thoroughly; the rest will be paid by the people of Dresden and Königsberg," and that doesn't leave you feeling so good. And you feel still worse if, like myself, you only started thinking and writing like this in 1961, the Year of the Wall. Are we to pay with Berlin too? And when is this payment at the expense of others going to stop?

Again Germany lies in a magnetic field of powerful interests that overlap and divide the country. The largest and most vital part is the Federal Republic between the North Sea and the Alps, between the Elbe and the Rhine. What place is it to fill in the world? What does the world expect of it? We know the world doesn't want to *am deutschen Wesen genesen,* an old nationalistic dream exploited by Hitler; translated into today's political idiom it means to "recover along the lines of the German image." May we expect that in spite of this the world would risk a third world war for this Germany? A war over the outcome of which only those could have any illusions who successfully keep their eyes shut, their ears shut, but unfortunately not their mouths shut?

It is quite possible that, since 1945, much has been neglected. "In the moment of its collapse, Germany might have shamed and stirred the world by an act of profound sincerity and remorse. At the time I hoped for a moment that the lost feature of humility, which seems so constructive in Dürer's drawings, might again be limned in or added to that strangely one-sided German face which has become so stubborn. Perhaps there were a few people who felt this, whose wishes and hopes were directed toward such a correction. Now the fact that it did not happen begins to show and take its revenge. Something was left undone which would have put all things in proportion. Germany failed to present its purest, its best dimension, as restored on the oldest foundations—it failed to renew and reorient itself basically; it failed to create for itself that fresh dignity which has humility for its root. All it thought of was salvation in a superficial, quick, suspicious and avaricious sense. It wanted to act, arise, and get away, instead of suffering, overcoming, and preparing for its miracle according to its most innate nature. It wanted to remain rigid instead of change. One feels therefore only: something was neglected. A date is lacking to which one might have clung. A rung is missing in the ladder, hence this indescribable anxiety, this fear, this premonition of a sudden and precipitous fall."

How the metaphors fit! How the words are suited! Every one of them could have been written today if someone were alive today who could write like that, like Rainer Maria Rilke in the year 1923.

Perhaps reality was never able to keep pace with such sublime expectations. I can see another, much less lofty possibility, one which could therefore be more easily realized: we were on our way to becoming a nation of happy consumers, loyal to the Western Alliance, otherwise totally disinterested in world politics; we seemed to be on our way to becoming slightly contemptible but utterly harmless. But we shunned the role like a star who is asked to be an extra. Perhaps we should have played it, but the director was of a different opinion.

Why did two great world ideologies have to meet head-on in Germany? There we are, saddled again with a mission and not at all sure which one. Bulwark against the east? Bulwark against Leipzig and Dresden? If it were a question of industry, thoroughness, organizing talent, we would have nothing to fear. Nor would we be found lacking in smartness, ability, bravery, and loyalty. But I am afraid they are going to ask of us just what we have least of: the imagination to understand somebody else's point of view and still preserve our own: the tough humility of the democrat; *suaviter in modo, fortiter in re*: the art of making compromises without falling flat on your face.

Meanwhile there isn't much point in deploring the chances lost or lamenting the "if only's" and "had we but's." After all, the Germans do bring with them two attributes which, if only they might be recognized and acknowledged as good, might someday bring desirable results: our childish admiration of all things foreign, and our vague but sincere enthusiasm for a United States of Europe. Neither is anything new; there is therefore a good possibility that they will still be ours the day after tomorrow.

"Would the Germans be what they are today," wrote the philosophical globe-trotter, Hermann Graf von Keyserling from the Baltic provinces, "without their notorious fault of preferring what is foreign?" And deputy Von Bismarck, in the Prussian Chamber, 1849, irascibly: "For us all things foreign always seem to have a certain distinguished aspect." As early as 1825, we find the following entry in Goethe's conversations with Eckermann, January 10: "It is the nature of the German to honor all things foreign in his own way, and to conform to alien peculiarities." And Bismarck again, this time in 1863: "The tendency to be enthusiastic about foreign nationalities, even when this can be achieved only at the expense of their own Fatherland, is a form of political sickness which is found unfortunately only in Germany."

What may have seemed a form of sickness to the man who saw his historic mission in a new formation of the German Reich, could turn out to be quite healthy today under different circumstances, not only for the Germans. Let us say also for Europa, although we don't enjoy saying "Europa" any more, since the word has had to serve far too often as camouflage for highly un-Europaic machinations. For the Germans of my generation, and for those a little younger, Albert Camus was the European writer we admired most, and loved. Whatever he had to say, fell on ready ears. And in his *Letters to a German Friend*, he says: "I must make a confession. During the entire time we were stubbornly and silently serving only our country, an idea and a hope were ever present within us, namely the idea of Europa, the hope of Europa. It is true that we haven't spoken about it for five years, but that is because *you* were speaking too loudly about it. And here, too, we don't yet speak the same language; our Europa is not yours."

I like to think that Camus might have found a point of agreement with Nietzsche, who wrote: "I look past all these wars of nationalities, new empires, and whatever may stand behind them. I am concerned with One Europa. I can see it evolving slowly and hesitantly. Actually it has been the total soul effort of all the more broad-minded and profoundly thinking people of this century to prepare this new synthesis, and to anticipate tentatively the European of the future: only in their weaker moments, or when they grew old, have they fallen back into the national narrow-mindedness of their fellow citizens—then they were patriots!"

"That's fine!" said Dick. "But what good is it going to do you in the next Berlin crisis?"

Tactically speaking—none. Writers should be careful not to interfere with the politician. It is the writer's job to take inventory, to describe what he sees and hears, to report what he has read and observed. He must be able to afford the luxury of complete freedom from prejudice. "The man who acts always lacks conscience; only the observer has a conscience." (Goethe.) All that he who is observing can do is draw maps, according to his best knowledge and conscience, and perhaps put in a few markers. To find passable routes is the concern of the man who acts.

"Really, Dick, I don't think you should ask him questions which the German Foreign Minister—no, the Bundeskanzler—should be answering. Or the President of the United States!" Yvonne speaking. "I've got a much more personal question. It was the first one I asked, and he still hasn't answered it."

"But I haven't forgotten it," I told her. " 'Do you like being a German?' Wasn't that it? And today, when you are not so apt to mis-understand me, I can say yes. Yes, I love this Germany, all of this Germany; and I love the Germans, those living in Hamburg, and those in Leipzig and Dresden. Sometimes it is a painful love, and there's a lot of defiance in it, a feeling of 'in spite of': in spite of the politicians, judges, and party functionaries of the DDR whose hatred of the Federal Republic is German hatred; in spite of some things in West Germany which may be hateful; in spite of Germany's past which nobody can deny; in spite of those people who don't seem to have learned anything from it; in spite of those Germans who can't derogate all things German enough as long as their scorn remains nicely gen-eral and abstract; and in spite of a lot of things that I have tried to describe in this book as I see them."

Why so much defiance yet so much love?

For that I have no sensible answer. An experience from my youth might explain it.

Before anti-Semitism became a state doctrine, it was considered re-fined, where I grew up, to be a little anti-Semitic. But we had only three Jewish families in our town, and all three "belonged." They weren't treated any differently than anyone else; they were friends. Caught up in the youthful superstition that life was conducted along sensible lines, this bothered me, so I asked, "How can you be anti-Semitic and have Jewish friends?" I shall never forget the answer. "Oh, you mean the Fürths, the Wolfs, and the Beermanns? They're excep-tions."

Today I know—let's say fifty Germans, the way one gets to know friends and close acquaintances. I don't find them less lovable than the English, French, Americans, Swiss, and Austrians I know. Can they possibly all be "exceptions"?

Of course they are individual Germans, and it is in Germany that so many foreign observers declare again and again how likable the in-dividual is, and how frightening the sum-total, the people as a whole, the *Germans*. And are they really likable? The provincial-European Germans and pseudo-big-industrialist Germans, who in some Swiss hotel or other see themselves as focal points and the personnel as people to yell at? The car supermen who weave through heavy traffic, take every advantage, and think they're great? The pseudo-brave, who with their heads obsequiously bowed, grow to super-dimensional heights of arrogance whenever they're sure nobody is going to rap their knuckles? The self-righteous apostles of freedom who think they are infallible, and don't want to grant anyone the most vital of all human freedoms: the freedom to err? Are all of them really likable?

Of course not. But look . . .

BIOGRAPHICAL INDEX

When not otherwise defined, the persons referred to in this index are German or wrote in German. The titles of books by post World-War II German authors, which have been translated into English, are given whenever available.

A

ADENAUER, KONRAD (1876———). Lawyer. Mayor of Cologne, 1917–1933. Removed from office by the National Socialists; reinstated by the Americans in March, 1945. Removed from office again by the British, October, 1945. One of the founders of the CDU (Christian Democratic Union). Its chairman since 1946. Became Chancellor of the Federal Republic in 1949. Resigned and was replaced by Chancellor Erhard, CSU (Christian Socialist Union) in 1963. 15, 32, 47, 99, 125, 127, 129, 131, 132, 133, 134, 135, 136, 137, 139, 140, 144, 207

ALTENBERG, PETER, pseudonym for RICHARD ENGLÄNDER (1859–1919). Writer of impressionistic prose. 150

ANDERSCH, ALFRED (1914———). Writer. (*Flight to Afar*, Coward-McCann, 1958. *The Redhead*, Pantheon, 1961.) 152, 154

ARNDT, ERNST MORITZ (1769–1860). Son of a peasant, university professor, freedom fighter. 48

ARNIM, ACHIM VON (1781–1831). Poet and writer. 149

ARNIM, BETTINA VON (1785–1859). Sister of Clemens Brentano. From 1811, wife of Achim von Arnim. 149, 203

AUERBACH, BERTHOLD (1812–1882). Writer. 151

B

BAMM, PETER, pseudonym for CURT EMMRICH (1897———). Writer. (*The Invisible Flag*, Day, 1956.) 33

BARTELS, ADOLF (1862–1945). History of Literature. Racial theorist. 145

BARTH, KARL (1886———). Swiss Protestant theologian. Professor at the University of Basel. 67, 116, 117

BECKMANN, MAX (1884–1950). Painter and illustrator. 33

BEHAIM, MARTIN (1459–1507). Explorer and geographer. 188

BENJAMIN, WALTER (1892–1940). Scholar and writer. 150

BENN, GOTTFRIED (1886–1956). Poet and writer. (*Primal Vision: Selected Writings*, New Directions, 1960.) 114, 115

255

ENZENSBERGER, HANS MAGNUS (1929——). Writer and poet. 154
ERHARD, LUDWIG (1897——). Co-responsible for the Federal Republic's "Economic Miracle." Since 1963, Chancellor of the Federal Republic. 57, 58, 129, 131, 133
ESCHENBACH, WOLFRAM VON See WOLFRAM VON ESCHENBACH.
EULENSPIEGEL, TILL See TILL EULENSPIEGEL.
EULER, LEONHARDT (1707–1783). Mathematics, physics, astronomy. 114

F

FABRE D'EGLANTINE, PHILIPPE FRANÇOIS NAZAIRE (1755–1794). French writer, dramatist, and revolutionary. 29
FECHTER, PAUL (1880–1958). Writer and journalist. 145
FEUCHTWANGER, LION (1884–1958). Writer. Emigrated to the United States in 1933. 150
FICHTE, JOHANN GOTTLIEB (1762–1814). Philosopher. 33, 145, 149
FISCHER, KUNO (1824–1907). Philosopher. 67
FISCHER, S. (SAMUEL) (1859–1934). Publisher. 150, 194
FLEMING, PAUL (1609–1640). Lyric poet. 114
FONTANE, THEODORE (1819–1898). Poet and writer. 151, 215
FOUQUÉ, FREIHERR DE LA MOTTE (1777–1843). Poet and writer. 149
FREYTAG, GUSTAVE (1816–1895). Writer and historian. 114, 151
FRICKE, GERHARD (1901——). Professor of Literature in Mannheim. 145
FRIEDELL, EGON (1878–1938). Austrian critic and writer. 222
FRINGS, THEODORE. German professor in Leipzig. 31
FRISCH, MAX (1911——). Swiss writer and dramatist. X, 152
FROBENIUS, LEO (1873–1938). Ethnologist and explorer. 145

G

GAISER, GERD (1908——). Writer. (*The Last Squadron*, Pantheon, 1956. *Final Ball*, Pantheon, 1959.) 151, 152
GEIBEL, EMANUEL (1815–1884). Poet. 114
GELLERT, CHRISTIAN FÜRCHTEGOTT (1715–1769). Poet and writer. Professor in Leipzig. 30, 33, 114
GENTZ, FRIEDRICH VON (1764–1832). Political writer. 149
GERHARDT, PAUL (1607–1676). Composer of hymns. 33
GIDE, ANDRÉ (1869–1951). French writer. Nobel Prize, 1947. 205
GLUCK, CHRISTOPH WILLIBALD (1714–1787). Composer. 211
GOERDELER, KARL FRIEDRICH (1884–1945). Executed in connection with the attempted assassination of Hitler. 213
GOETHE, JOHANN WOLFGANG VON (1749–1832). Poet, dramatist, writer, and statesman. 7, 30, 33, 34, 68, 99, 110, 151, 153, 186, 190, 192–194, 202, 204, 210, 225, 236, 239, 252, 253
GOLLWITZER, HELMUT (1908——). Theologian. Professor in Berlin. 67
GÖRING, HERMANN (1893–1946). Airforce Chief under Hitler. 82, 212
GOTTSCHED, JOHANN CHRISTOPH (1700–1766). Professor of Philology, Leipzig University. 30, 114
GRASS, GÜNTER (1927——). Writer. (*The Tin Drum*, Pantheon, 1962. *Cat and Mouse*, Harcourt Brace, 1963.) 152, 154
GRILLPARZER, FRANZ (1791–1872). Austrian dramatist. 149
GRIMM, JACOB (1785–1863). Founder of German philology. With his brother Wilhelm, collected, edited, and published *Grimm's Fairy Tales*. Also the German Dictionary.
GRYPHIUS, ANDREAS (1616 1664). Poet. 114
GUNDOLF, FRIEDRICH (1880–1931). Historian of literature. Friend and disciple of Stefan George, member of the George Circle. 68

H

HAAS, WILLY (1891——). Writer and Journalist. Formerly editor of the Berlin weekly, *Literarische Welt*. 150

K

KAFKA, FRANZ (1883–1924). Writer. 150

KAISEN, WILHELM (1887——). Politician, SPD (German Socialist Party). Bremen senator, 1928–1933. Political arrest. Since 1945 Mayor of Bremen and President of the Senate. 137

KAISER, GEORGE (1878–1945). Dramatist. Emigrated to Ascona, 1938. 150

KANT, IMMANUEL (1724–1804). Philosopher. 98, 99, 100, 113, 145

KÄSTNER, ERICH (1899——). Poet and writer. (*Emil and the Detectives*, Double-day, 1930. *Lisa and Lottie*, Little, Brown, 1951. *The Animals' Confernce*, McKay, 1953. *A Salzburg Comedy*, Ungar, 1957. *Emil and the Three Twins, 35th of May, When I Was a Boy*, Watts, 1961.) 20, 33

KELLER, GOTTFRIED (1819–1890). Swiss writer and poet. 151

KERR, ALFRED, pseudonym for *Kempner*. (1867–1948). Drama critic. 150

KESTEN, HERMANN (1900——). Writer. (*The Children of Guernica*, Longmans Green, 1939. *Copernicus*, Roy, 1945. *The Twins of Nürnberg*, L. B. Fischer, 1946. *Ferdinand and Isabella*, Wyn, 1946. *Happy Man*, Wyn, 1947. *Casanova*, Harper, 1955, Collier, 1962.) 150

KEYSERLING, HERMANN GRAF VON (1880–1946). Writer. 99, 252

KINDERMANN, HEINZ (1894——). Germanist. Professor of Theatre Science in Vienna. 145

KIRCHHOFF, ALFRED (1838–1907). Geographer. 67

KIRST, HANS HELMUT (1914——). Writer. (*The Lieutenant Must Be Mad*, Har-court Brace, 1951. *Forward Gunner Asch*, Little, Brown, 1956. *The Return of Gunner Asch*, Little, Brown, 1957. *The Seventh Day*, Doubleday, 1959. *Officer Factory*, Doubleday, 1963. *Night of the Generals*, Harper, 1964.) 151, 152

KISCH, EGON ERWIN (1885–1948). Communist writer and reporter. 150

KLEE, PAUL (1879–1940). Painter. 156

KLEIST, HEINRICH VON (1777–1811). Writer and dramatist. 20, 82, 204, 211

KLOPSTOCK, FRIEDRICH GOTTLIEB (1724–1803). Poet. 30, 33

KLUGE, KURT (1886–1940). Writer. 33

KOCH, FRANZ (1888——). Austrian. Professor of German at the University of Berlin, 1935–1945. 145

KOEPPEN, WOLFGANG (1906——). Writer (*Death in Rome*, Vanguard, 1960.) 152, 154, 183

KOGON, EUGENE (1903——). Political writer. First president of the Europa Union. Since 1951, Professor in Darmstadt. 57

KÖRNER, THEODORE (1791–1813). Poet. 33

KRAFFT, ADAM (*circa* 1460–1508/9). Nürnberg sculptor in stone. 188

KRAUS, KARL (1874–1936). Austrian writer, journalist, satirist, and pacifist. 150

KUHN, RICHARD (1900——). Chemist. Nobel Prize, 1938. 66

L

LAGARDE, PAUL ANTON DE, pseudonym for BÖTTICHER (1827–1891). Orientalist. Outstanding representative of national conservatism. 147

LAMPRECHT, KARL (1856–1915). Historian. 114

LANGE, FRIEDRICH ALBERT (1828–1875). Professor of philosophy, socialist. 232

LASSALLE, FERDINAND (1825–1864). Socialist. Founded the *Allgemeine Deutsche Arbeiterverein*, Leipzig, 1863, which was a forerunner of the SPD, or German Socialist Party. 91

LEHR, ROBERT (1883–1956). Politician, CDU (Christian Democratic Union). Minister of the Interior, 1950–53. 137

LEIBNIZ, GOTTFRIED WILHELM (1646–1716). Philosopher. 30, 33

LENZ, JACOB MICHAEL REINHOLD (1751–1792). Poet. 154

LENZ, SIEGFRIED (1926——). Writer and dramatist. (*The Lightship*, Hill & Wang, 1962.) 114, 152, 154

LESSING, GOTTHOLD EPHRAIM (1729–1781). Poet and critic. 30, 33, 114

LILIENCRON, DETLEV VON (1844–1909). Poet and writer. 180, 211

LINNÉ, CARL VON (1707–1778). Swedish naturalist. 114

INDEX